HILMA AF KLINT

NOTES AND METHODS

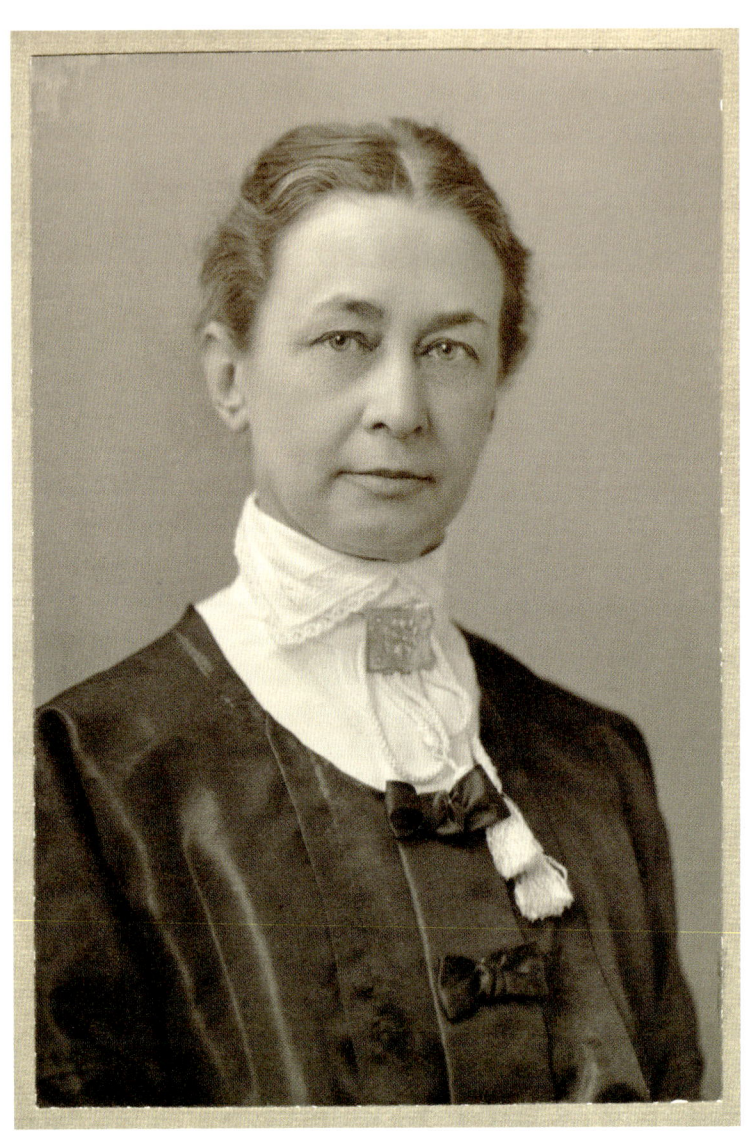

HILMA AF KLINT

NOTES AND METHODS

Introduction and commentary by
Iris Müller-Westermann

Afterword by Johan af Klint

Edited by Christine Burgin

Translations by
Kerstin Lind Bonnier
Elizabeth Clark Wessel
Anne Posten

CHRISTINE BURGIN | THE UNIVERSITY OF CHICAGO PRESS

This book is published with the full cooperation of the Hilma af Klint Foundation.
All images are reproduced courtesy of the Hilma af Klint Foundation.
Photographs: Moderna Museet, Stockholm, Sweden

Publication of this book has been aided by a grant from the Neil Harris Endowment
Fund, which honors the innovative scholarship of Neil Harris, the Preston and Sterling
Morton Professor Emeritus of History at the University of Chicago. The fund is supported
by contributions from the students, colleagues, and friends of Neil Harris.

Hilma af Klint: Notes and Methods is a copublication by
Christine Burgin and The University of Chicago Press.

Christine Burgin books are published by
Christine Burgin | 245 West 18th Street | New York, New York 10011
www.christineburgin.com

The University of Chicago Press, Chicago 60637
The University of Chicago Press, Ltd., London
© 2018 Christine Burgin
Introduction and commentary © 2018 Iris Müller-Westermann

Published 2018
Printed in China

29 28 27 26 25 24 23 22 21 20   4 5 6 7

ISBN-13: 978-0-226-59193-3 (cloth)

Designed and typeset in Scotch Text by Laura Lindgren

Image preparation by Jason Burch

Printed on 115 gsm Kasadaka White

Front cover: Hilma af Klint, Blue Book 1179 (pp. 129, 133, 142)
Back cover: Hilma af Klint, Blue Book 1177 (p. 102)
Frontispiece: Hilma af Klint, c. 1910

Library of Congress Cataloging-in-Publication Data
Names: Klint, Hilma af, 1862–1944, author, artist. | Müller-Westermann, Iris, writer of
introduction, writer of added commentary. | Wessel, Elizabeth Clark, translator. | Bonnier,
Kerstin Lind, translator. | Posten, Anne, translator. | Klint, Hilma af, 1862–1944. Paintings.
Selections. 2018.
Title: Hilma af Klint : notes and methods / introduction and commentary by Iris Müller-
Westermann ; translations by Kerstin Lind Bonnier, Elizabeth Clark Wessel, Anne Posten.
Description: Chicago : The University of Chicago Press ; New York City : Christine Burgin, 2018.
Identifiers: LCCN 2018010066 | ISBN 9780226591933 (cloth : alk. paper)
Subjects: LCSH: Klint, Hilma af, 1862–1944—Aesthetics. | Painting, Abstract—Sweden. | Spirit
art—Sweden. | Spirituality in art. | Painting, Abstract—Sweden—Pictorial works.
Classification: LCC ND793.K63 A35 2018 | DDC 759.85—dc23
LC record available at https://lccn.loc.gov/2018010066

♾ This paper meets the requirements of ANSI/NISO Z39.48-1992 (Permanence of Paper).

Contents

21/6 1907

Till utgångspunkt tages
följande tre begrepp:

∞ 0 ∞

6/21/1907 The following three concepts are taken as a starting point: ∞ 0 ∞

Introduction

At the turn of the century, Swedish artist Hilma af Klint (1862–1944) created a body of work that left visible reality behind, exploring the radical possibilities of abstraction years before Vasily Kandinsky, Kazimir Malevich, František Kupka, or Piet Mondrian, acknowledged fathers of twentieth-century abstraction.

From 1882 to 1887, Hilma af Klint studied at the Royal Swedish Academy of Fine Arts in Stockholm, where she was part of the first generation of female students to study alongside male colleagues. Up until the beginning of the twentieth century, she primarily painted naturalistic portraits, landscapes, and detailed nature studies. Her accurate and systematic observation of nature followed in the tradition of the Swedish botanist Carl von Linné. Works from this period reflect a young artist who meticulously observed the world around her.

But, like many of her contemporaries, af Klint was also interested in the invisible relationships that shape our world. Around the turn of the twentieth century, sweeping scientific discoveries forever changed the common understanding of matter and space. Heinrich Hertz had proved the existence of electromagnetic waves that spread in a manner and at a speed similar to light waves. In 1886 he succeeded in transmitting these waves from a sender to a receiver. His discoveries formed the basis for wireless telegraphy and later for radio. X-rays, discovered by Wilhelm Röntgen in 1895, made it possible to see structures that lie under the surface of the visible world.

Af Klint devoted her life and her work to an exploration of an invisible realm. She strongly believed in a spiritual dimension and became a part of the growing movement of forward-thinking members of Swedish society who were interested in spiritual investigation. She joined the Theosophical Society in 1889, the same year it was established in Sweden, and she later spent many years attending lectures and doing research at the Goethe-anum in Dornach, the home of Rudolf Steiner's Anthroposophical movement. While af Klint chose not to share the work she made after 1906 with the art world, she was an active member of a group that included poets,

From Letters and Words Pertaining to Works by Hilma af Klint (see pages 247–85)

inventors, journalists, doctors, scientists, and a proportionally high number of women. If there was little room for advancement for women in the art world of her time, the Theosophical world was one in large part founded and run by women.

Hilma af Klint's first experiments in spiritual investigation date back to 1879. In 1896 af Klint and four other women formed The Five, a group devoted to the systematic study of mediumship. After ten years of regular meetings, af Klint was chosen by the higher powers with whom The Five were in communication to create a series of largely abstract paintings known as *The Paintings for the Temple*. Between 1906 and 1915, af Klint created 193 paintings, a body of work that, in scale and scope of imagery, was like none other of the time. Botanically inspired imagery, which after 1912 became increasingly abstract and geometric, mystical symbols, diagrams, and a vast array of words and letters make up a complex abstract vocabulary that would not become part of the language of art until years later. Hilma af Klint understood that *The Paintings for the Temple* were her most important work, a gift of knowledge from the spiritual world, and she spent much of the rest of her life searching for the deeper meaning in these works. She explored world religions, atoms, and the plant world and wrote extensively about her discoveries. At the time of her death in 1944, she left behind a vast body of work: paintings and works on paper as well as 126 annotated notebooks, a dictionary to her own work, and more than twenty thousand pages of text describing her spiritual investigations. Concerned that the world was not yet ready for the knowledge revealed in her work, but ever a believer in the spiritual evolution of mankind, she had requested of her family that the work not be shown until twenty years after her death.

Hilma af Klint's process of investigation took many forms and drew on systems and symbols outside the traditional language of art. *Notes and Methods* traces the origins of her powerful abstract work and demonstrates the ways in which with great courage and openness she used her own work to understand the world—in all its manifestations, visible and invisible. Included are mediumistic drawings created with The Five; the handmade book *Flowers, Mosses, and Lichens*, a spiritual explication of the plant world; *The Atom Series*, in which she outlines her method of diagramming the spiritual planes; and, reproduced in their entirety, the invaluable Blue Books, ten hand-painted and annotated books in which af Klint catalogued *The Paintings for the Temple*, her attempt to preserve for more enlightened

Untitled nature study HaK 1335, c. 1890.
Watercolor and pencil on paper, 6¾ × 6¹¹⁄₁₆ in. (17.3 × 17 cm)

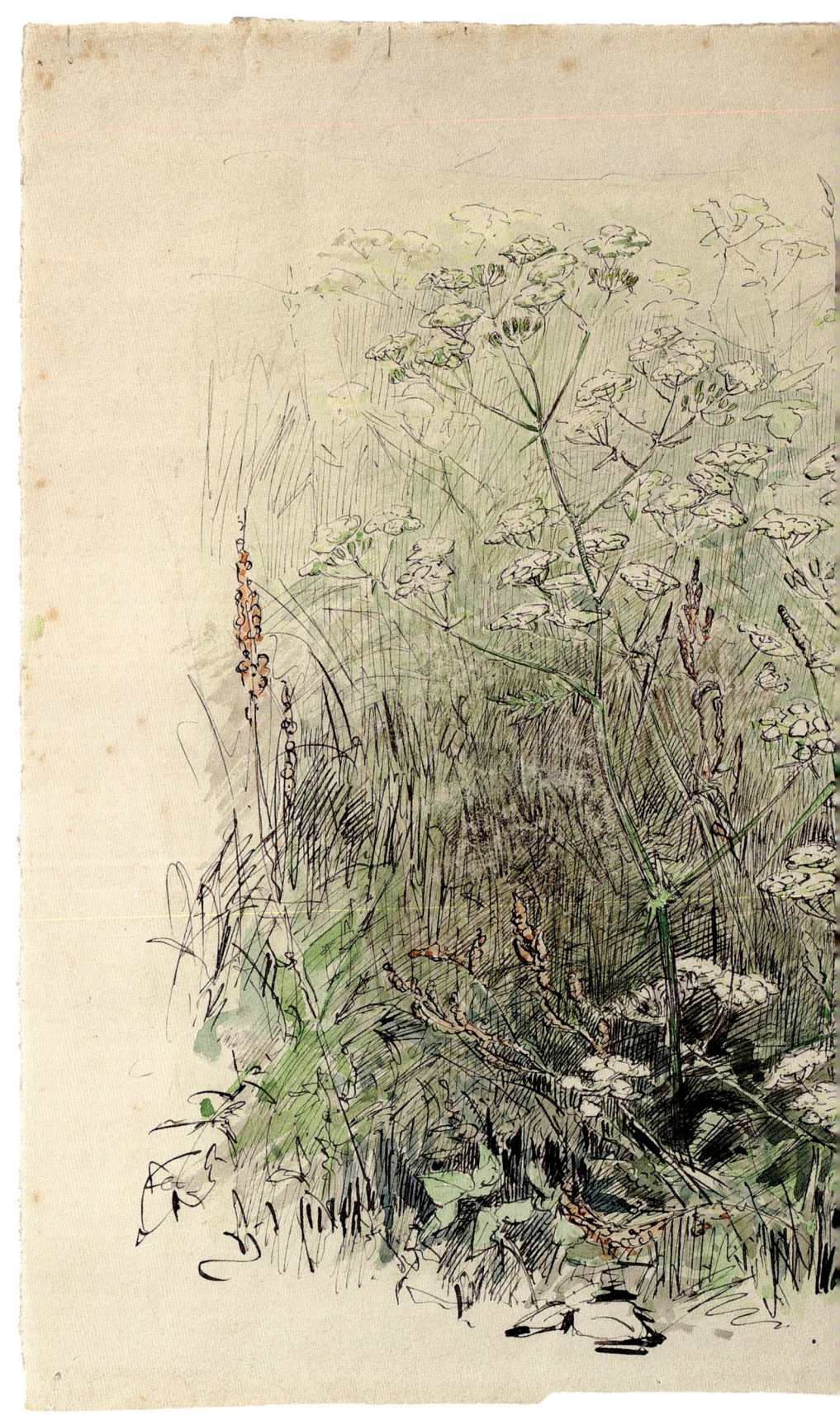

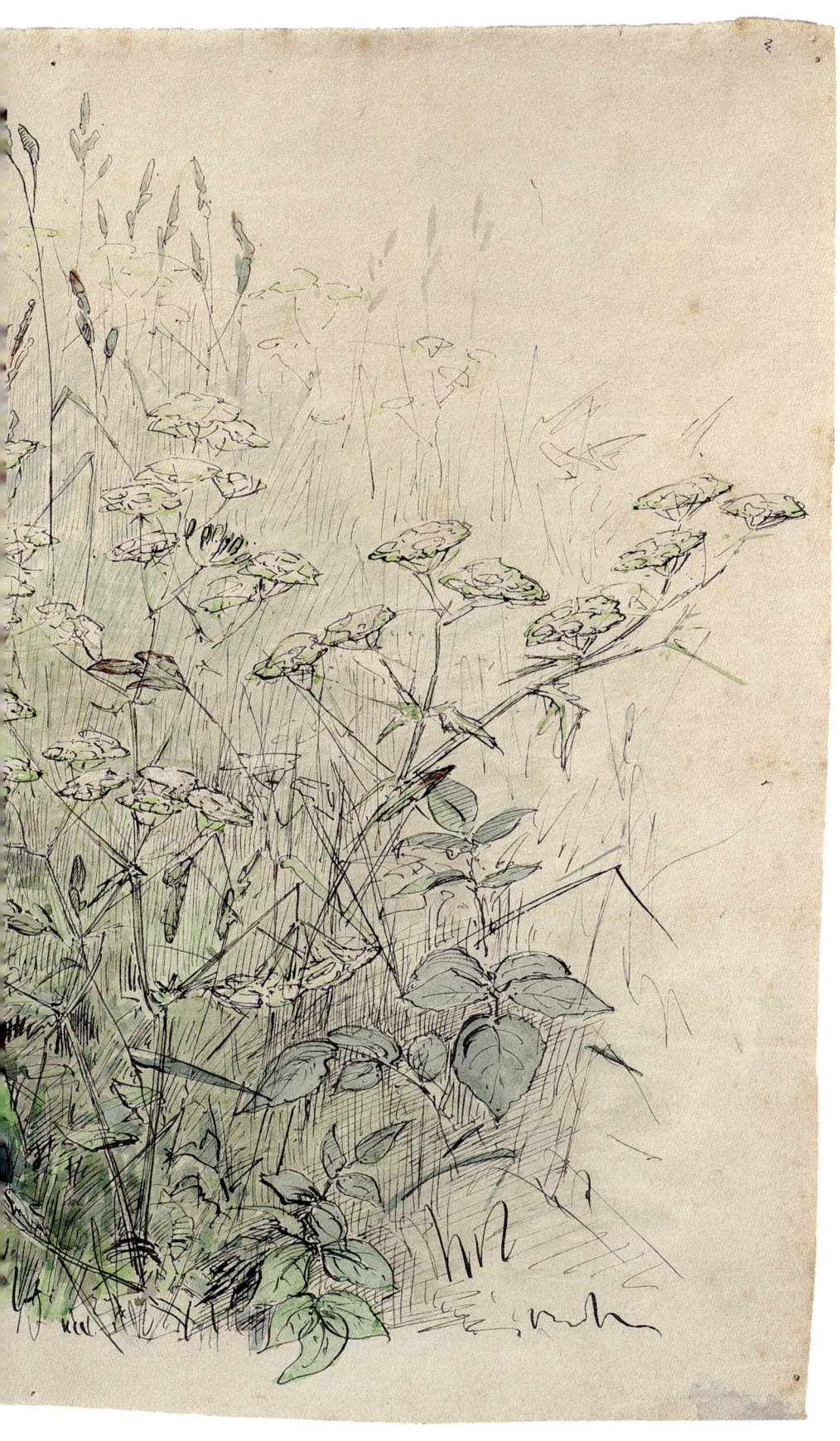

generations to come the progression, development, and conclusions of what she considered to be her most profound and important body of work.

Notes and Methods is the first extensive English translation of the writings of Hilma af Klint. In addition to translations of all notebooks reproduced, the book also includes the first English translation of *Letters and Words Pertaining to Works by Hilma af Klint*, a guide to the meaning contained in the work, compiled by Hilma af Klint herself.

Jean Dubuffet, the great supporter and promoter of art brut, describes the art brut artist as someone who can "draw everything . . . from their own depths and not from clichés of classical art or art that is fashionable. Here we are witnessing an artistic operation that is completely pure, raw, reinvented in all its phases by the author." Dubuffet discovered in art brut a direct and powerful connection between artist, work, and the world that was of central importance yet that was somehow irretrievably lost to him and to his generation. Dubuffet could, however, have been describing Hilma af Klint. Af Klint was neither an art brut nor outsider artist. She was trained as an artist yet she chose to leave the traditional sphere of art behind and to embark instead on an investigation of the spiritual world. In setting aside the language of the art of her time, af Klint was free to use other visual languages: the language of science, of mathematics, of esoteric texts, and mysticism. Language and abstraction were, however, only tools to be used in her search for meaning. Af Klint's primacy as an abstract artist is what has brought her to the attention of the contemporary art world, but it is her belief in the power of images and her search for meaning that we may come to recognize as her more profound and remarkable achievement.

Note to the reader: Hilma af Klint's notebook texts and annotations are accompanied by English translations throughout this publication. The letters and words that appear in her paintings and drawings, however, are not. Translations and definitions for these can be found in the English translation of *Letters and Words Pertaining to Works by Hilma af Klint*, which appears on pages 255–65 and 268–85.

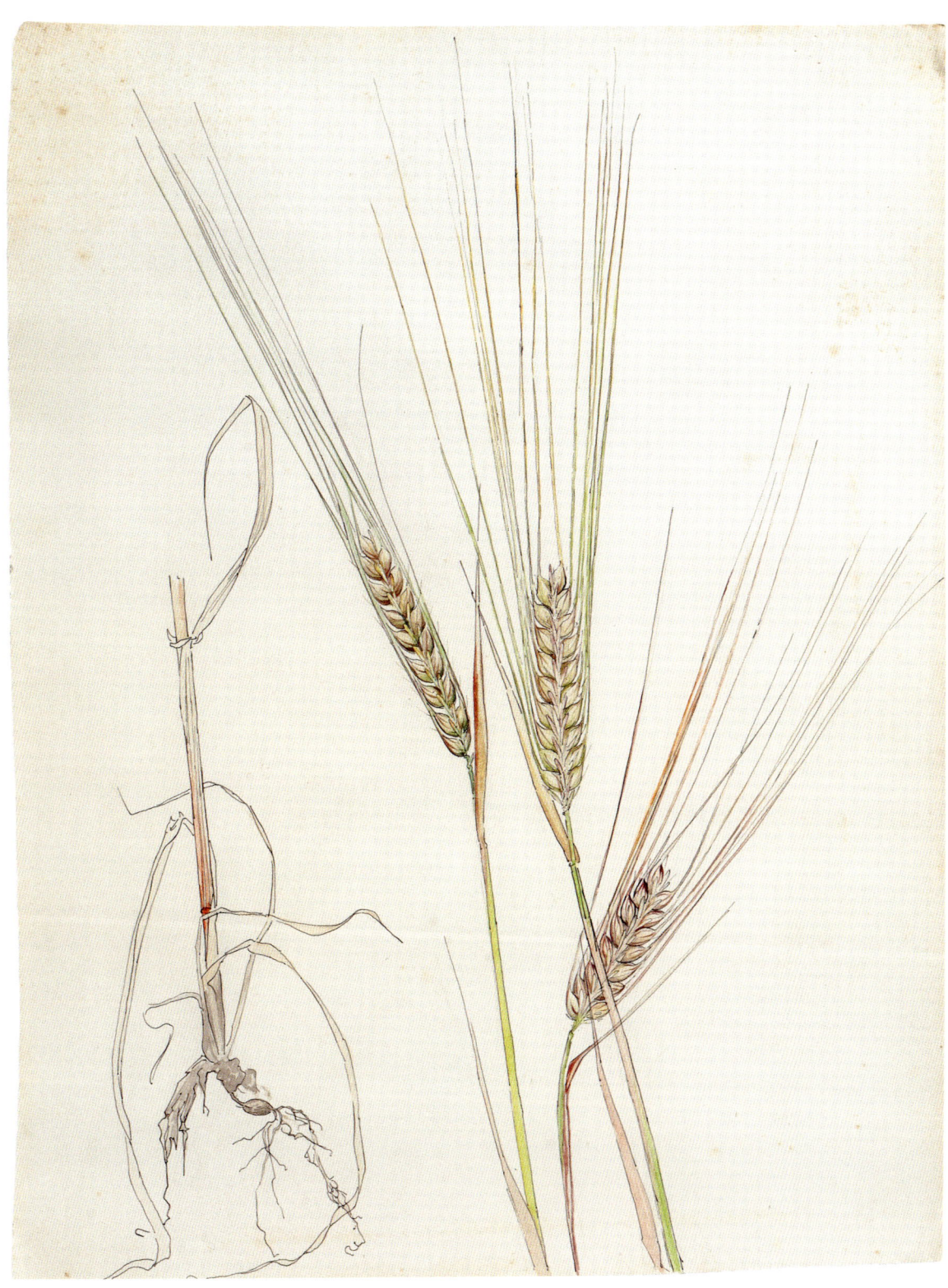

The Five

The Paintings for the Temple, which Hilma af Klint embarked upon in 1906, grew out of a ten-year period of experimentation with the group of women who called themselves The Five (De Fem). The Five—Anna Cassel, Cornelia Cederberg, Sigrid Hedman, Mathilda Nilsson, and Hilma af Klint—shared a strong belief in the existence of a reality beyond the material world, and between 1896 and 1906 they met on a regular basis to study mediumship as a means of communicating with this spiritual dimension.

The Five began their association as members of the Edelweiss Society (Edelweissförbundet). Founded by Huldine Beamish in 1890, the Edelweiss Society embraced a combination of the Theosophical teachings of Helena Blavatsky and spiritualism. Mathilda Nilsson, a practicing medium and the publisher of a spiritualist journal, was one of the founding members of the society. In addition to the members of The Five, the society included a large number of women. In 1889 Hilma af Klint joined the Theosophical Society and remained a member until 1914/1915. She later became interested in the teachings of Rudolf Steiner and became a member of the Anthroposophical Society in 1920.

The Five had a systematic method of working. Each meeting started with a prayer, followed by meditation, a Christian sermon, and a review and analysis of a text from the New Testament. This was followed by a séance. The Five carefully documented their meetings and collected the drawings and messages received in sketchbooks. Five notebooks dating from 1896 to 1907 describe their meetings with detailed information regarding each séance. For each session it is noted who acted as medium, who was doing the drawings, what the received content was, and the names of the High Masters with whom The Five were in contact: Gregor, Clemens, Amaliel, and later Ananda. Two notebooks contain mediumistic messages given to The Five by Gregor and one of messages from Clemens. In addition to these notebooks, there exist nine sketchbooks of received drawings. Each page is dated and signed. Many of the drawings are collectively signed D.F. (De Fem [The Five]); in other cases the initials of the names of the individuals who made the drawings appear. To The Five, it was not authorship

Pages 17–27: selections from The Five notebook HaK 1522, 1904.
Pencil on paper, 12 × 10¼ in. (30.8 × 26 cm)

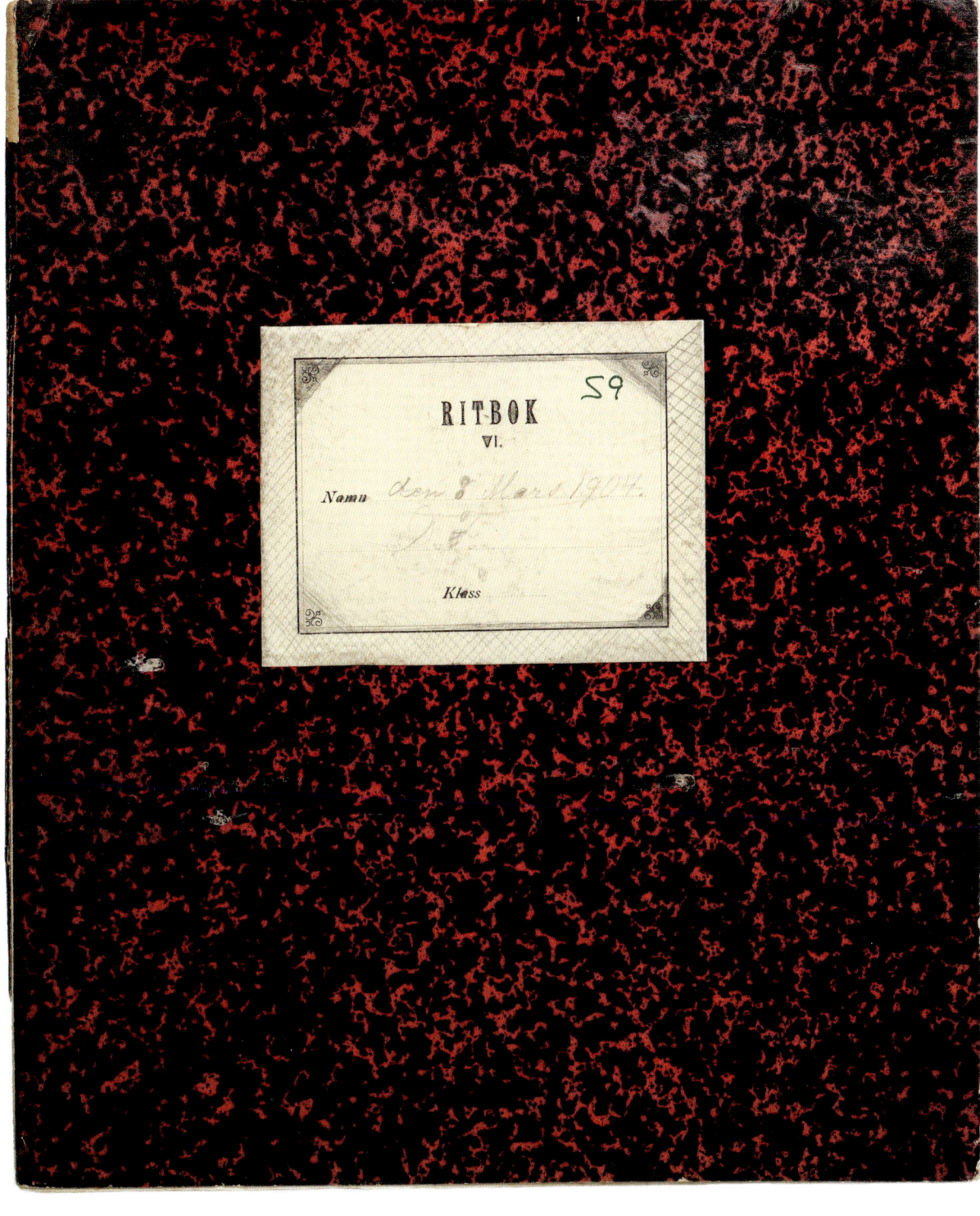

RITBOK

VI.

Namn ~~den 8 Mars 1904.~~

Klass

59

that was important but the message received. All of the notebooks of The Five remained with Hilma af Klint until her death and were an invaluable reference for her, especially later in her life, when she revisited these notebooks and sketchbooks frequently. The pages reproduced here are from a sketchbook that dates from 1904.

Of The Five only two were trained as artists: Hilma af Klint and her friend from the Royal Academy Anna Cassel. Initially Cornelia Cederberg was in charge of drawing, but this work was eventually ceded to Hilma af Klint. In 1905 she was commissioned by the High Master Amaliel to create a series of paintings that became known as *The Paintings for the Temple*: ". . . Amaliel presented me with a task and I immediately said Yes. The expectation was that I would dedicate a year to this task. In the end it became the greatest work of my life." [1/1/1906, HaK 555, p. 8]

When Hilma af Klint first began to work on *The Paintings for the Temple*, she did not know what she was about to depict, only that she was an instrument and that, as such, her role was to remain as open as possible. Af Klint continued to receive the work in this way until 1908. Between 1908 and 1912 af Klint devoted herself full time to the care of her blind mother. In 1912, when she began to work again on the paintings that would complete the series, she found that her method of working had changed. Her hand was no longer led through the process of creation; she instead received the works—a combination of images, sounds, and words—fully formed. With this new method came a new freedom of interpretation.

It is clear from the drawings and sketches contained in the notebooks of The Five that some of the abstract language of *The Paintings for the Temple* was received by The Five between 1896 and 1906. The snail, the rose, a wide array of botanical imagery, an elaborate system of diagrammed dualities, a geometrical language were all arrived at during this time. For Hilma af Klint this imagery continued to be of central importance. Maybe of equal importance was the method of working she realized at this time: drawing and painting not as an end in itself but as an ongoing method of investigation.

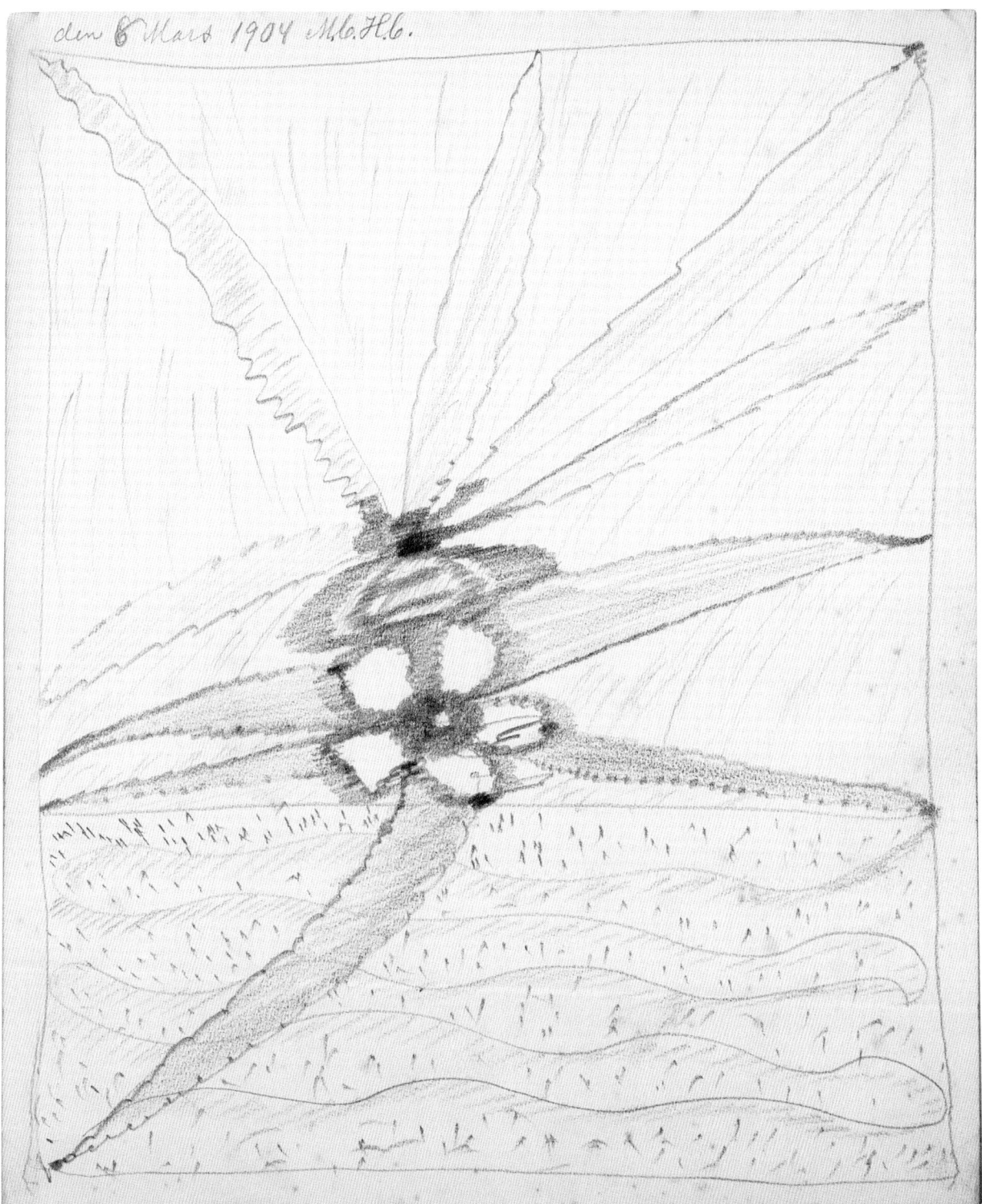
den 8 Mars 1904 M.6.H.6.

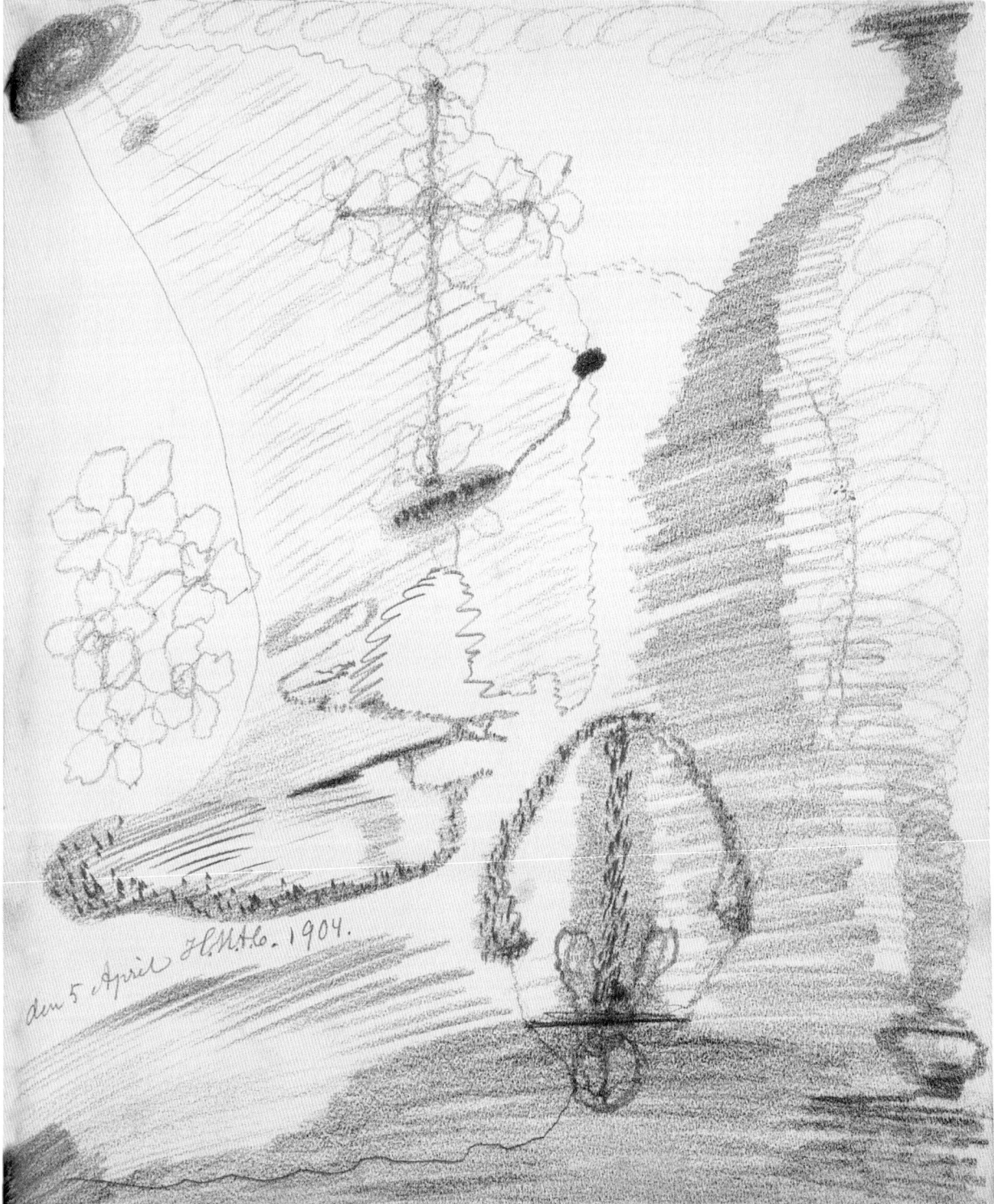

den 5 April H.N.H.G. 1904.

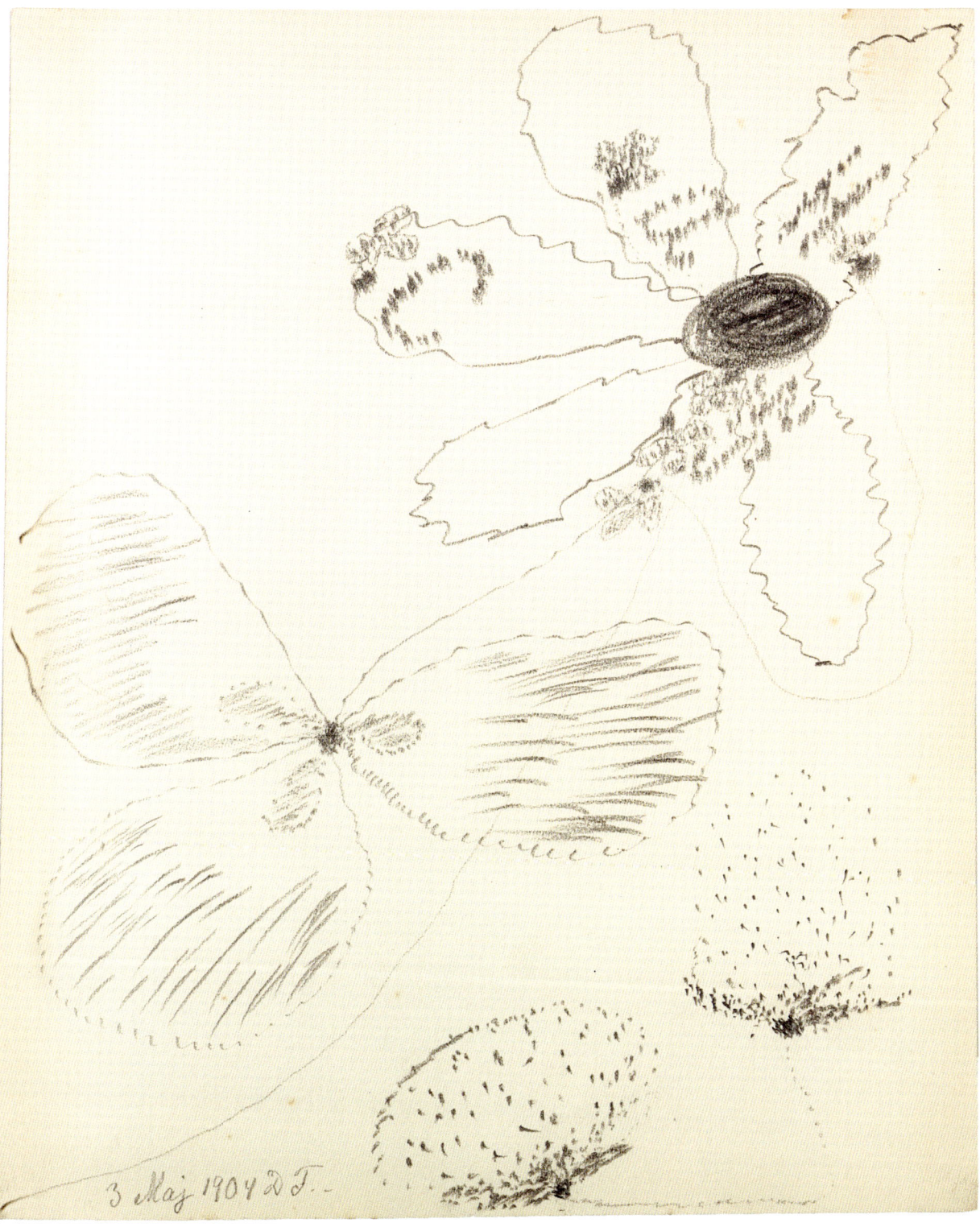

3 Maj 1904 2 J.

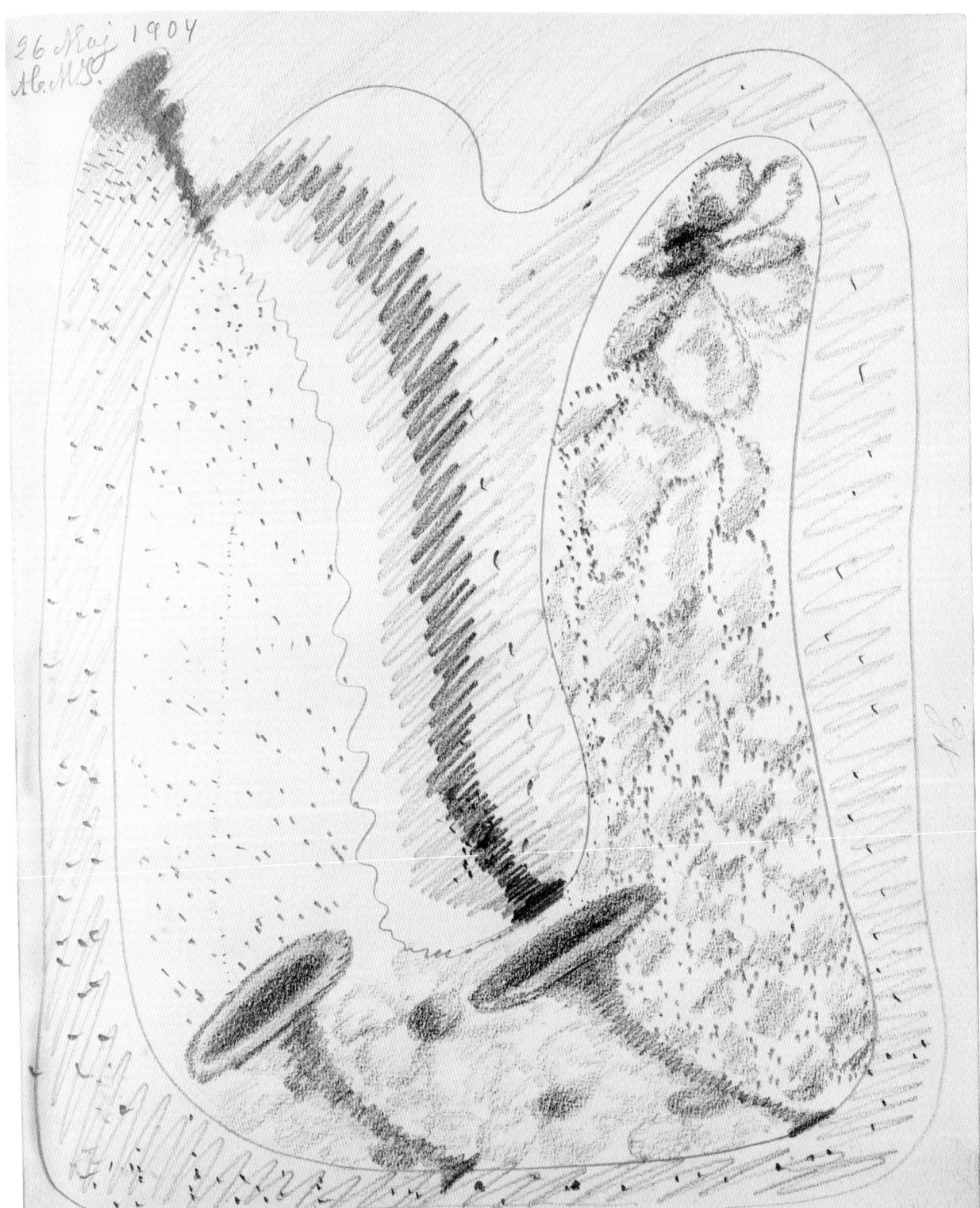

26 Maj 1904
Aften.

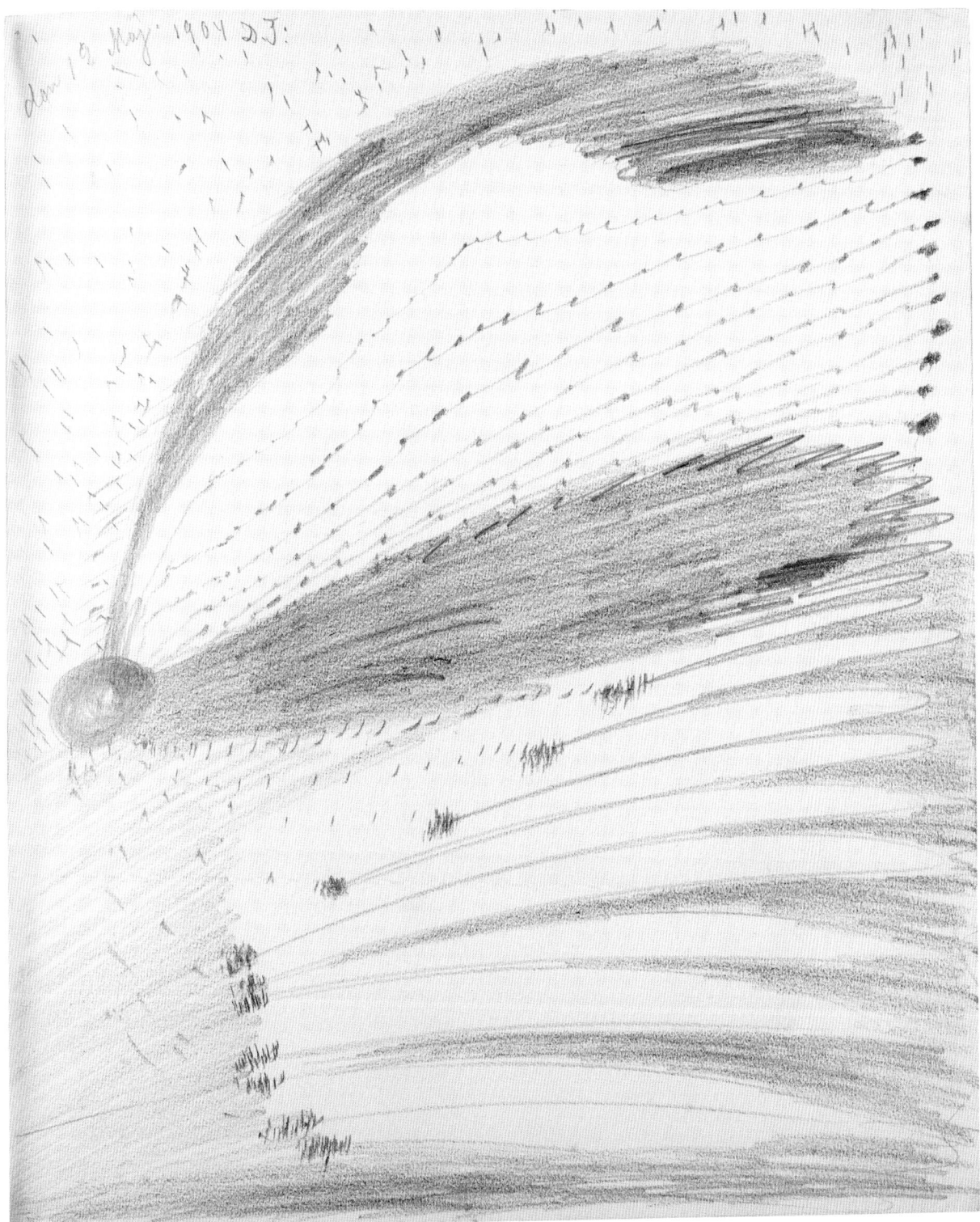

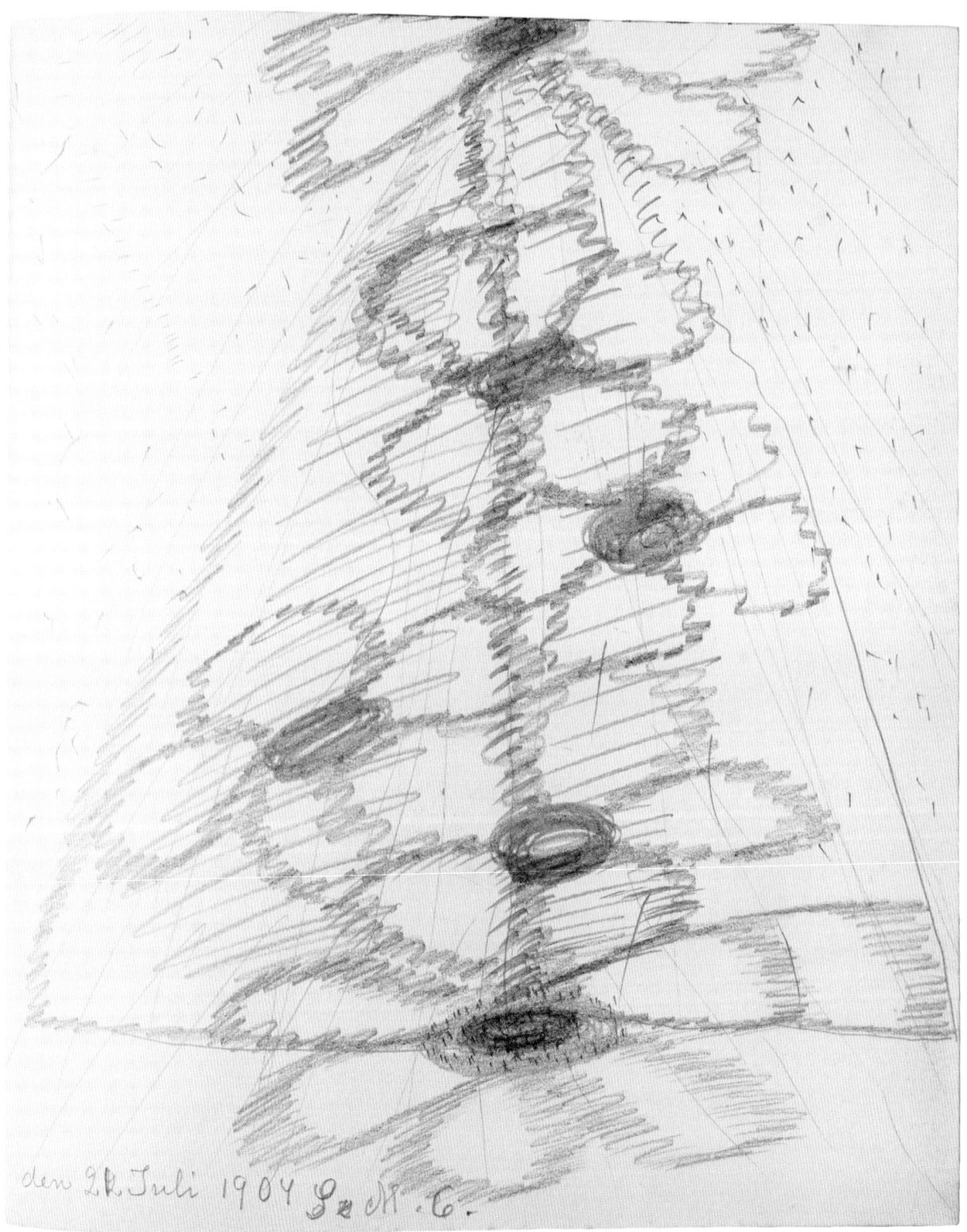

den 24 Juli 1904 S₂ M. 6.

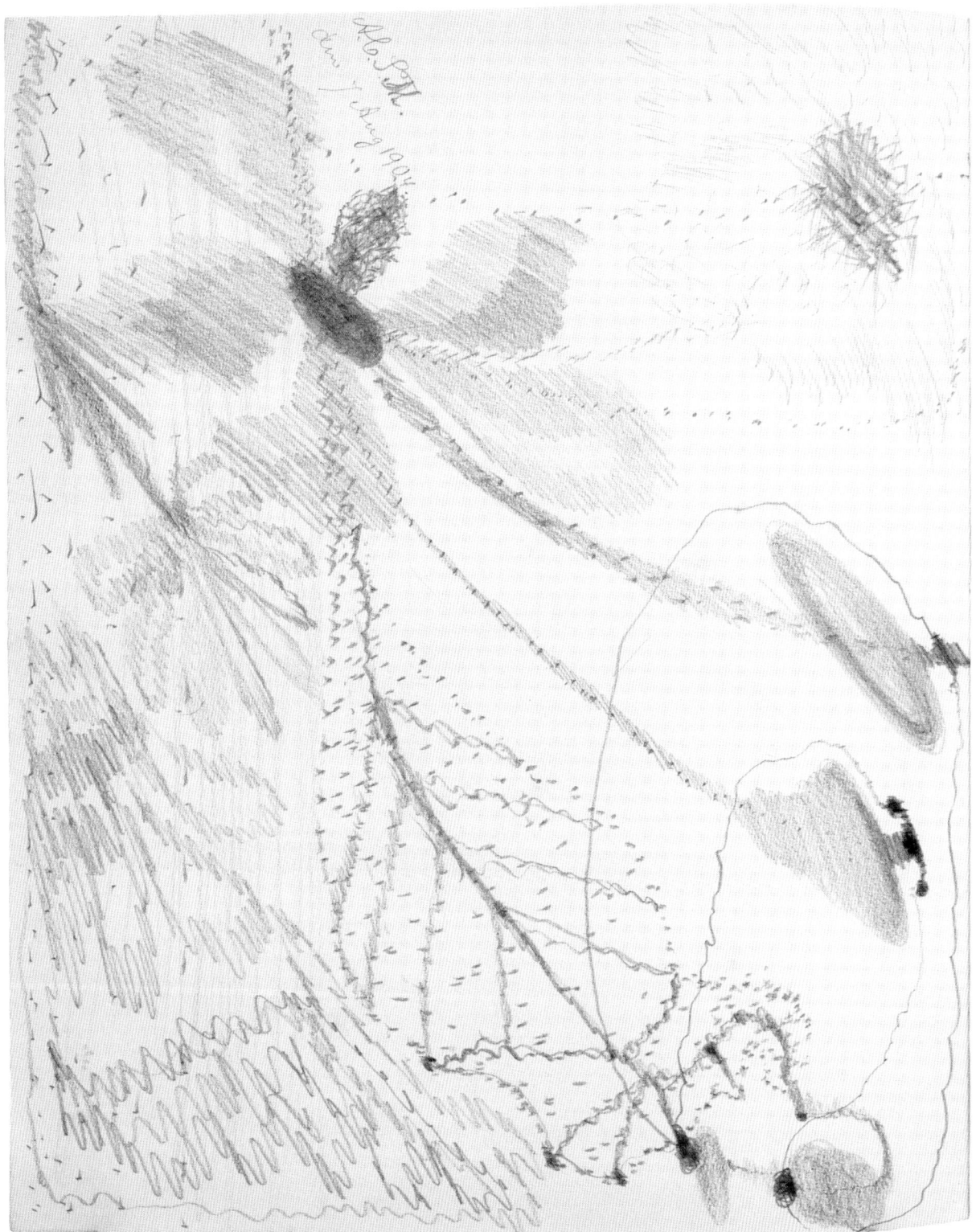

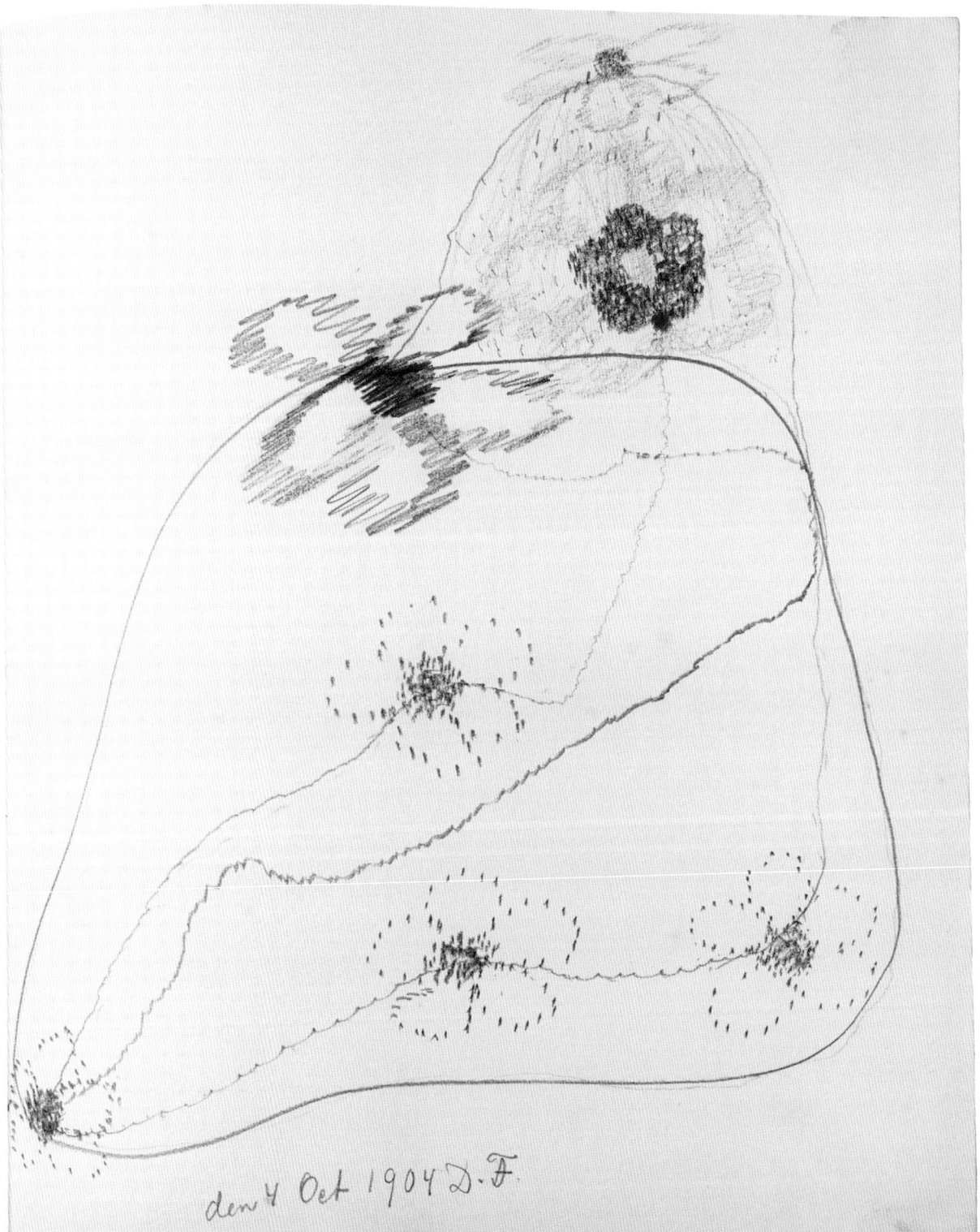

den 4 Oct 1904 D. F.

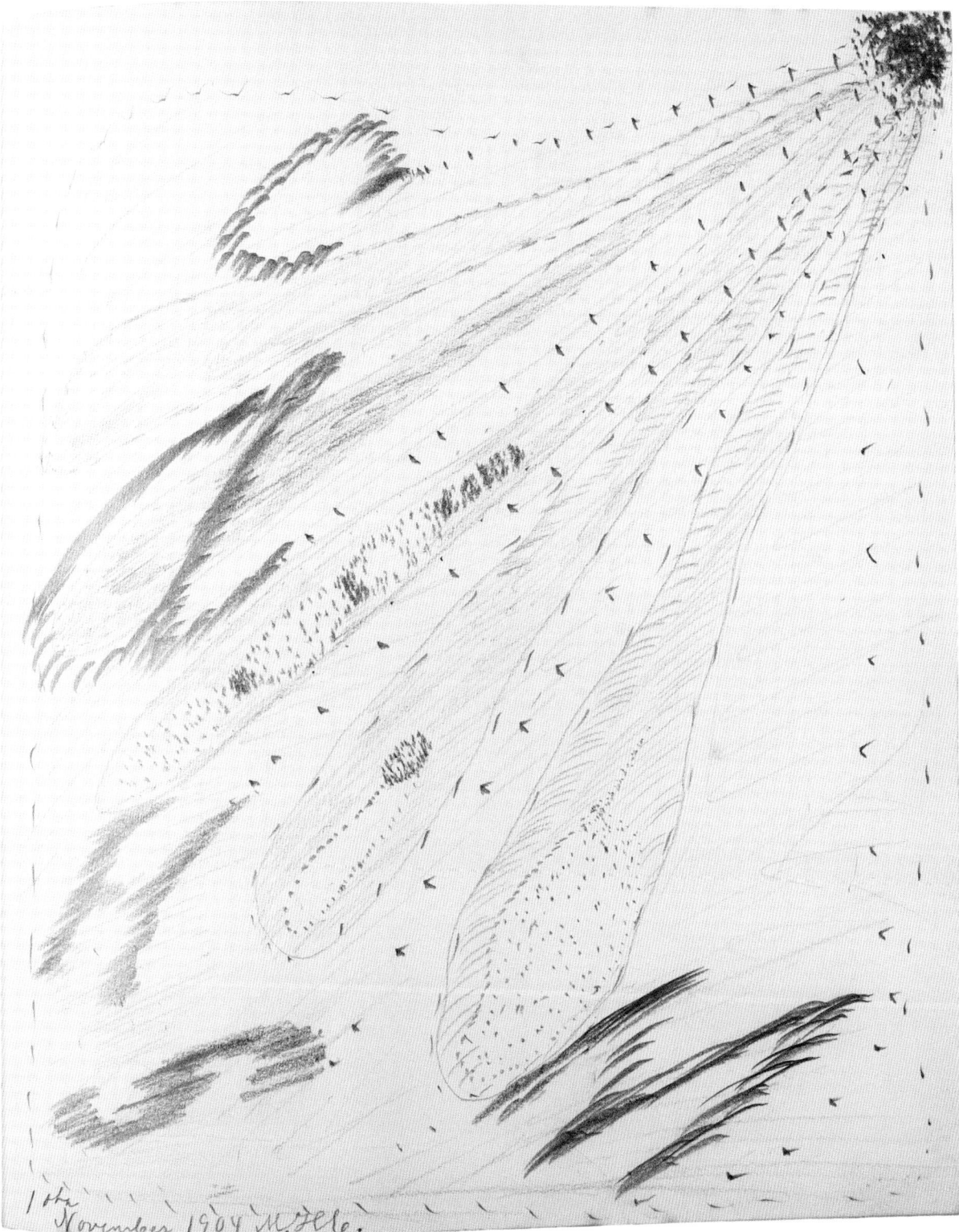

10th
November 1904 M.H.C.

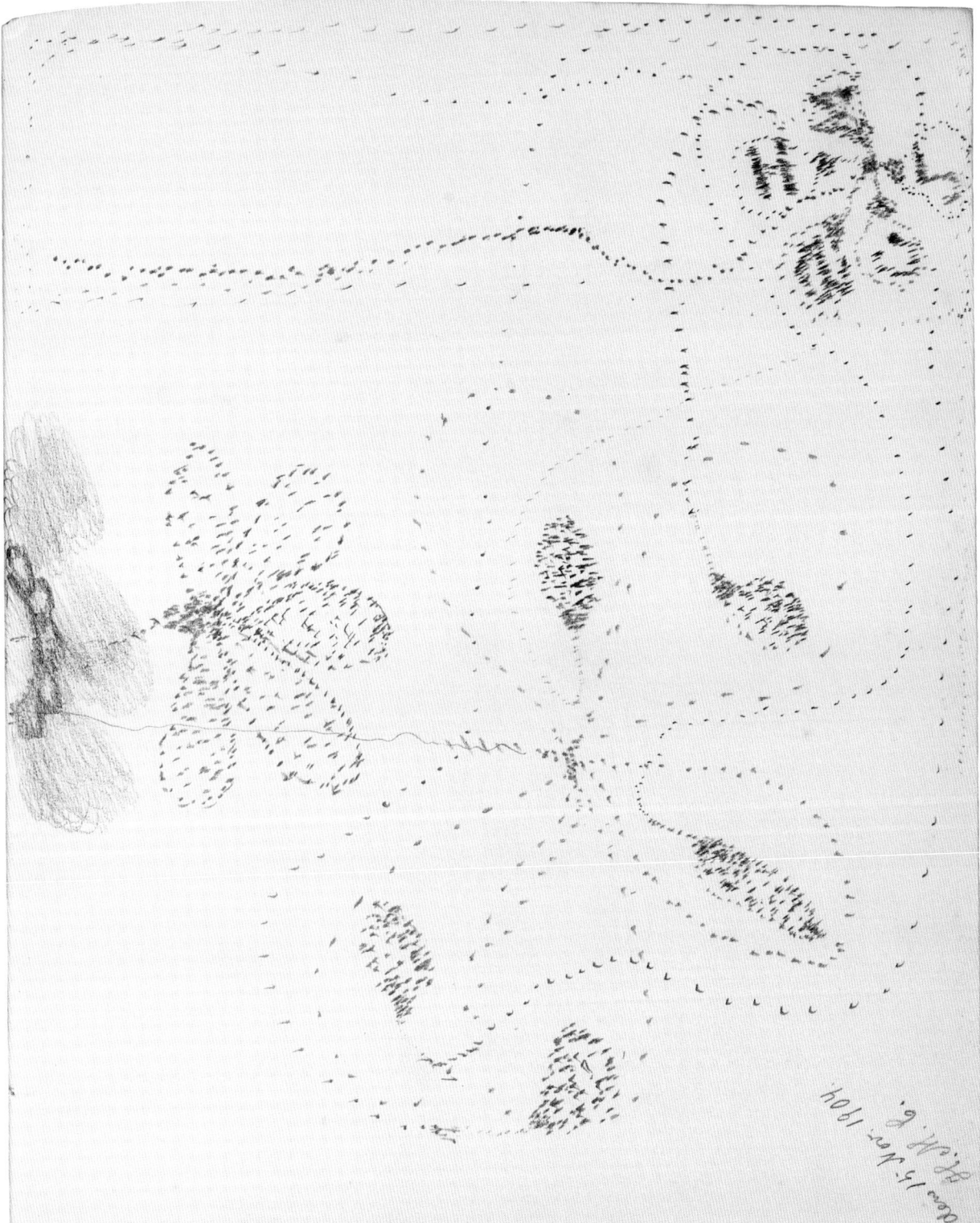

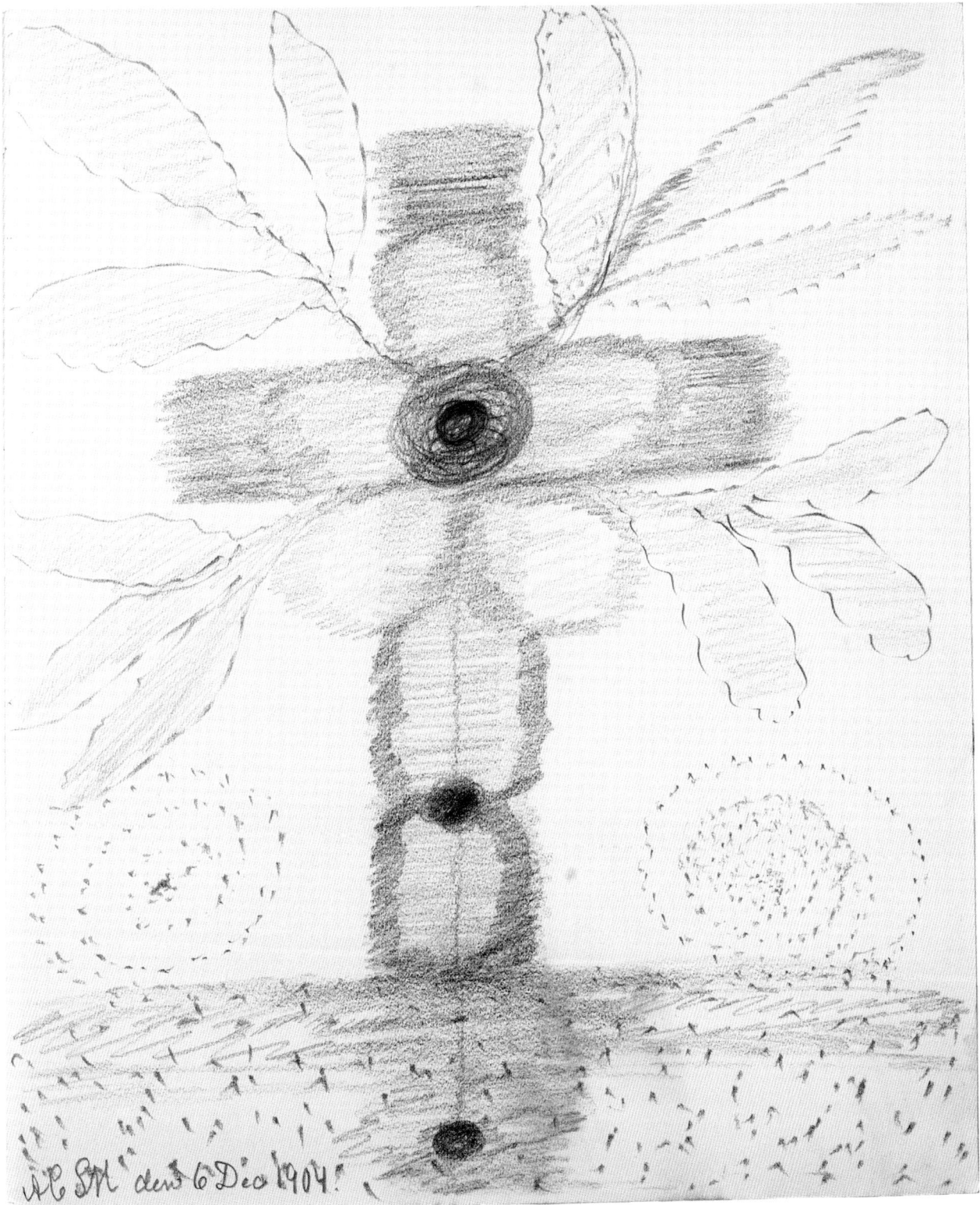

AC SM den 6 Dec 1904.

Den 13 Sept. 1903

J förvänden Eder öfver vårt utkast, men förunderlig är isanning ock den förställen af hvilken vi härmed försöka gifven Er en bild. Men hvad är då detta för en förställelse säga J? Jo J'älskade det är den som vi vilja kalla det försvarliga växandets. Men ofta hören vi ej Eder säga allt är än så gagnlöst, aldrig blir det något resultat. Likt oformliga växtdelar skjuta Edra försök att växa fram ät alla håll J sen endast på huru formlöst allt är och gömmen därvid att tänka på huru då allt detta betecknar ett växande lif

...

Men det oformliga tagen småningom allt bestämdare konturer från den allt rikare roten skjuter ständigt i höjden en allt kraftigare växt som till sist tagen en bestämd gestalt med ymnighet af blad och blommor. O så än är veten J men detta vetande måste J söka fatta så lefvande att J ock vägen bygga därpå. J måsten såsom visshet känna att hvarje äfven det minsta försök att växa i det goda lämnar ett alldeles tydligt spår i Edert inres form att J ej sen deta

...

Såsom ett yttre resultat sen ej nedli Edert mod eller trötte Eder sträfven ty på alldeles samma sätt som osynligt händer högre och inom hvarje plant på Jordens mark så värdes och gestaltes och höjnes hvarje spirande grodd i det goda af osynliga mäkter hvilka vi stunder är inne en gång skola öppna Edra ögon så att J ock sen den sköna växt som i det fördolda spirat ur Edra ädla bemödanden och Edert rena uppsåt Tagen detta som vi tecknat som en hälsning från oss att aldrig J skulen

...

trötta en äfven allt ser hopplöst ut

These four loose sheets were found slipped into the notebook of The Five in which the preceding drawings appear. It is not known to whom this is addressed.

September 16, 1903

You are bewildered by what we have told you, but the phenomenon we are trying to explain is truly bewildering. What is this phenomenon, you ask? Well, beloved, it is that which we want to call the secret growing. How often have we heard you say that everything is futile, that nothing comes of all your labors. Yet like amorphous buds your endeavors sprout in all directions. You see everything as formless and you forget that this is a sign of life. Gradually the formlessness takes on more precise contours and the steadily growing roots feed an ever stronger plant, which will one day explode with an abundance of leaves and flowers. You know this is so, but you must perceive this knowledge with such vividness that you dare to build on it. You have to feel with certainty that even the smallest effort to grow in goodness leaves a clear trace inside you. When you do not see an outer result, this must not discourage or tire you in your efforts, for just as invisible hands help and tend every plant on this green Earth, so every budding sprout of goodness is tended and shaped and protected by invisible powers and when the time comes your eyes will open and you too will see the beautiful plant that grew in secrecy, the product of your noble endeavors and your pure intentions. Accept our account as a greeting from us so that you shall never tire when all seems lost.

The Blue Books

The Blue Books are a catalogue, meticulously and beautifully assembled by Hilma af Klint, of the paintings she considered to be her most important body of work. In these ten books she organizes *The Paintings for the Temple* into a sequence of discrete series, preserving both the images and the progression of the work, together with a summation of the spiritual knowledge that she devoted her life to understanding and she wished to preserve intact for generations to come. The Blue Books are reproduced in this publication in their entirety.

It is not known when af Klint began work on the Blue Books, but it was most likely after 1917. For much of the time she was painting *The Paintings for the Temple*, af Klint was working either in her studio in Stockholm or at her family's summer home. The women who shared her studio complained that she took up too much room and the building she used at her family's home was habitable only in the summer. In 1917 Anna Cassel, her good friend, fellow artist, and member of The Five, built a studio for af Klint on the island of Munsö in Lake Mälaren. Here she was able to consolidate all her artwork including *The Paintings for the Temple* and the archive of notebooks created by The Five.

With this new space it became possible for her to unpack the 193 works that make up *The Paintings for the Temple* and to have them photographed. Given the scale of many of these works, this would not have been an easy undertaking, but she managed to have all but two series documented with black-and-white photographs. She mounted these photographs in small (8⅞ × 6⅞ in. [22.5 × 17.5 cm]) blue clothbound books and on the facing page affixed a watercolor version of the original to which she often added notes or details illuminating as if under a microscope various areas of the original. It seems likely, given the accuracy of these watercolors, that they were made with the original paintings close at hand. Easy to carry, the Blue Books served af Klint as a portable way to share her work with others.

On the opening page of each book she notes the sizes of the original works and the dates when they were created. She begins with Group I, "Primordial Chaos" or the WU/Rose series (HaK 1171), the first series of

Pages 31–147: HaK 1171–HaK 1180. Mixed media on paper and black-and-white photographs mounted in ten blue clothbound books, each 8⅞ × 6⅞ in. (22.5 × 17.5 cm)

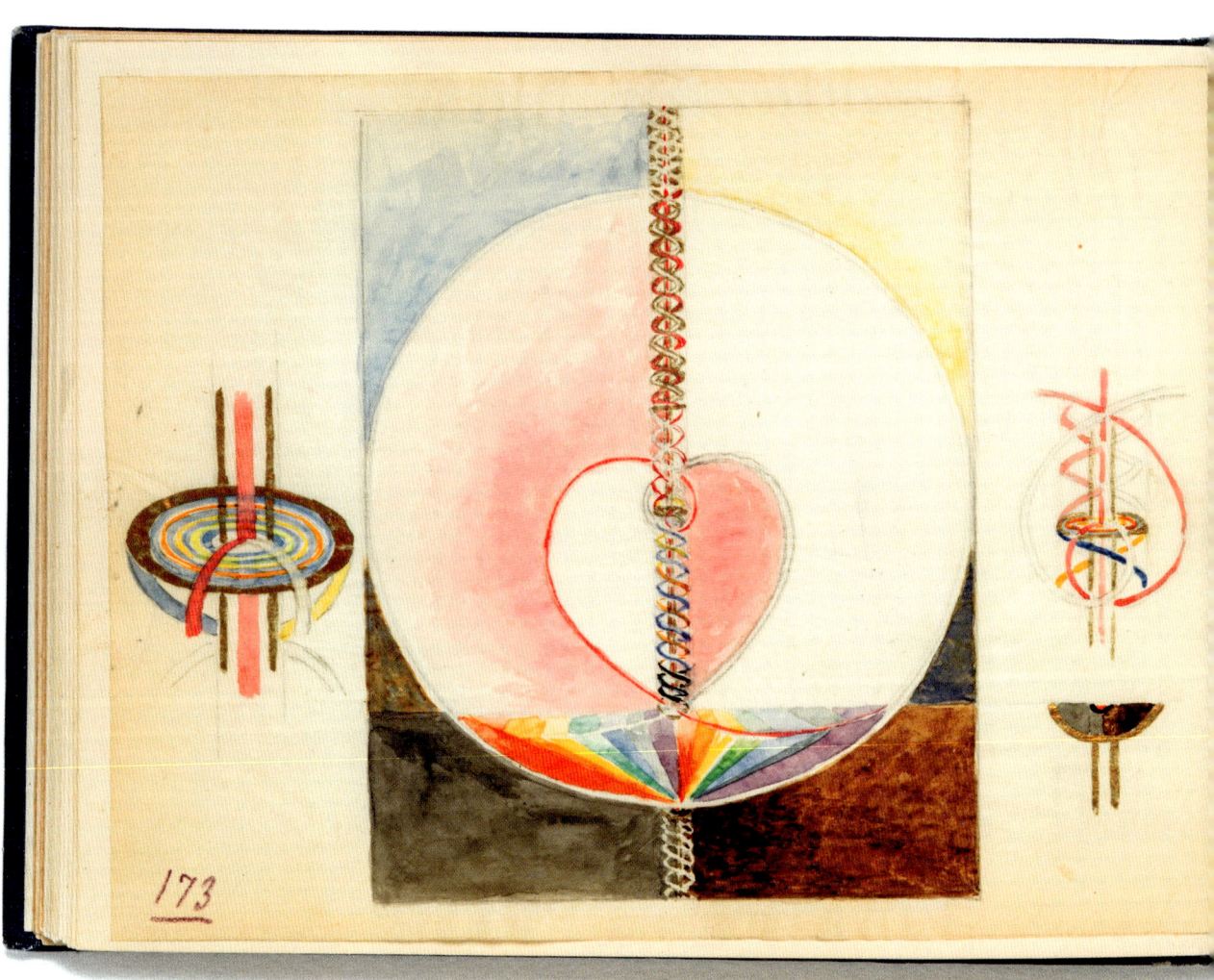

173

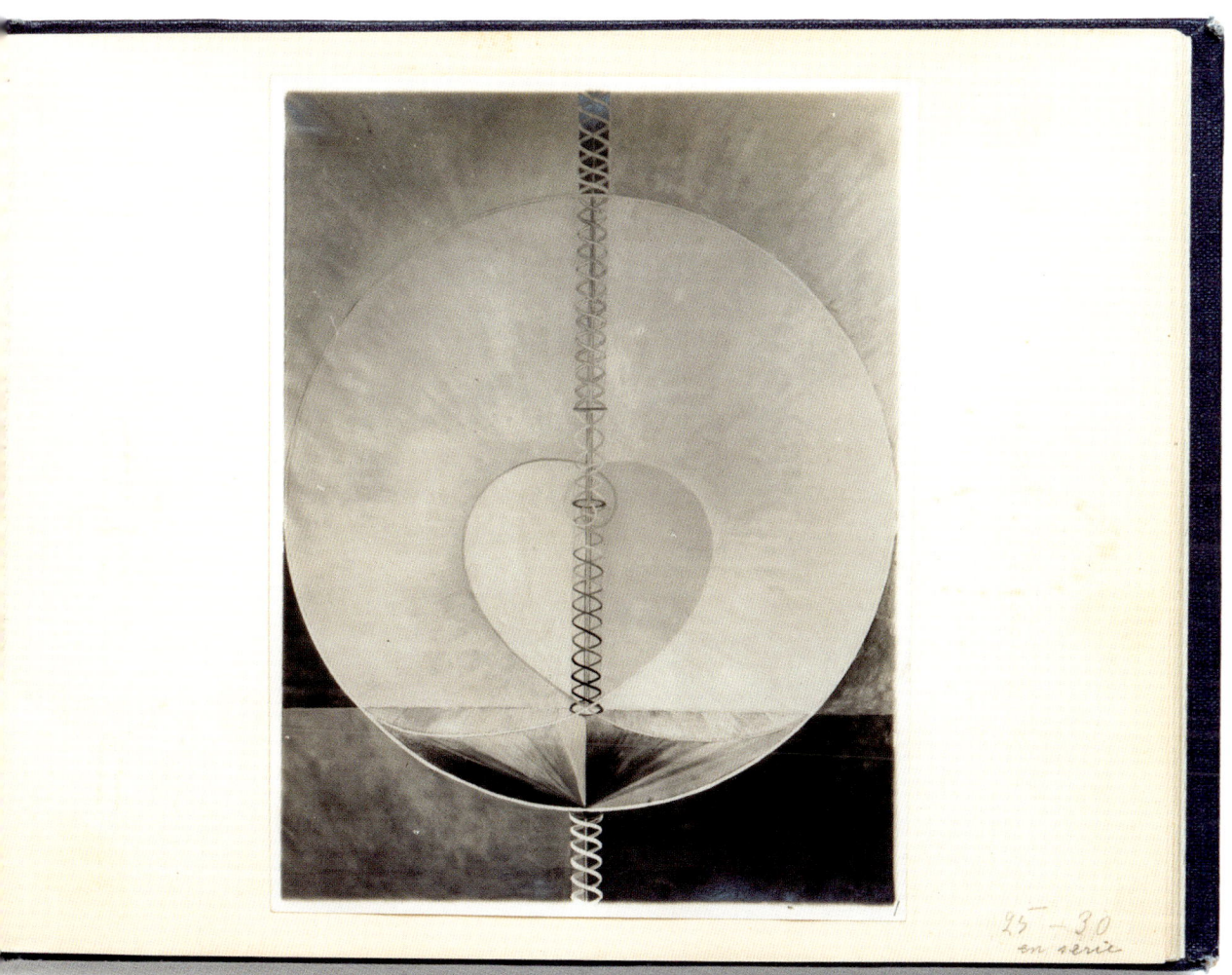

The Paintings for the Temple. Here the development of matter out of spirit is explored. "U" stands for the spiritual and "W" for matter; yellow represents the masculine and blue the feminine. (For af Klint's own definition of these and all terms in the work see *Notes on Letters and Words Pertaining to Works by Hilma af Klint* in this volume.) She continues through each series systematically exploring principles of polarity in its many forms: light and dark, good and evil, male and female. Polarity is understood by af Klint as a basic organizing principle of life into which is embedded a yearning for the return to unity. This desire for unity leads to spiritual evolution, which eventually culminates in a return to Oneness. For Hilma af Klint, the heart has a central role in this process. The three *Altarpiece* paintings of the final book, Group X (HaK 1180), depict the development of the material world from unity into multiplicity, experience in the world, and finally the return to Oneness. They are described by af Klint as "a summary of the whole work."

It is important to note that for Hilma af Klint evolution is not used in the Darwinian sense but refers instead to spiritual evolution. Both the Theosophists and Rudolf Steiner believed that humans were once pure spirit but that they had been separated from their spiritual selves by the material world. Evolution for Steiner and for af Klint is the process that will ultimately lead to the respiritualization of humankind.

Hilma af Klint continued to make new work for the rest of her life— including a new body of work for which she developed a "wet on wet" or "floating color" method influenced by Steiner's theory of color—but a large part of her time later in life seems to have been devoted to cataloging the work she had made up to this point.

The archive she compiled with almost scientific precision became an important tool in her lifelong investigation. She annotated, edited, and created indexes for the notebooks of The Five and wrote a text of more than two thousand pages describing her spiritual experiences. Her most important contribution from this period may be the compilation of the Blue Books, which preserve for what she hoped would be a respiritualized world of the future the messages she had received so long ago.

Pages 32–33: Inv. 173 from book HaK 1179, n.d. Blue Book catalogue entry for the painting *The Dove, No.4, Group IX/The SUW/UW Series*, 1915

1171, Inv. 1-26. Original size: 0.50 × 0.38 m. Made 11/7/1906–3/15/1907 by Hilma af Klint

No. 13,14, 15, 16, 17, 18, and 19 are described by Doctor Steiner as the best symbolically.

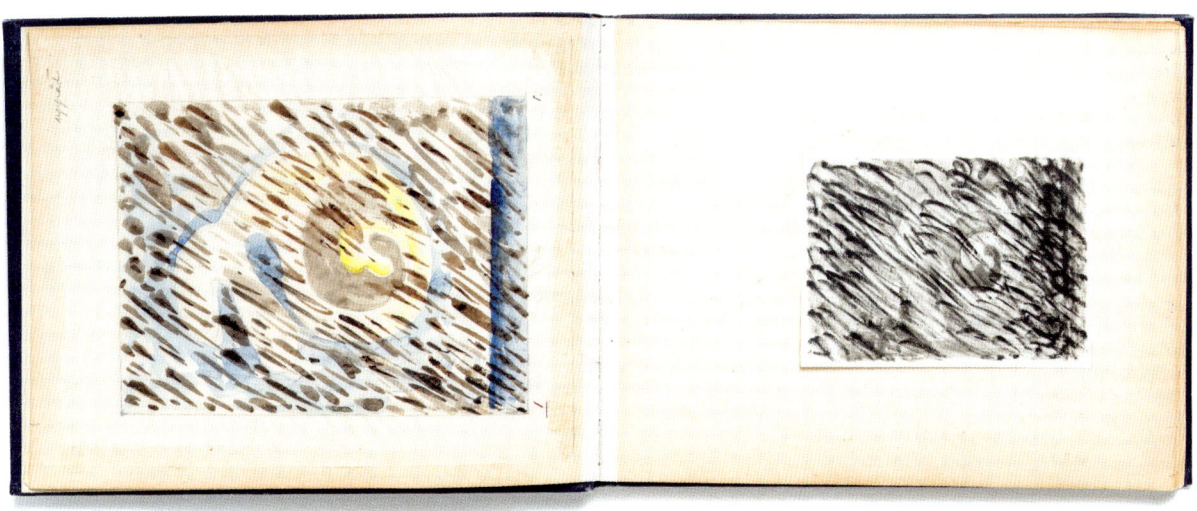

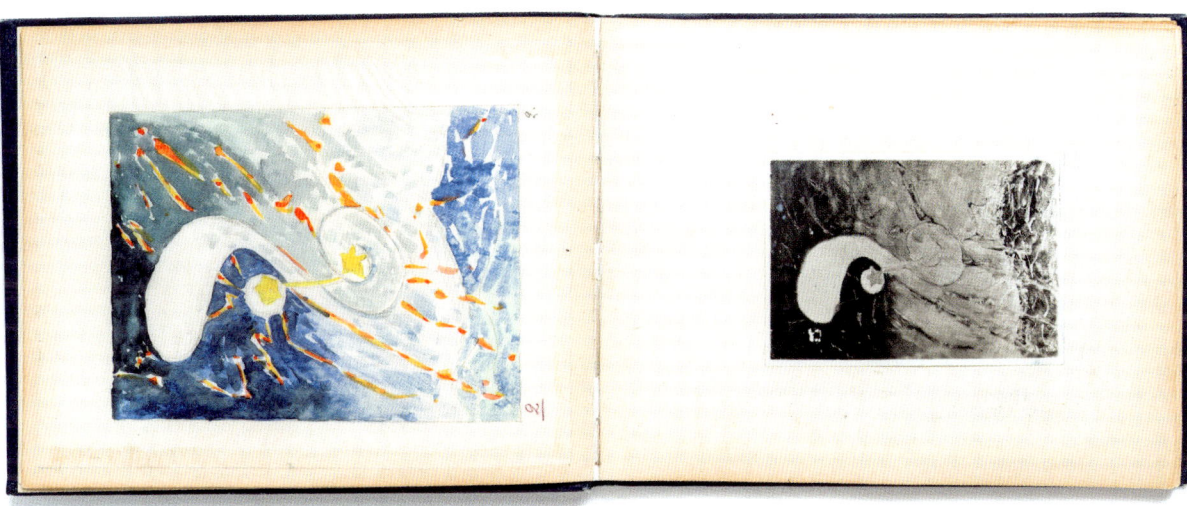

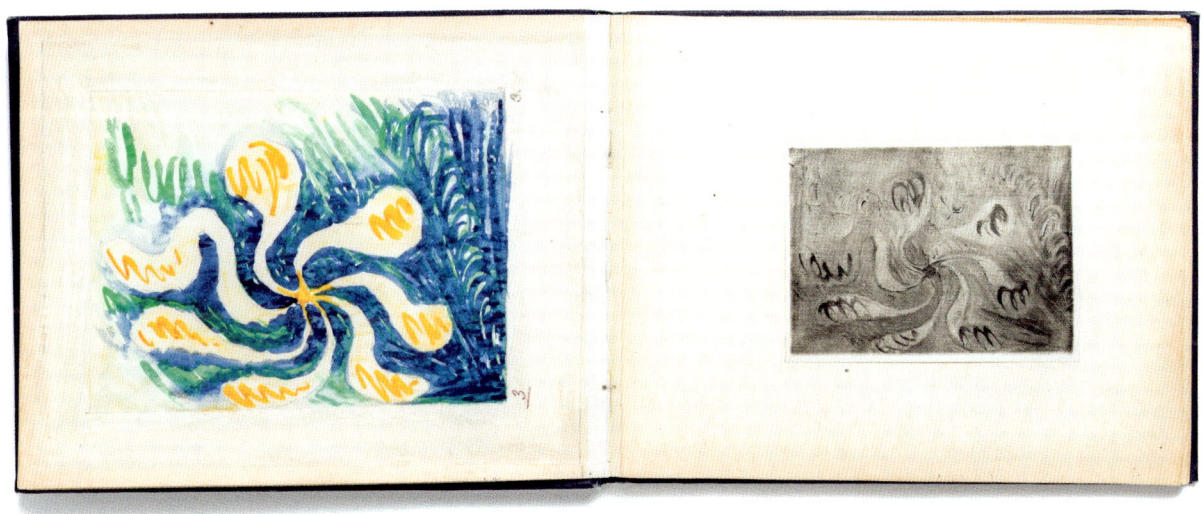

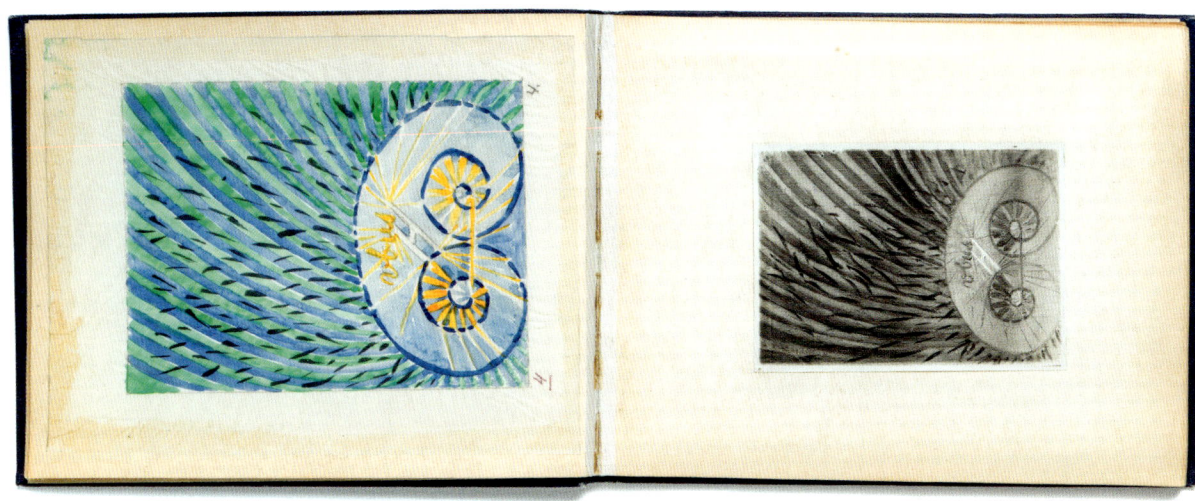

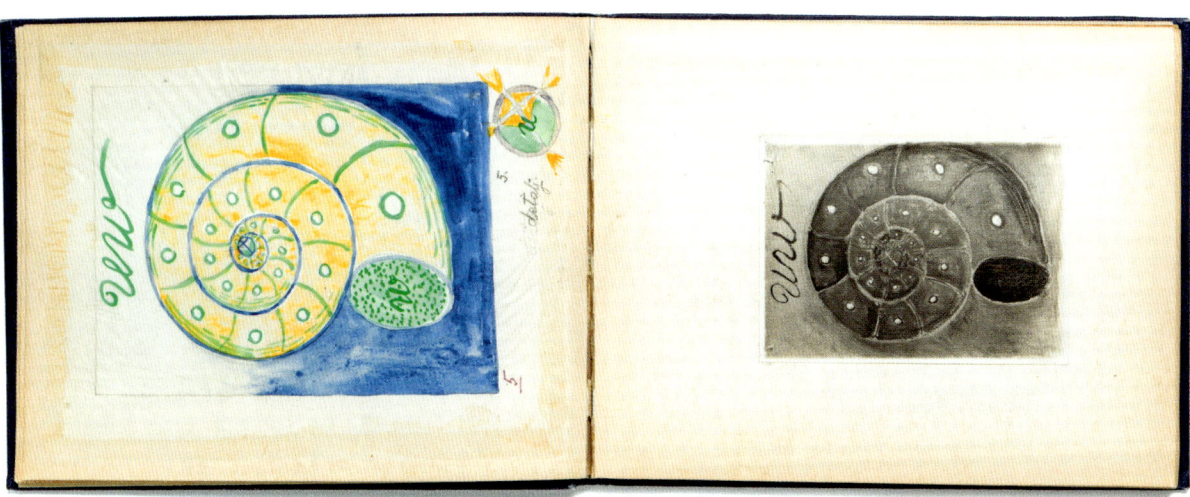

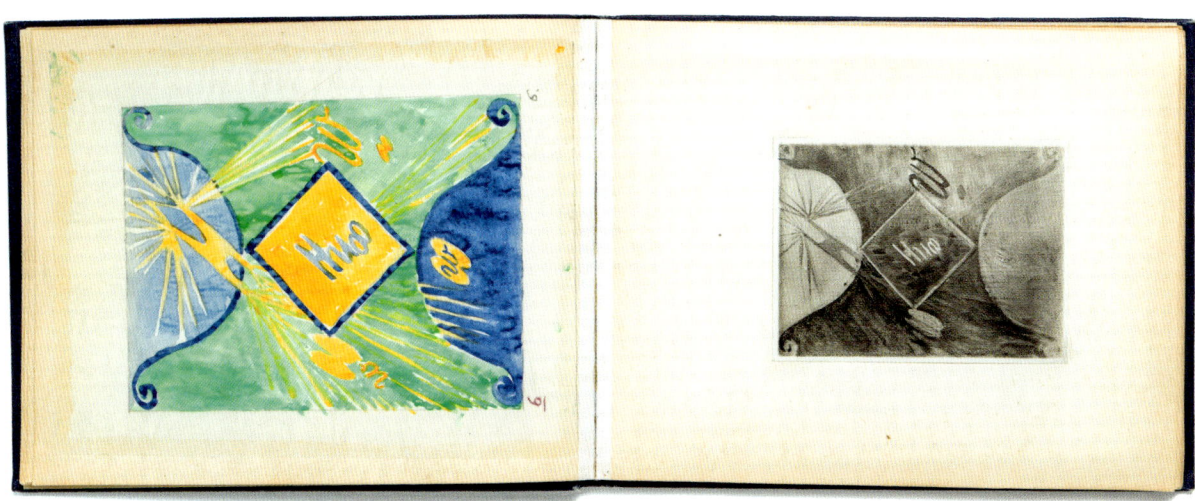

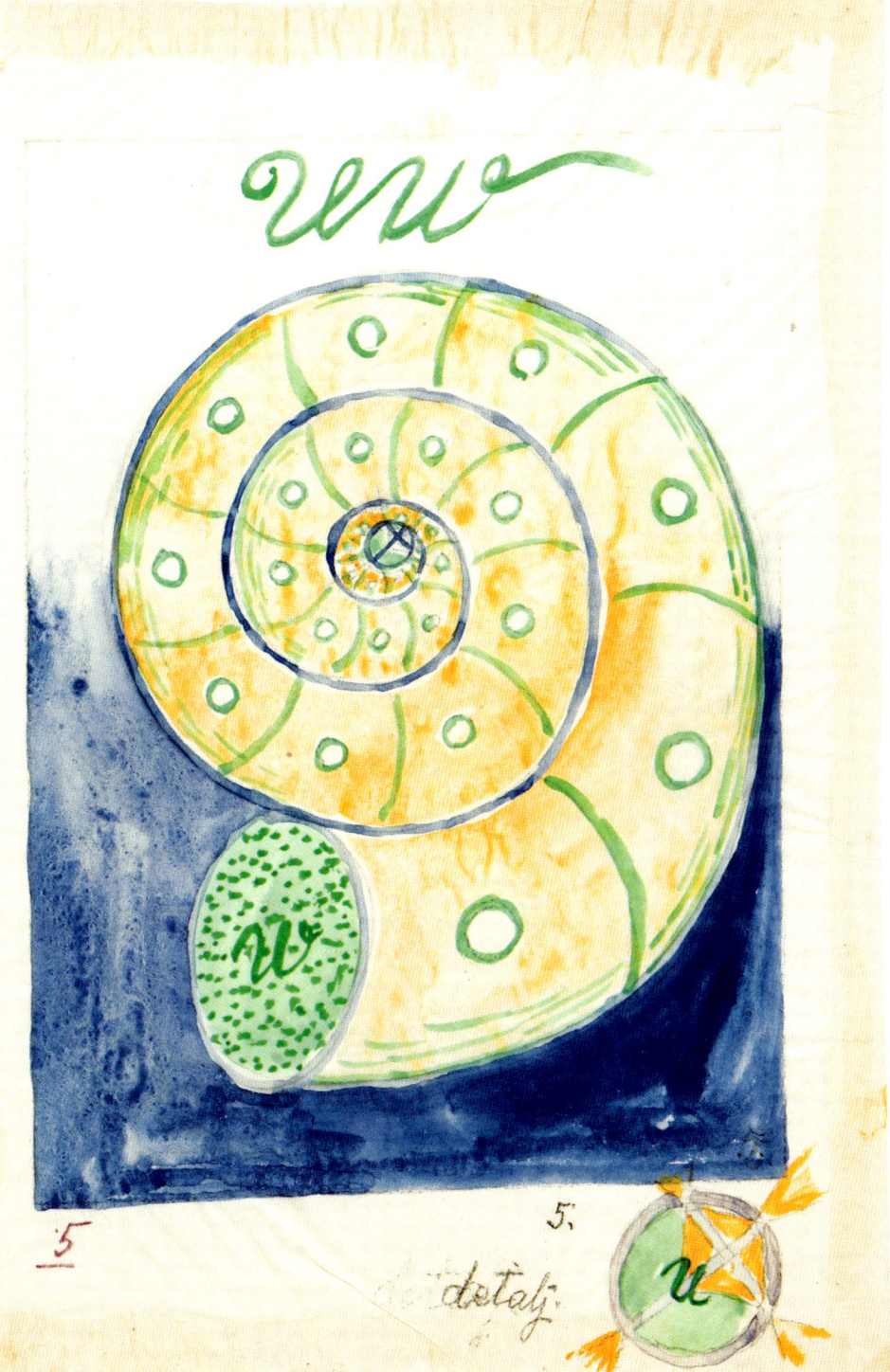

5

5.

detalj.

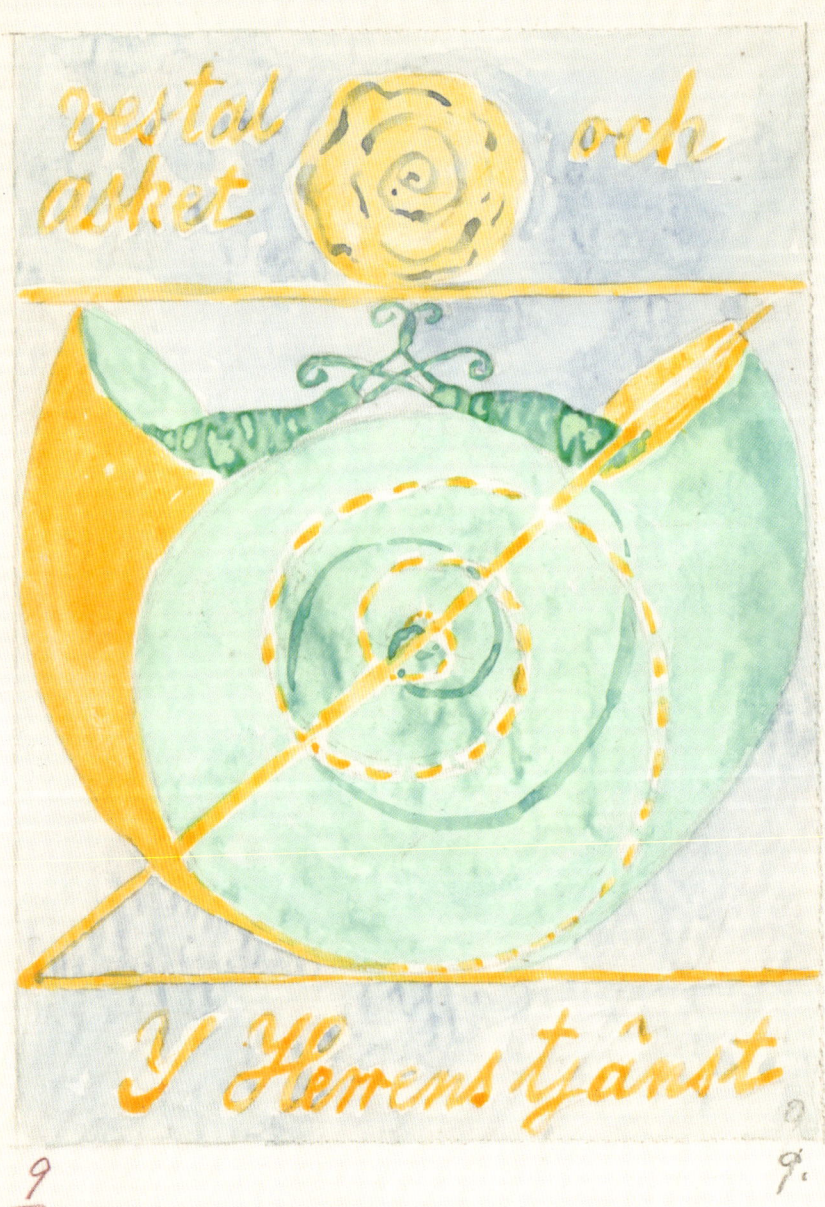

9

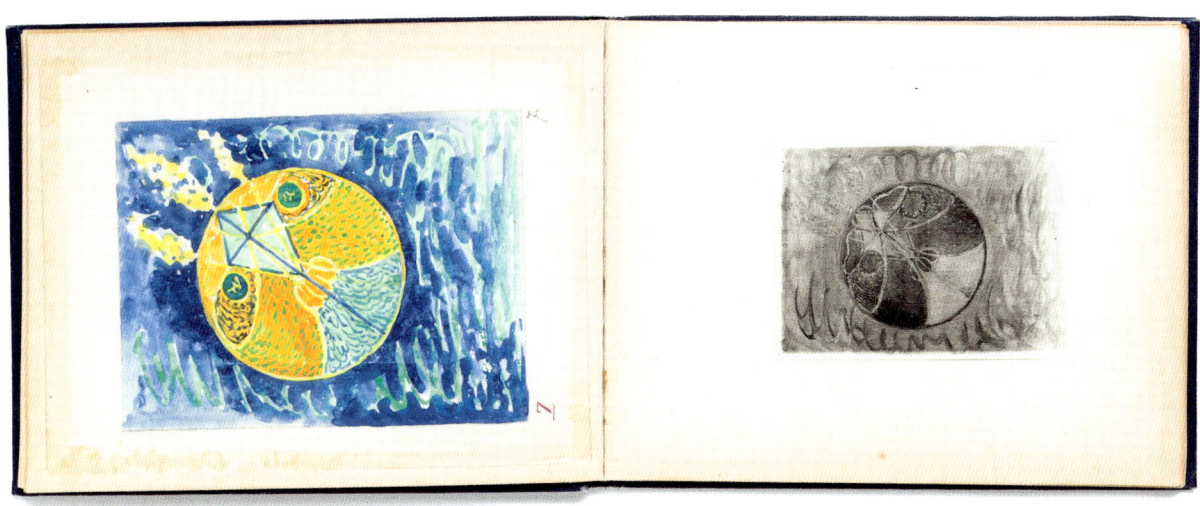

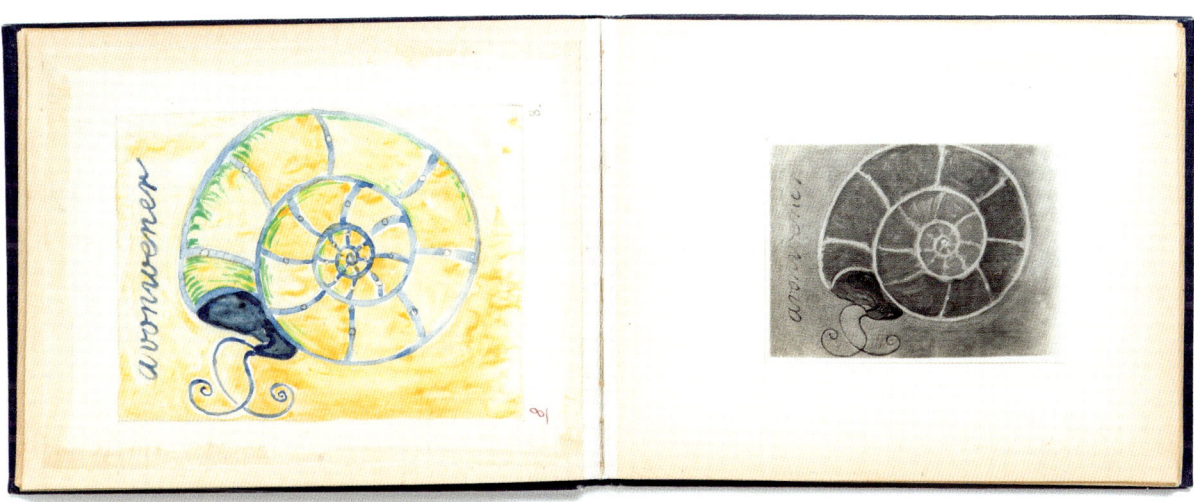

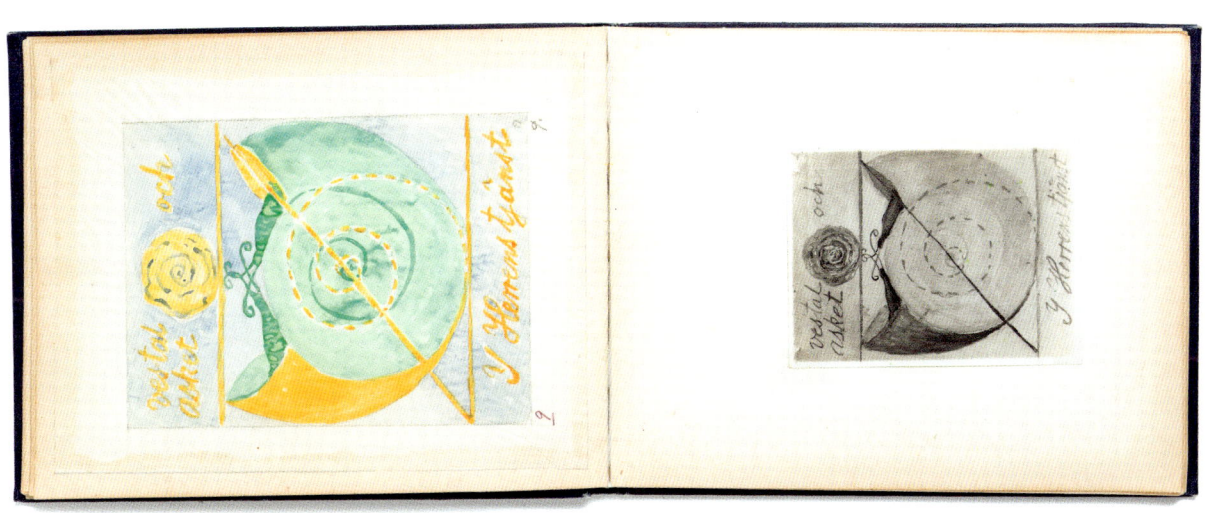

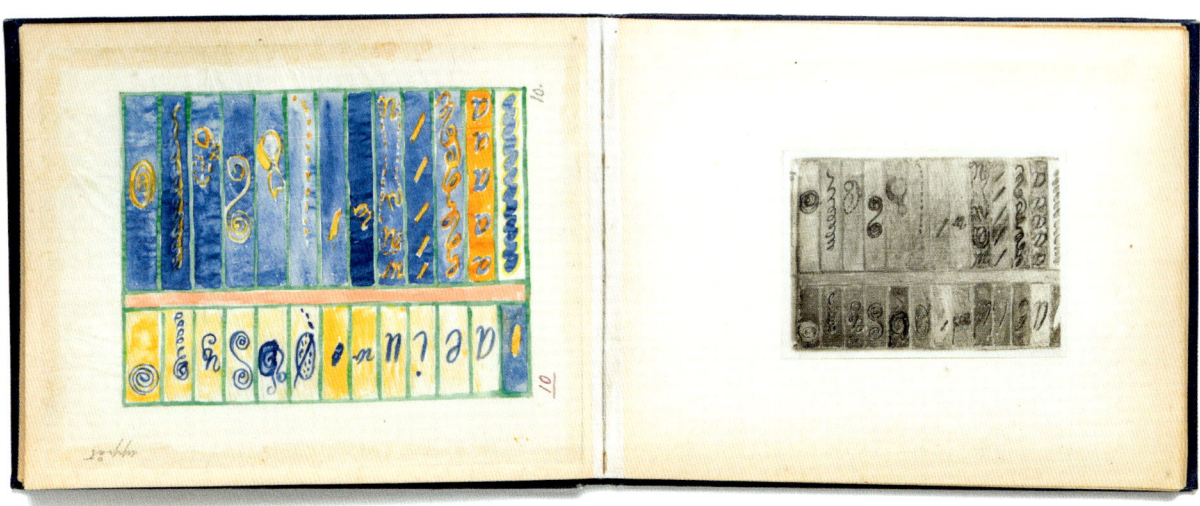

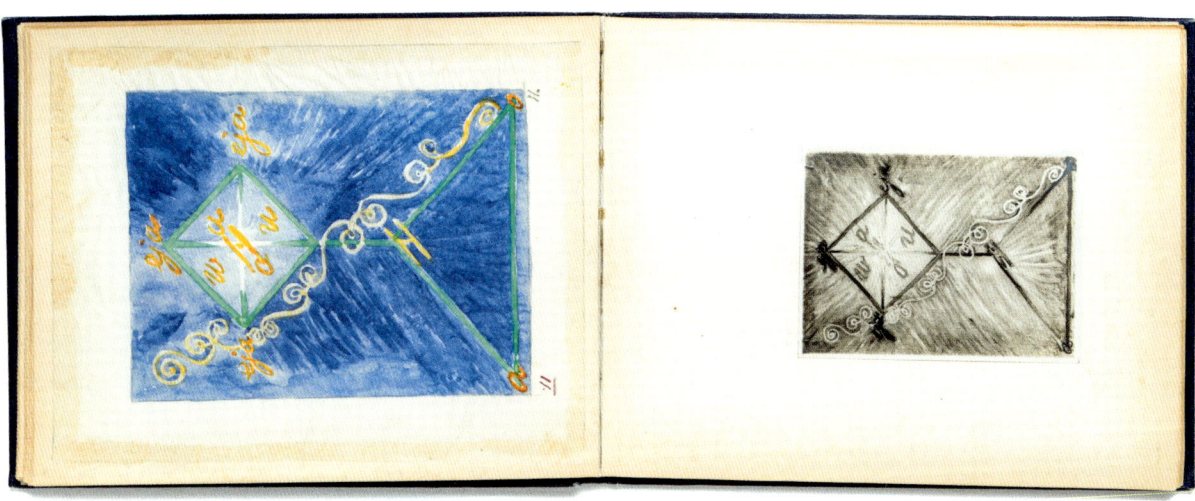

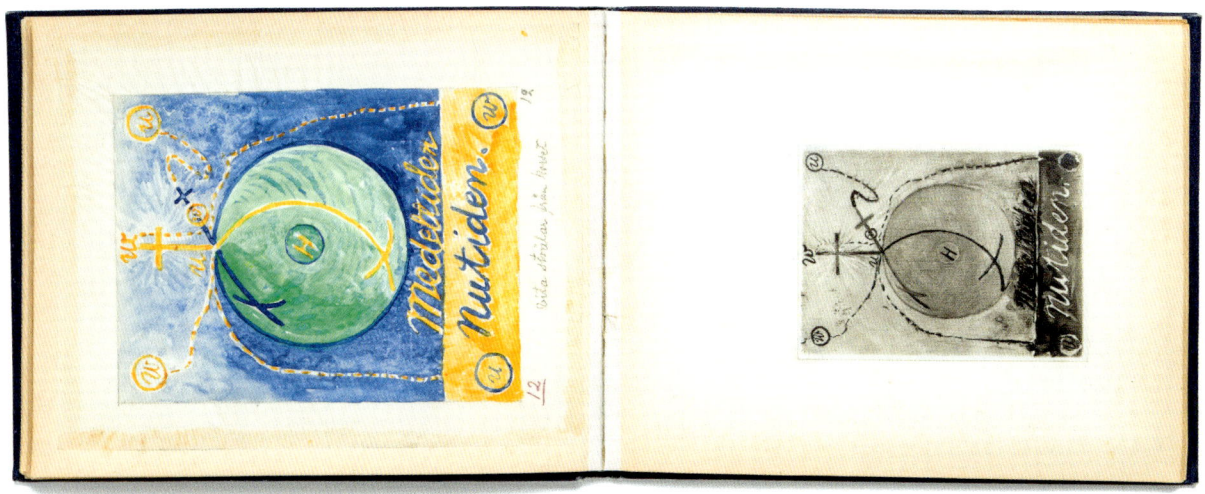

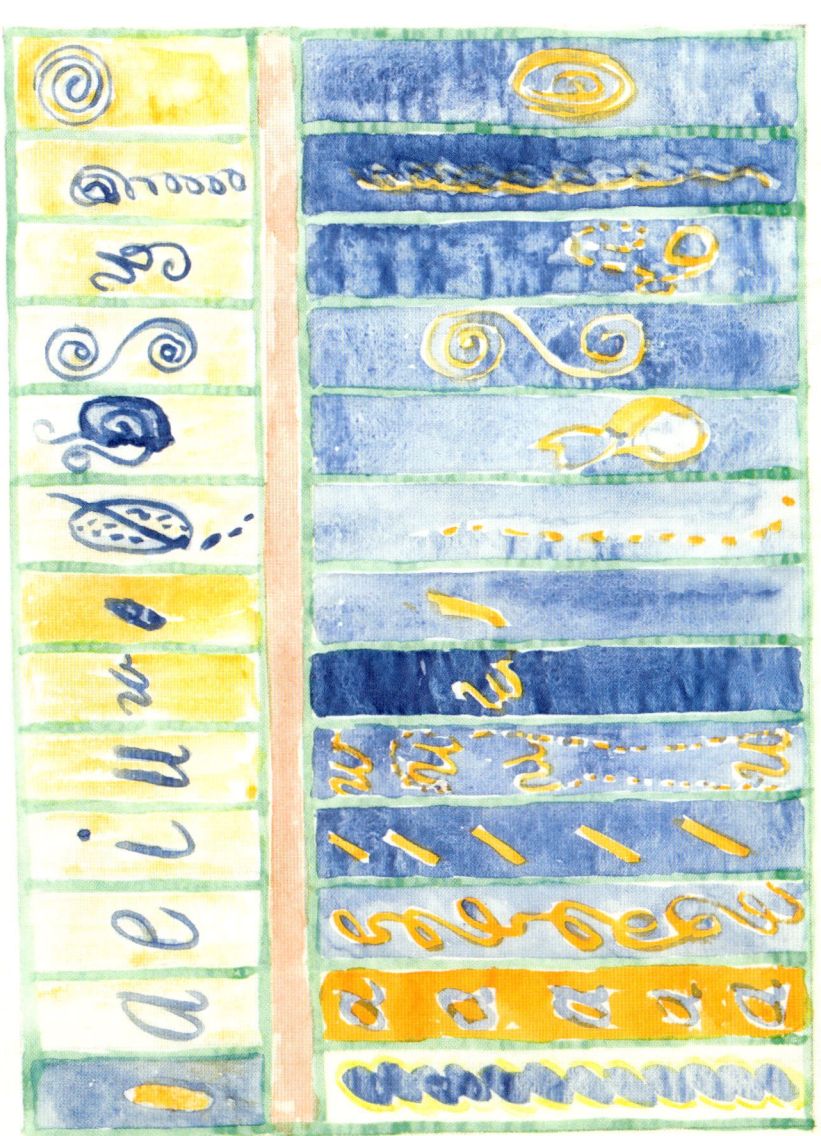

10   10.

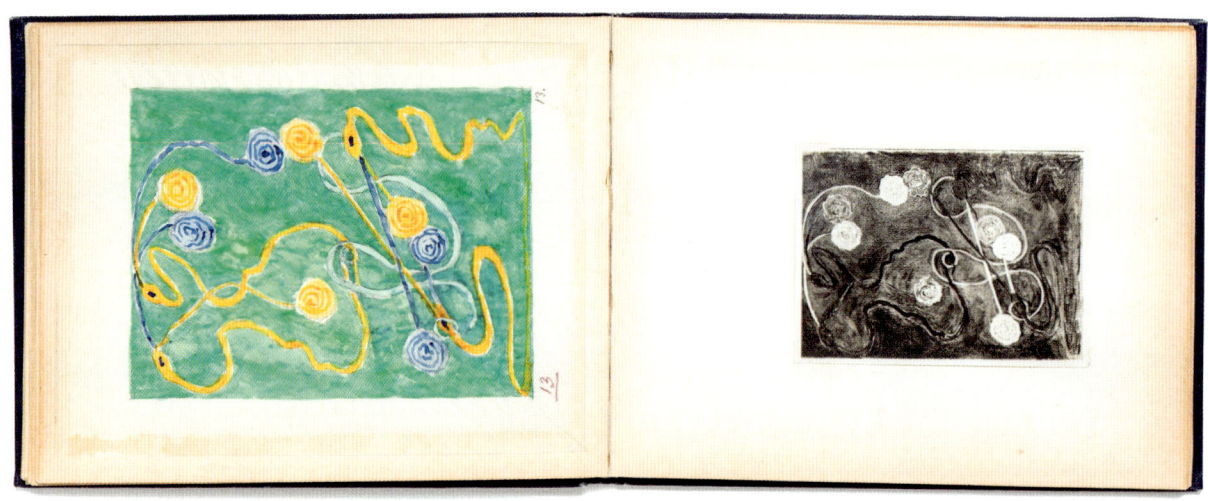

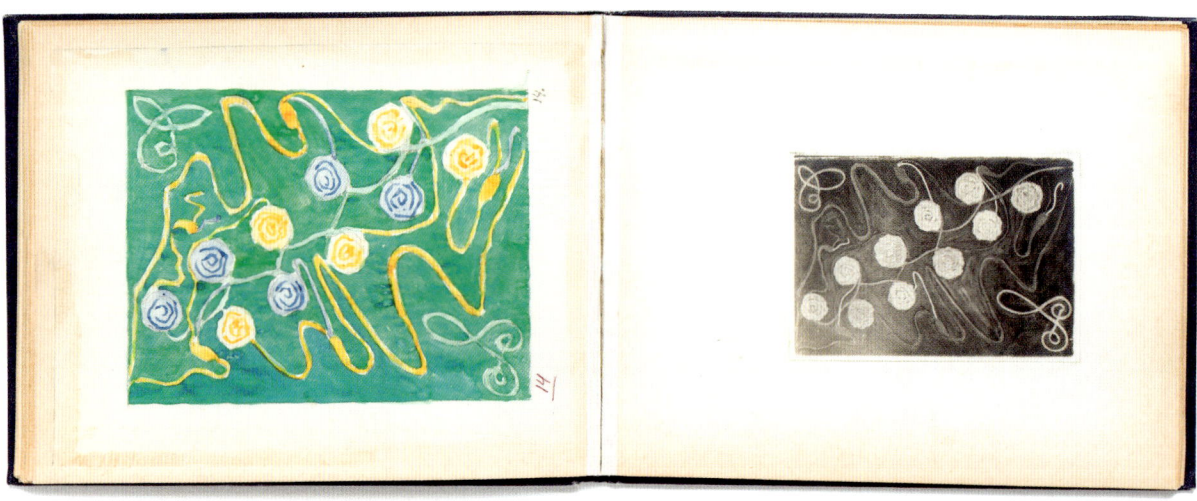

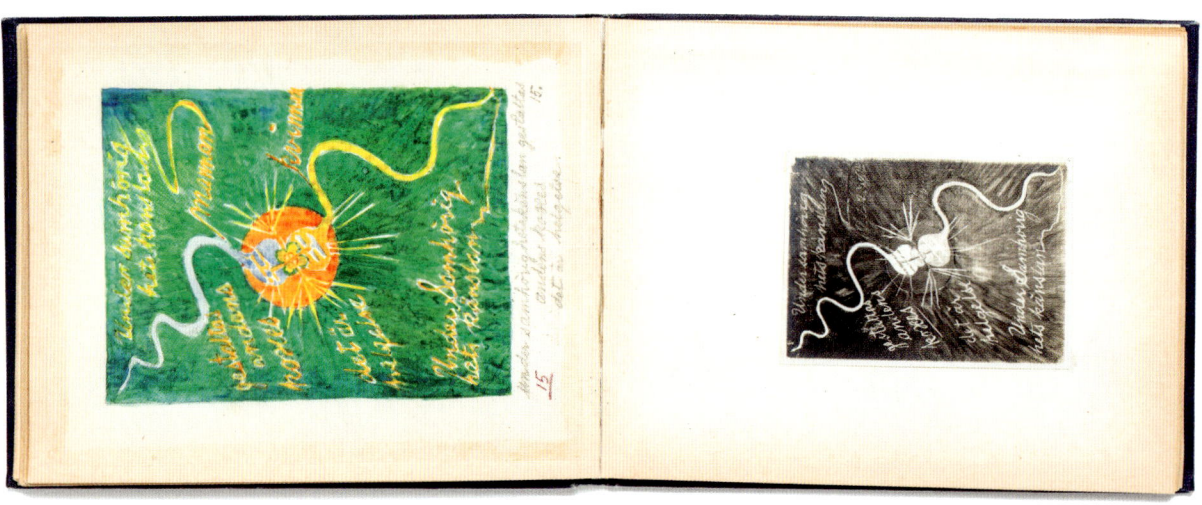

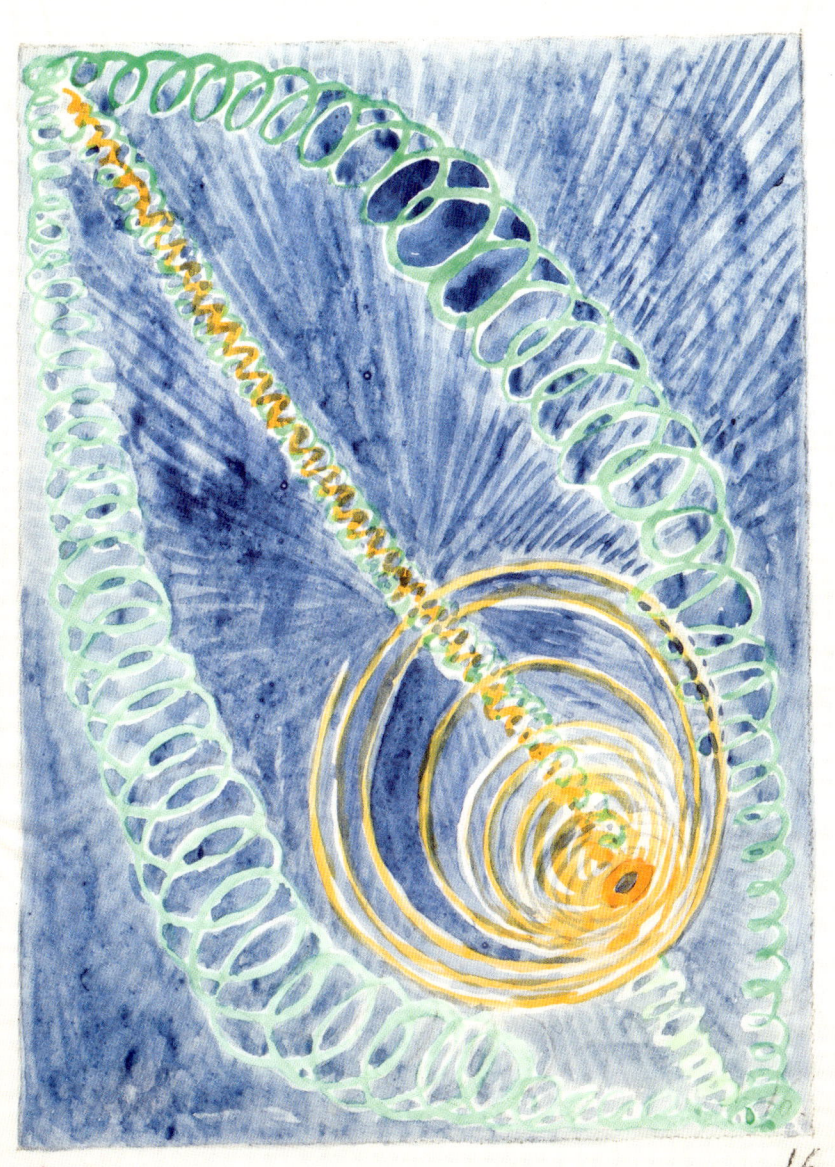

16

16.

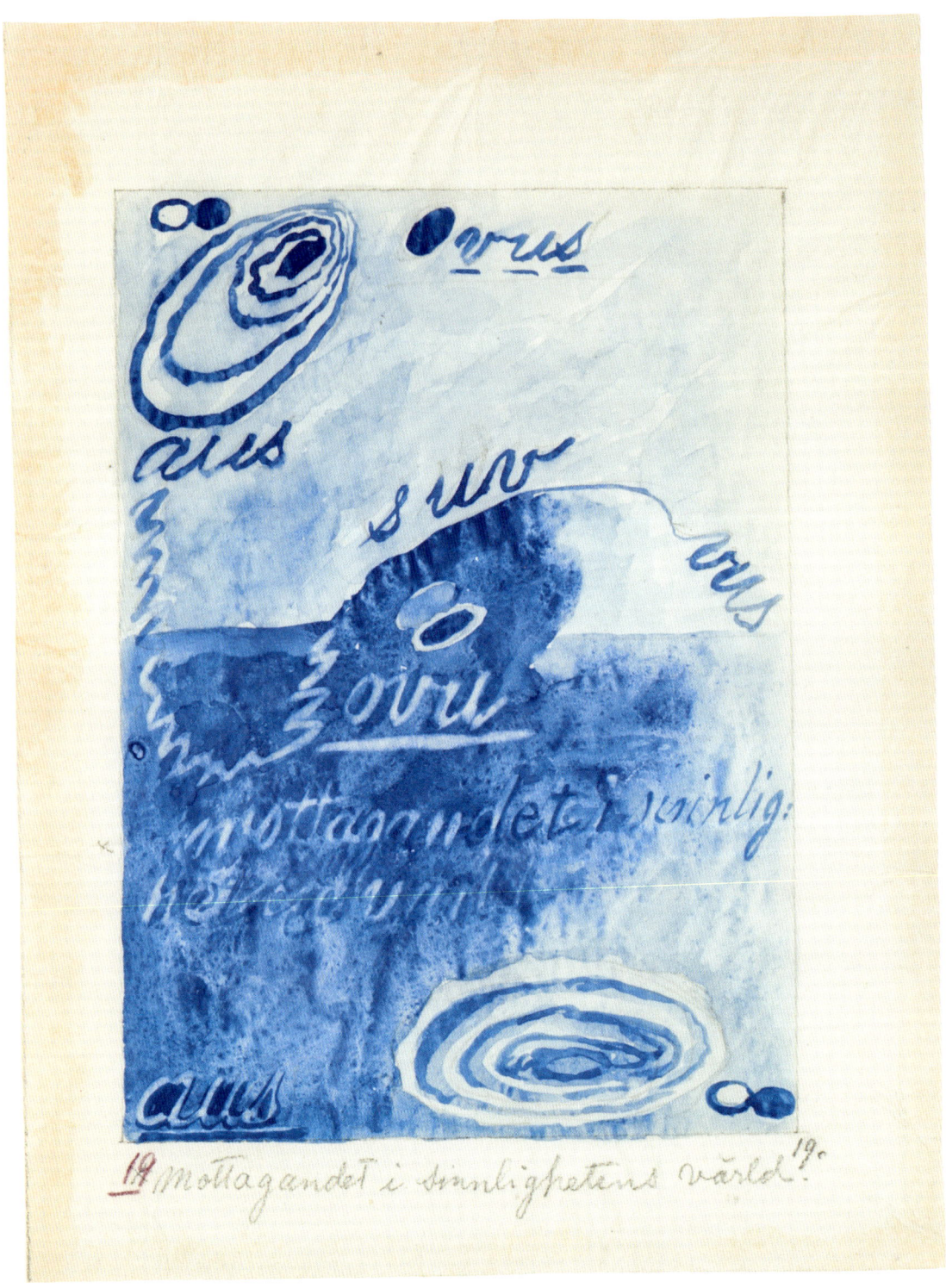

The reception into the sensual world.

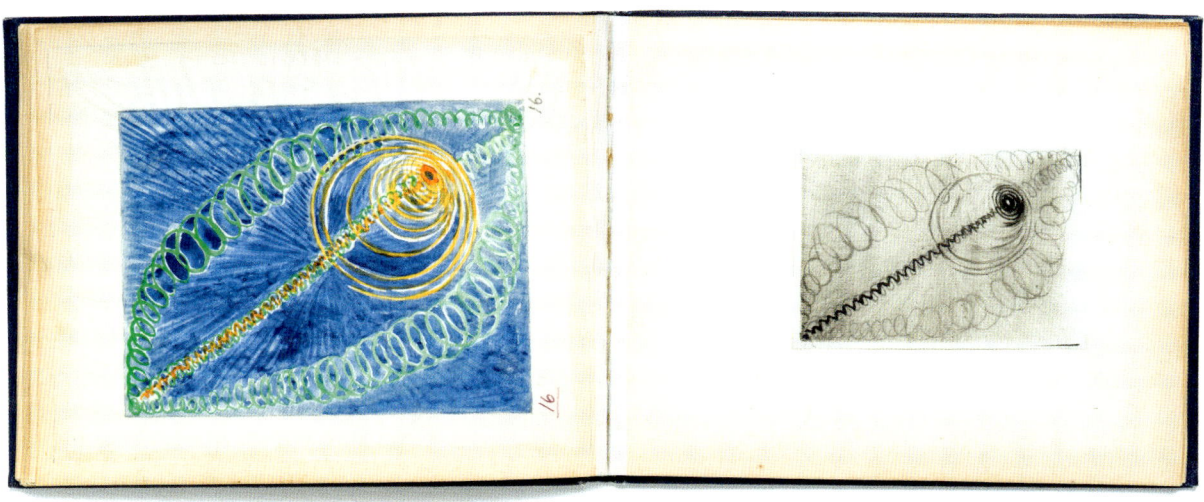

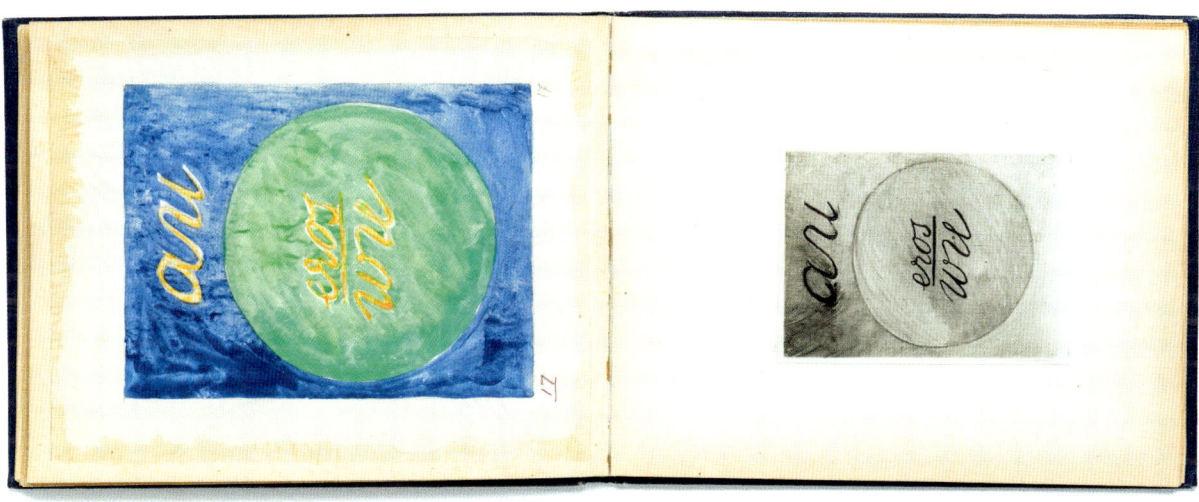

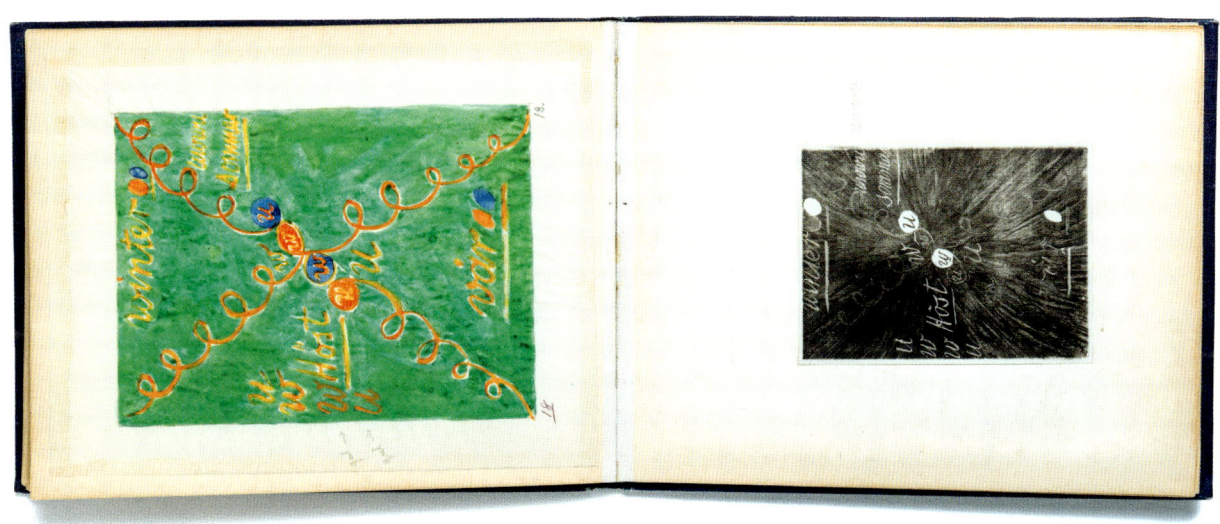

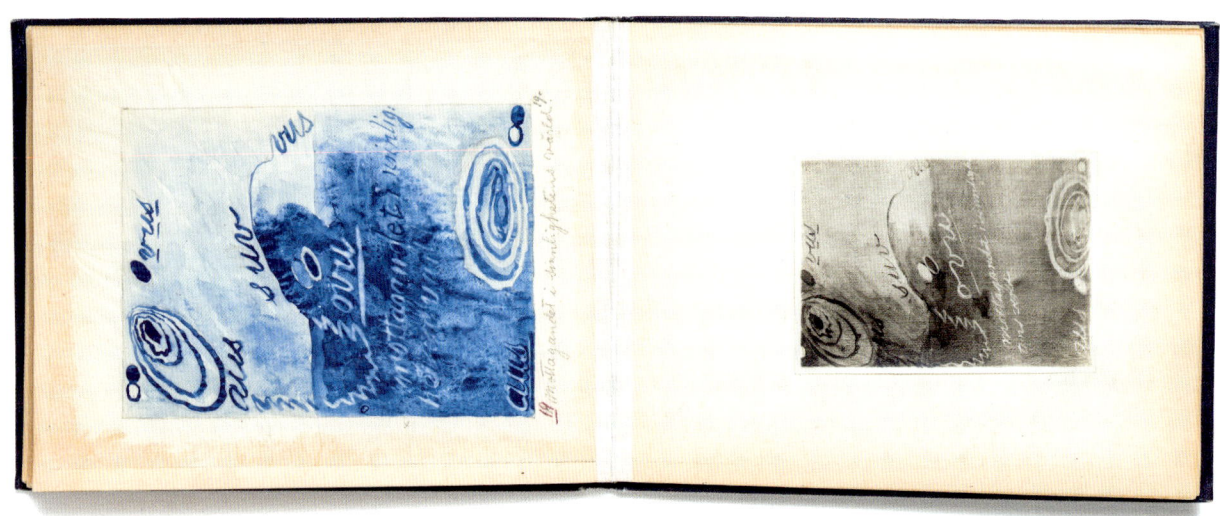

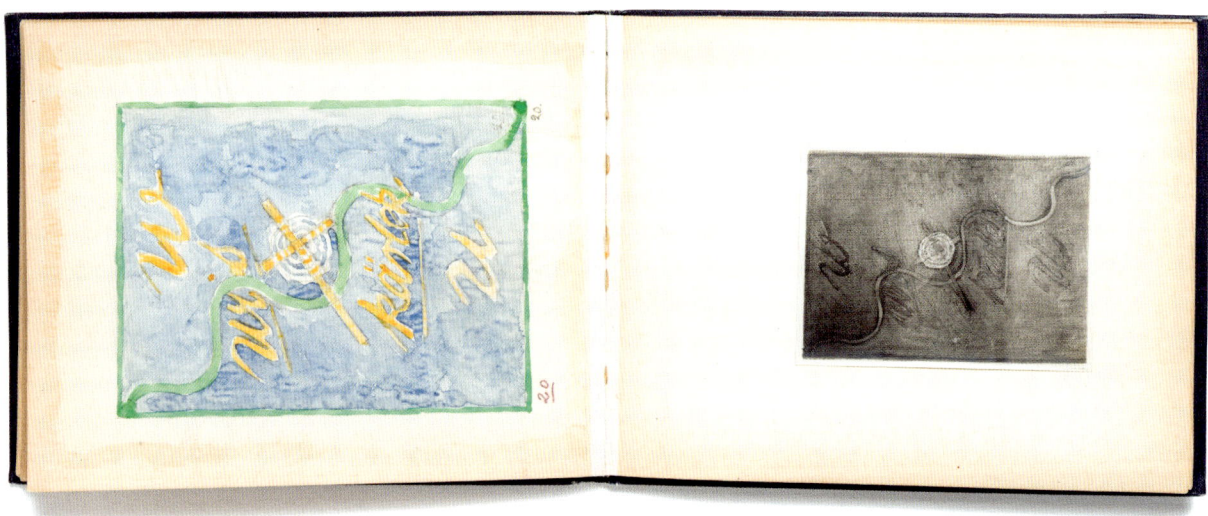

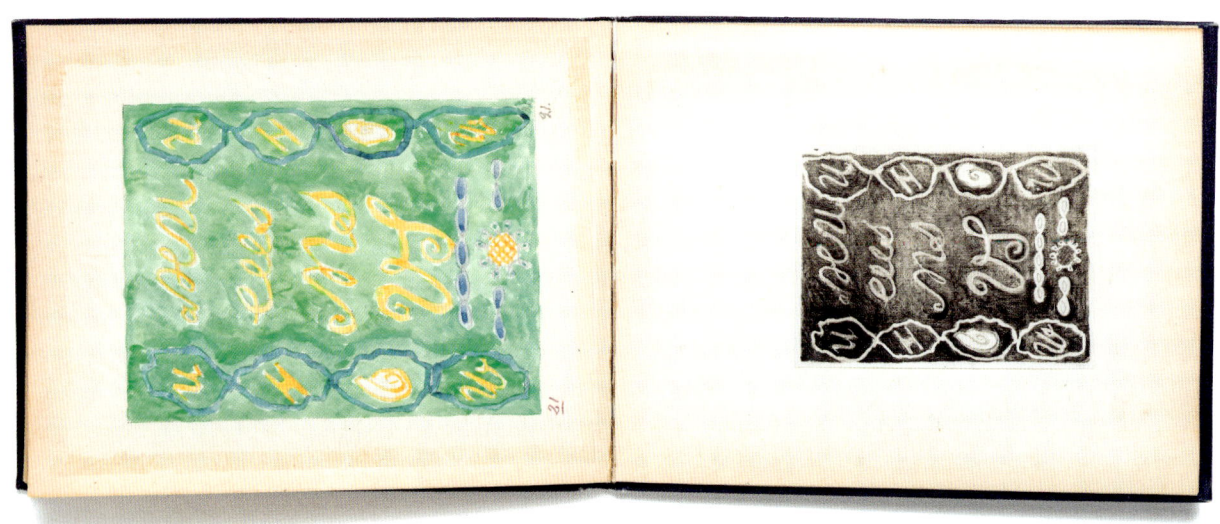

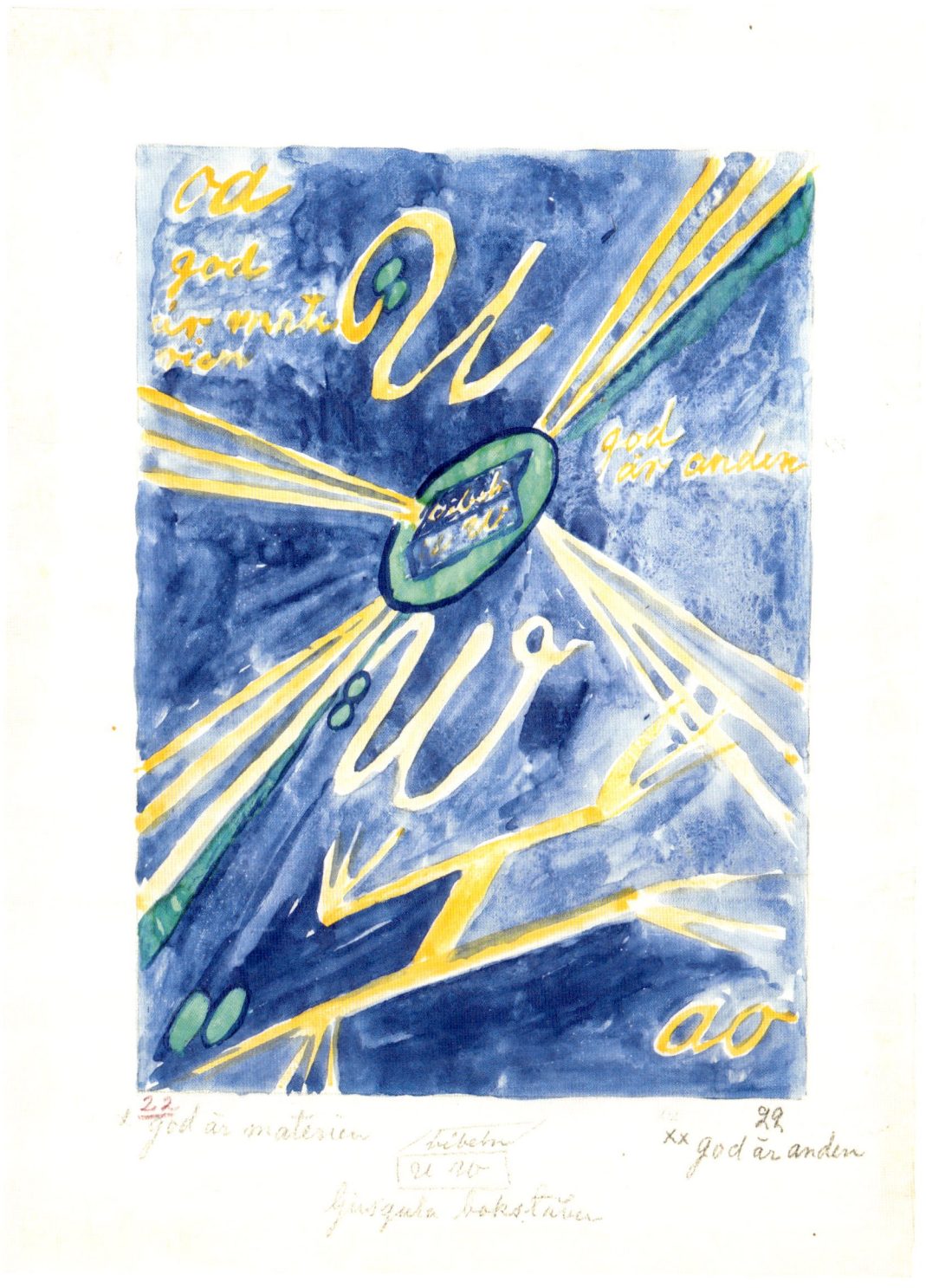

× *Matter is good* ×× *The spirit is good*
The bible / U W
letters in pale yellow

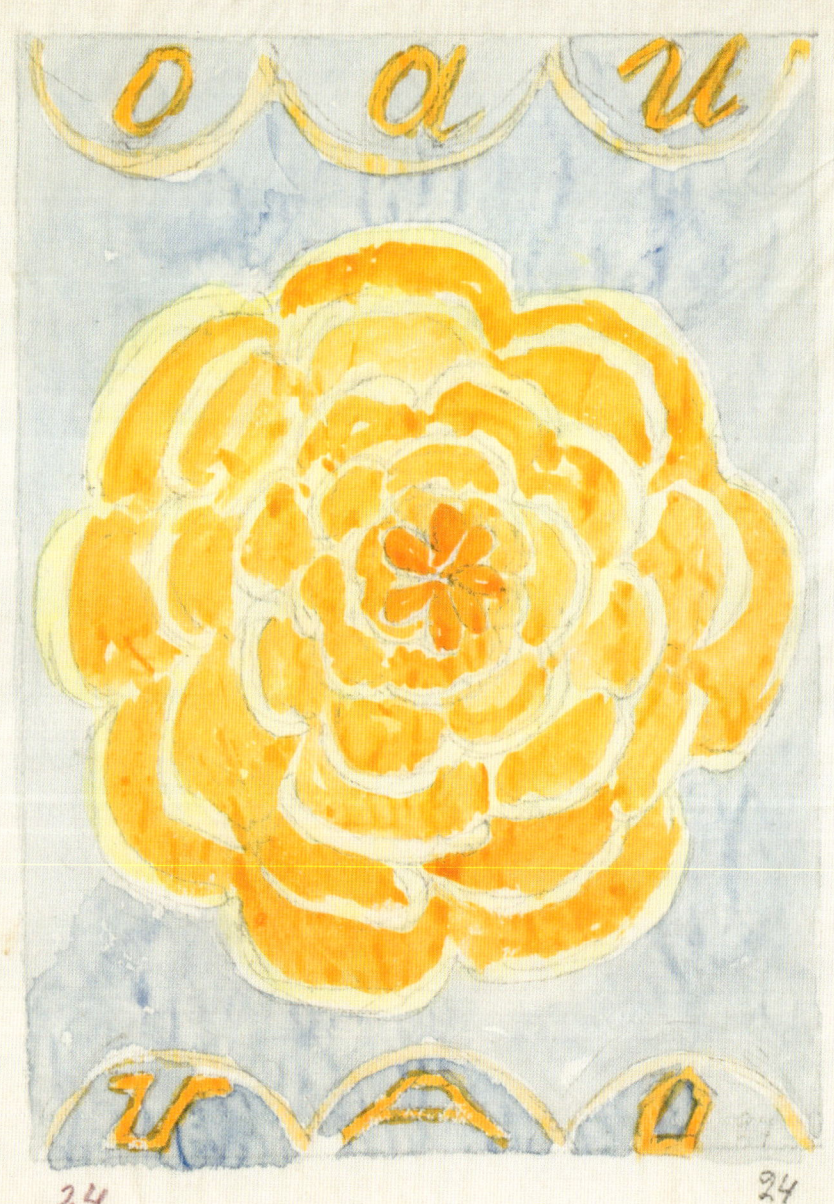

24   24

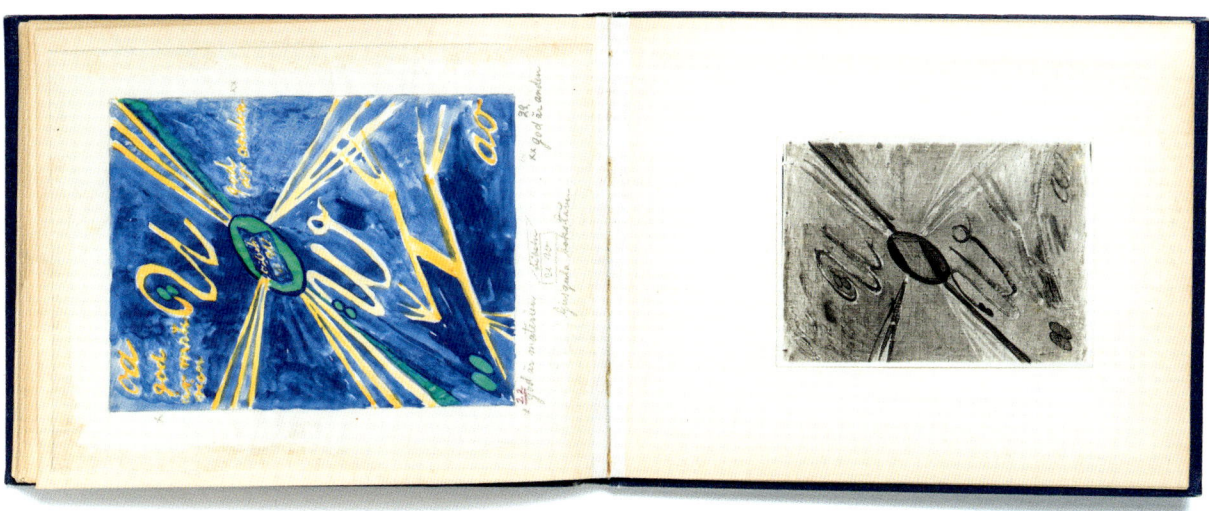

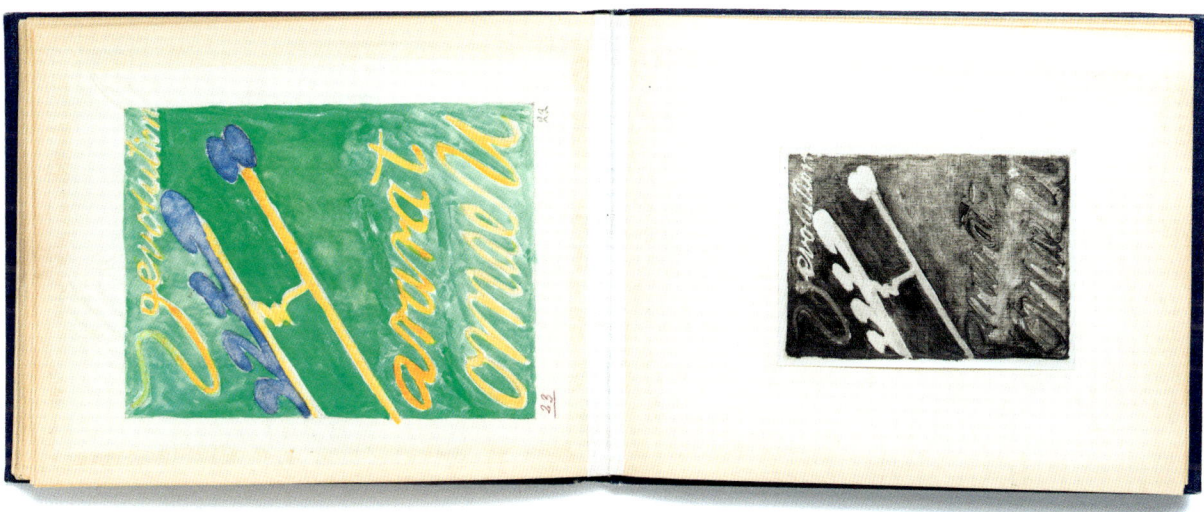

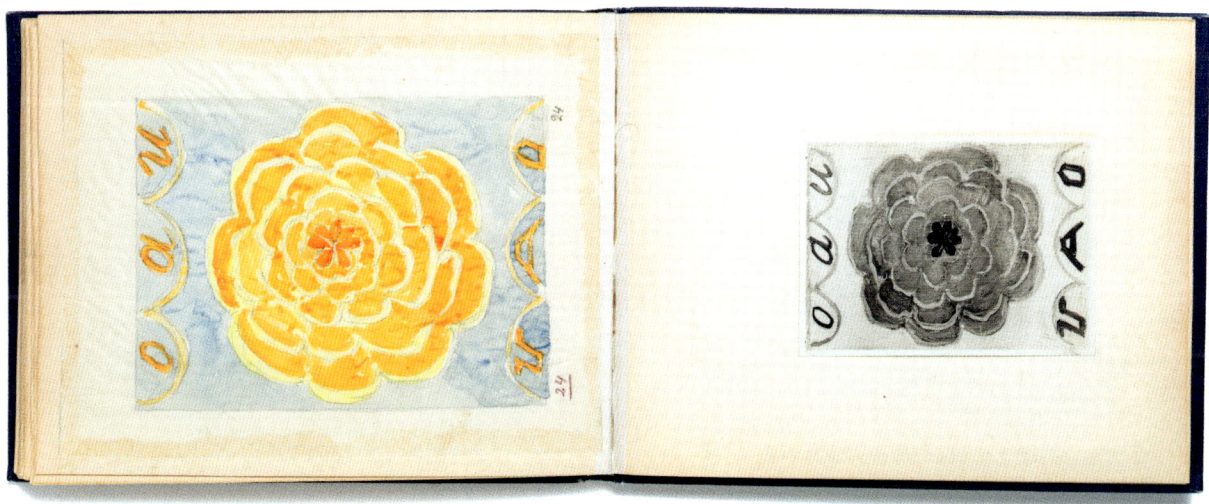

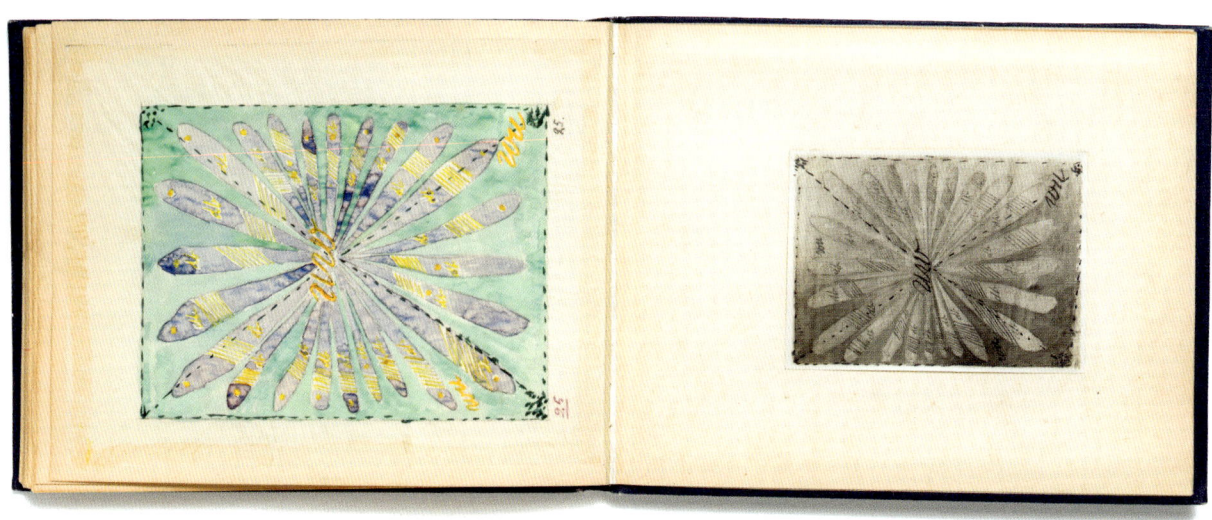

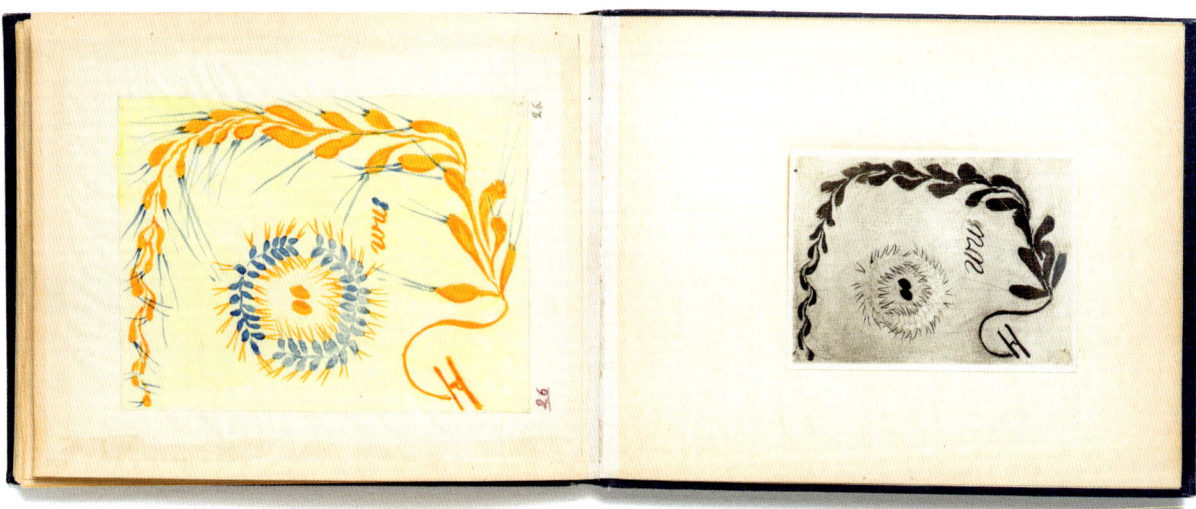

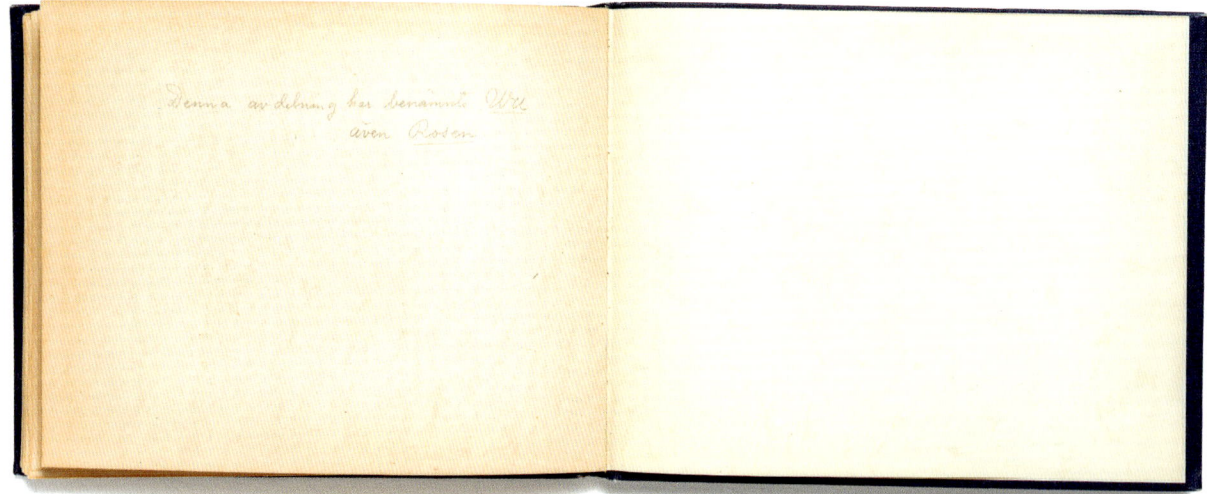

This section has been called WU and the Rose

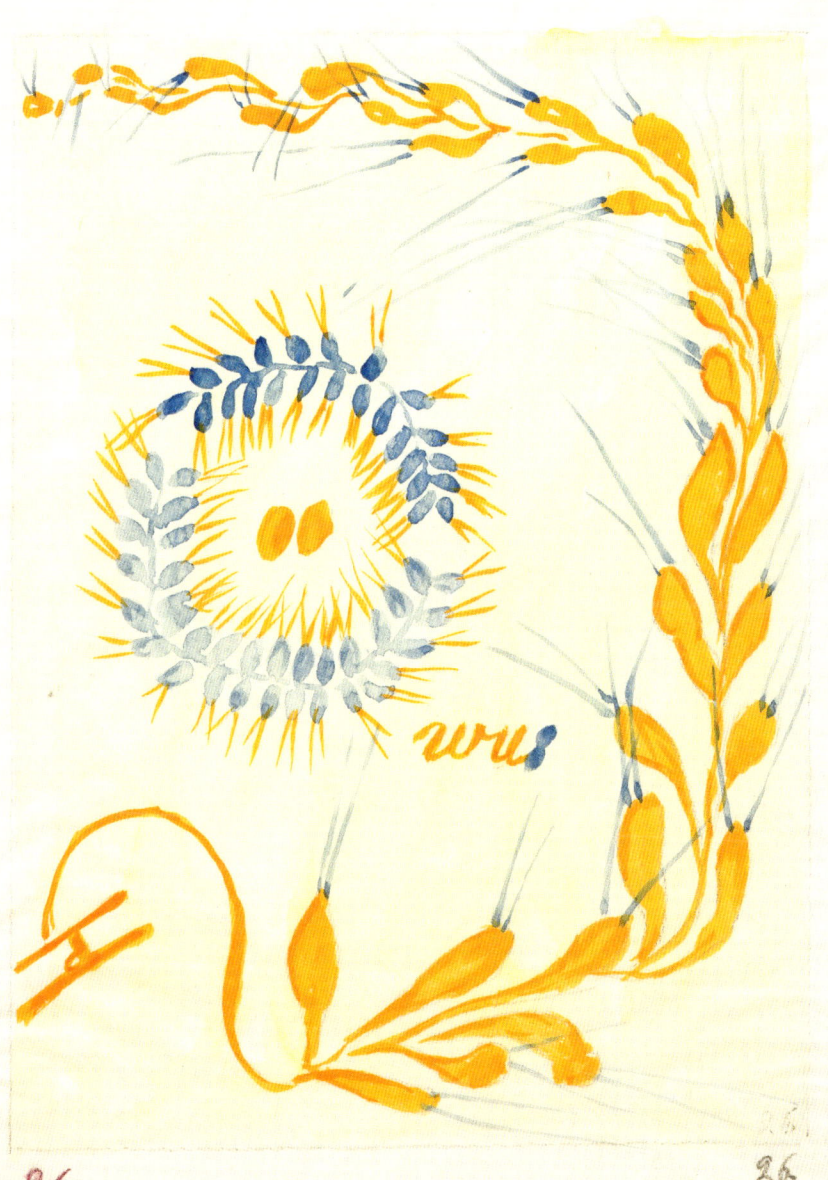

26

26

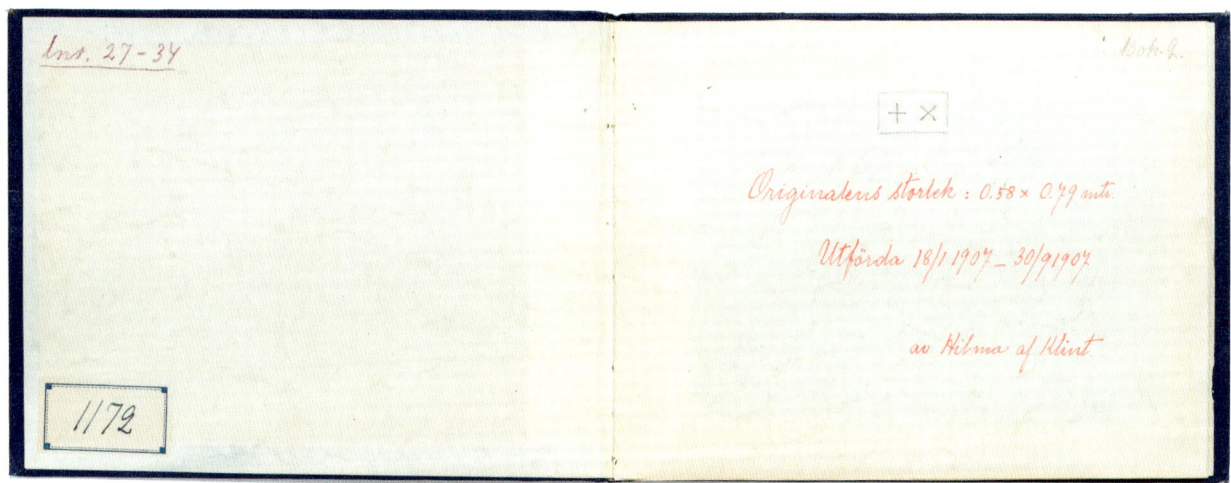

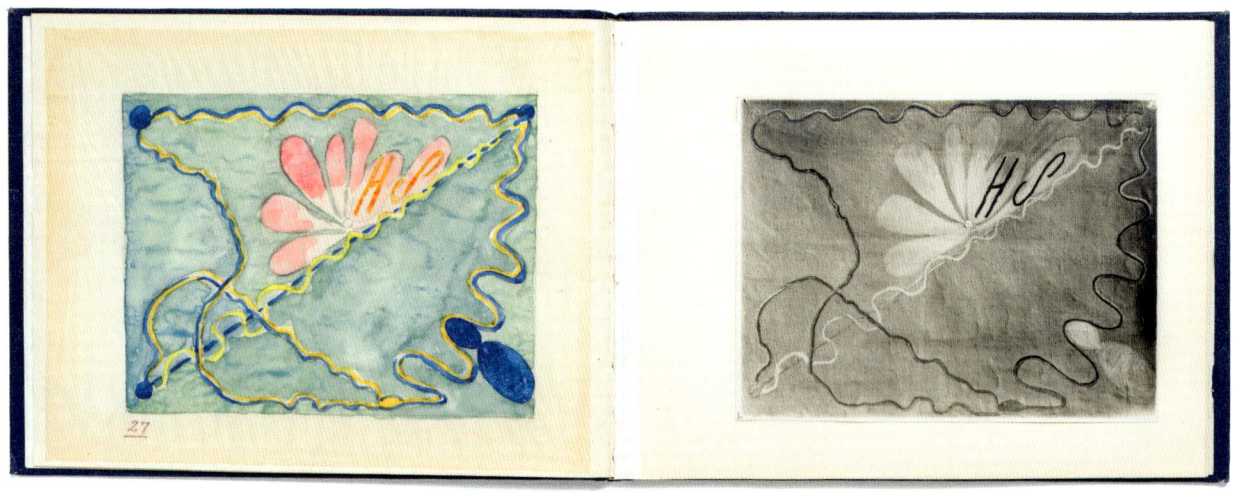

1172, Inv. 27–34. Original size: 0.58 × 0.79 m. Made 1/8/1907–9/30/1907, by Hilma af Klint

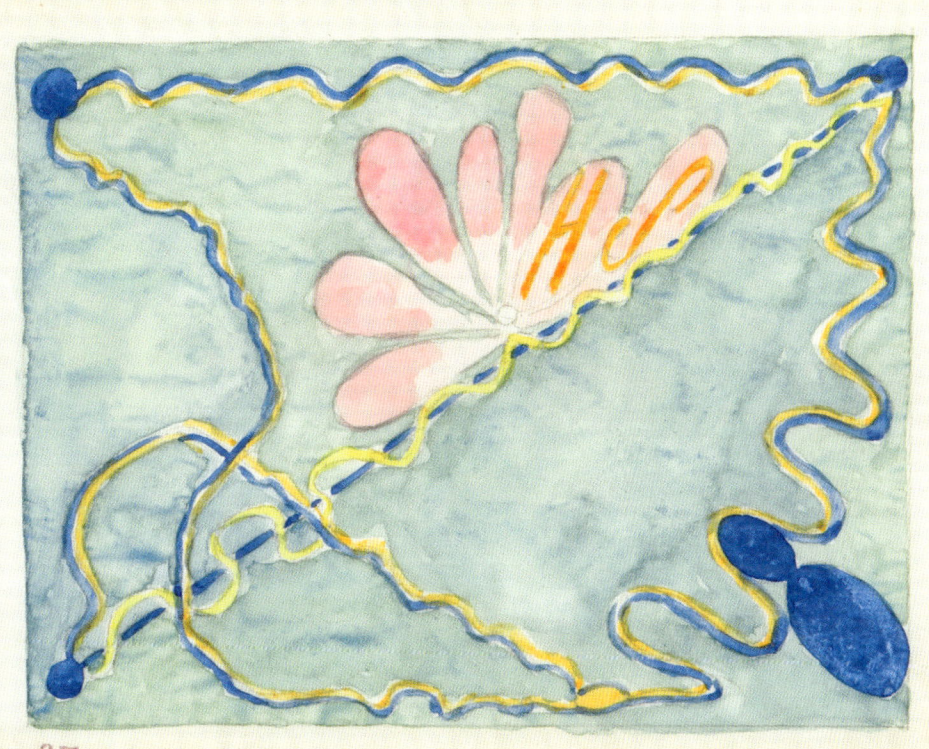

27

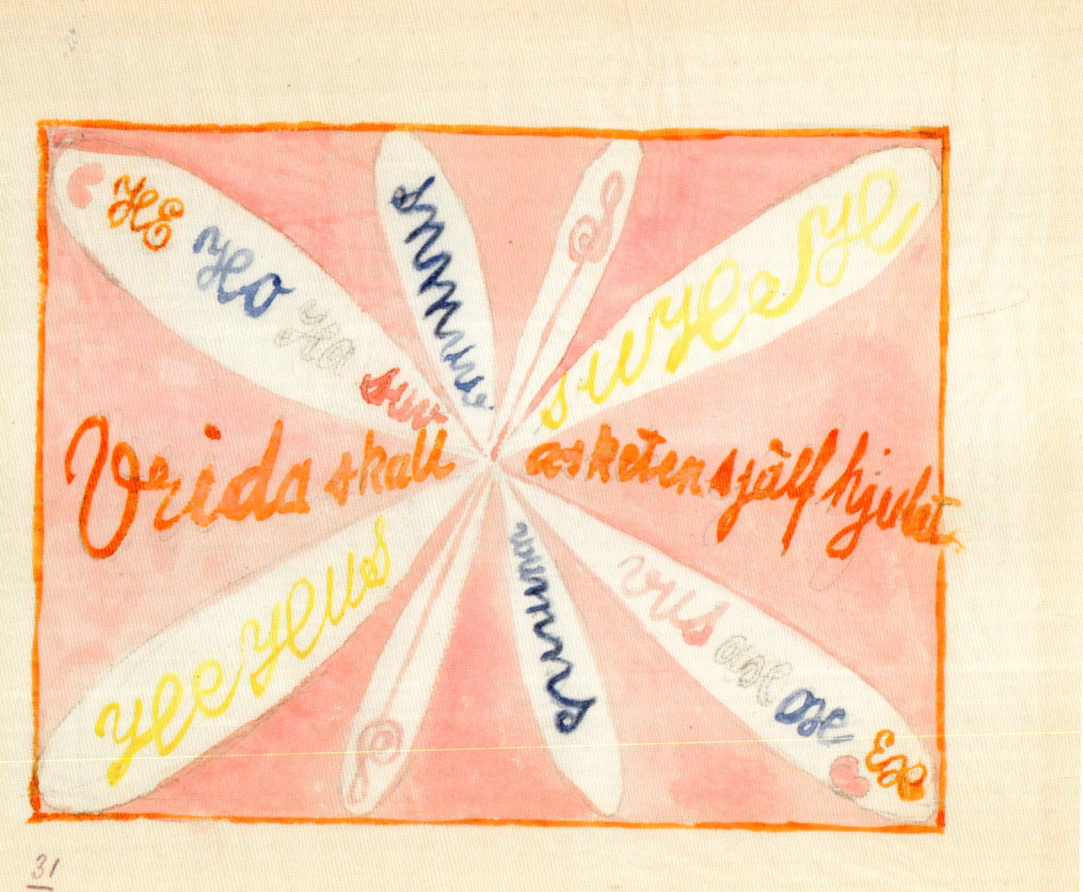

31

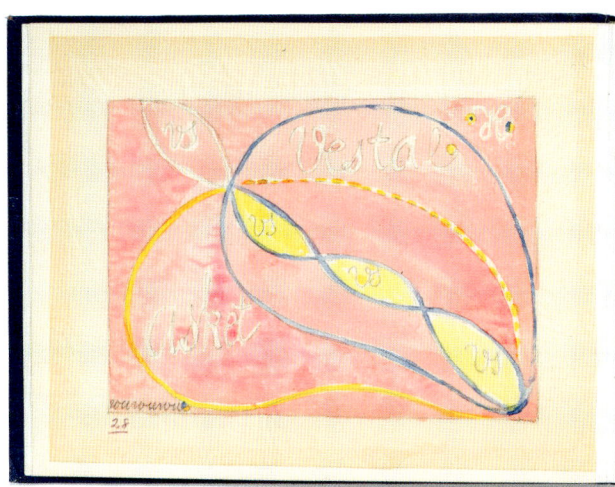

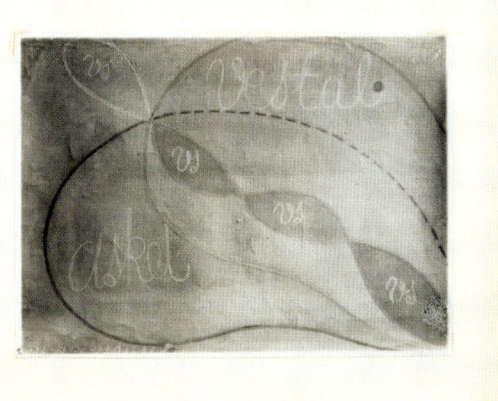

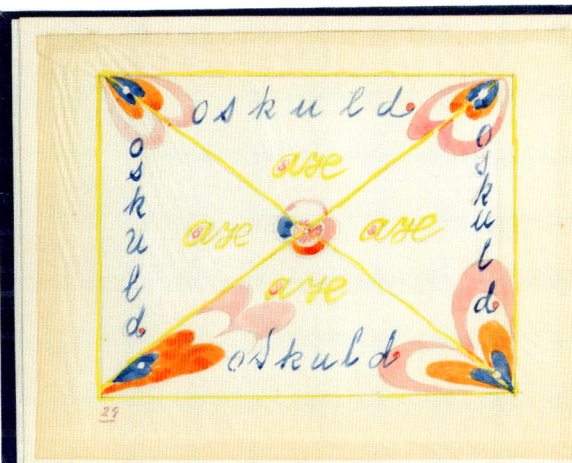

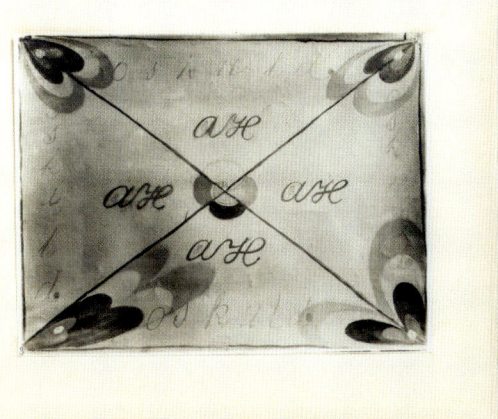

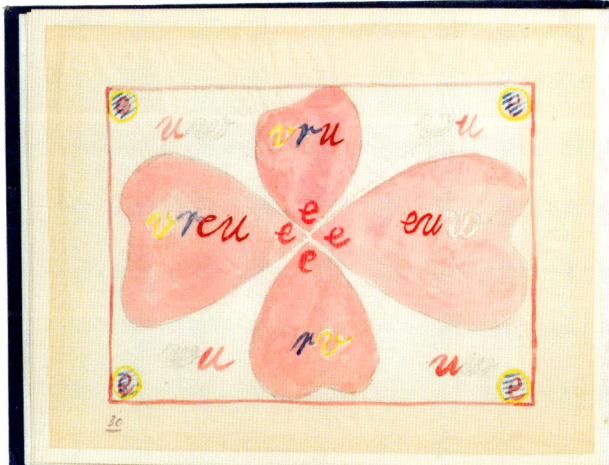

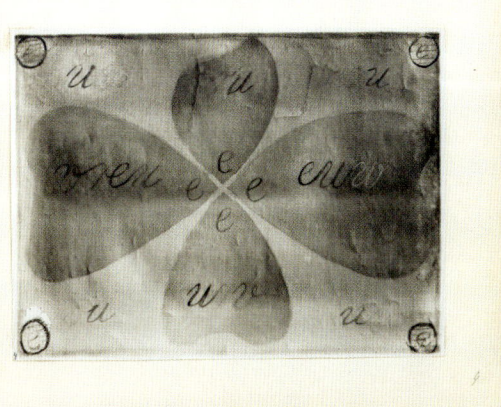

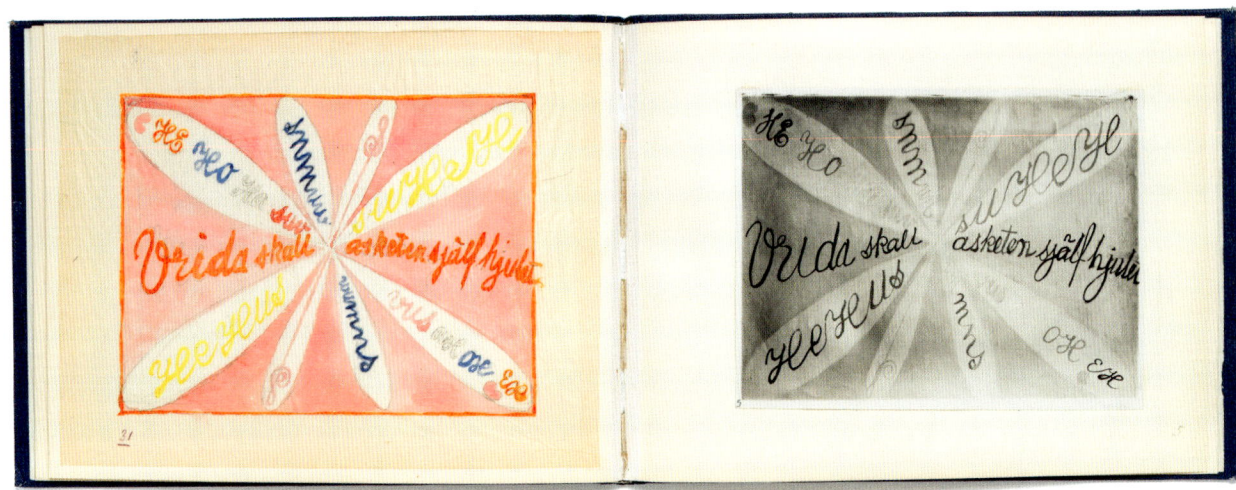

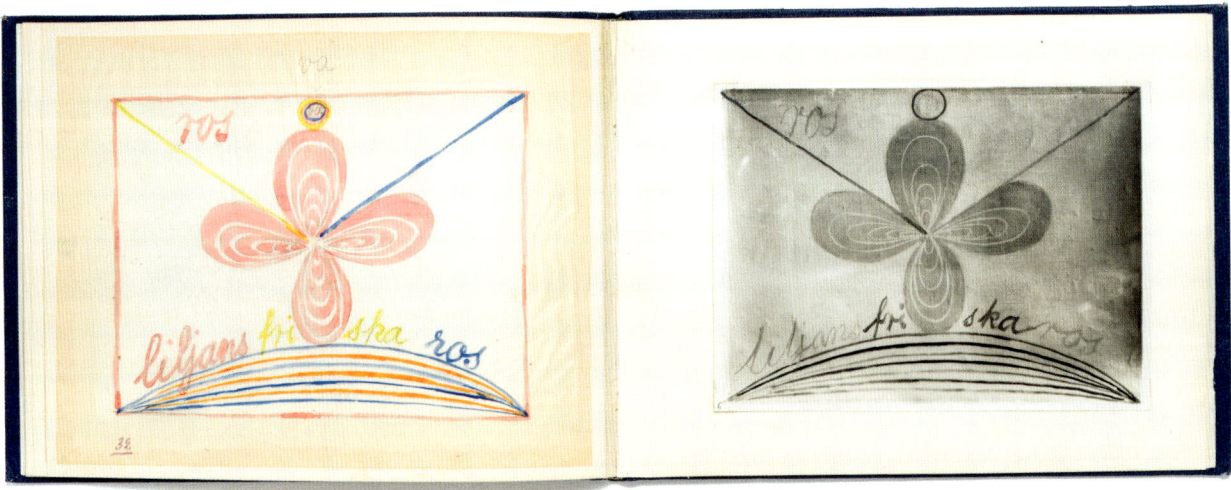

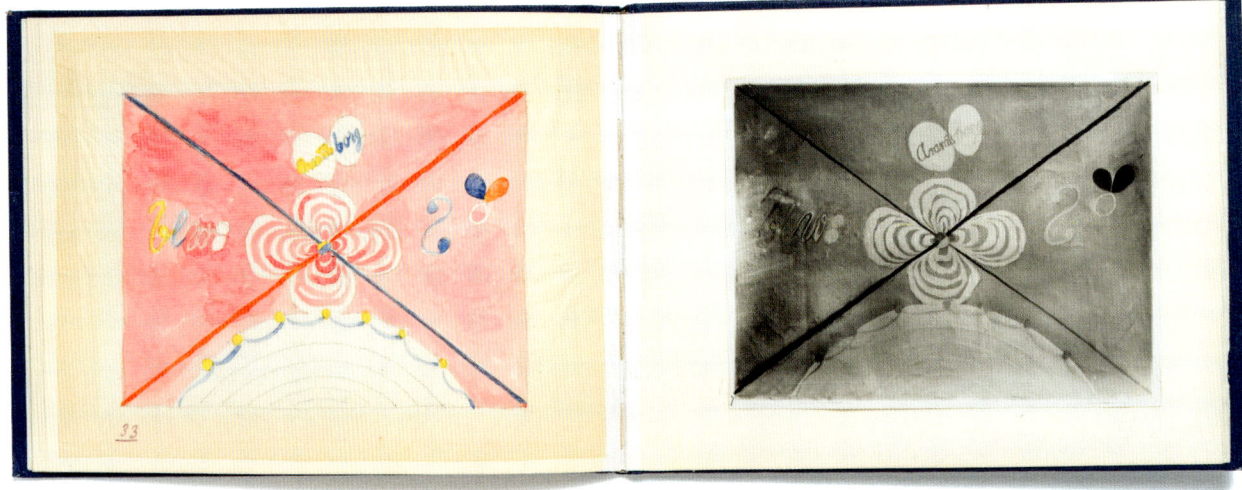

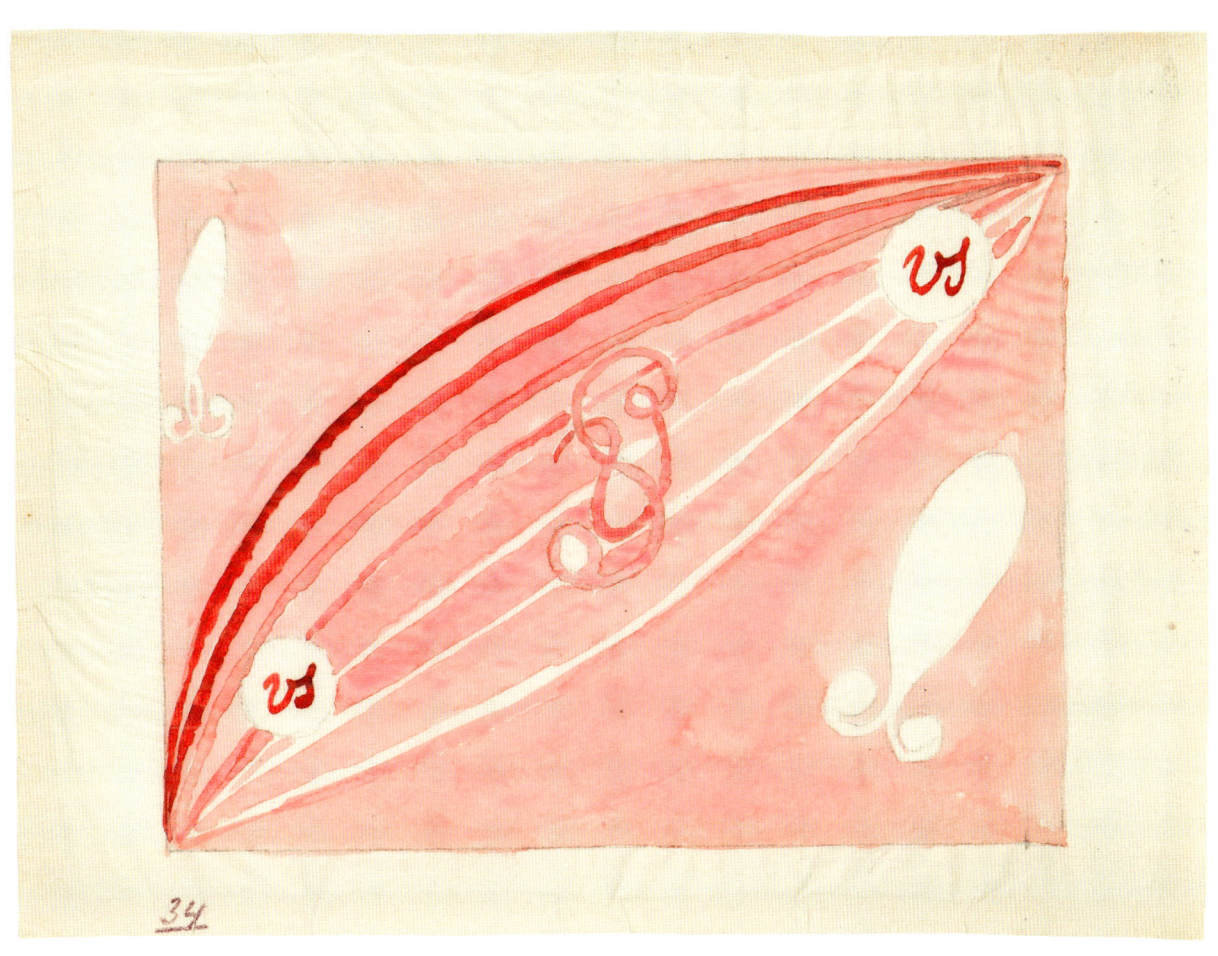

34

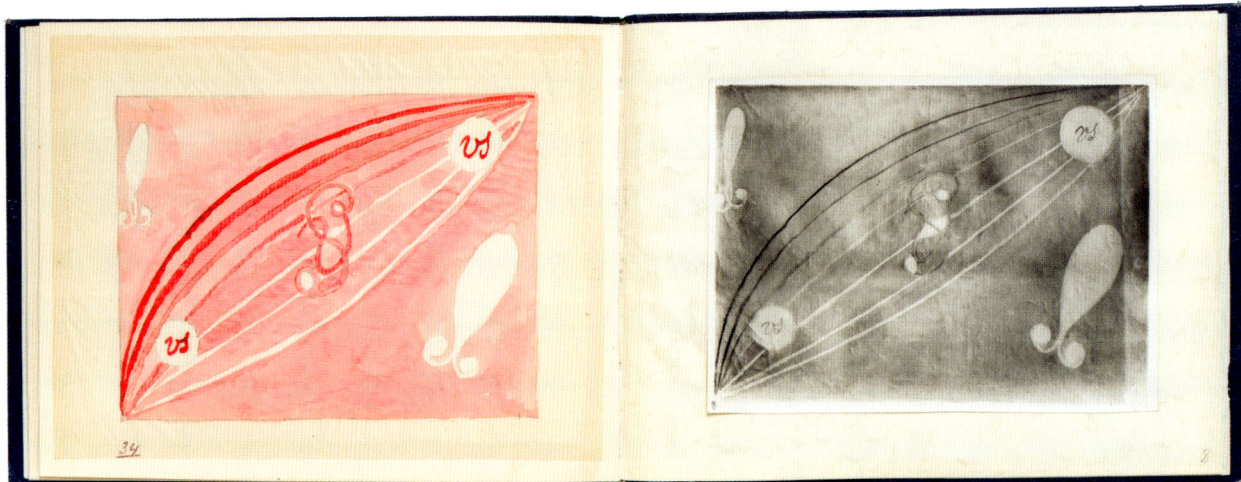

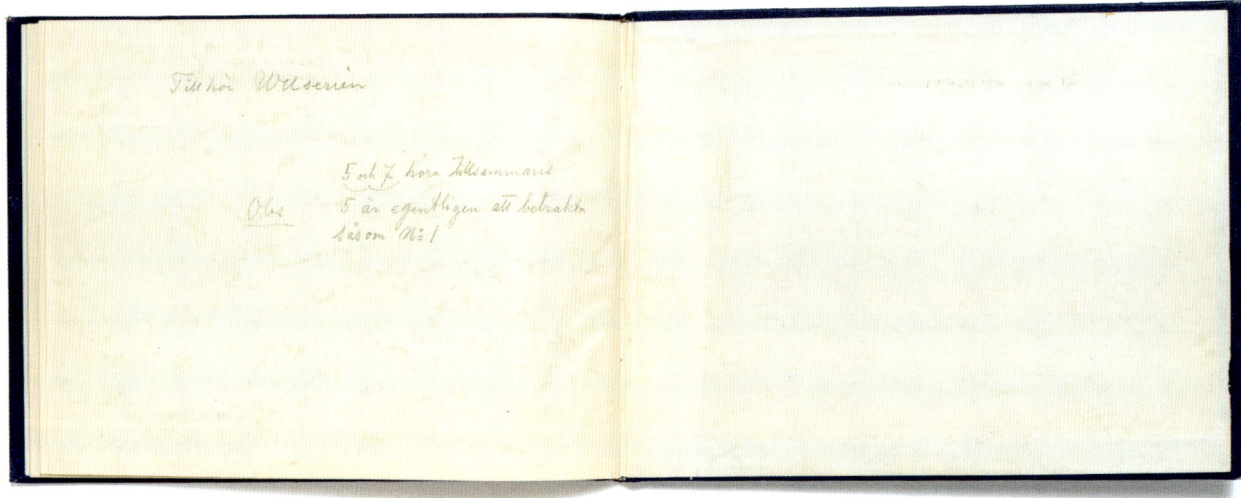

Belongs to the WU series. 5 and 7 belong together. Note 5 should really be seen as No. 1

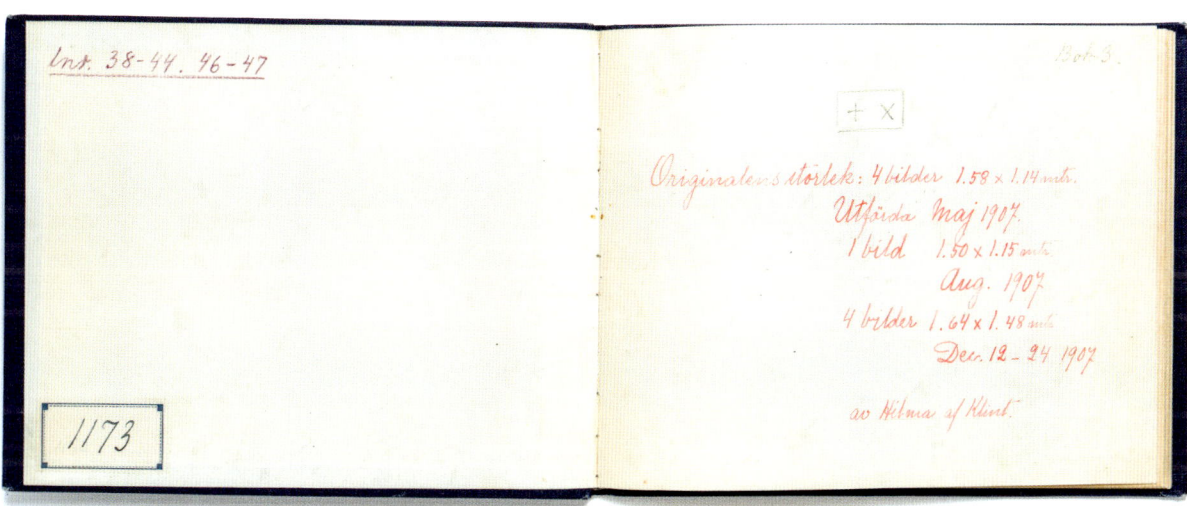

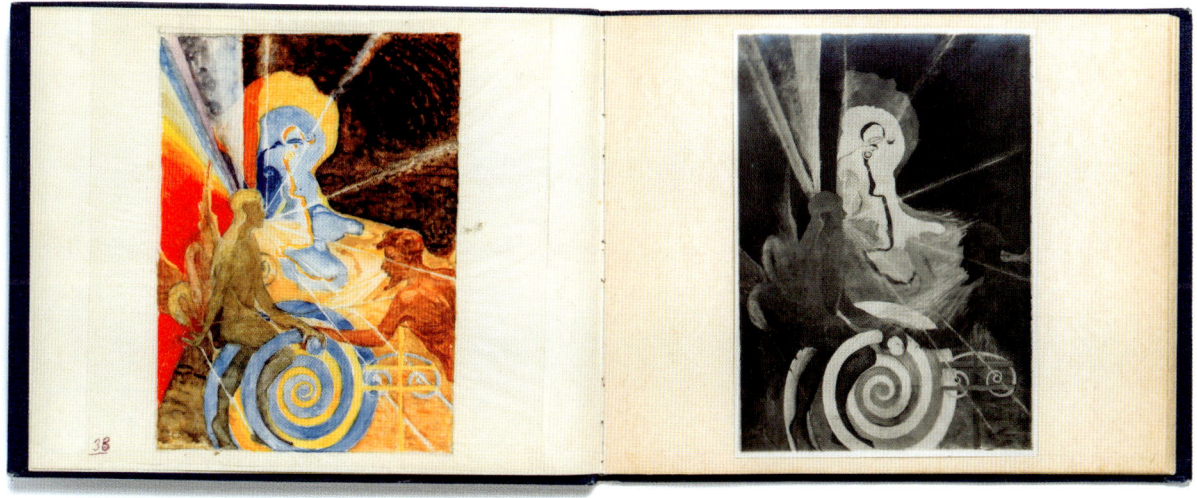

1173, Inv. 38–44.46–47. Original size: 4 pictures 1.58 × 1.14 m. Made May 1907,
1 picture 1.50 × 1.15 m, Aug. 1907, 4 pictures 1.64 × 1.48 m, Dec. 12–24 1907, by Hilma af Klint

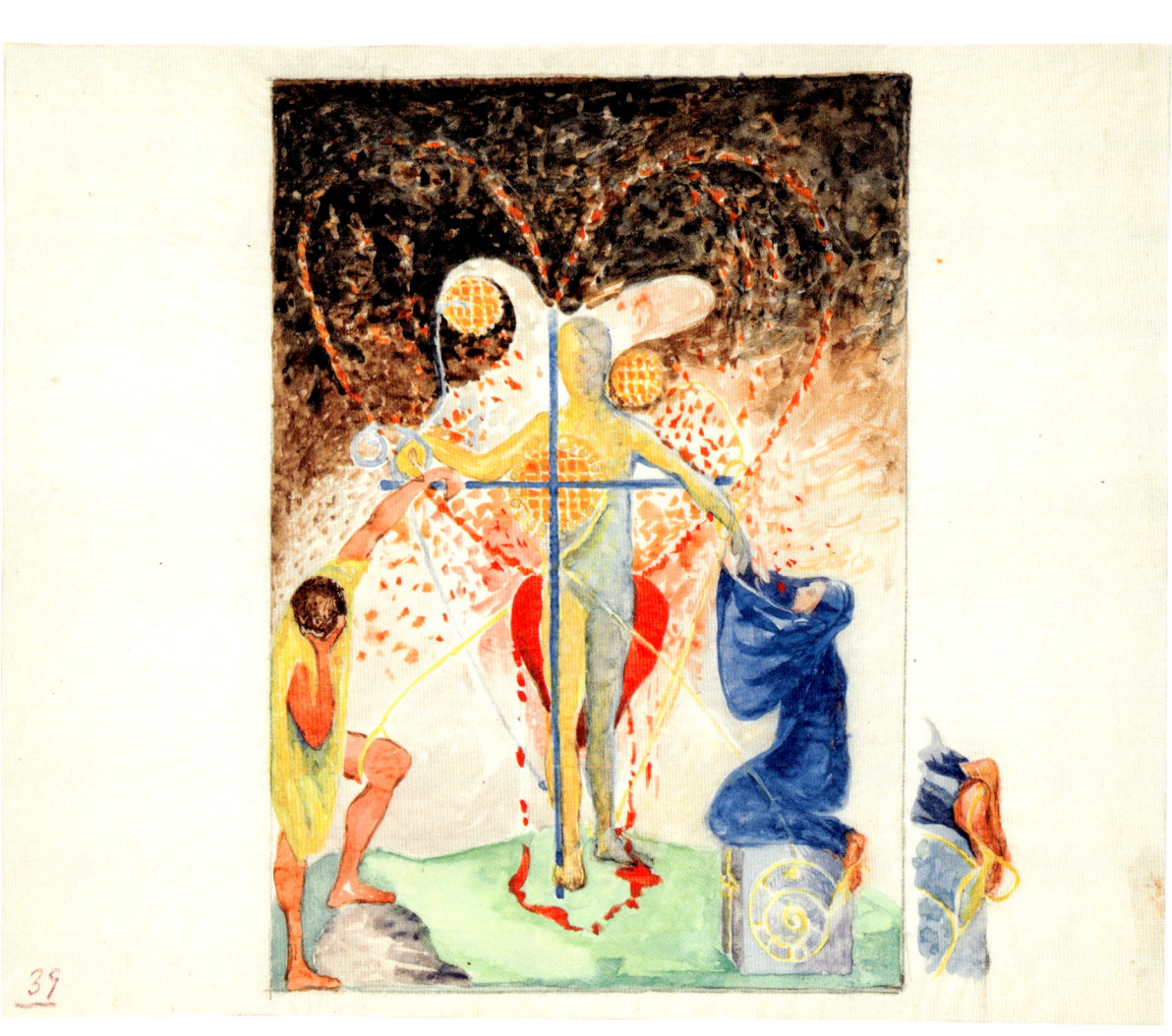

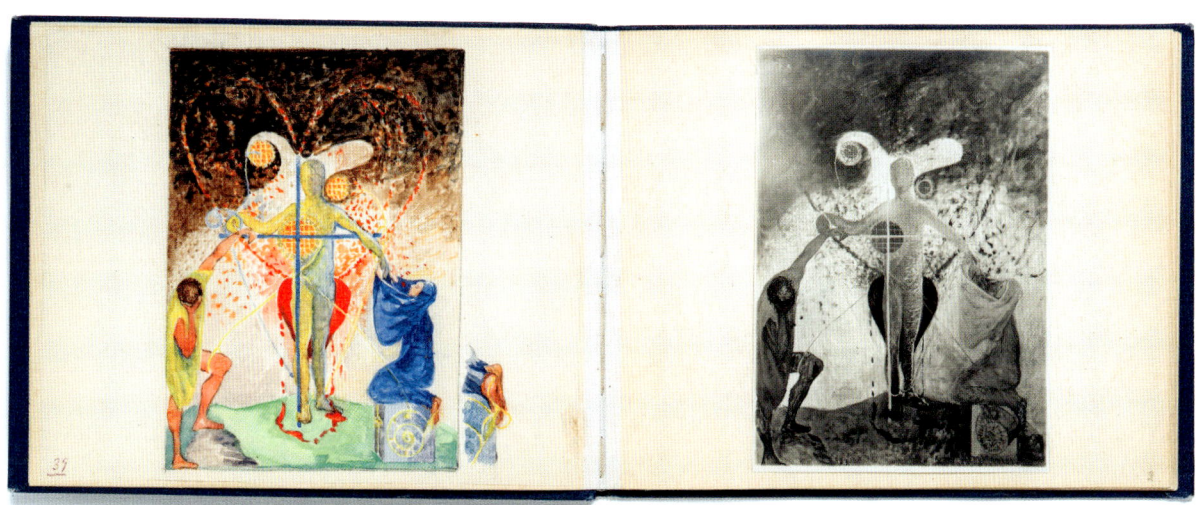

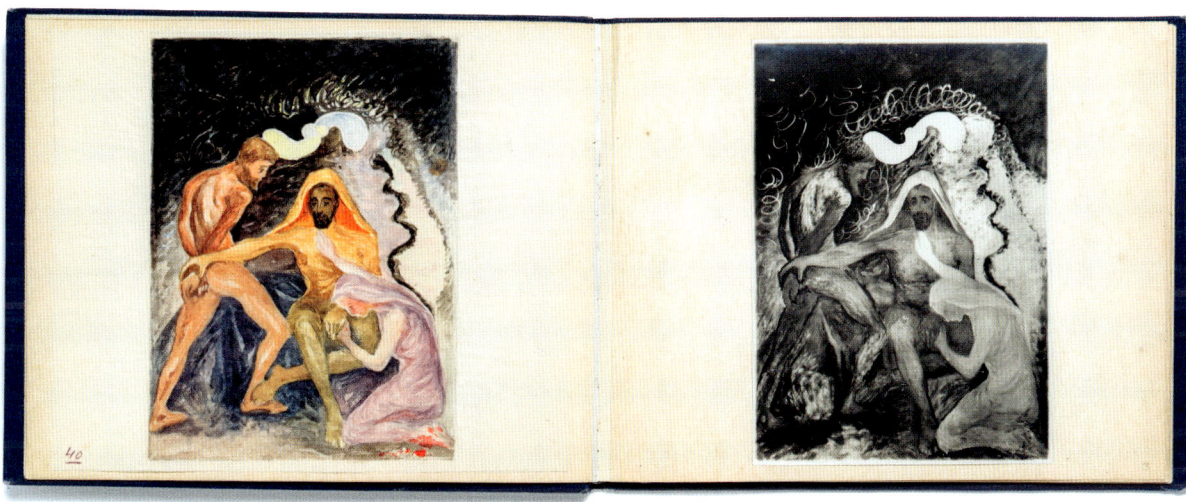

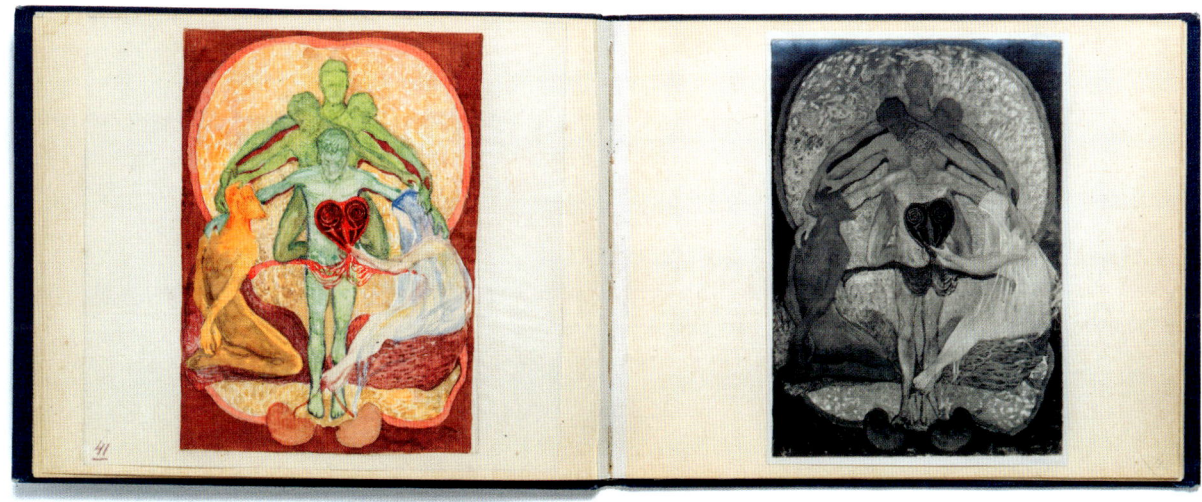

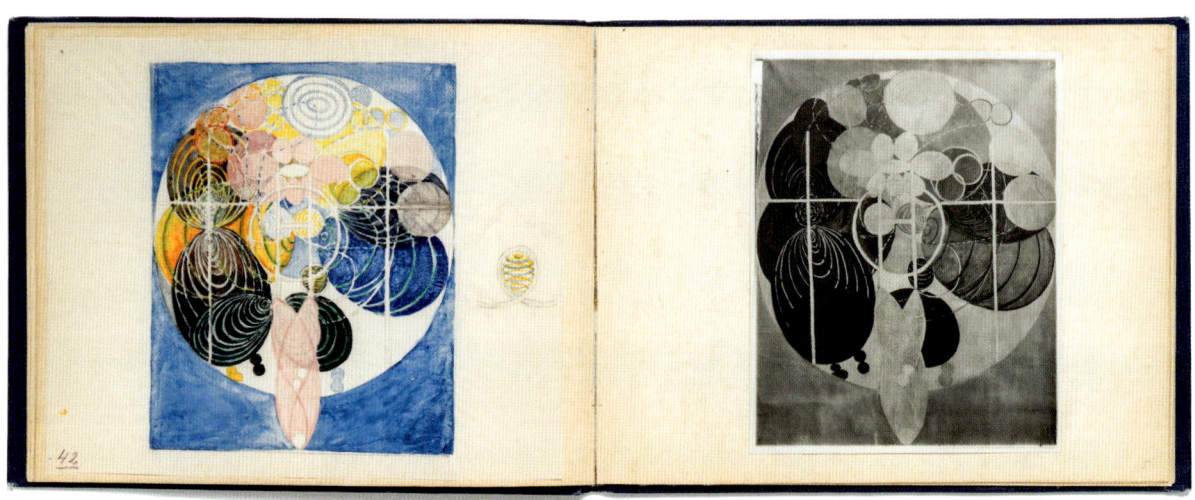

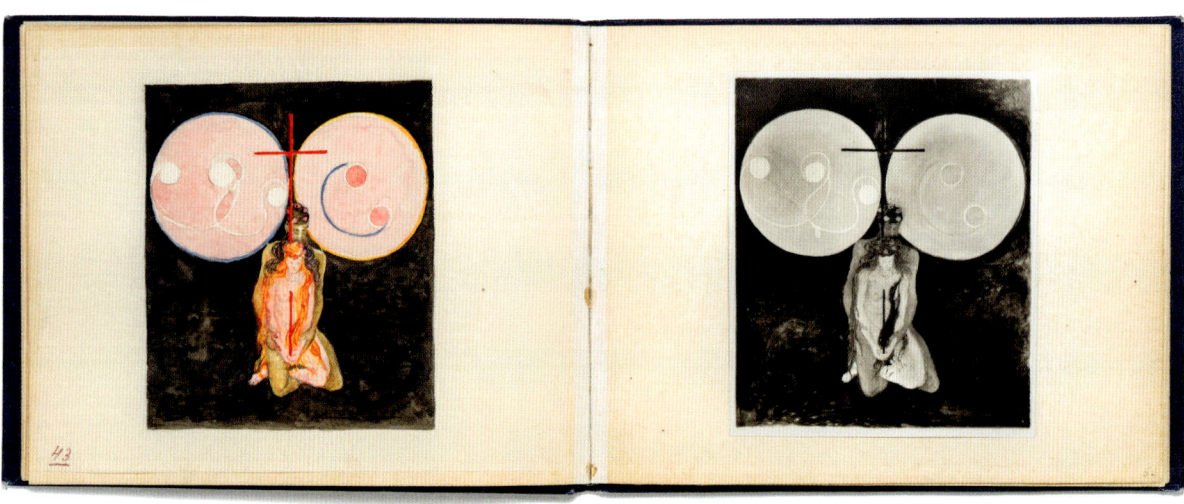

Finnes icke fotograferad
i stort format

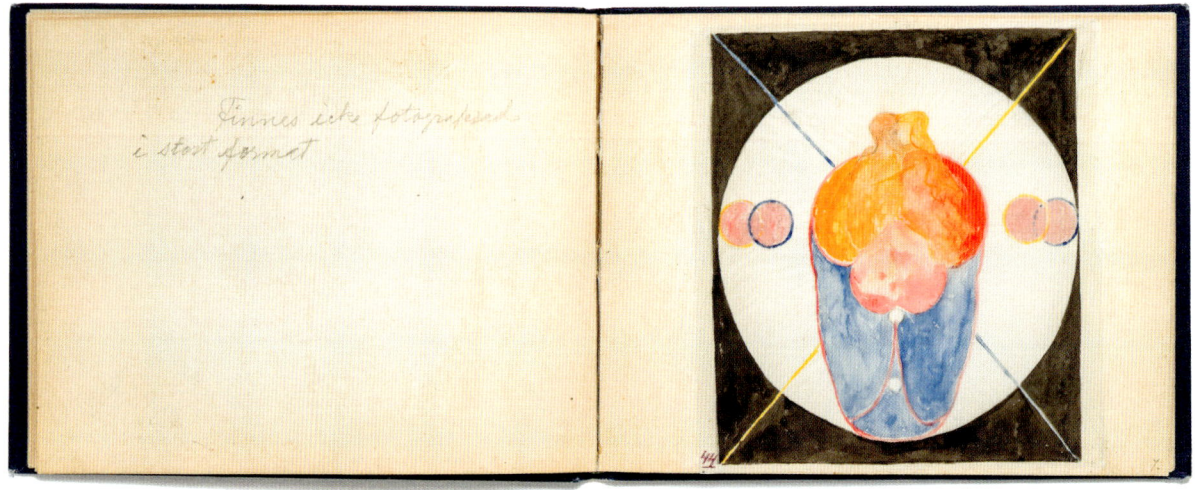

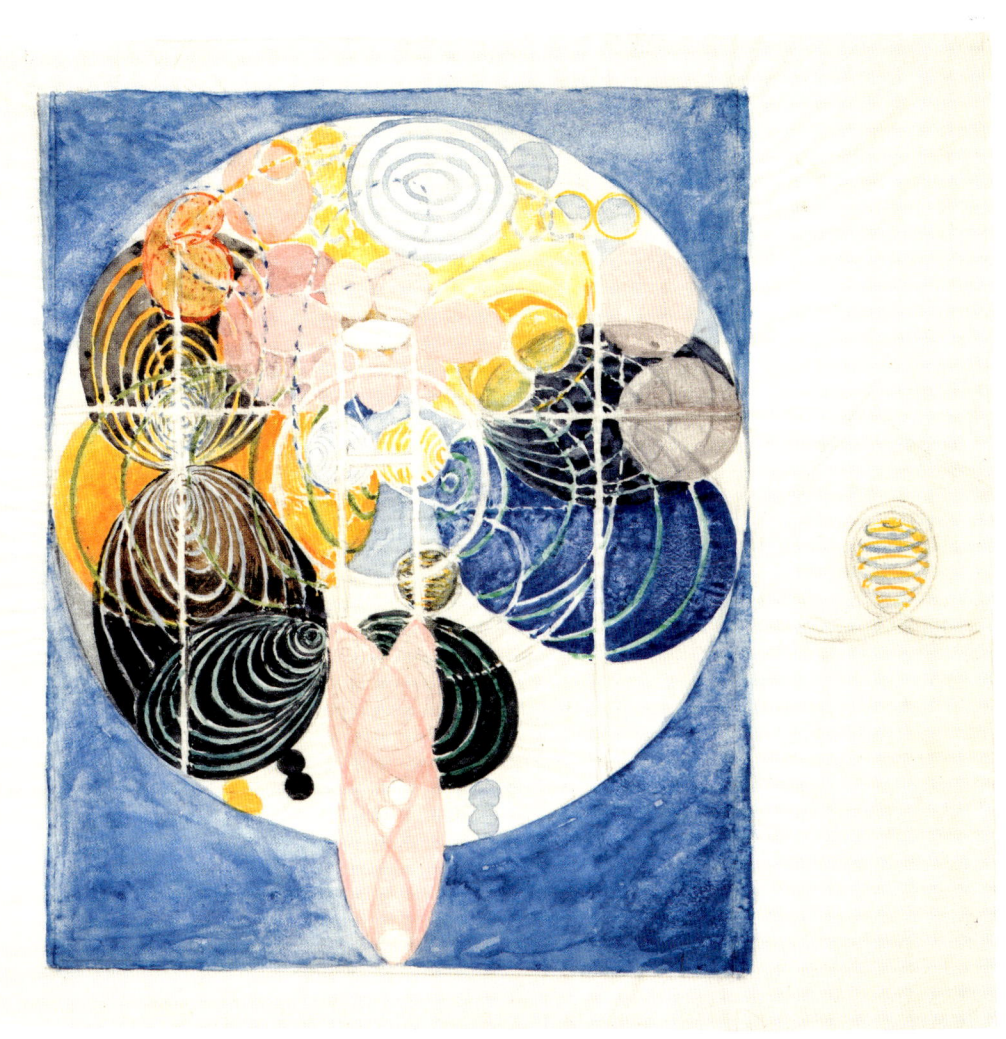

42

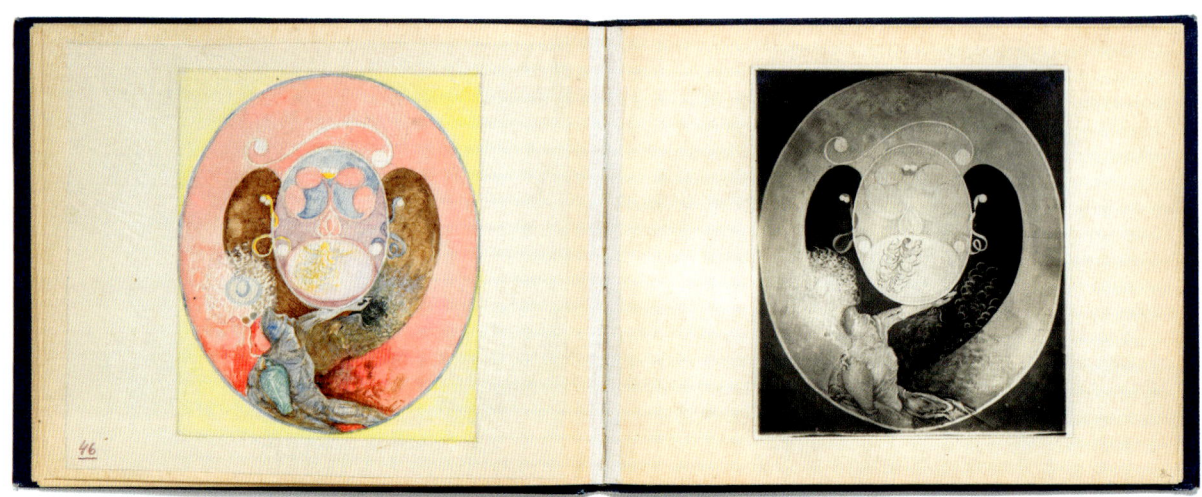

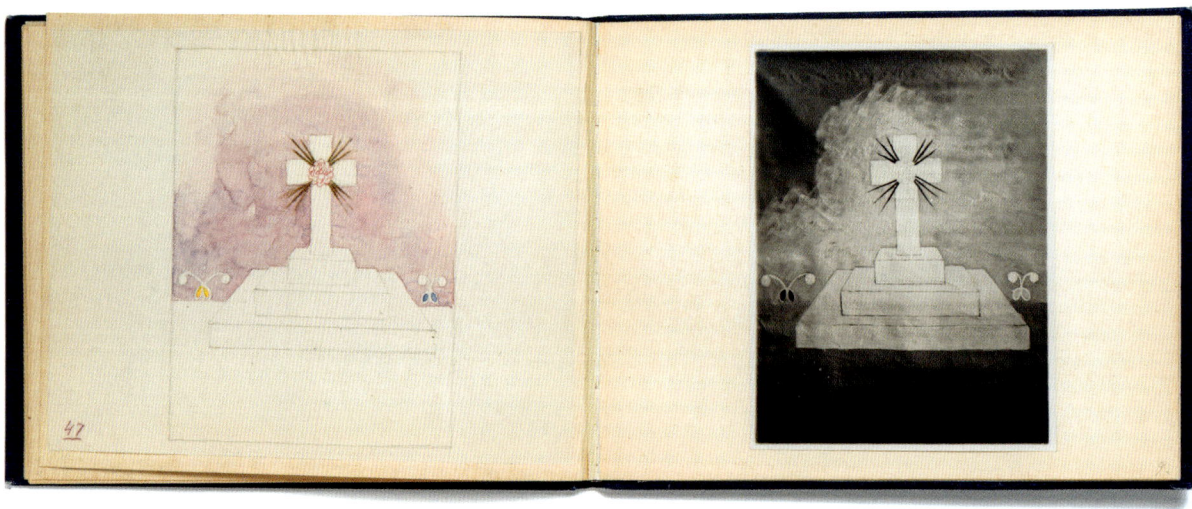

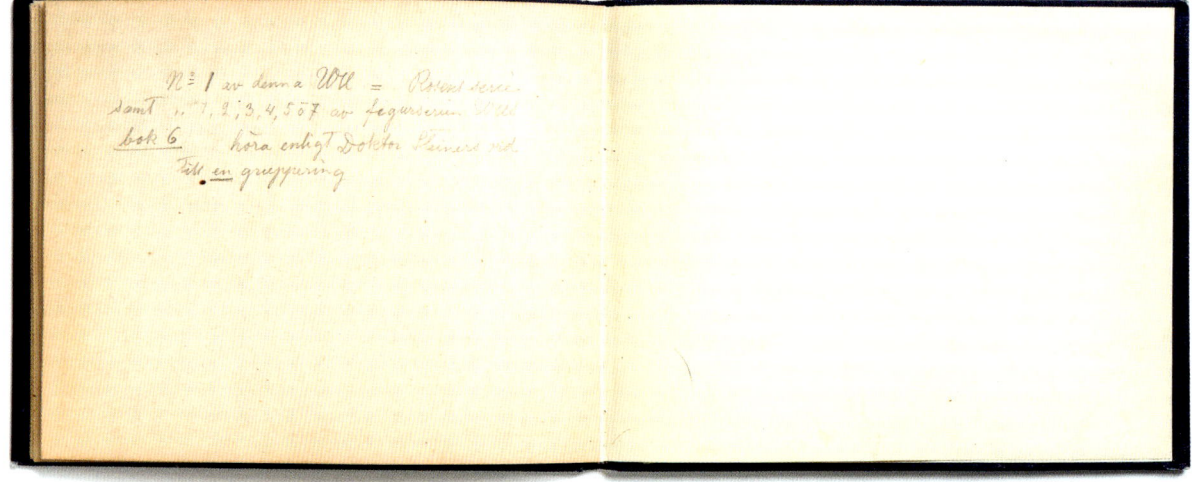

No. 1 of this WU= the Rose series and No. 1, 2, 3, 4, 5, and 7 of the figurative series WUS

Book 6 belongs, according to the words of Doctor Steiner, to one grouping.

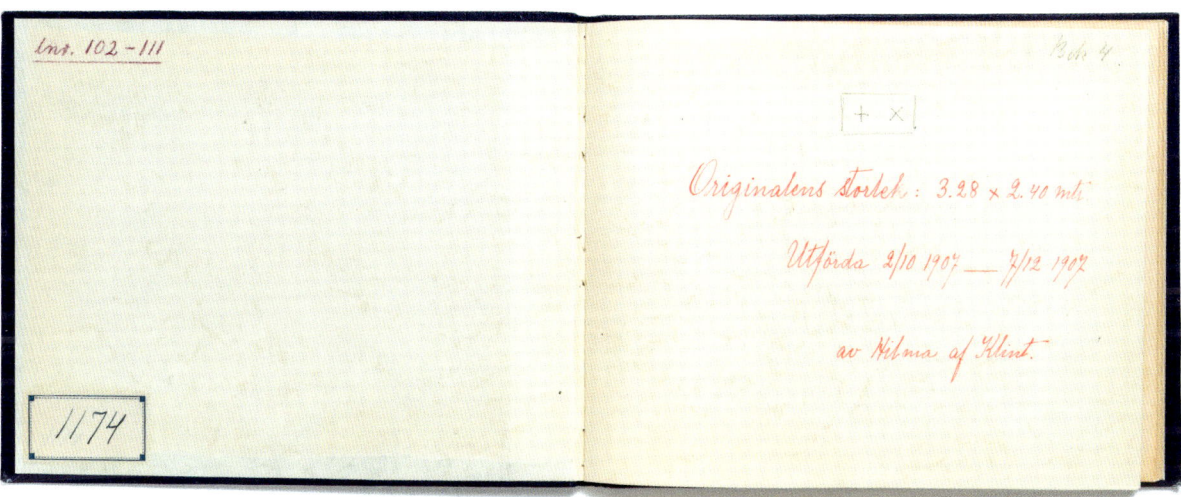

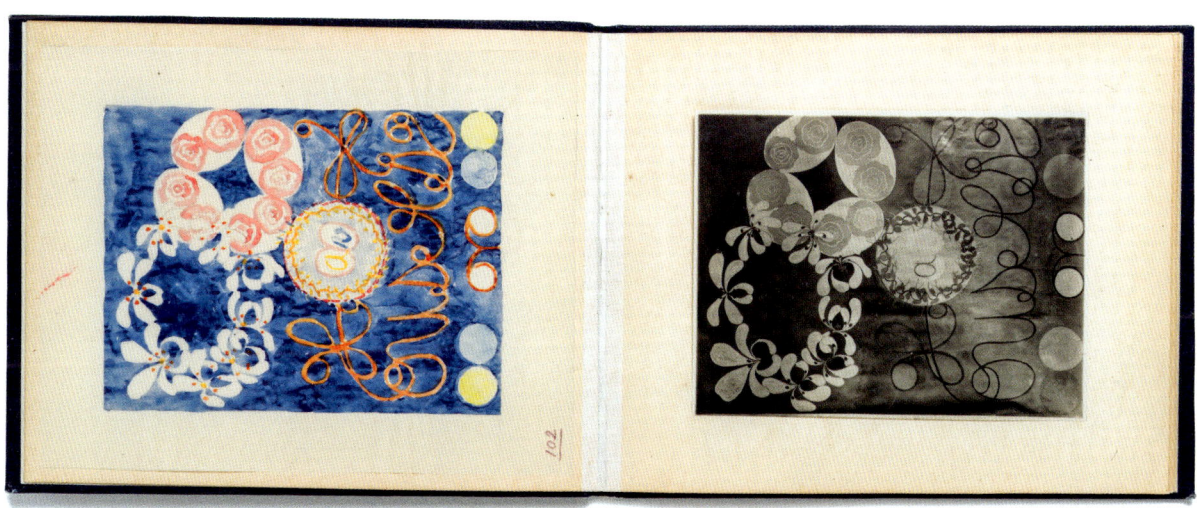

1174, Inv. 102–111, Original size: 3.28 × 2.40 m. Made 10/2/1907–12/7/1907, by Hilma af Klint

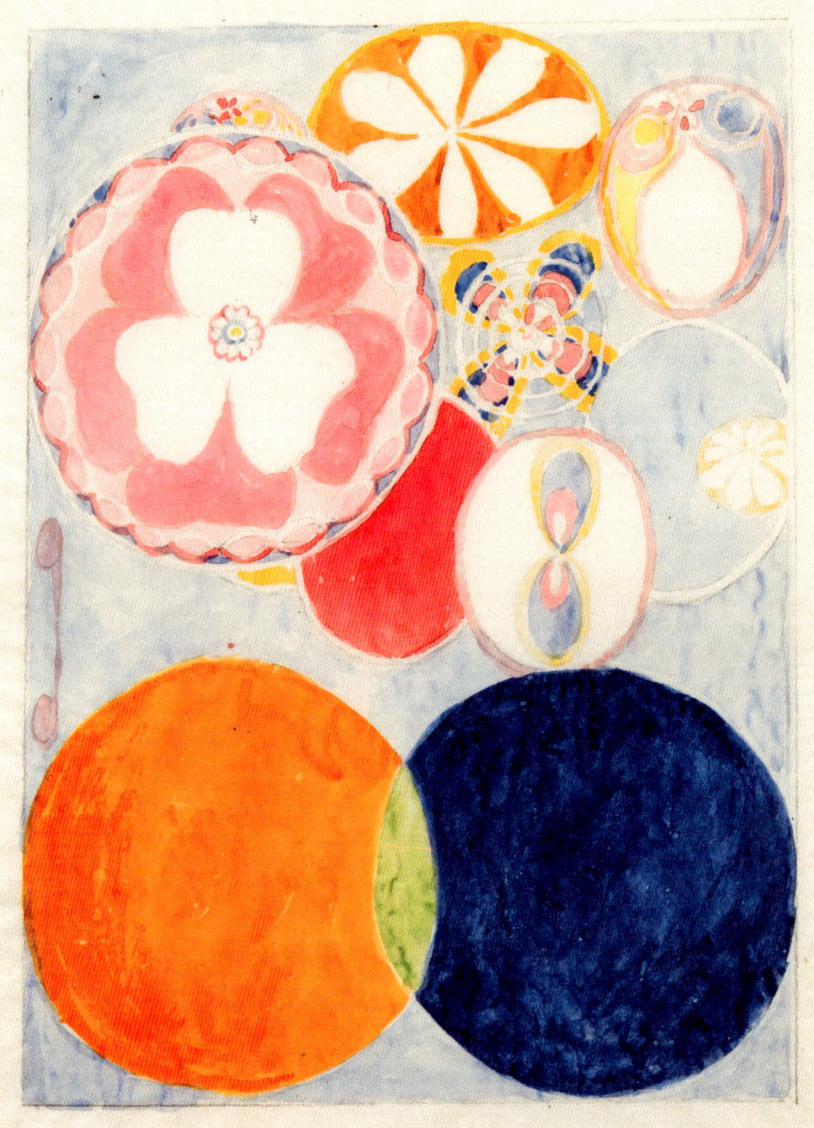

103

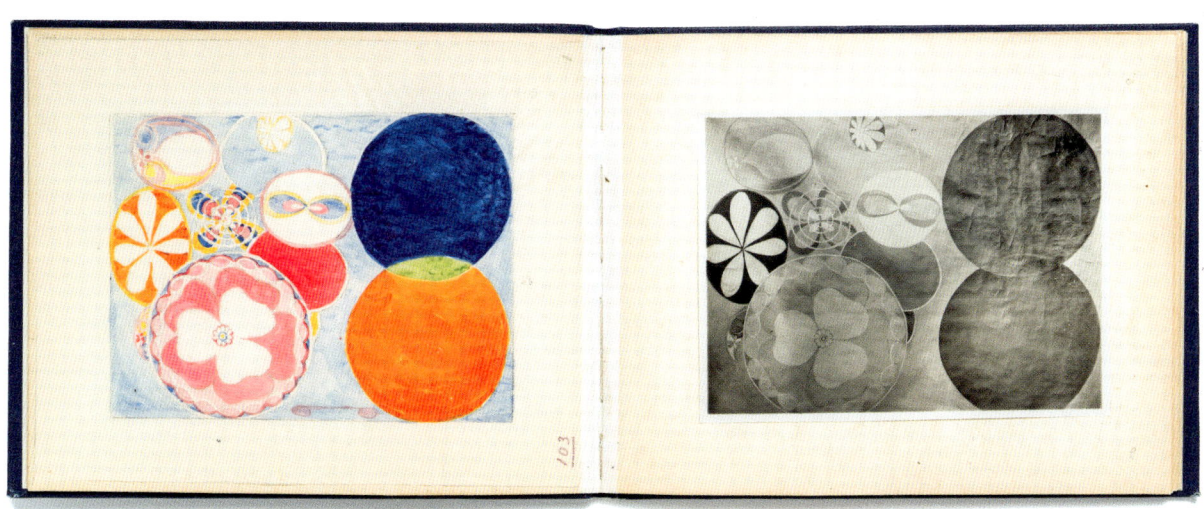

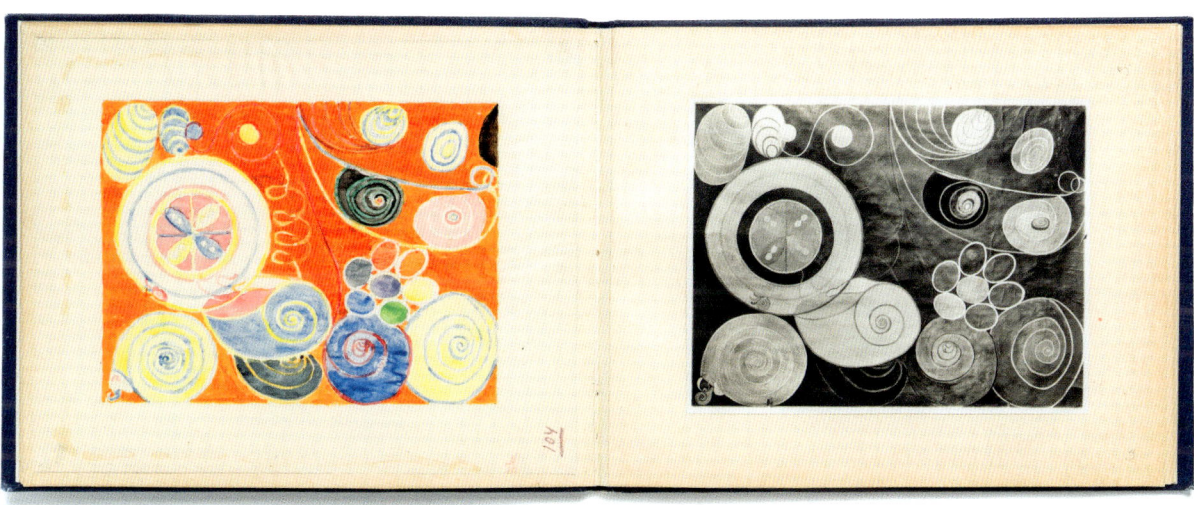

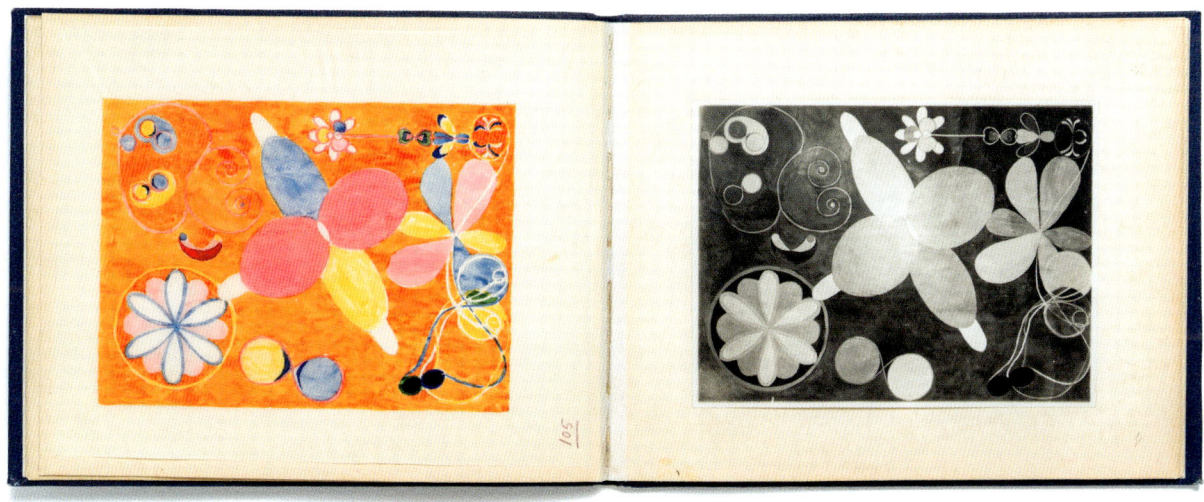

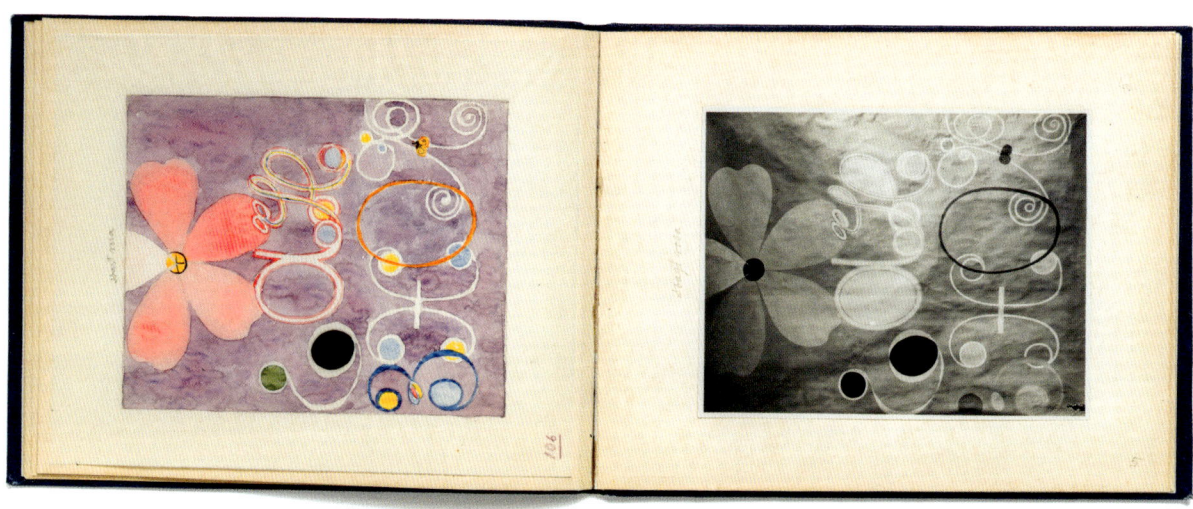

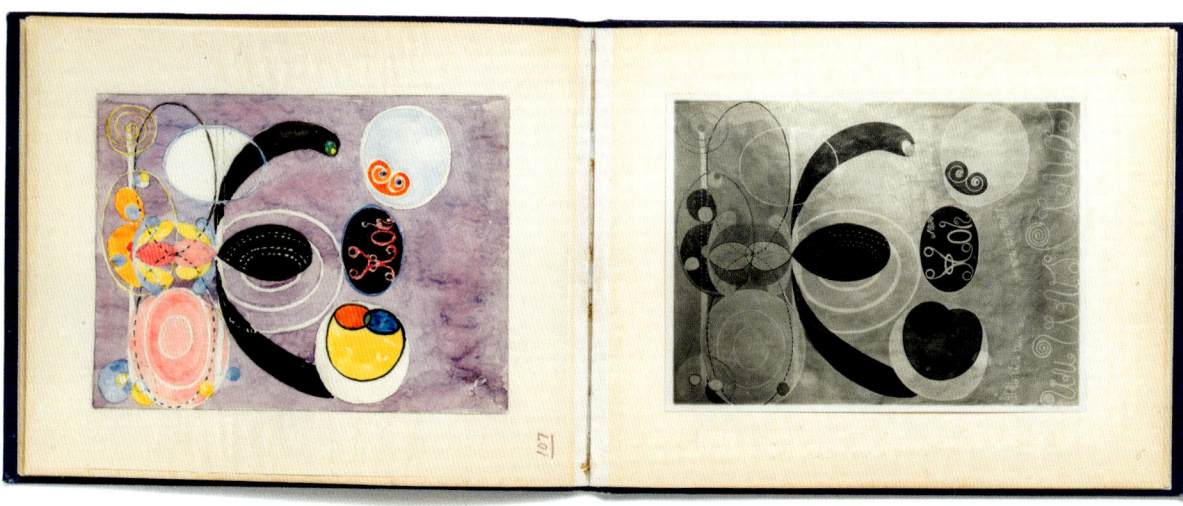

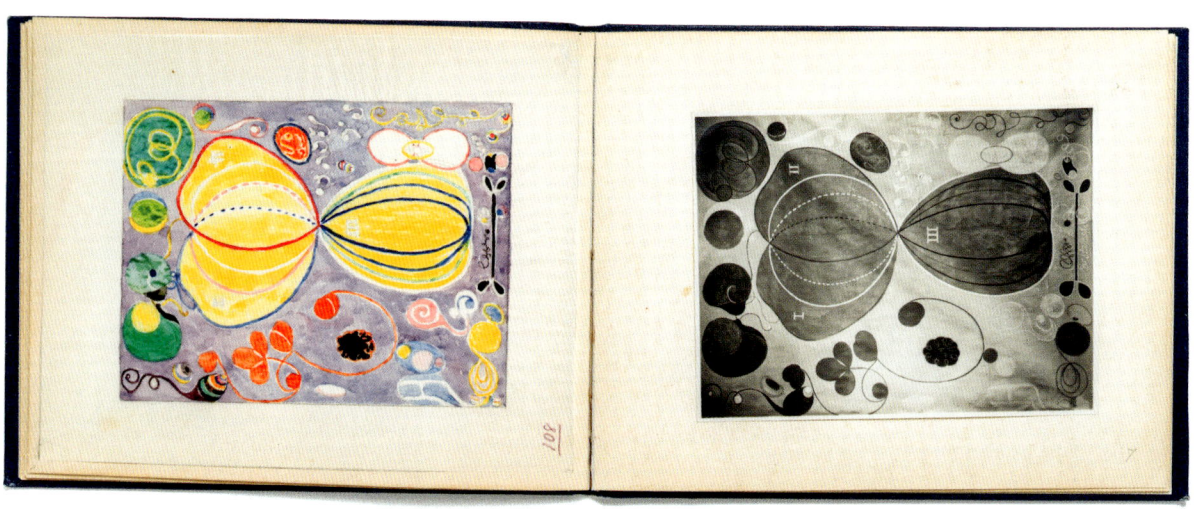

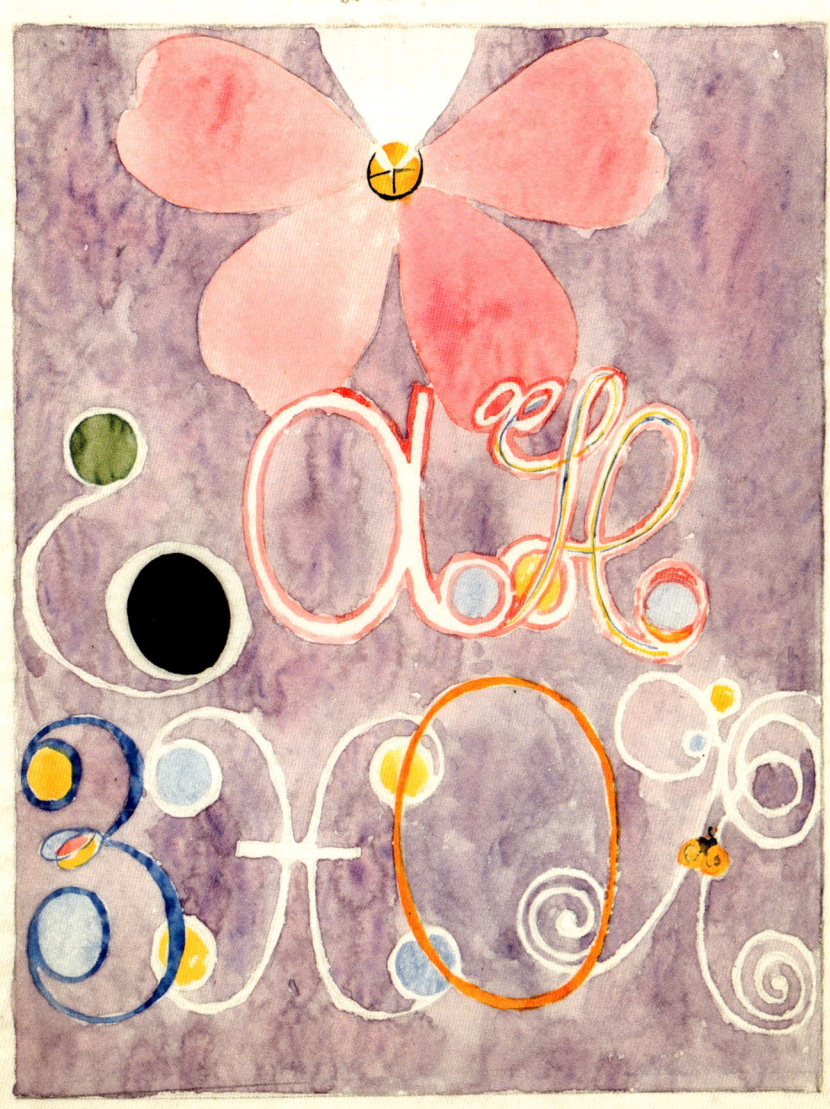

106

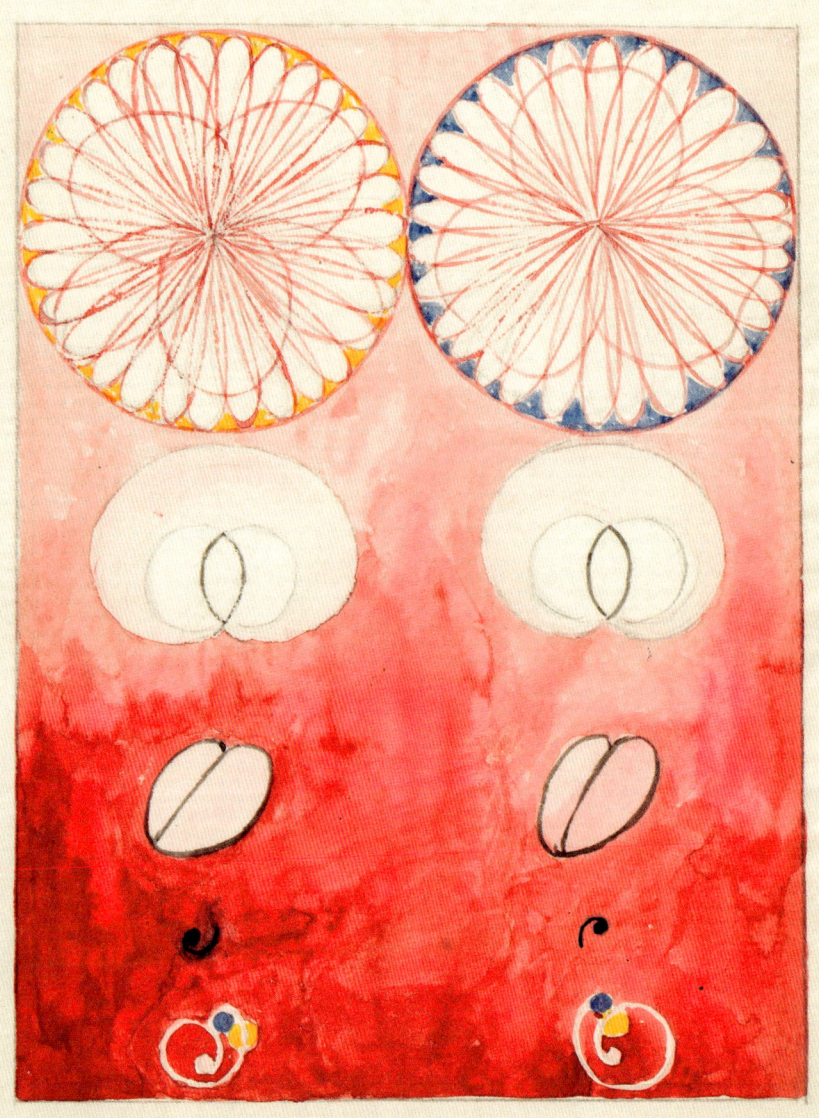

110

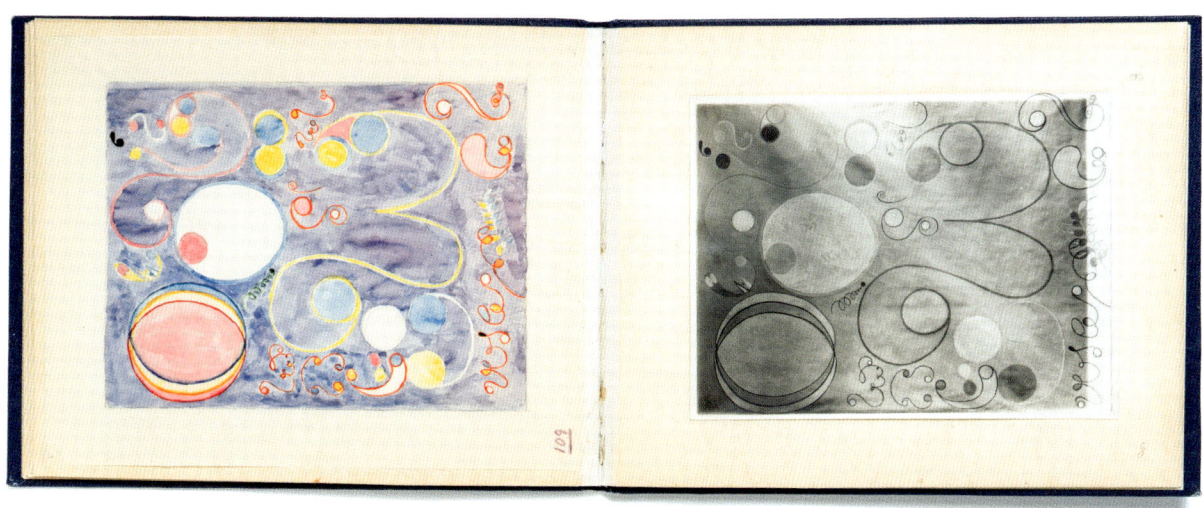

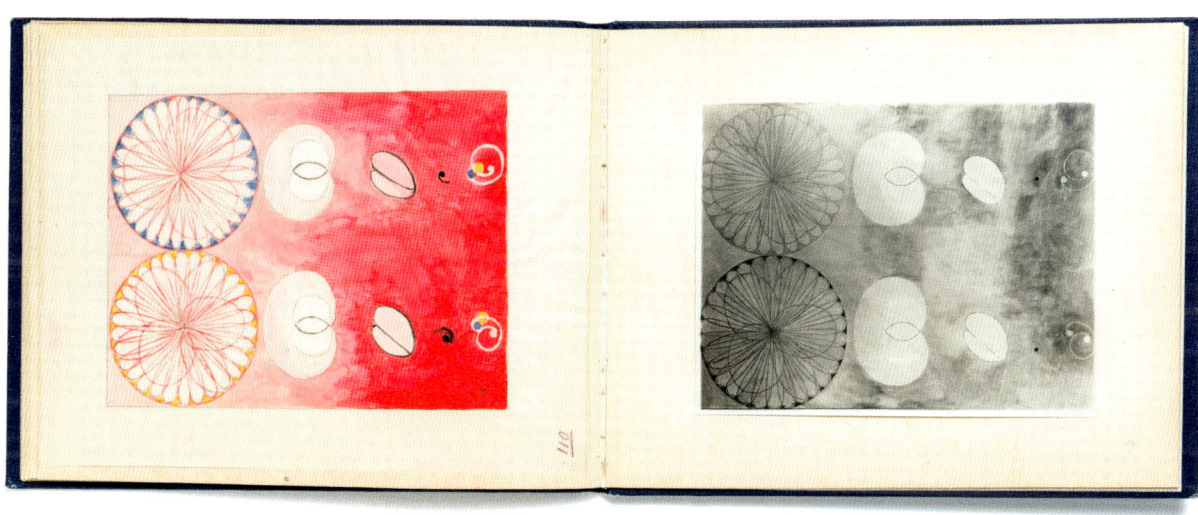

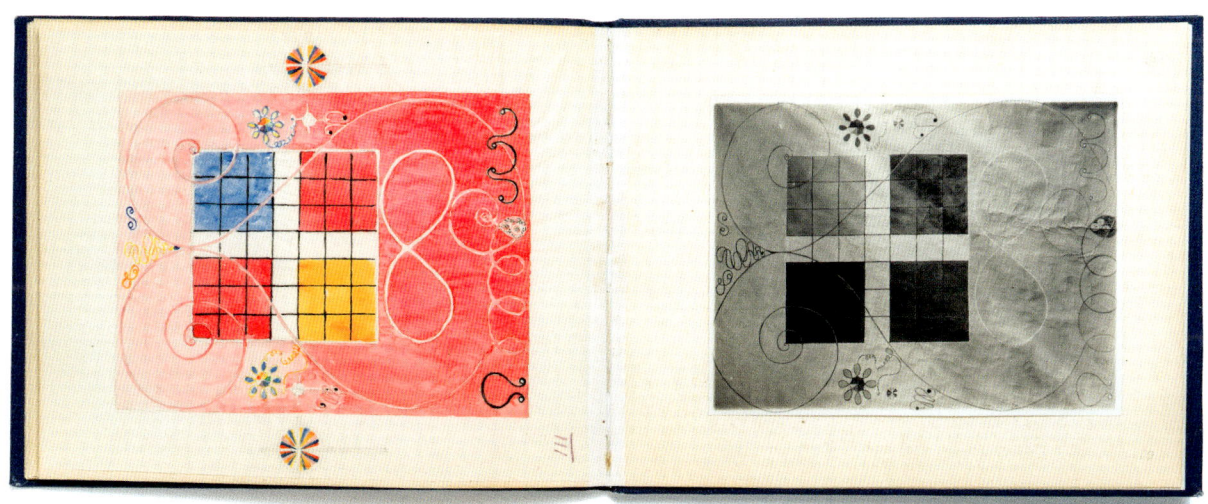

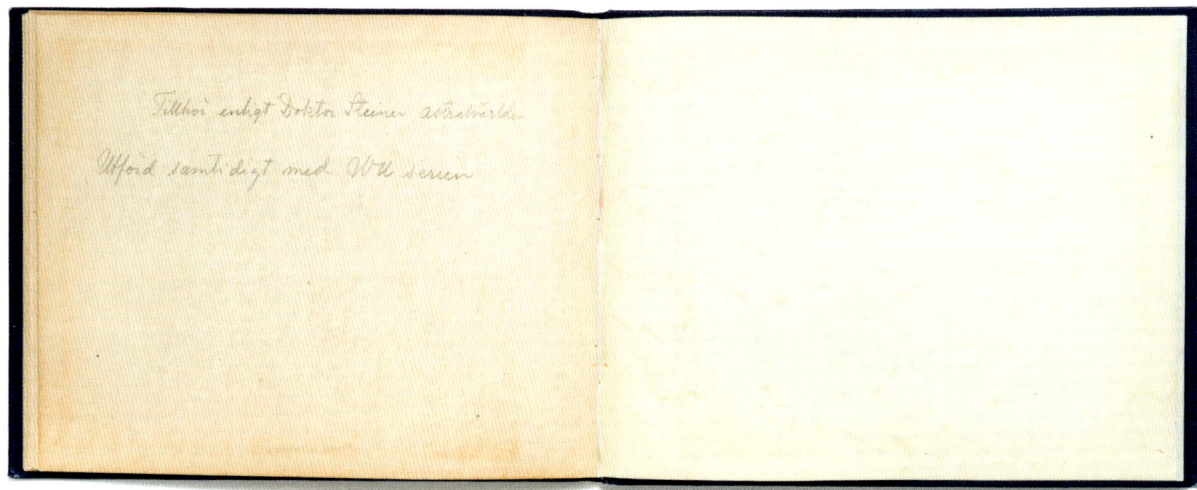

Belongs to the astral world according to Doctor Steiner
Made at the same time as the WU series

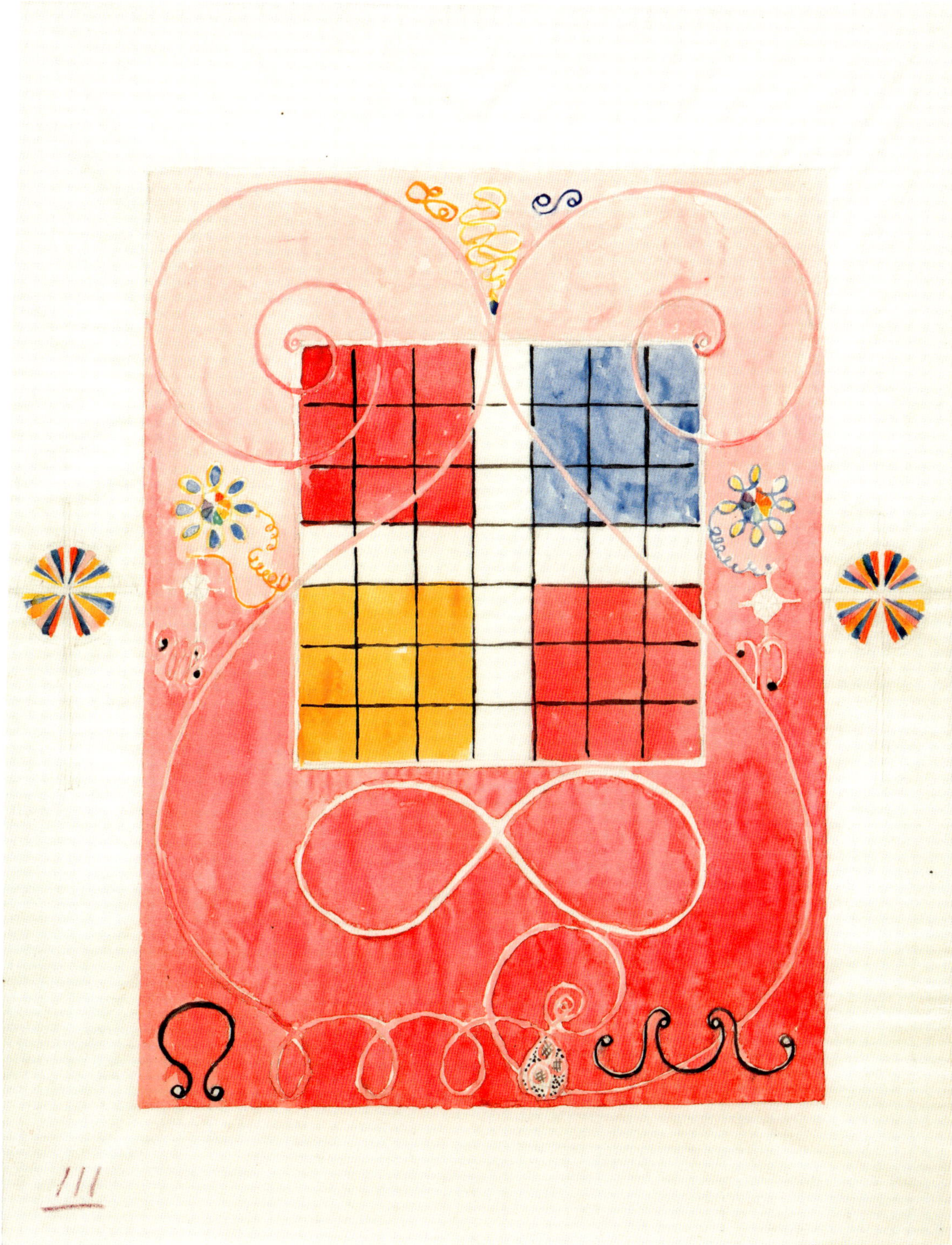

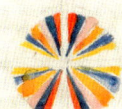

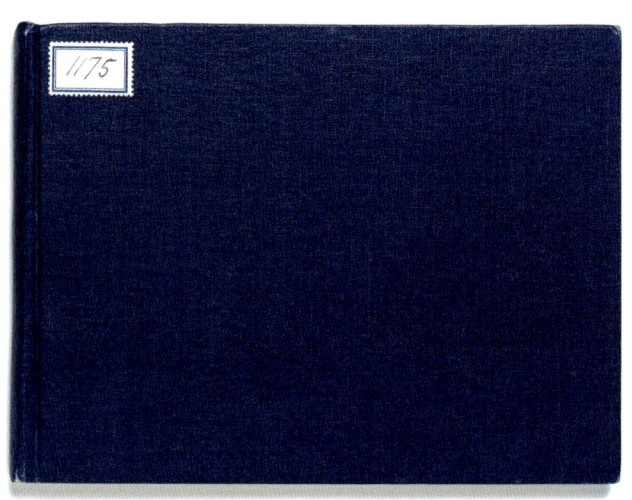

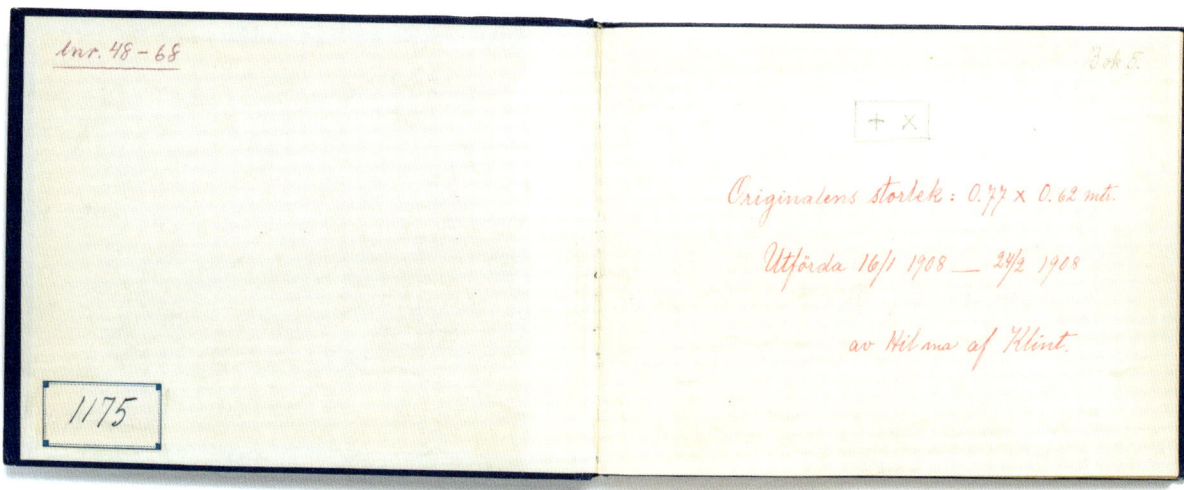

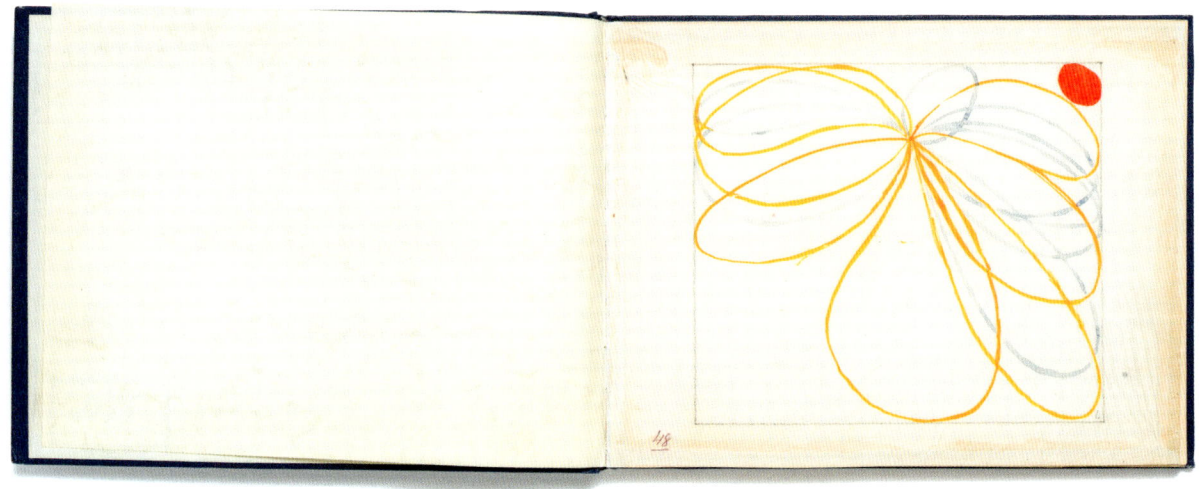

1175, Inv. 48–68, Original size: 0.77 × 0.62 m. Made 1/6/1908–2/24/1908, by Hilma af Klint

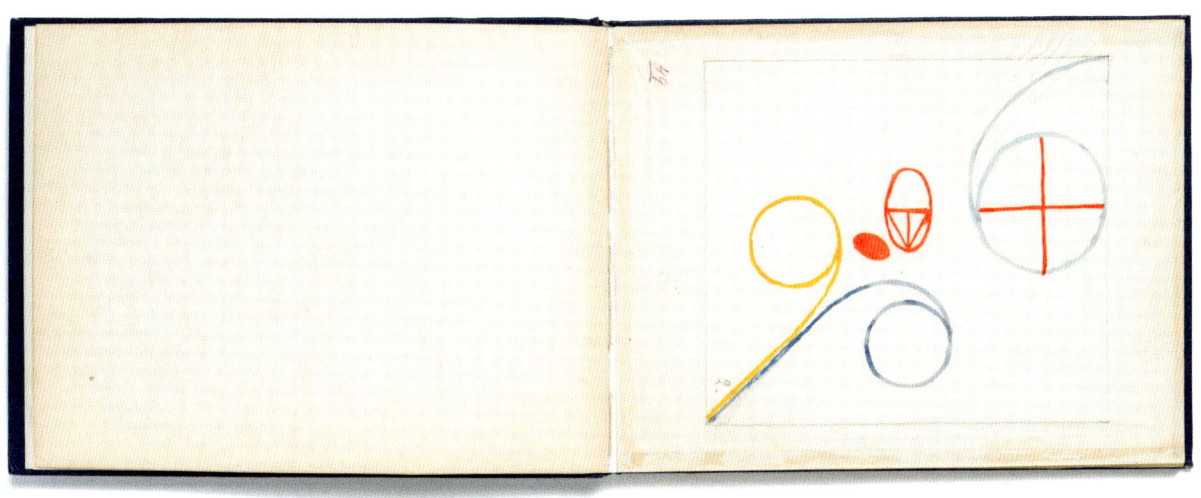

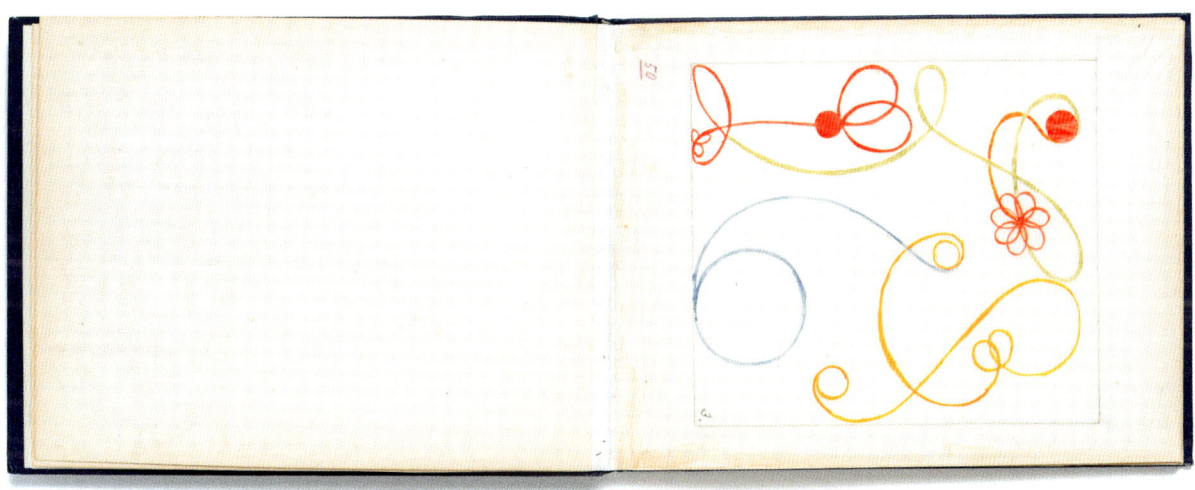

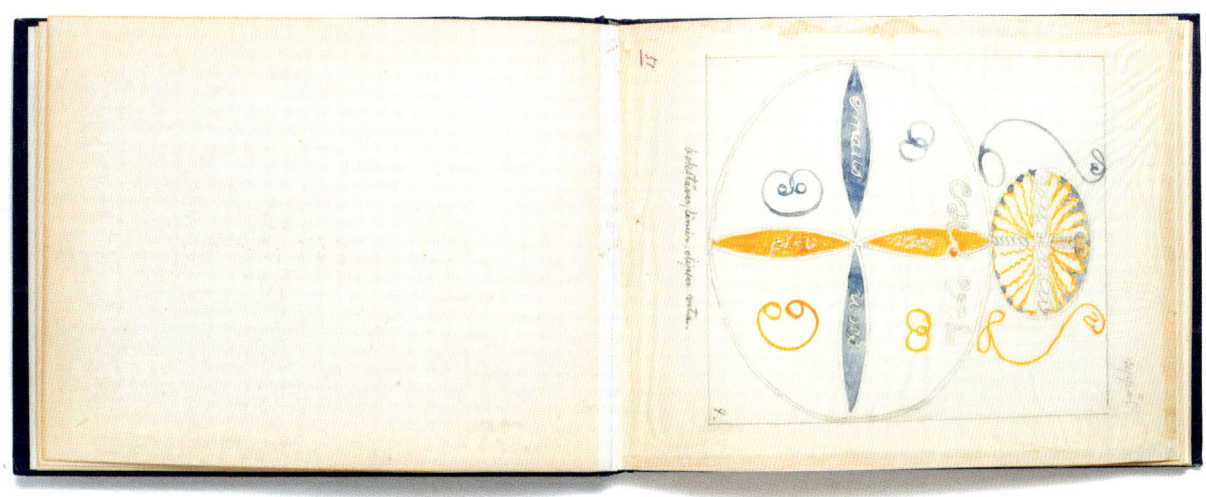

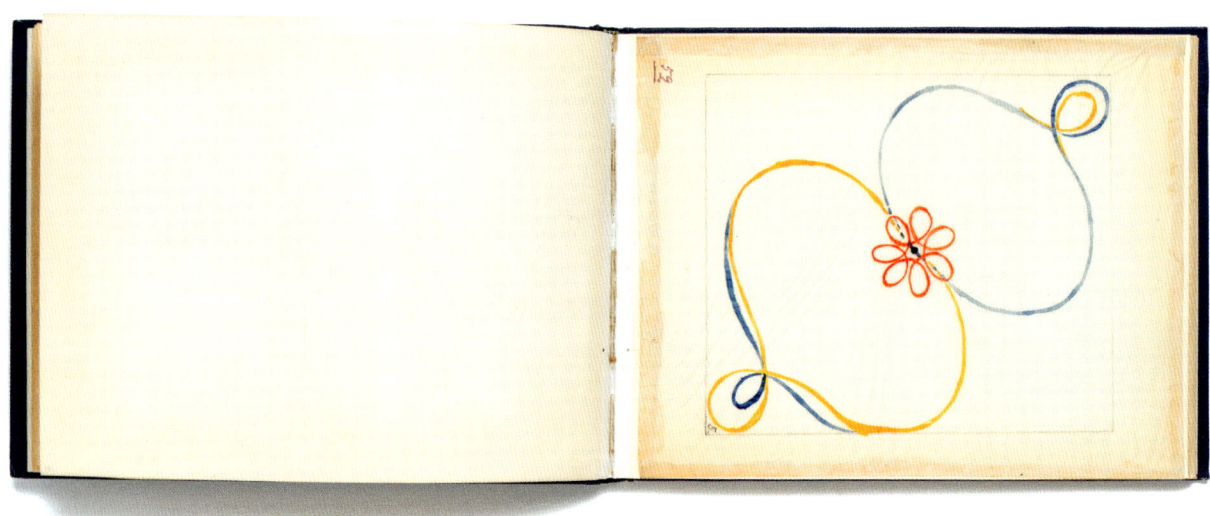

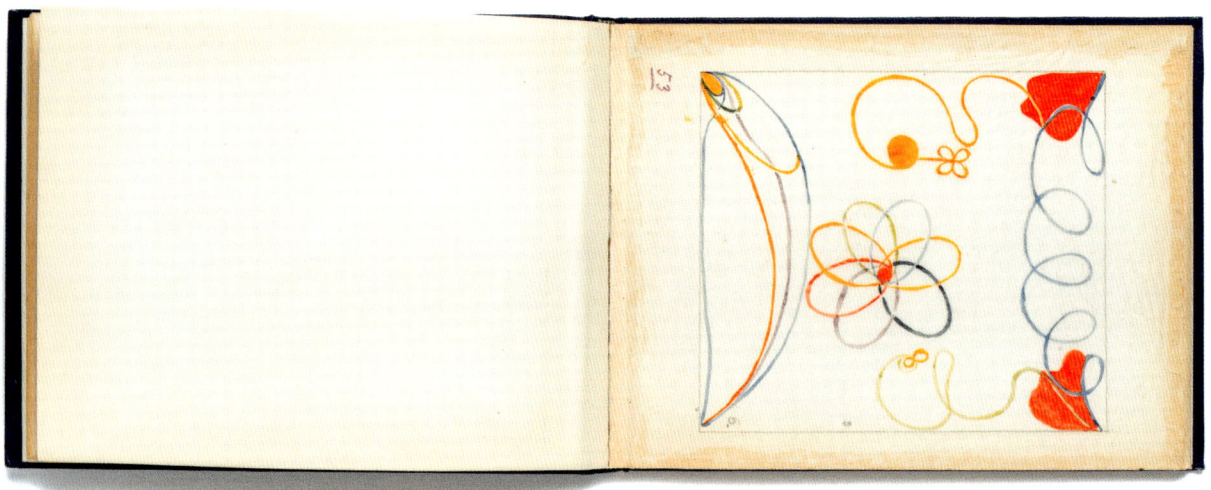

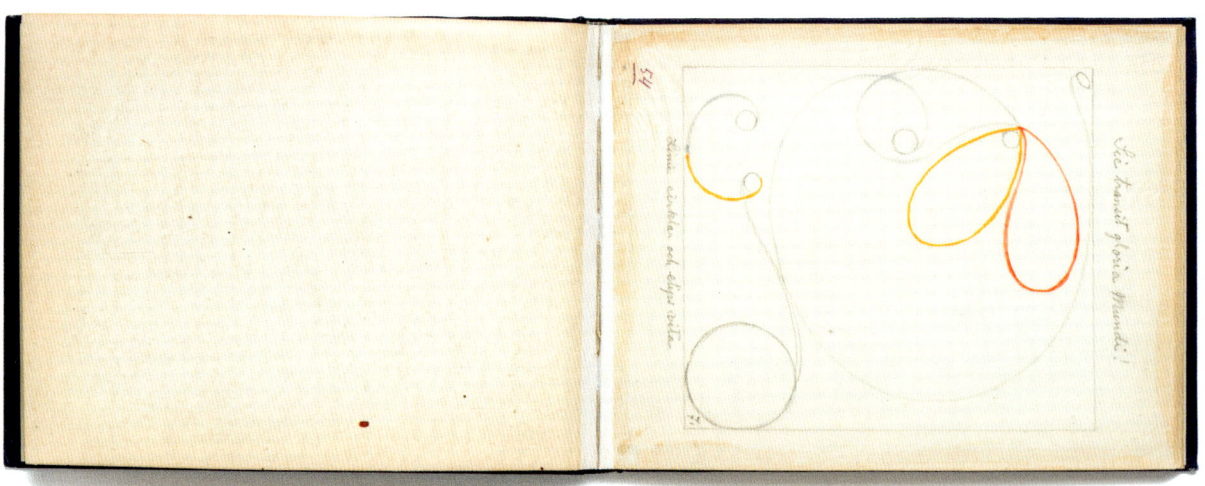

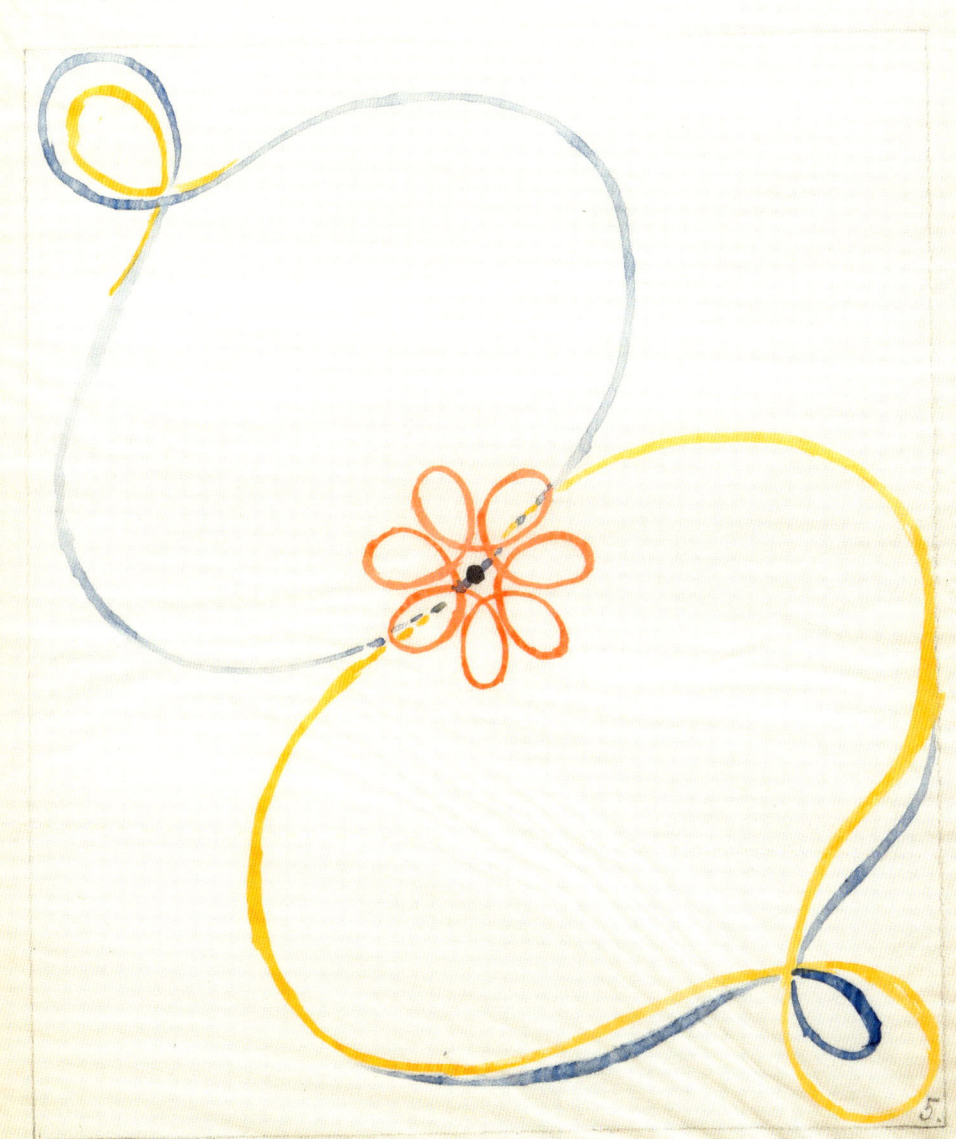

59

5

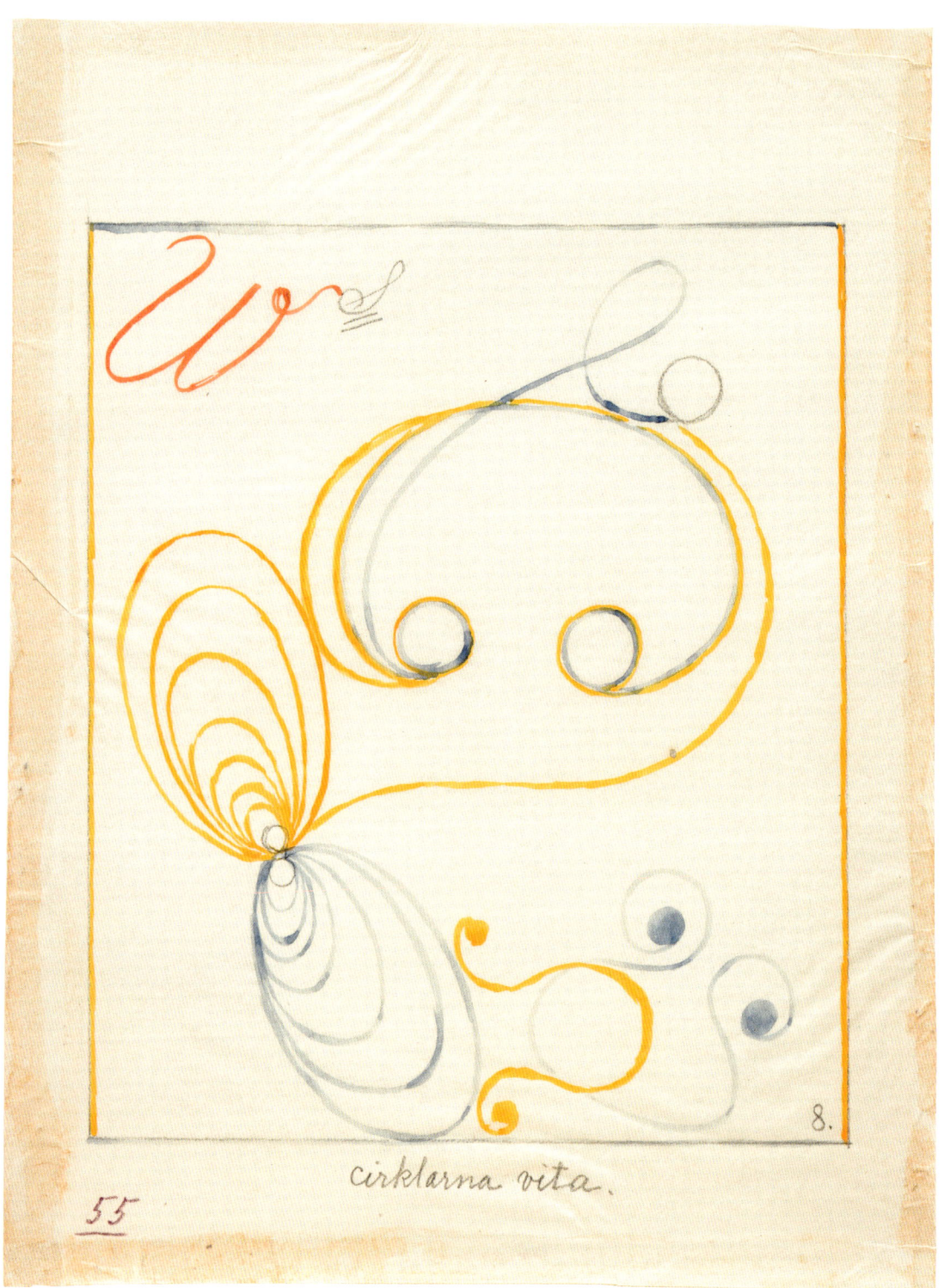

cirklarna vita.

8.

55

white circles

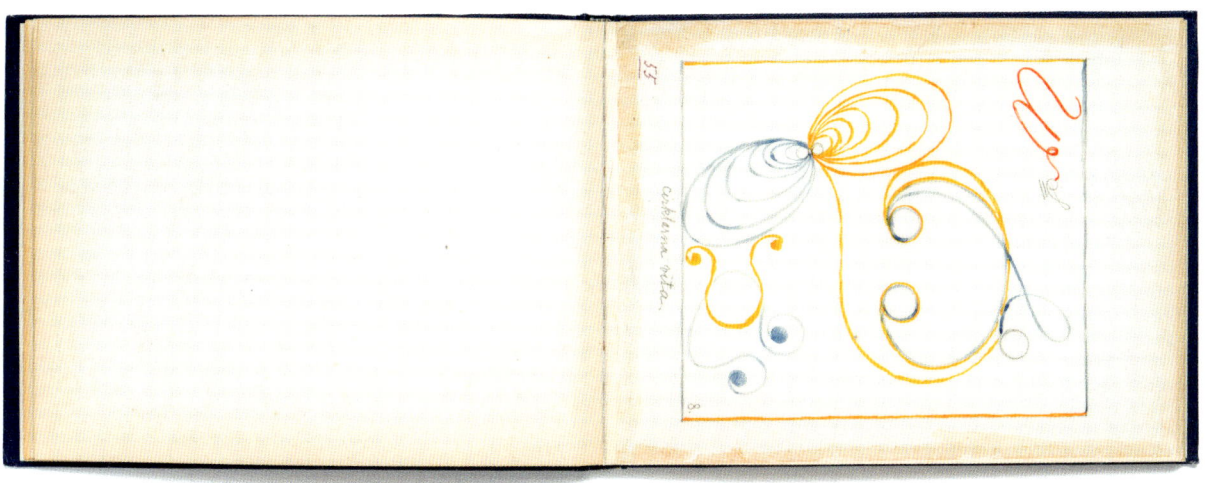

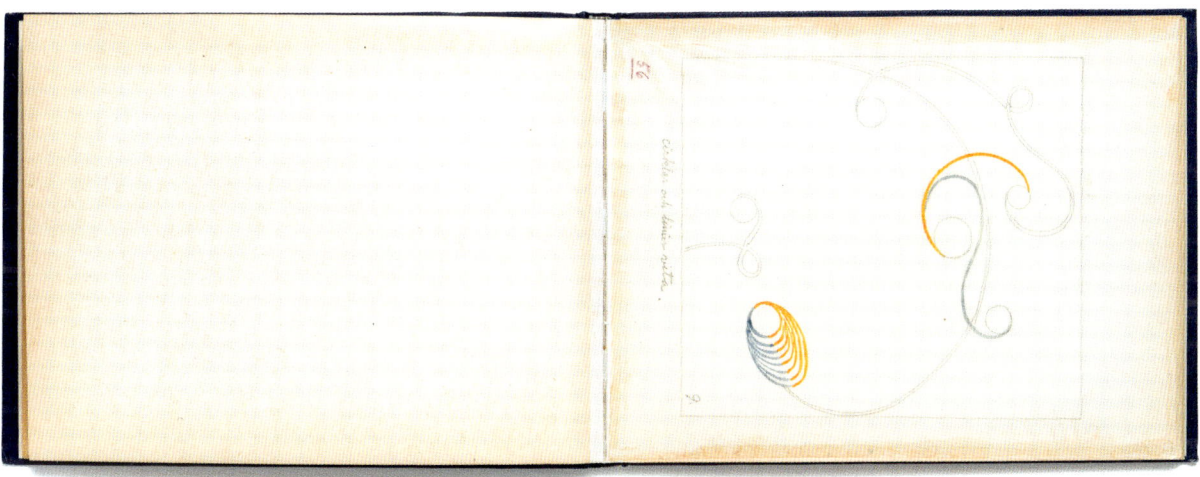

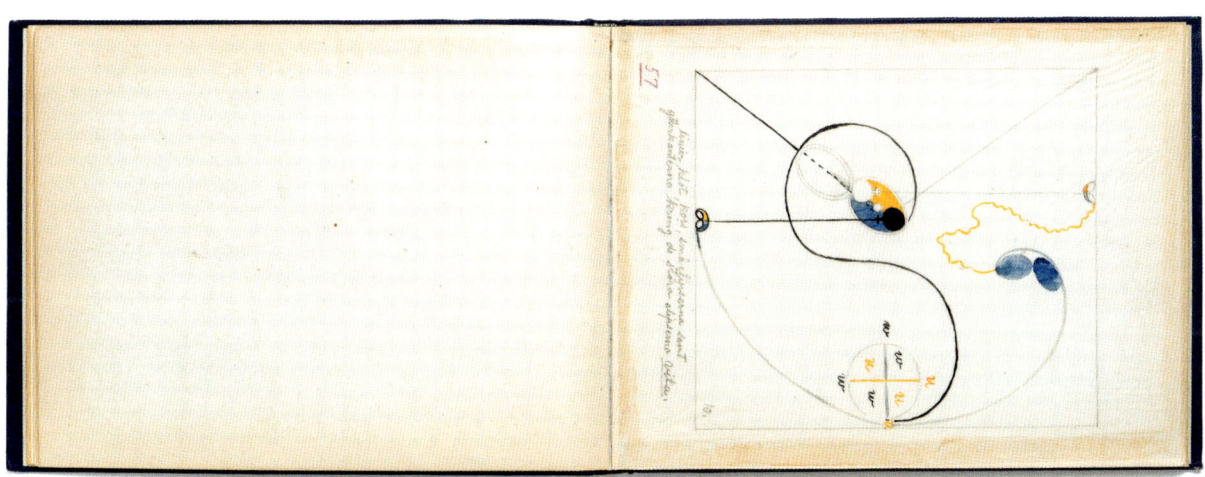

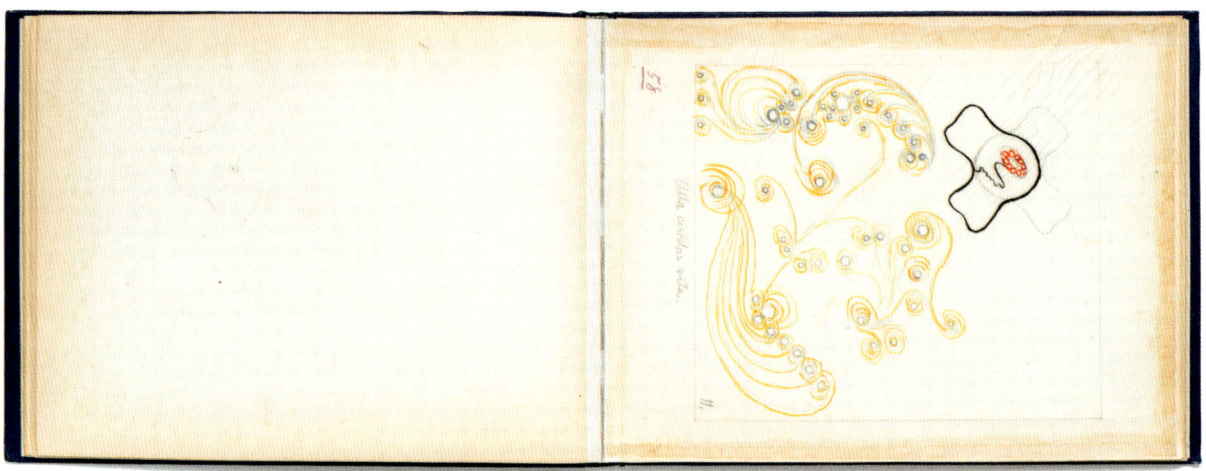

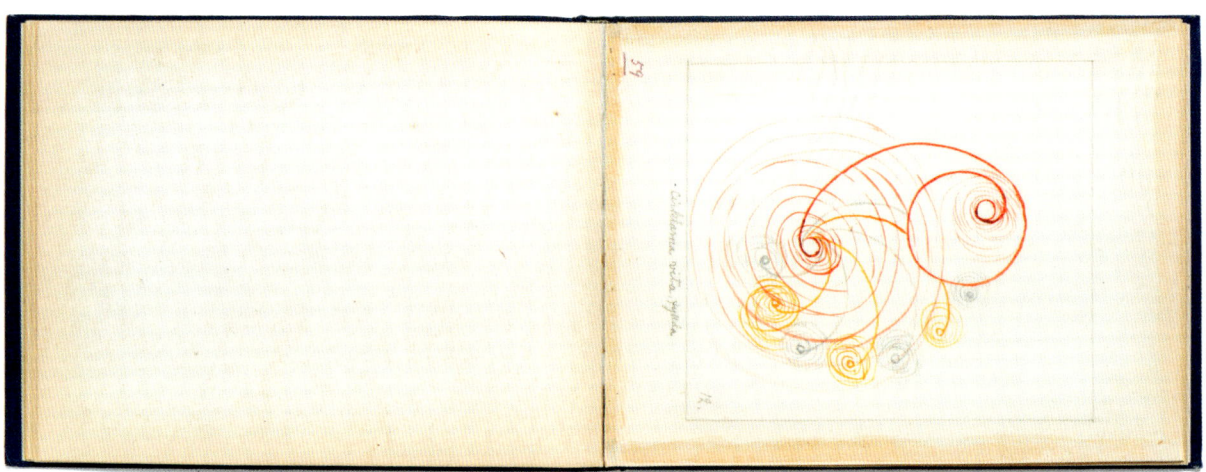

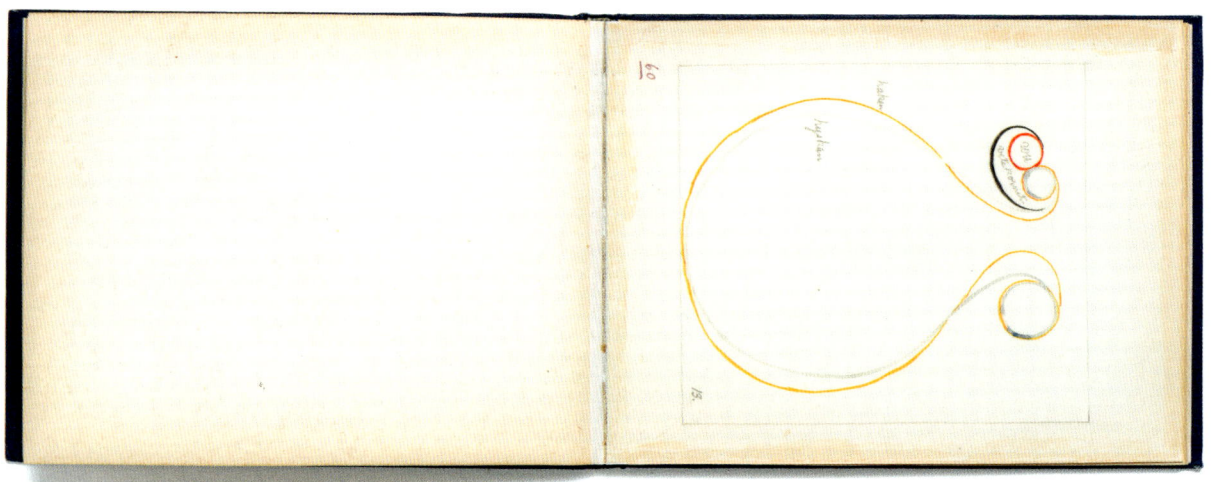

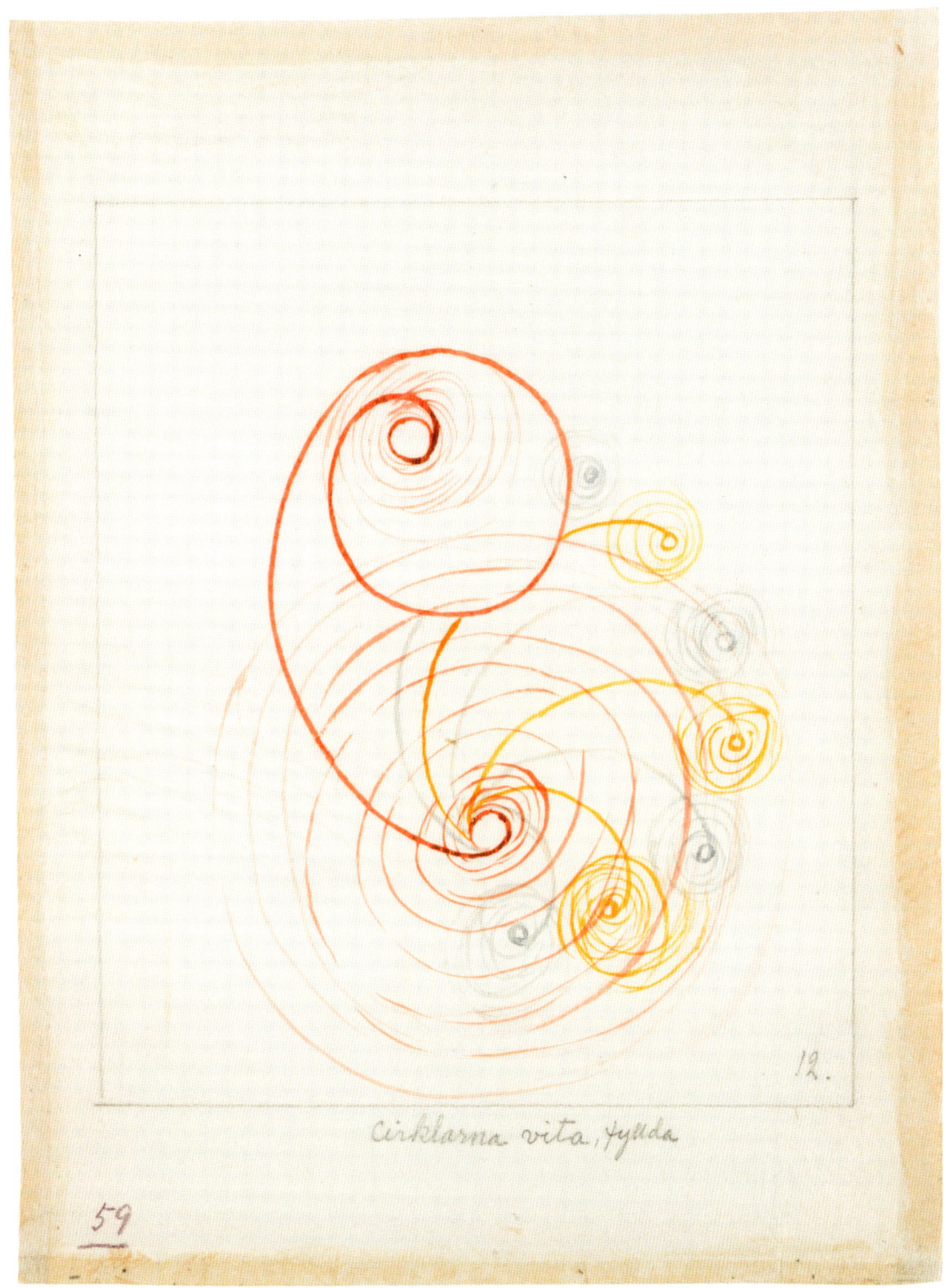

cirklarna vita, fyllda

12.

White circles, filled

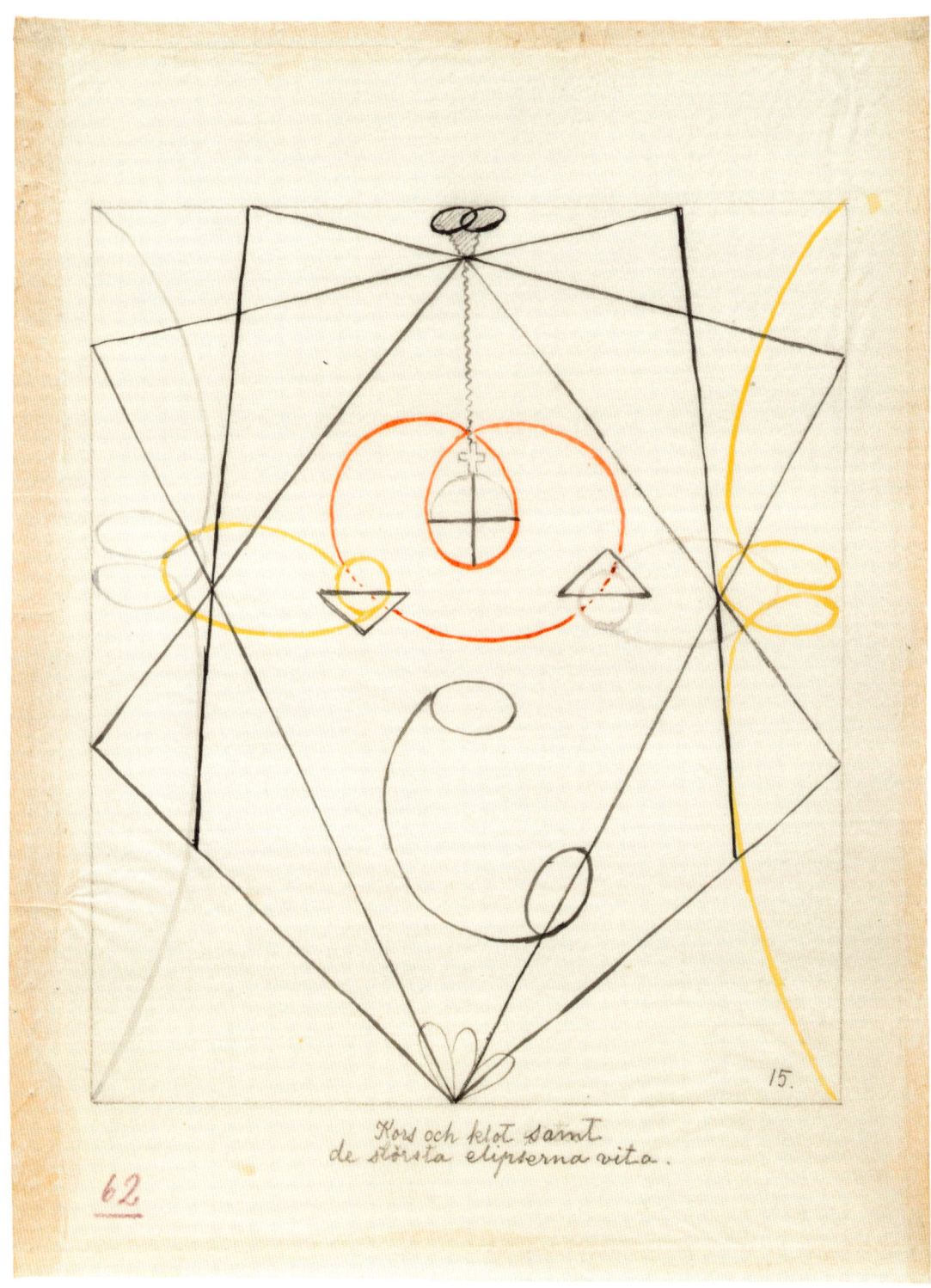

15.

62

*Kors och klot samt
de största elipserna vita.*

cross and sphere and the largest ellipses are white

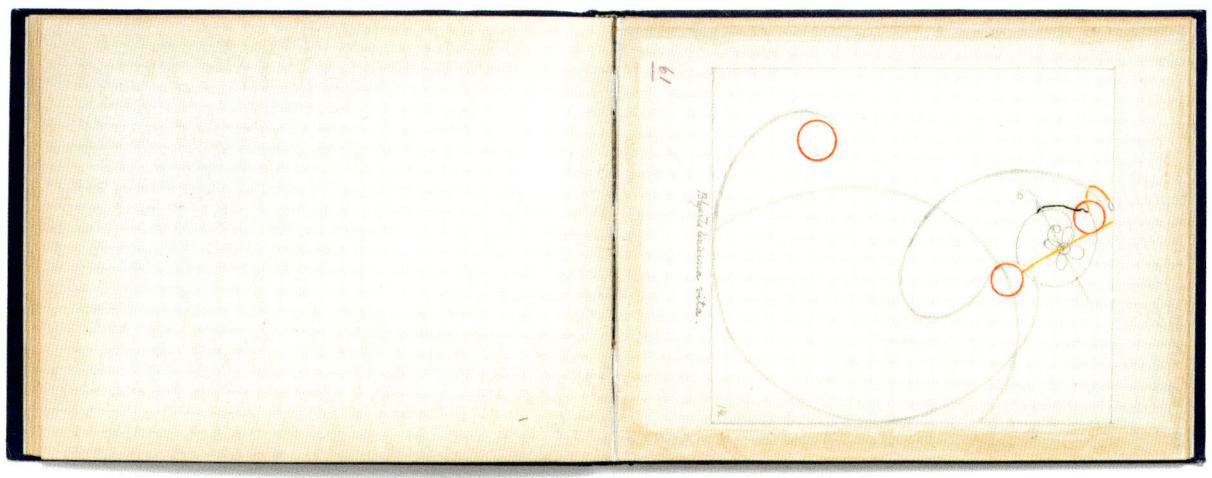

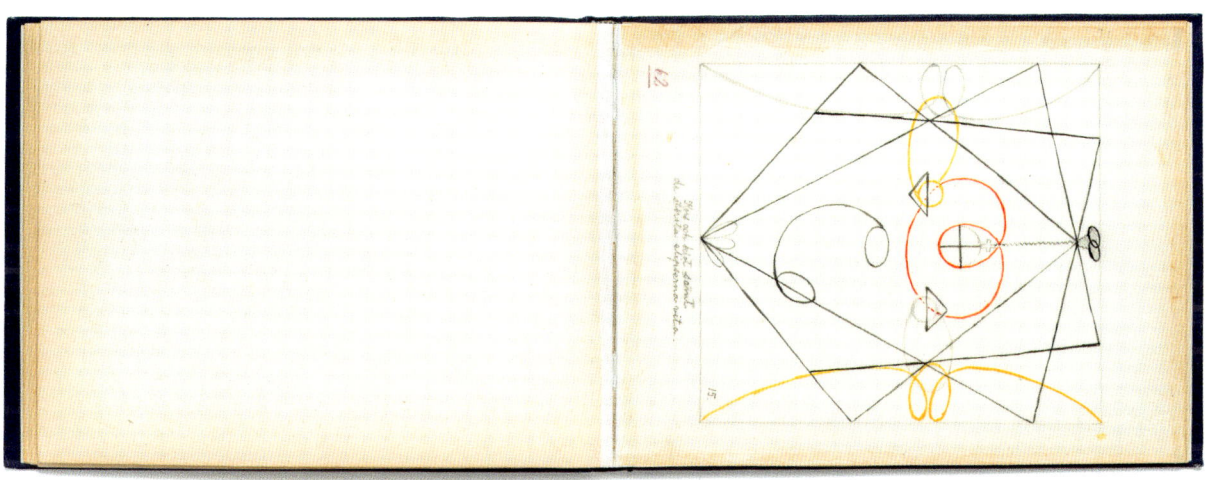

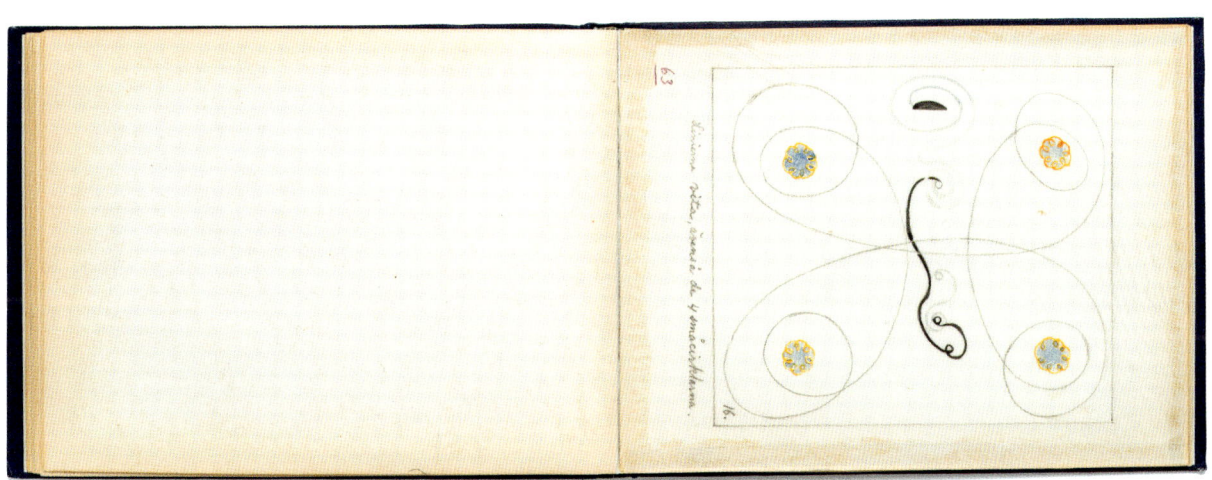

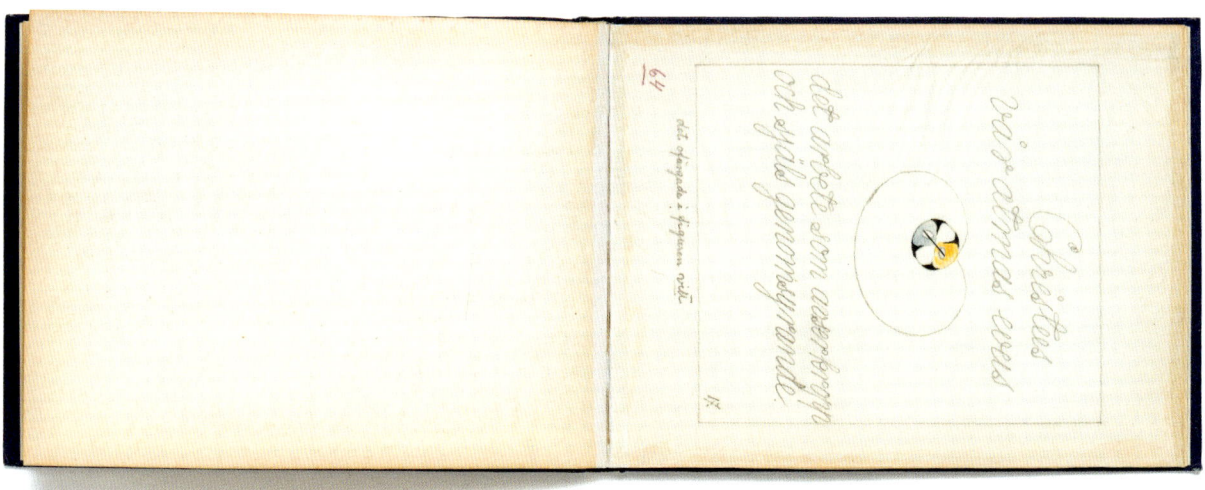

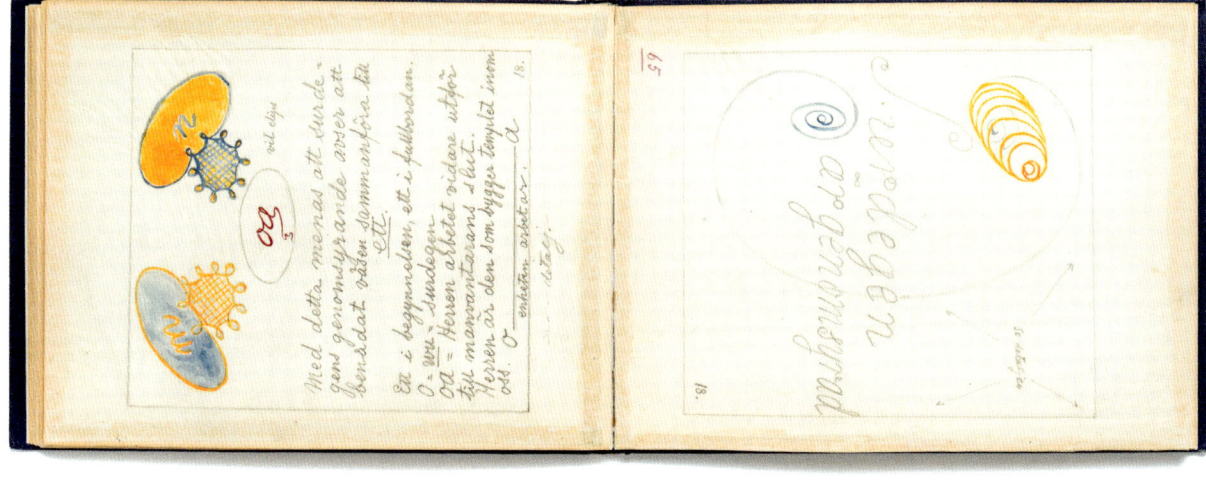

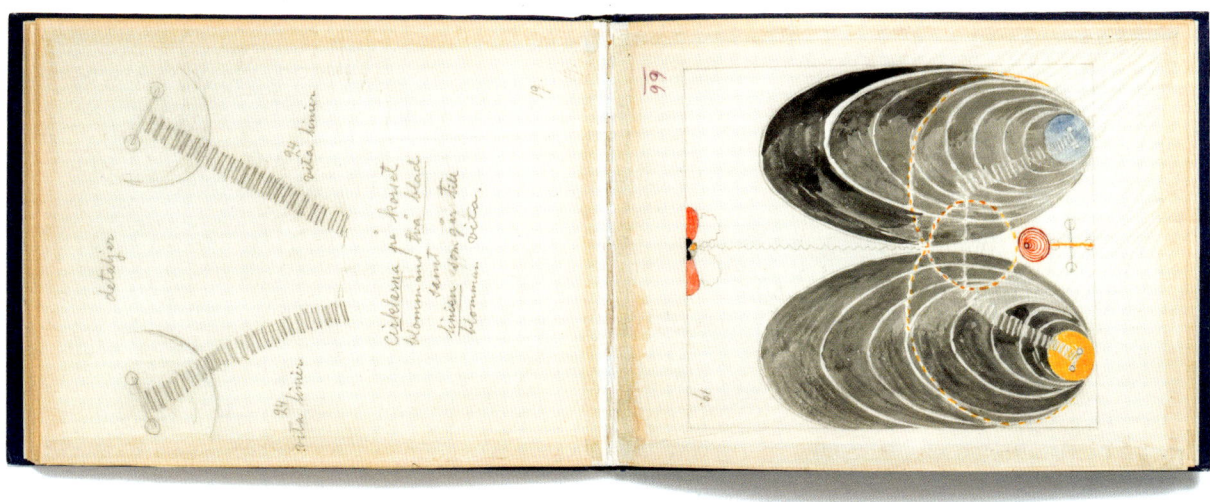

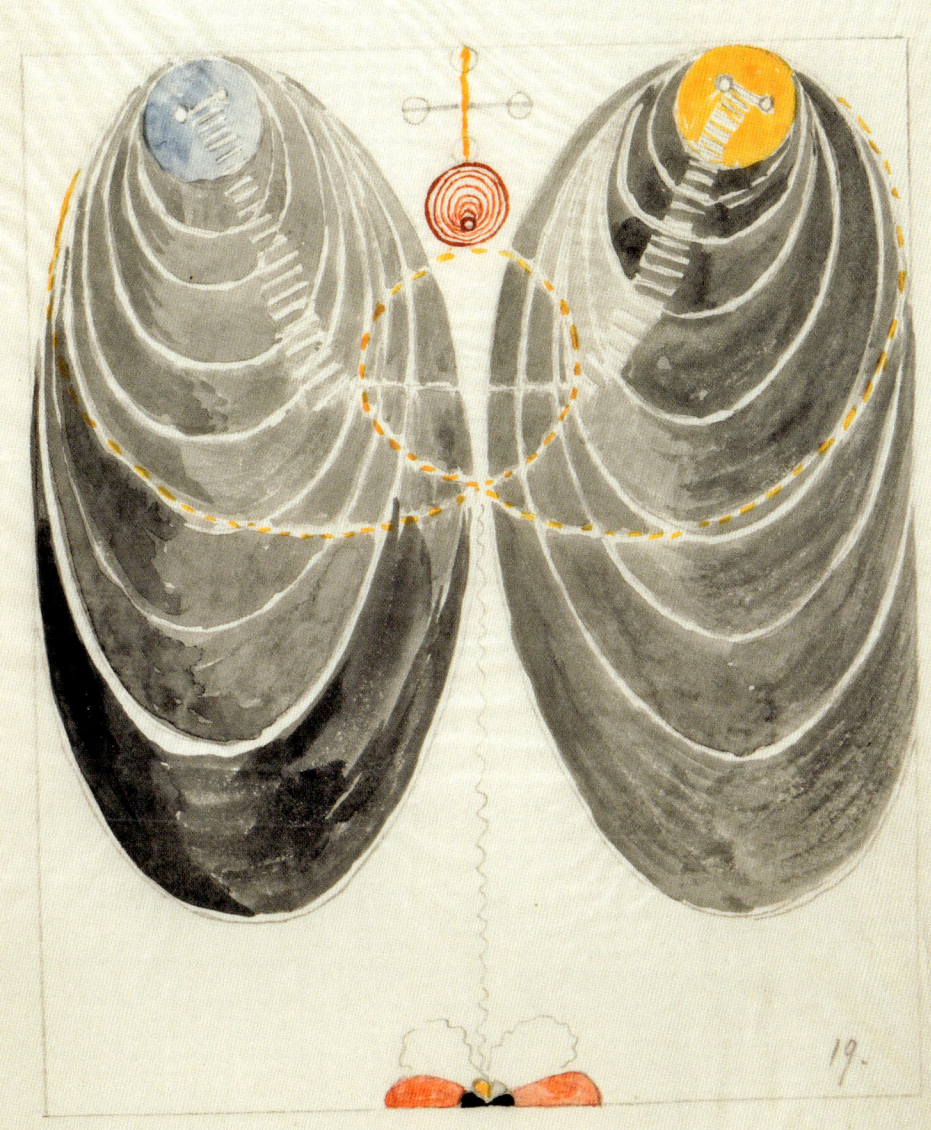

66

19.

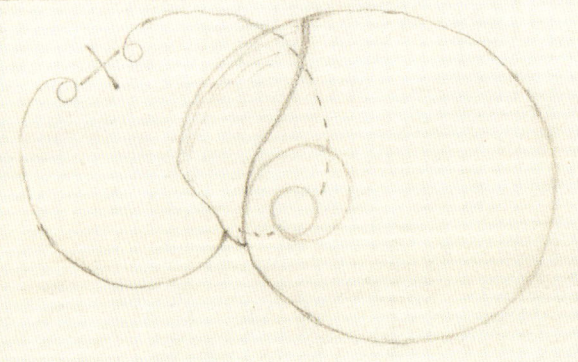

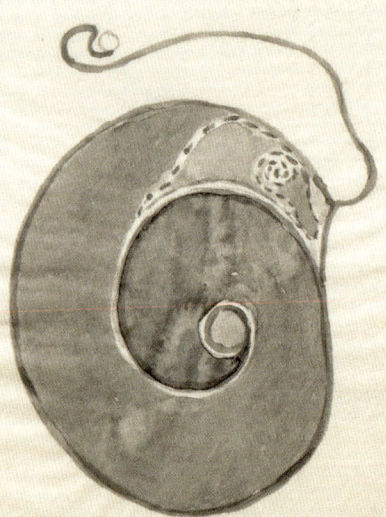

20.

67

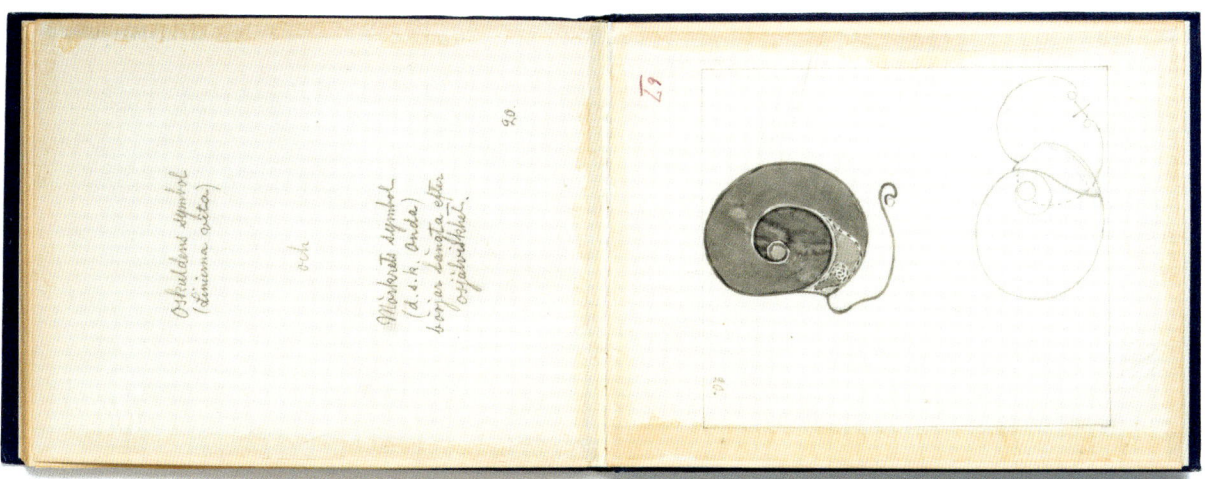

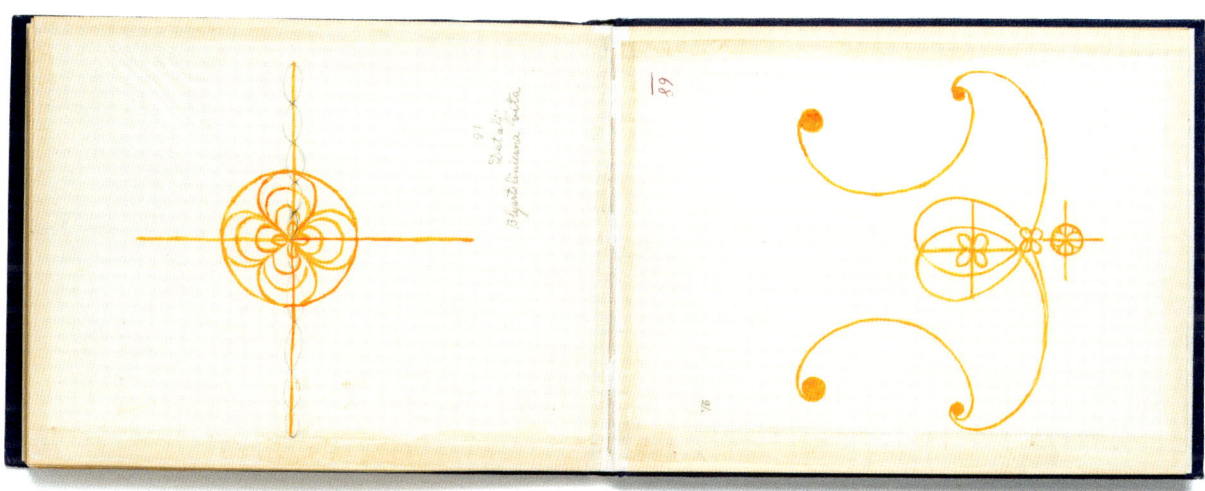

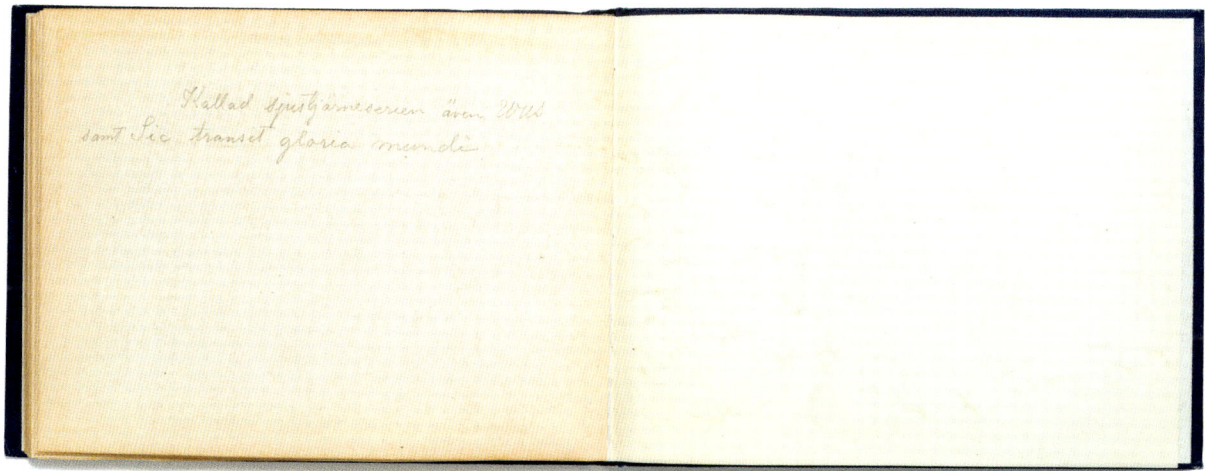

Called the Seven Sisters series also WUS as well as Sic transit Gloria mundi

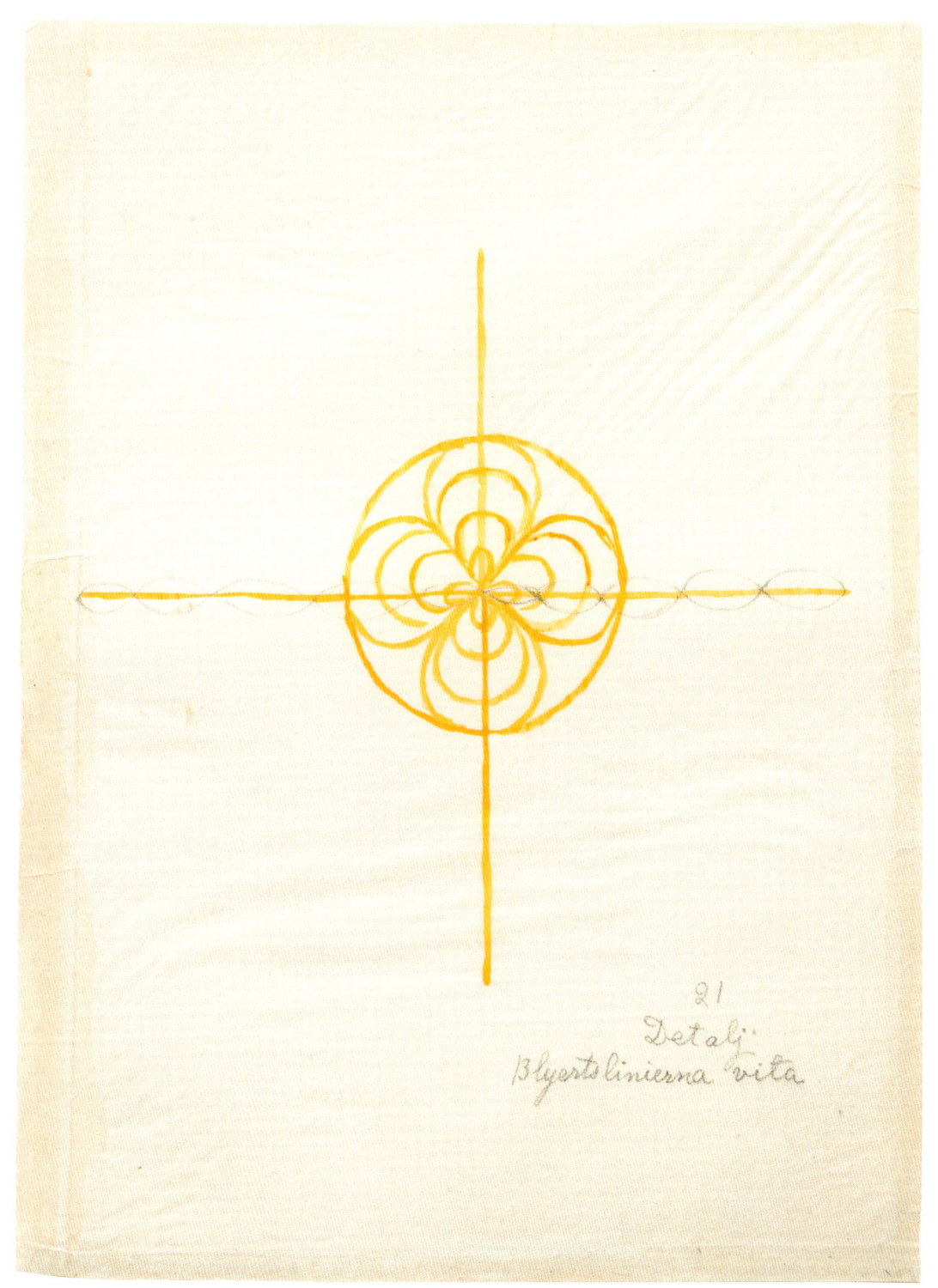

Detail. White pencil lines

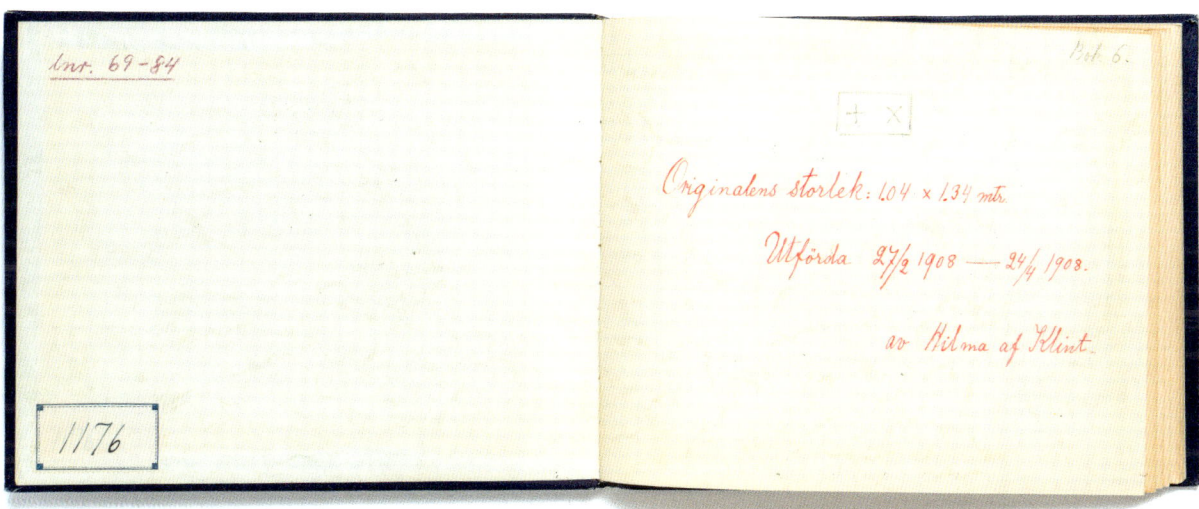

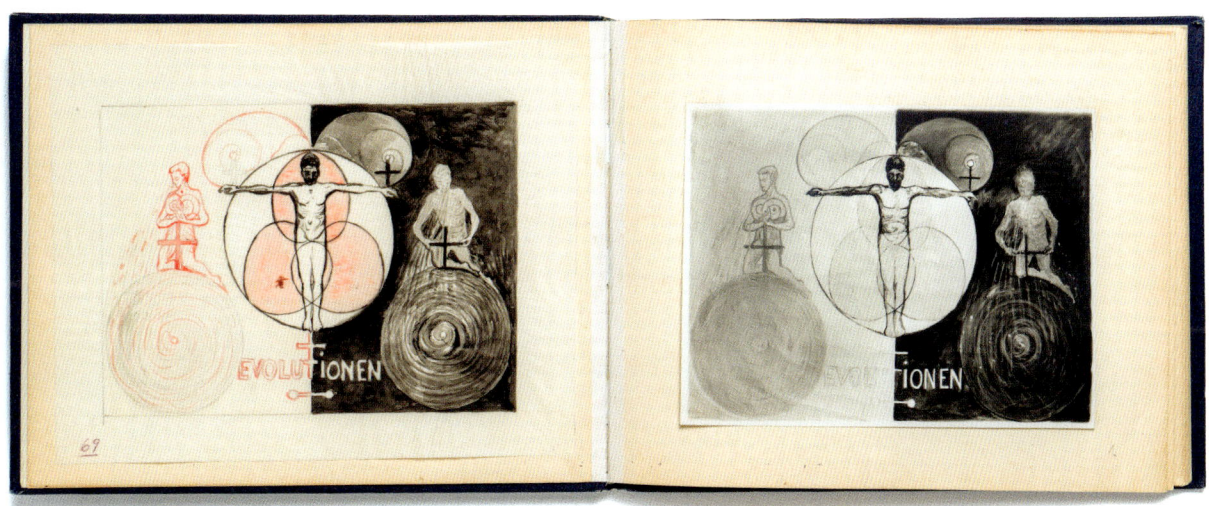

1176, Inv. 69–84. Original size: 1.04 × 1.34 m. Made 2/27/1908–4/24/1908, by Hilma af Klint

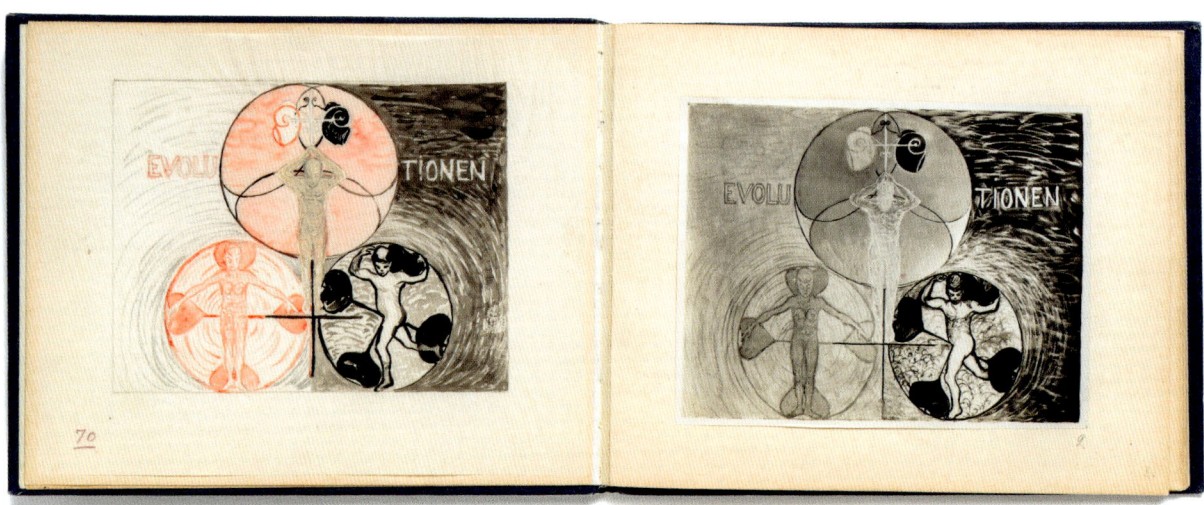

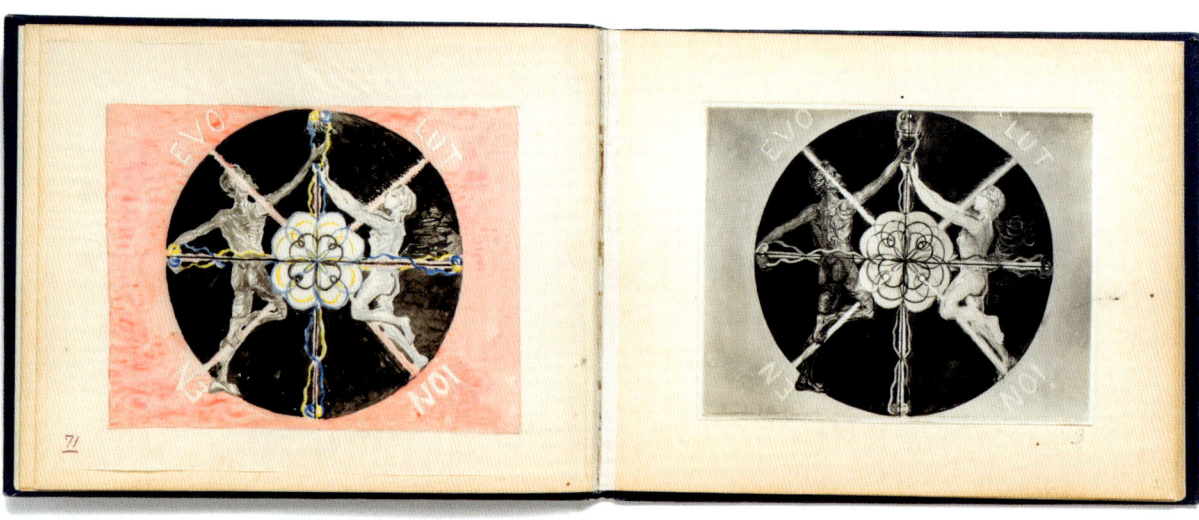

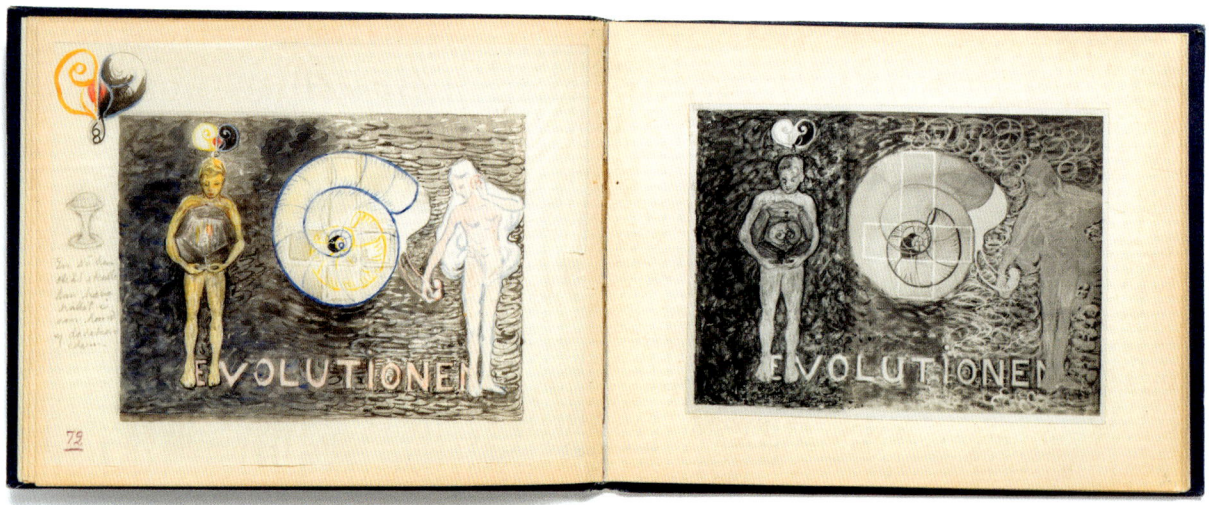

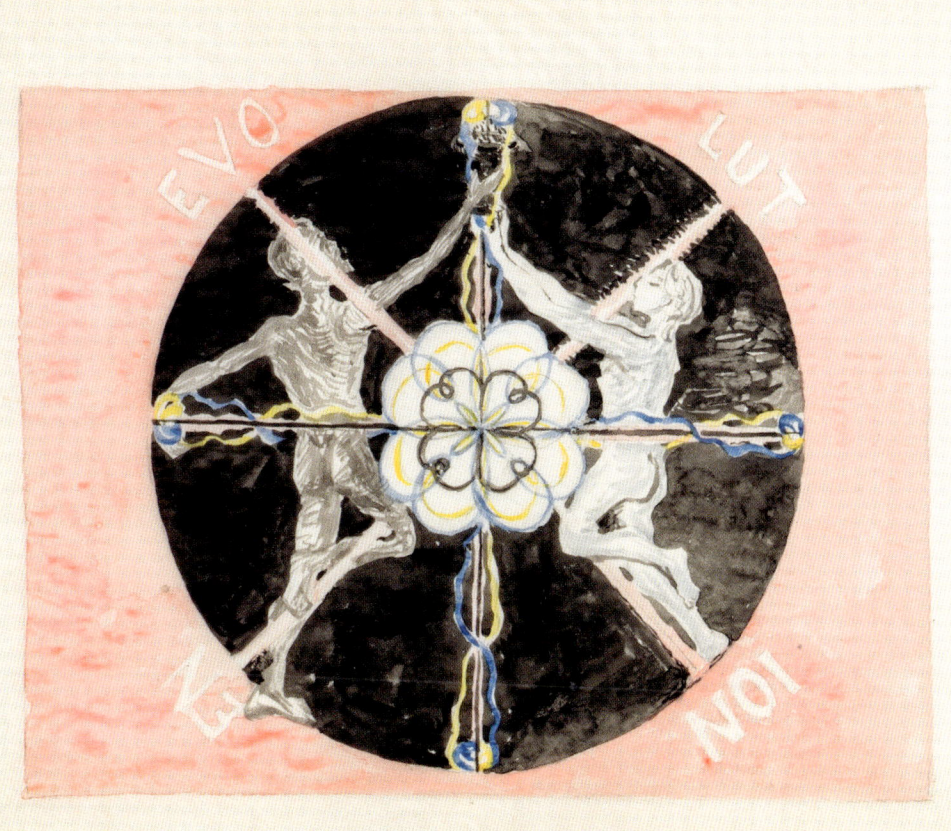

71

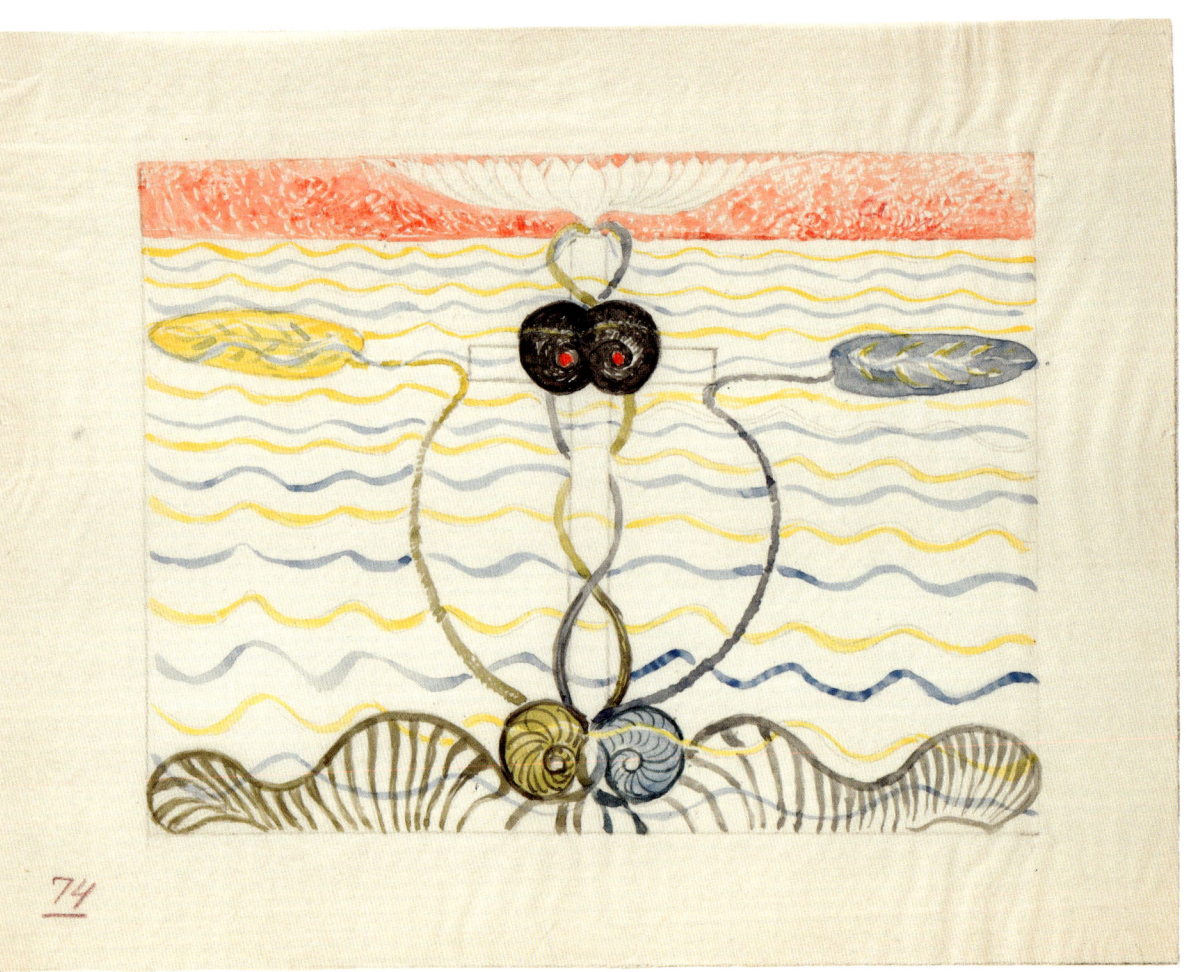

74

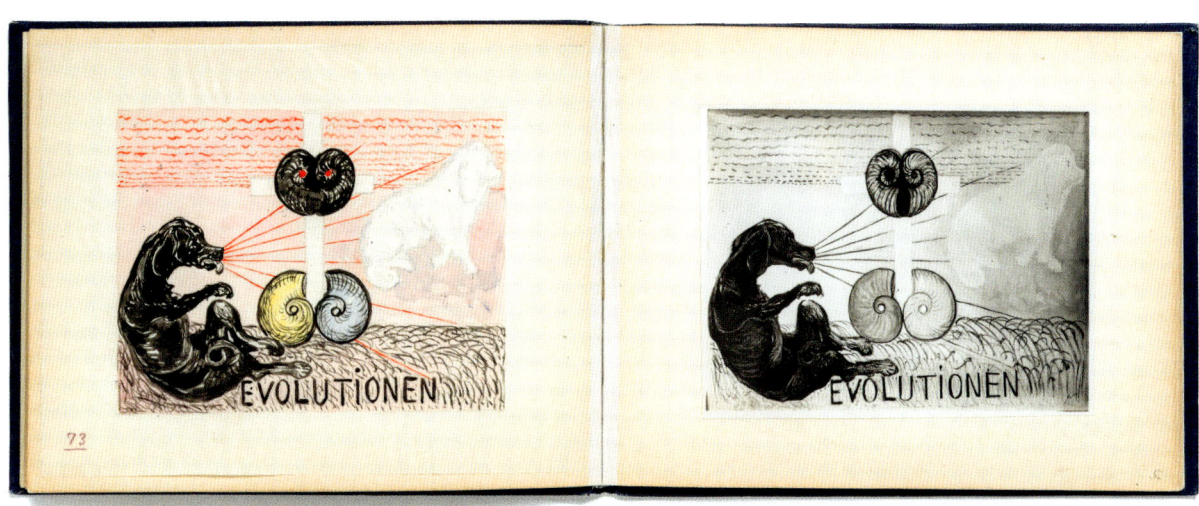

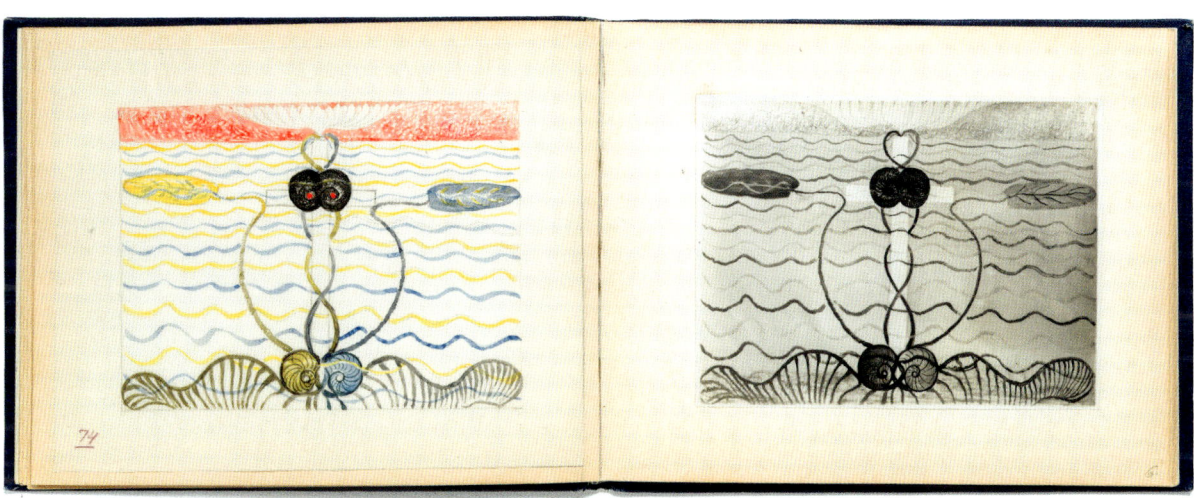

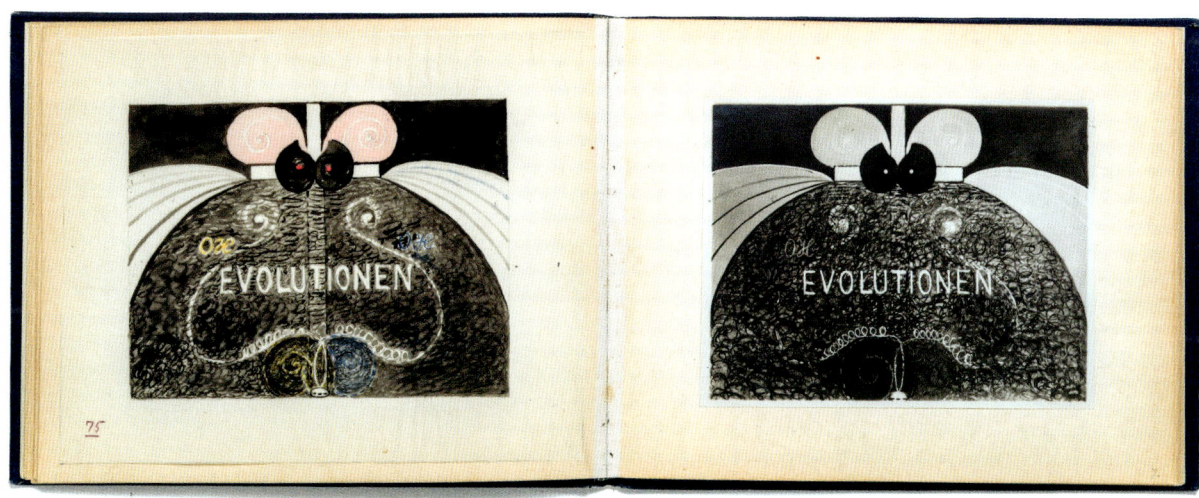

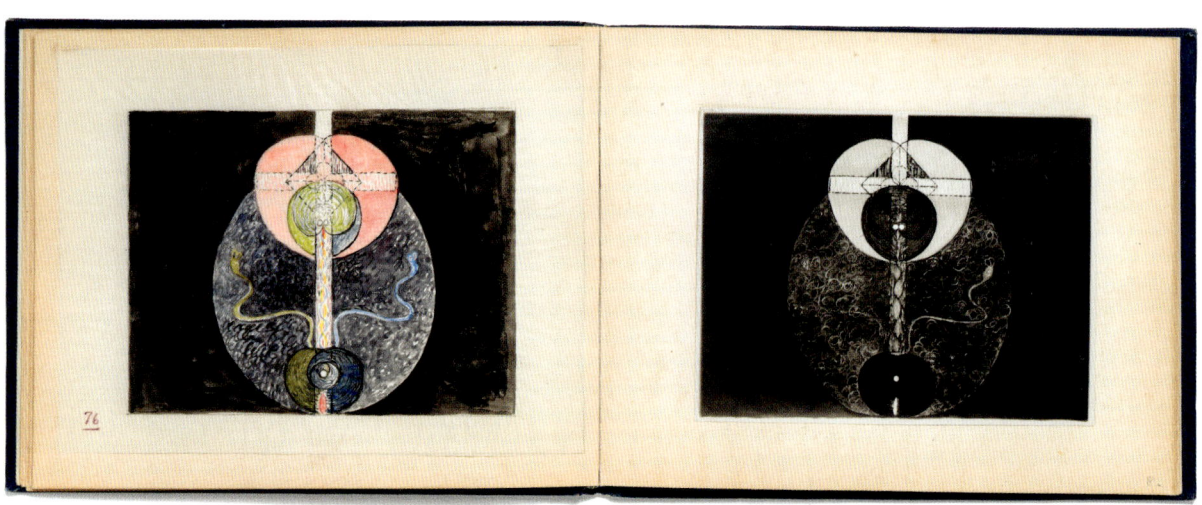

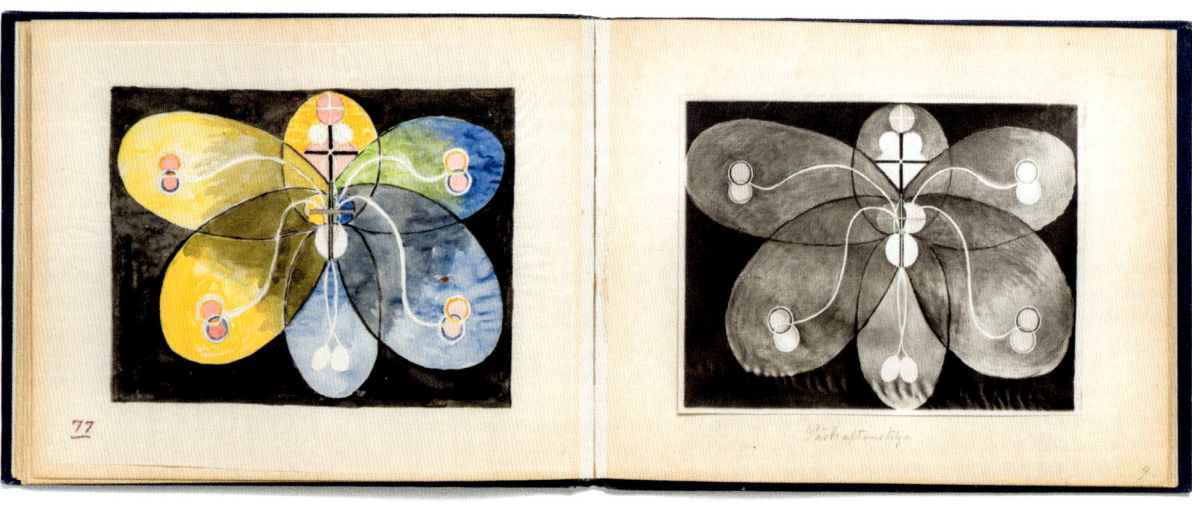

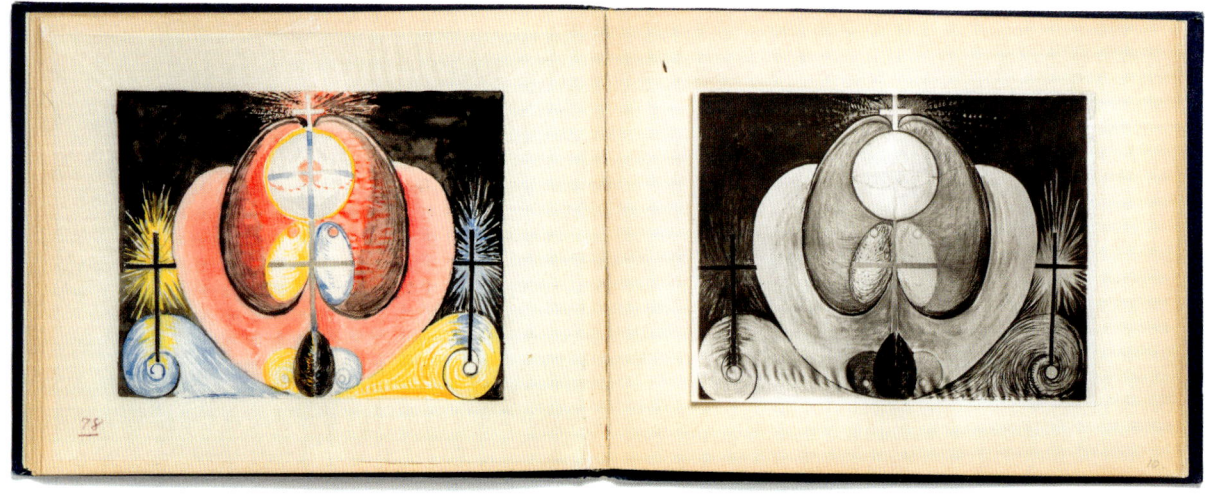

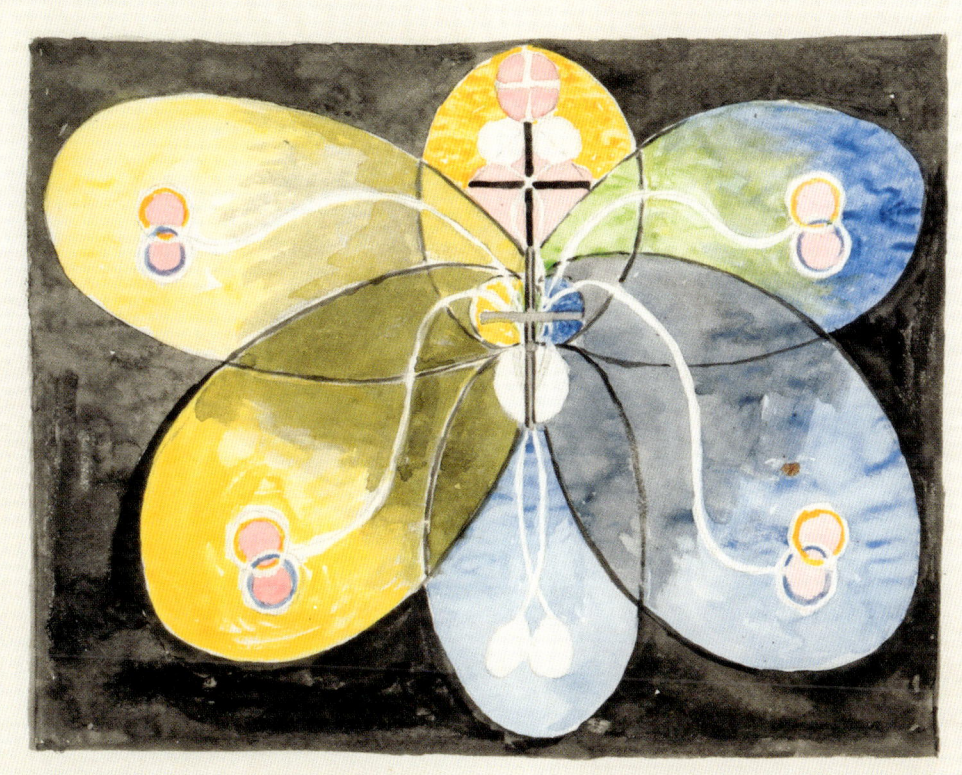

77

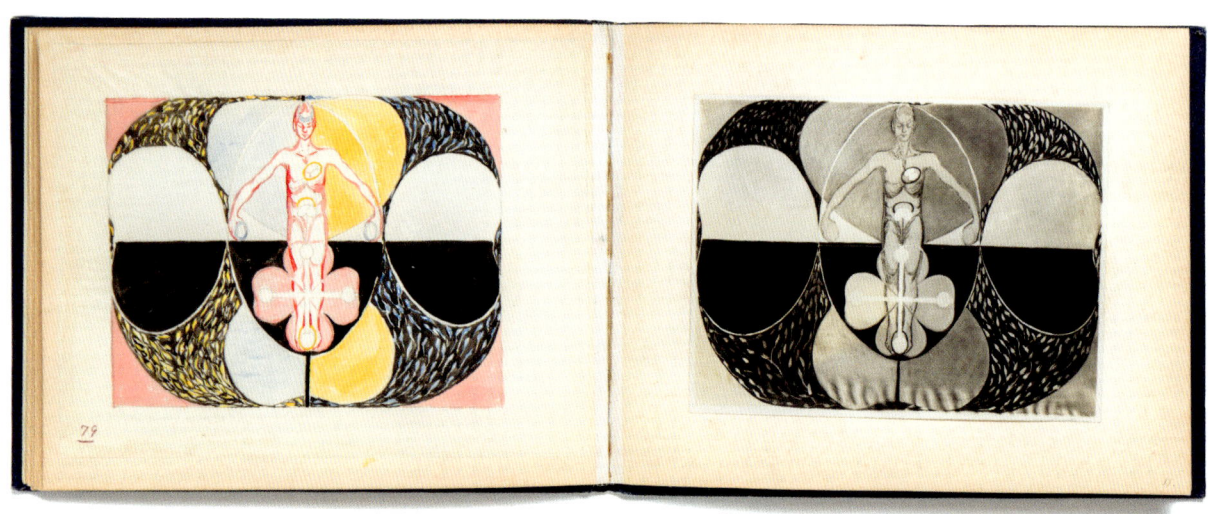

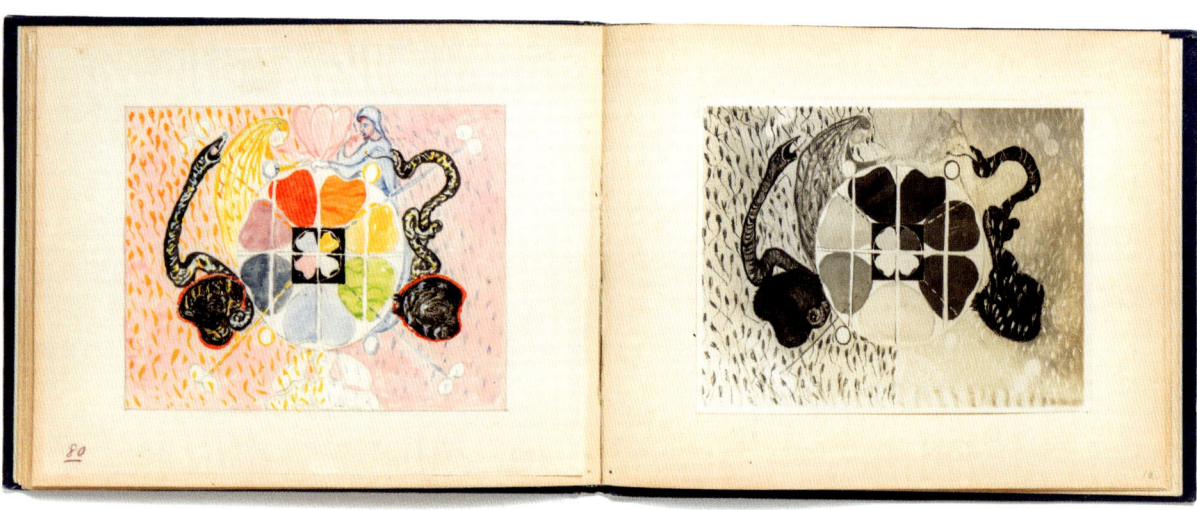

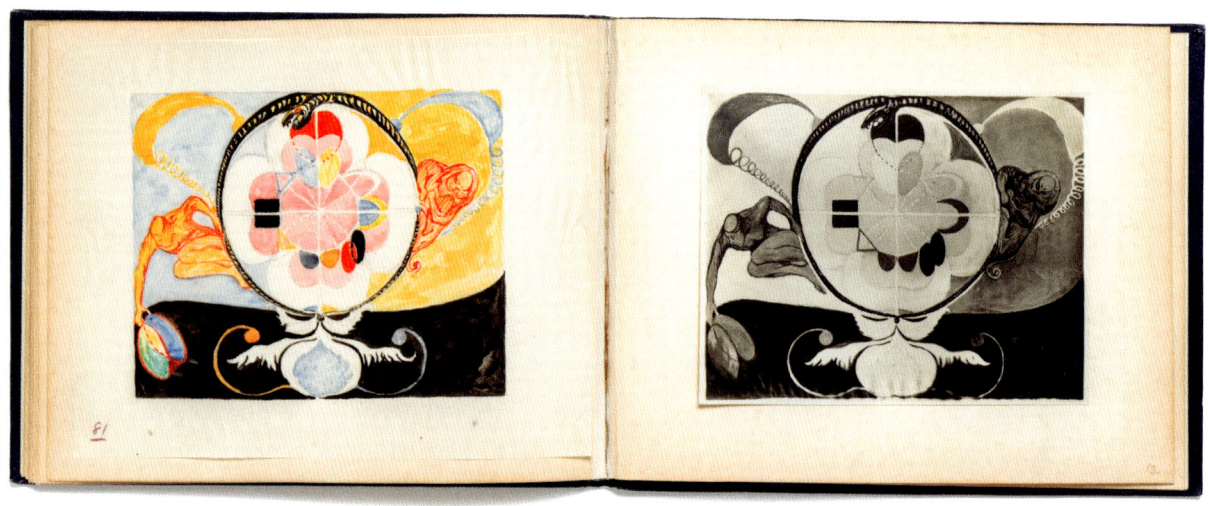

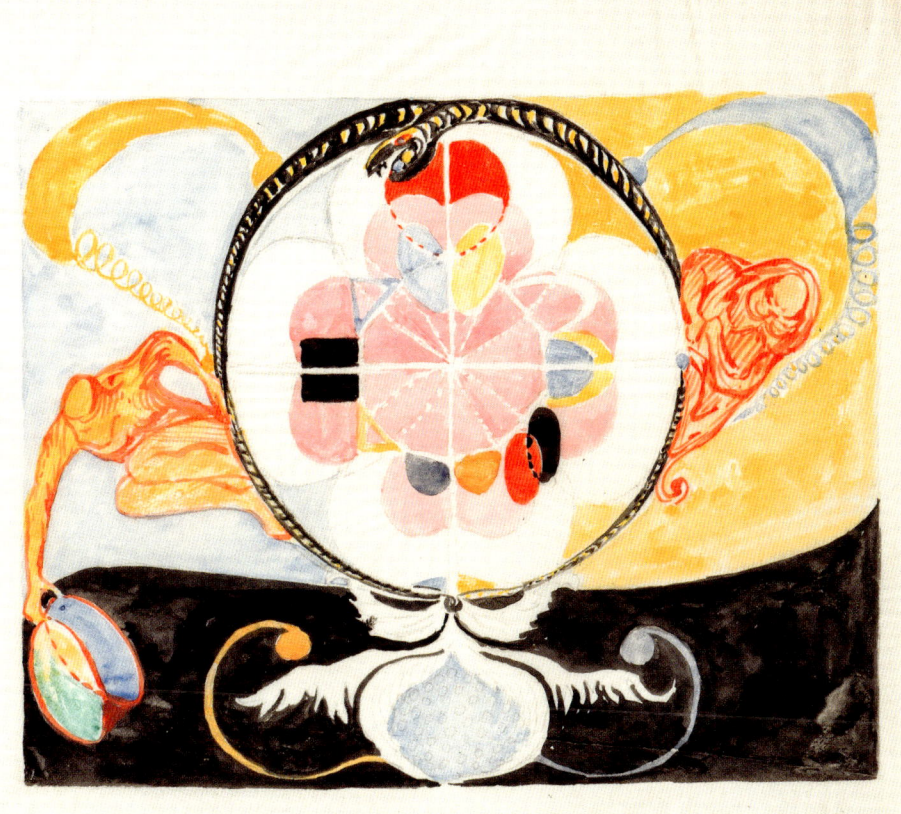

81

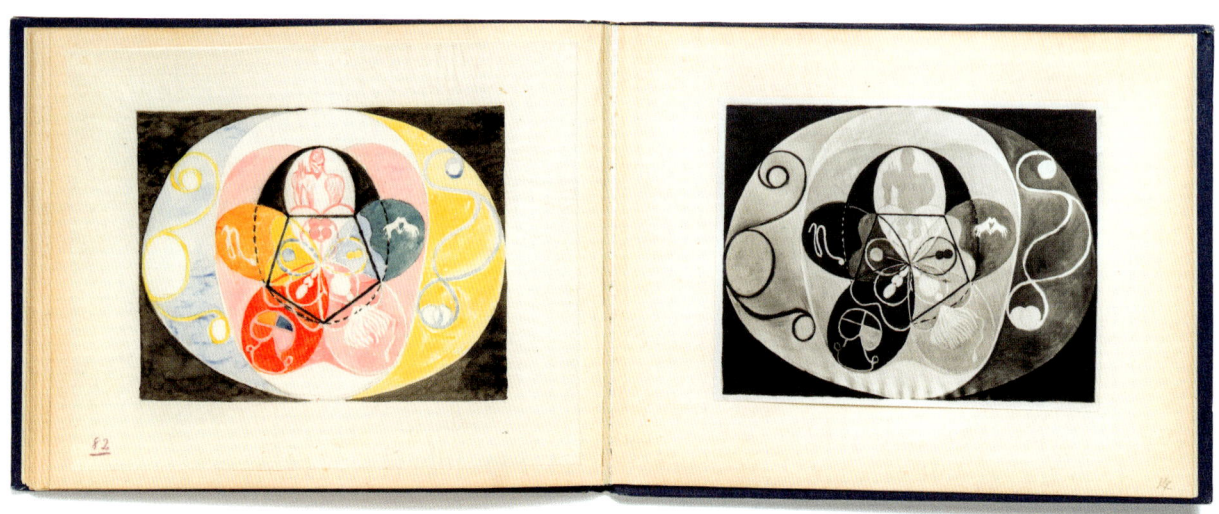

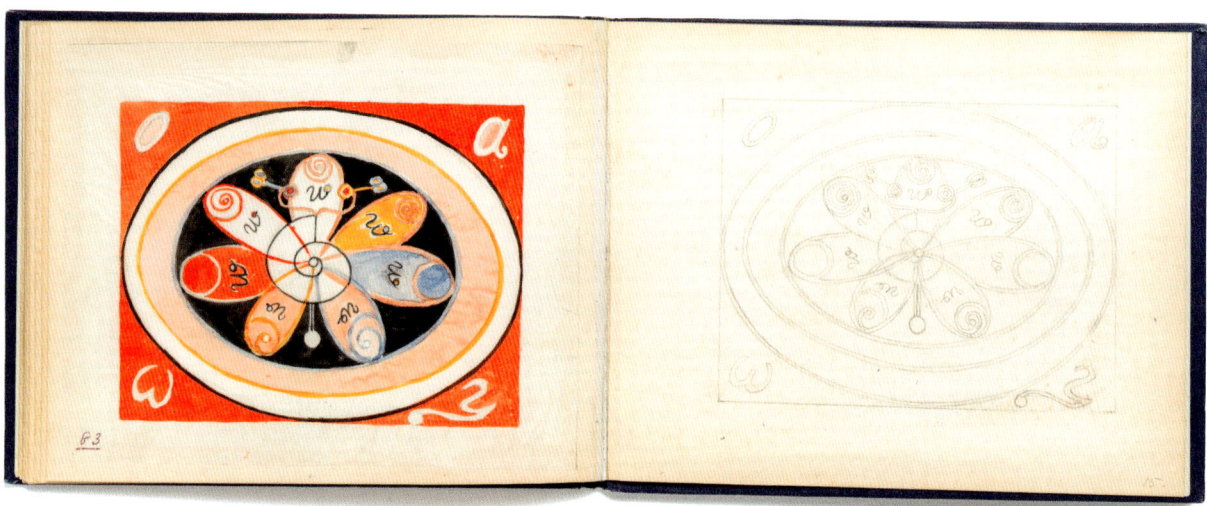

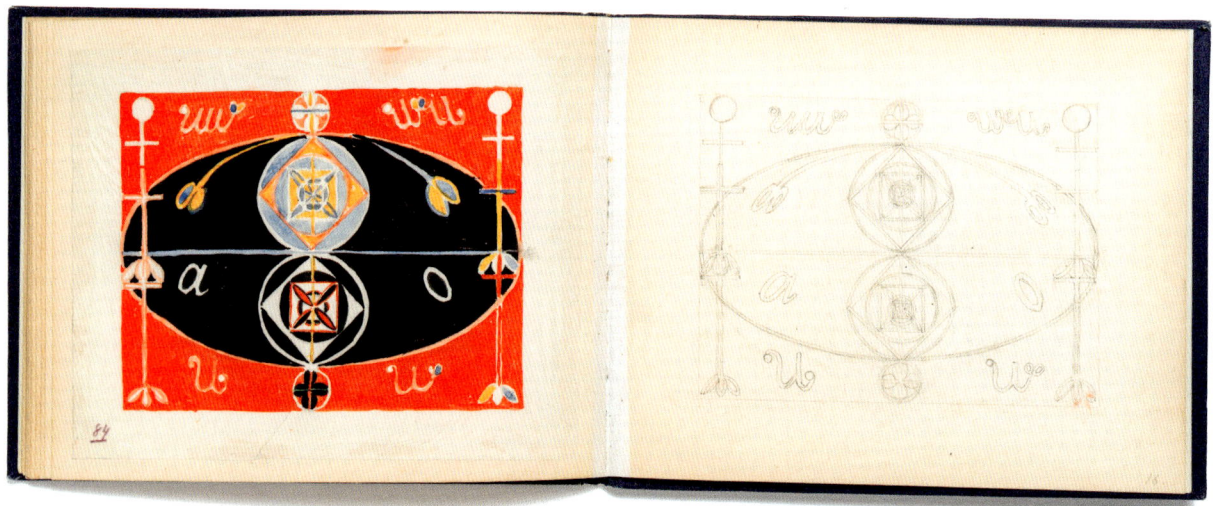

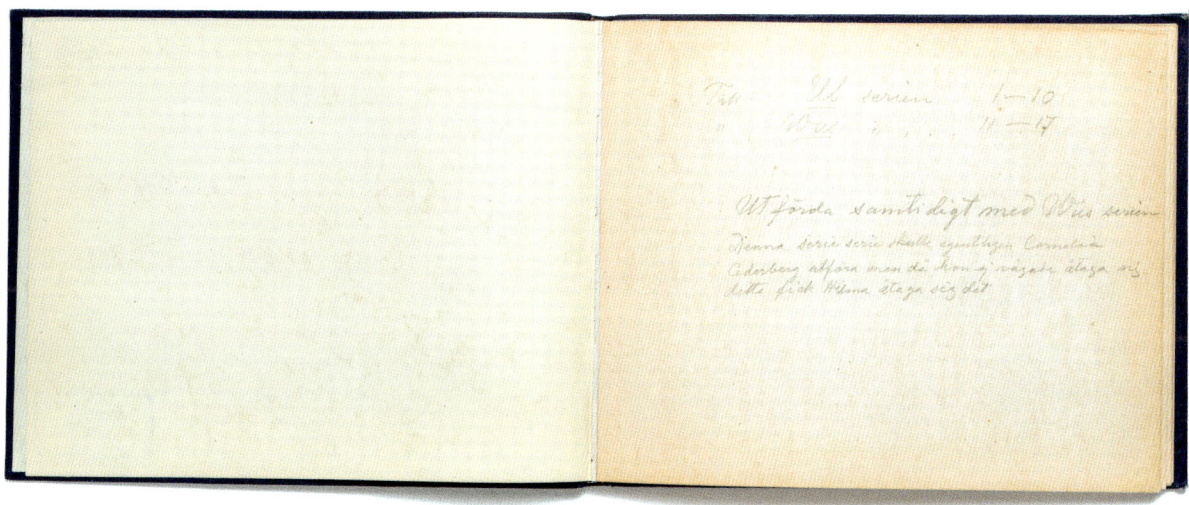

1177, Inv. 85–101. Original size: 0.36 × 0.26 m. Made 3/27/1908–4/24/1908, by Hilma af Klint
To the US series 1–10. To the WUS series 11–17. Made at the same time as the WUS series

This series series [sic] was actually to have been made by Cornelia Cederberg, but since she did not dare undertake it, Hilma had to.

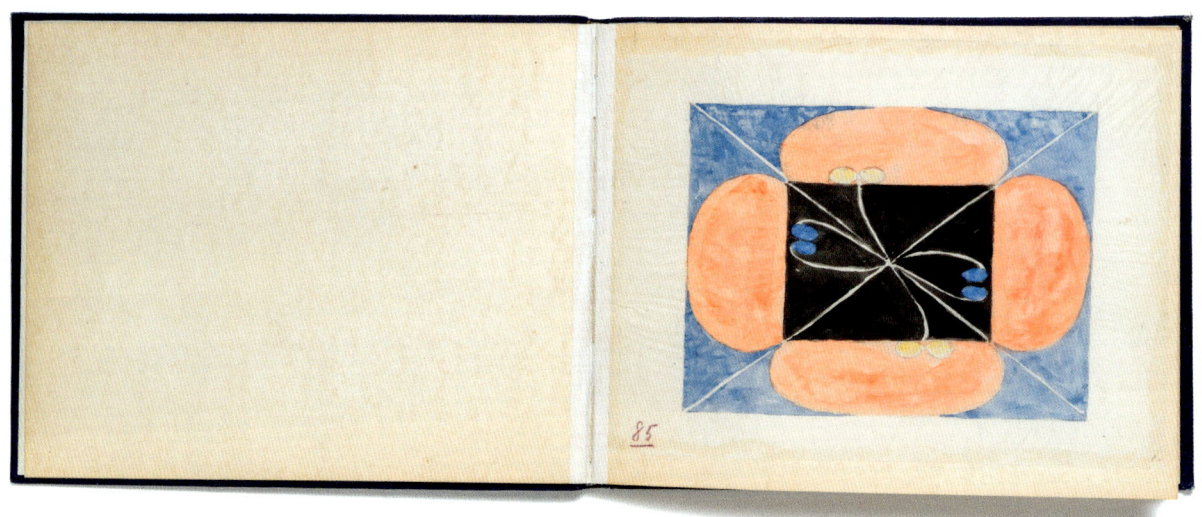

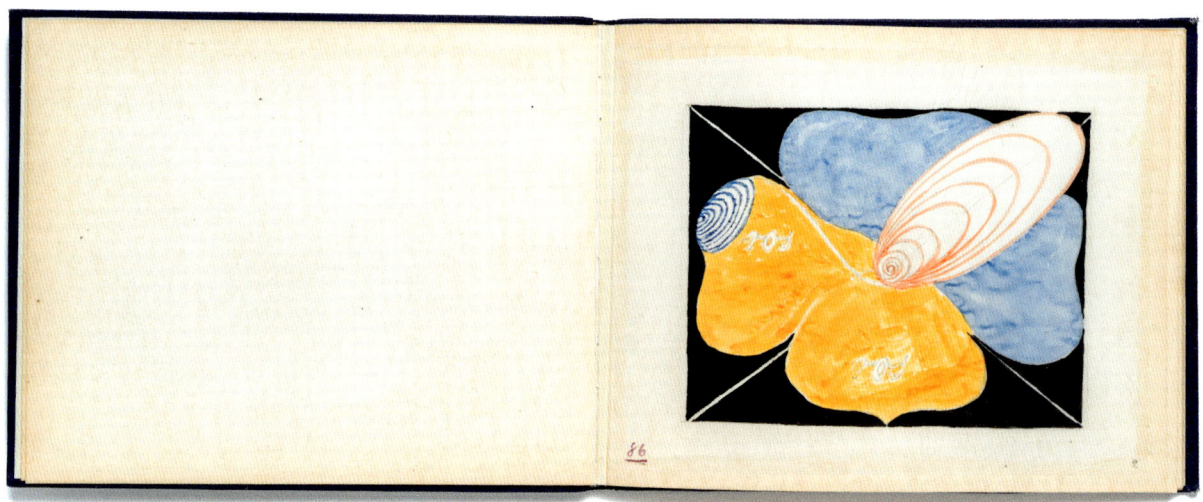

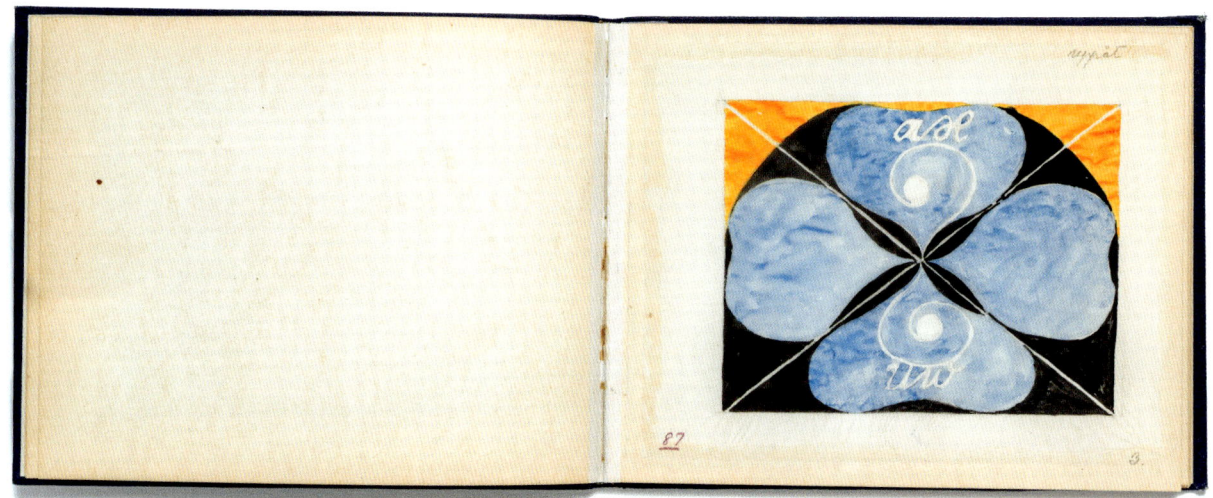

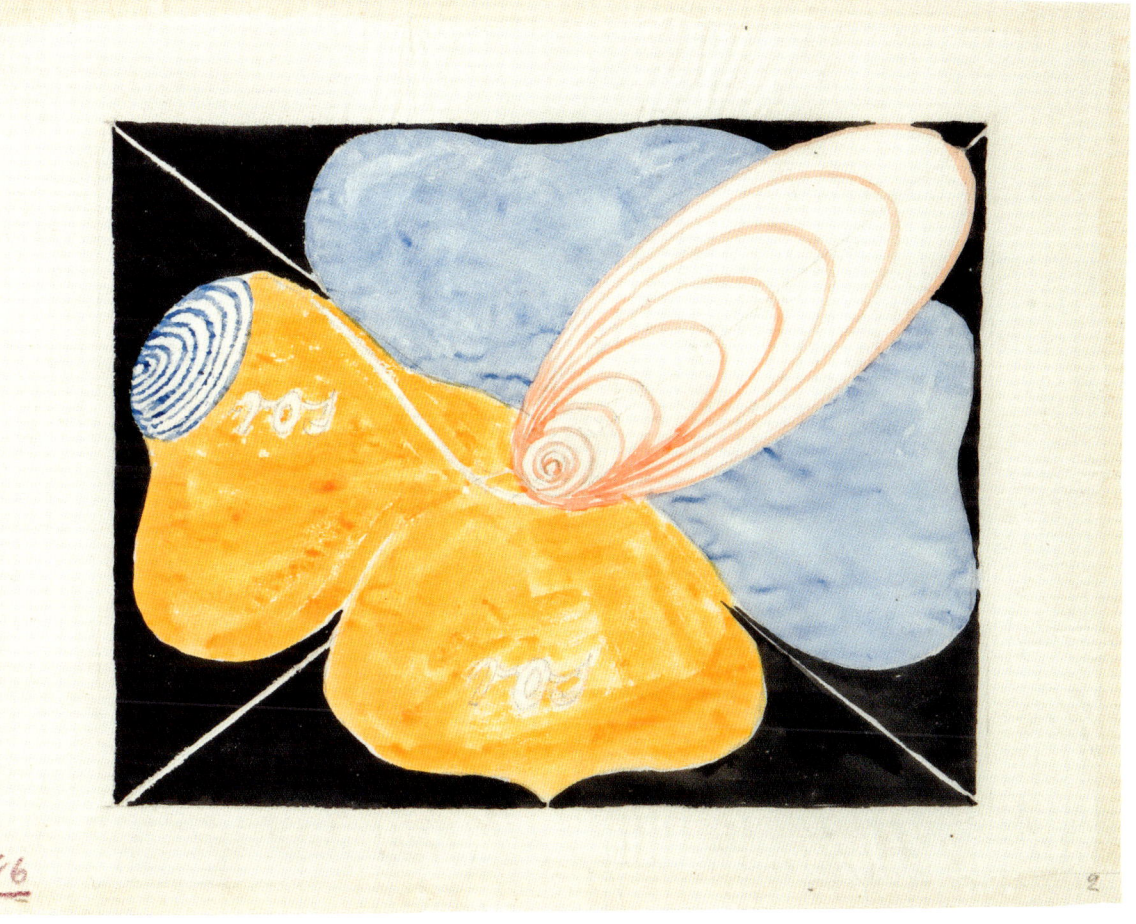

86

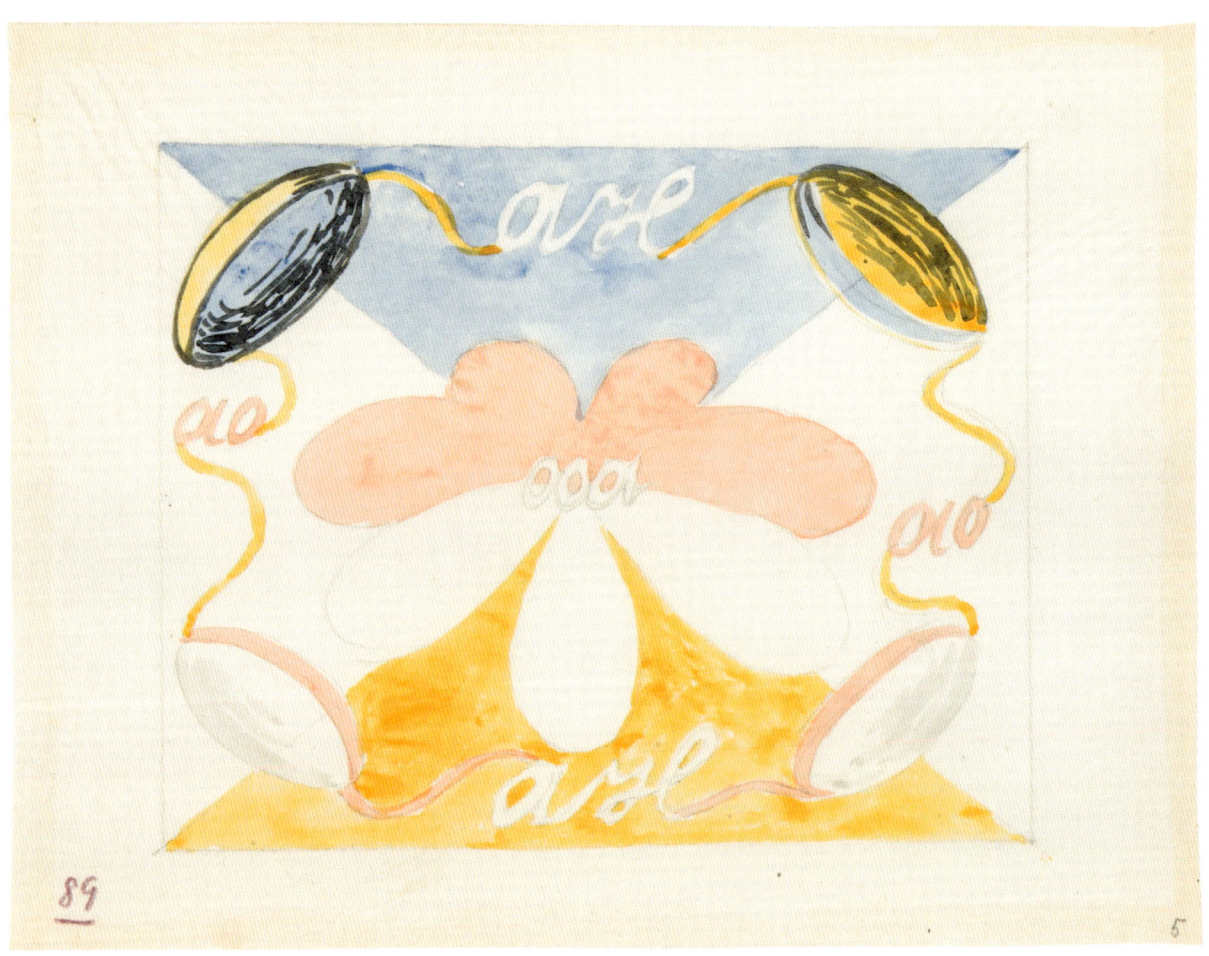

89

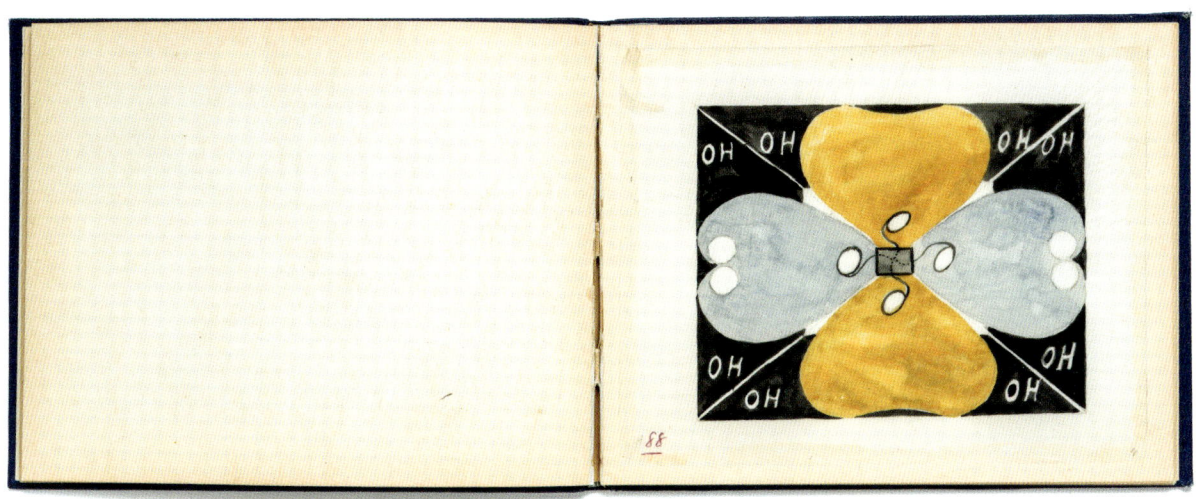

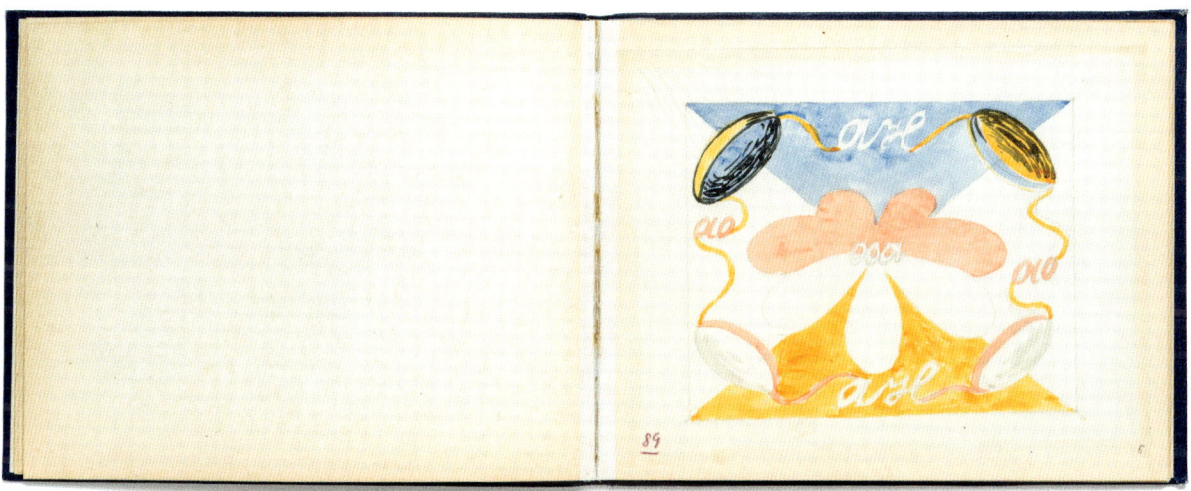

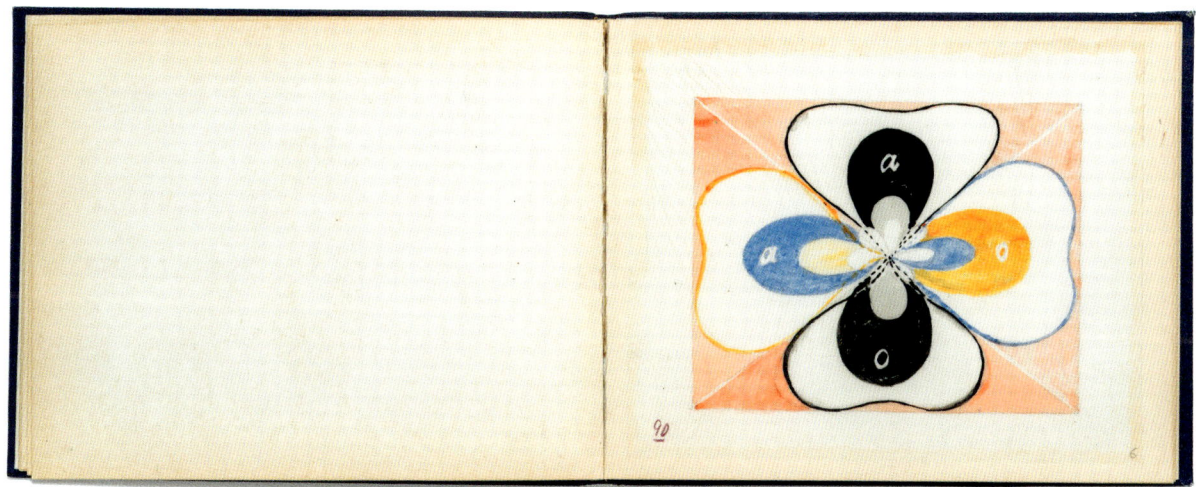

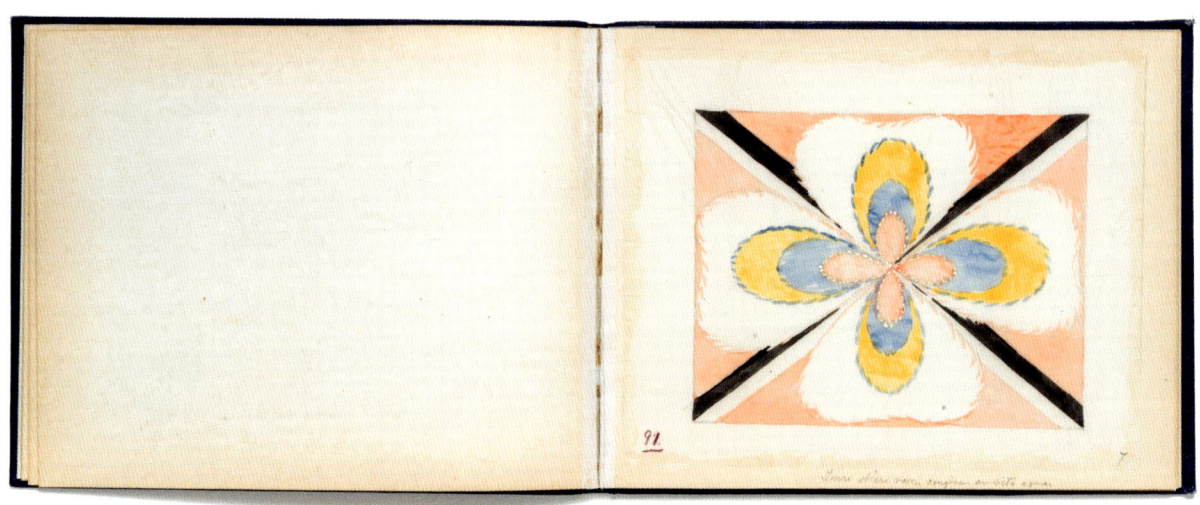

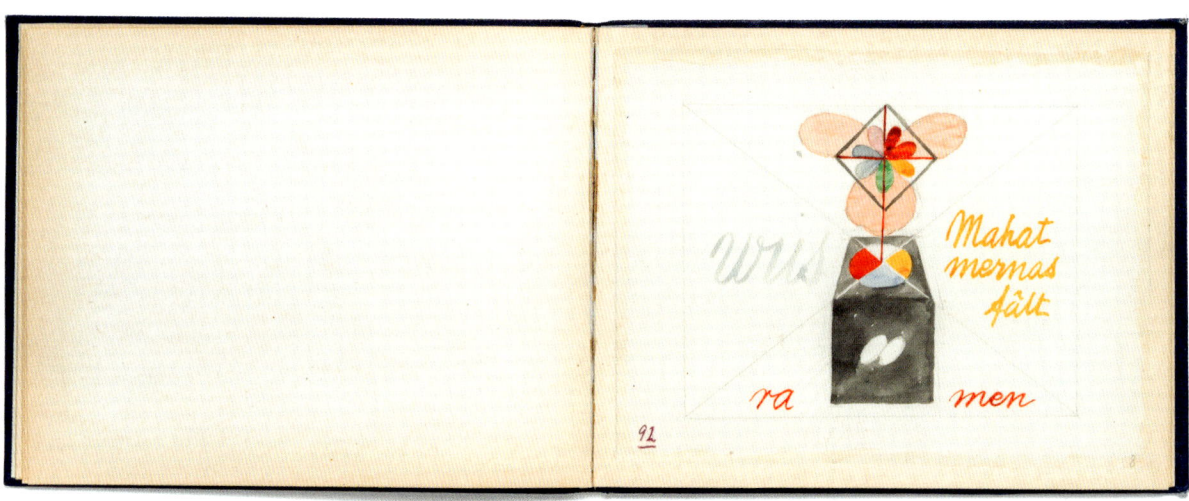

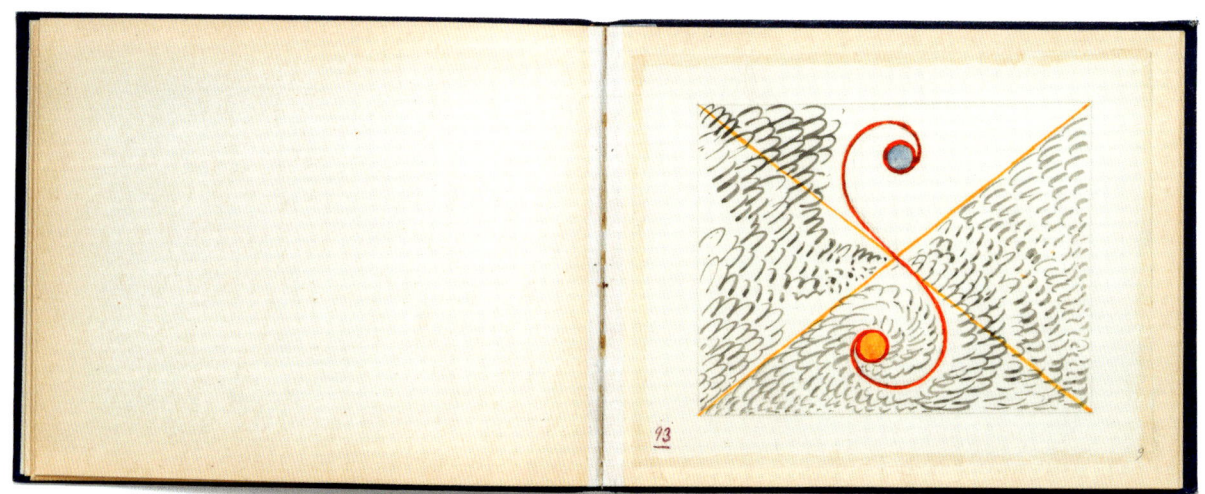

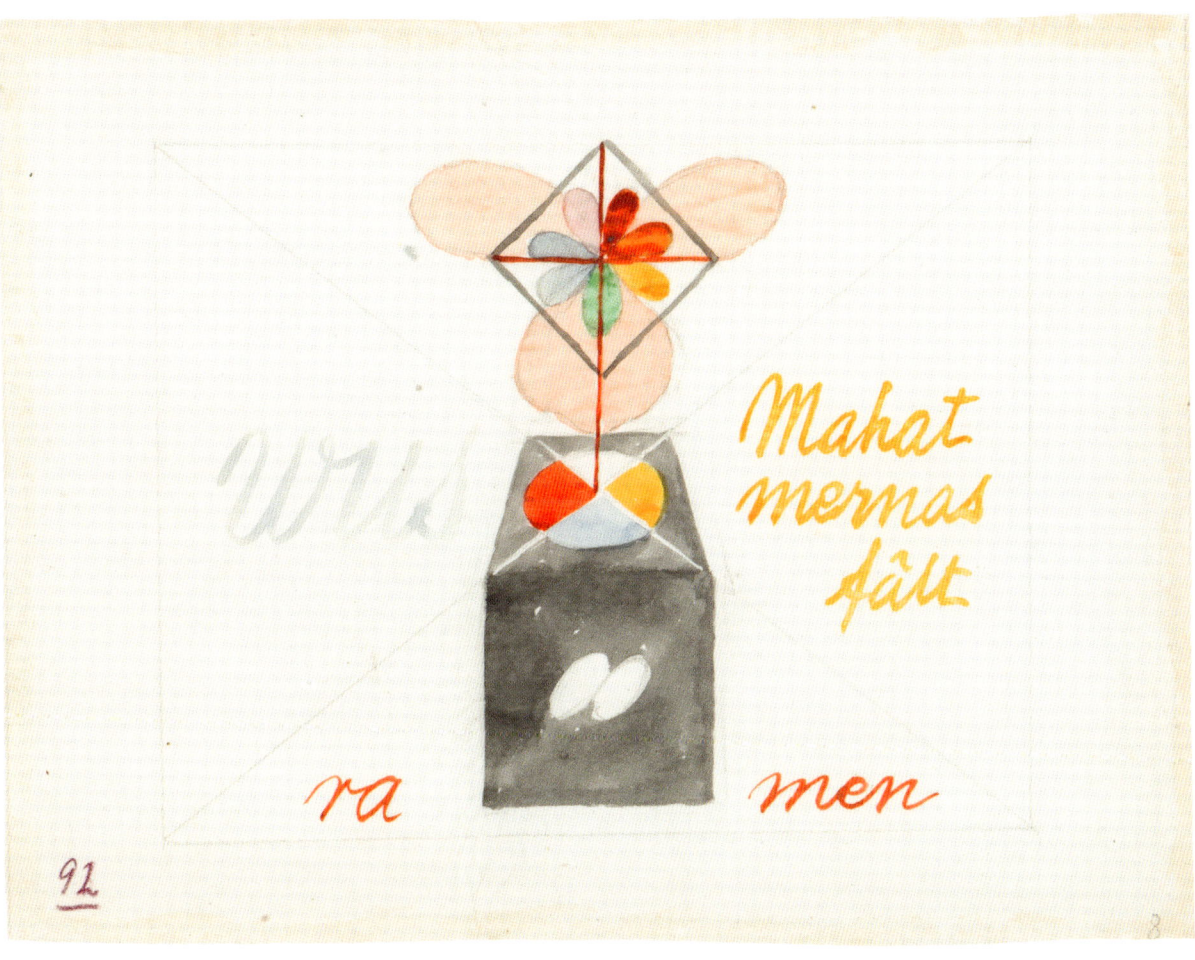

Mahat
mermas
dålt

ra   men

92

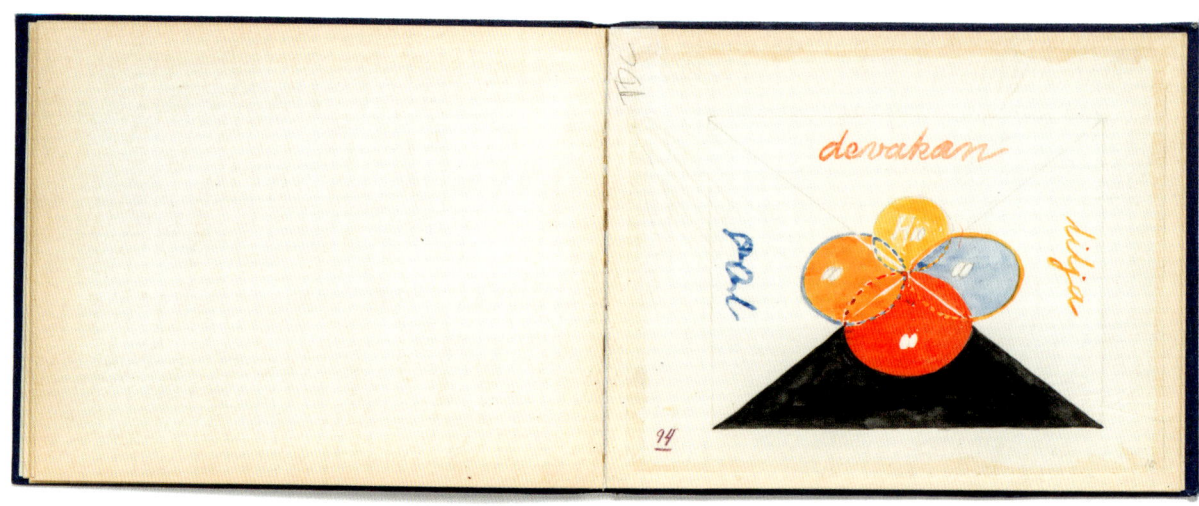

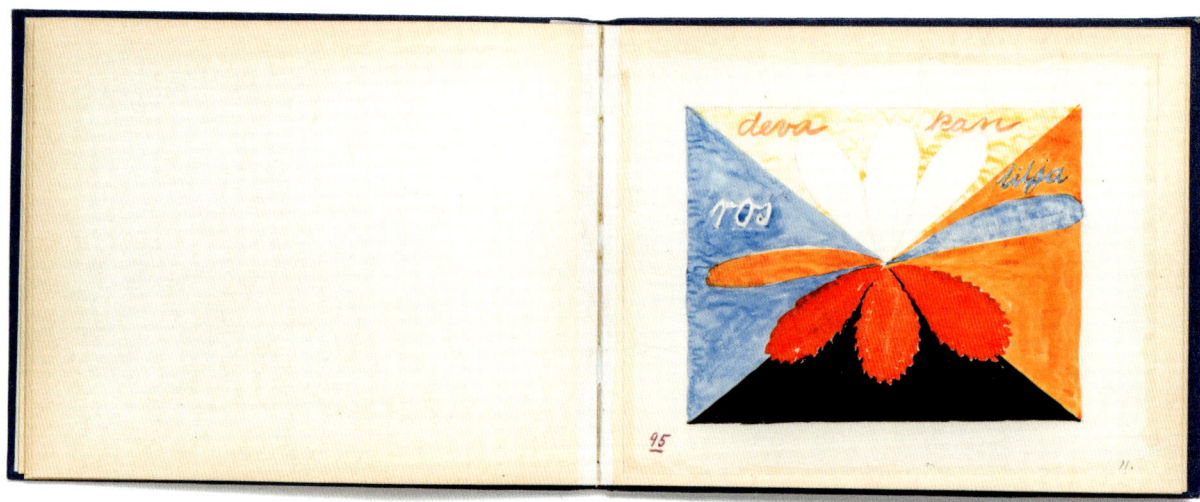

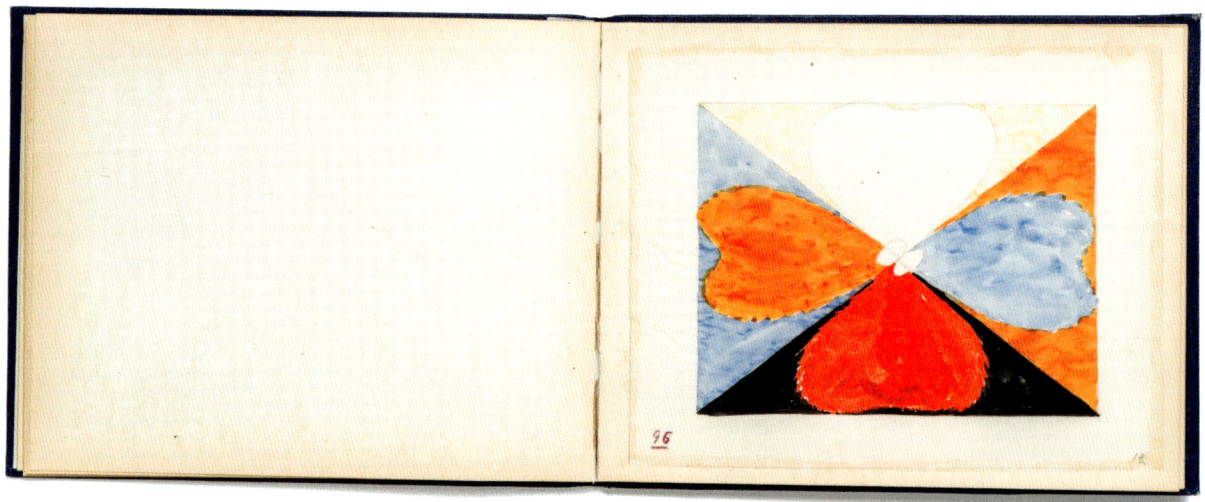

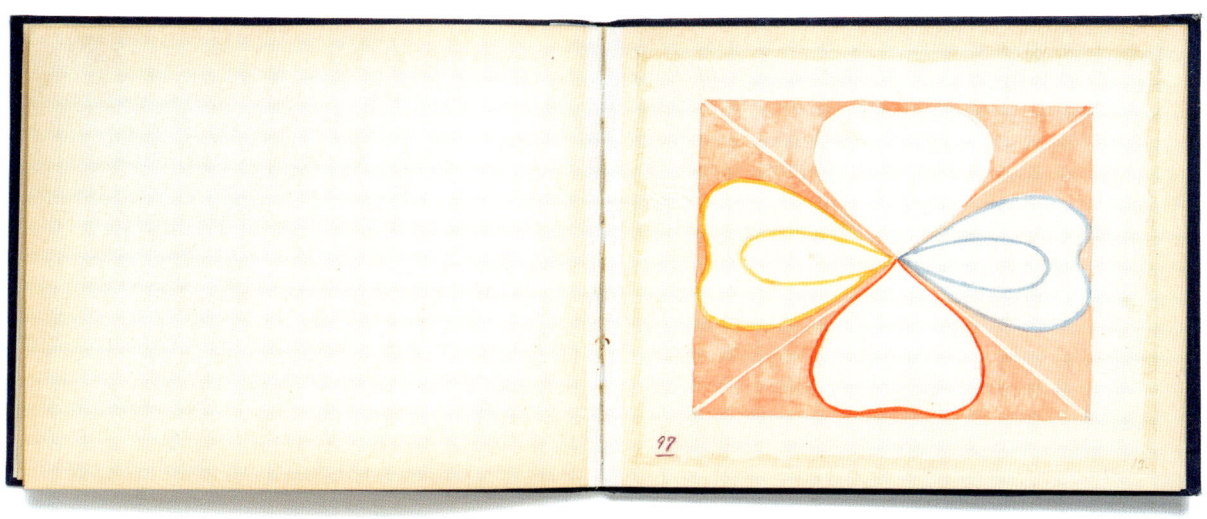

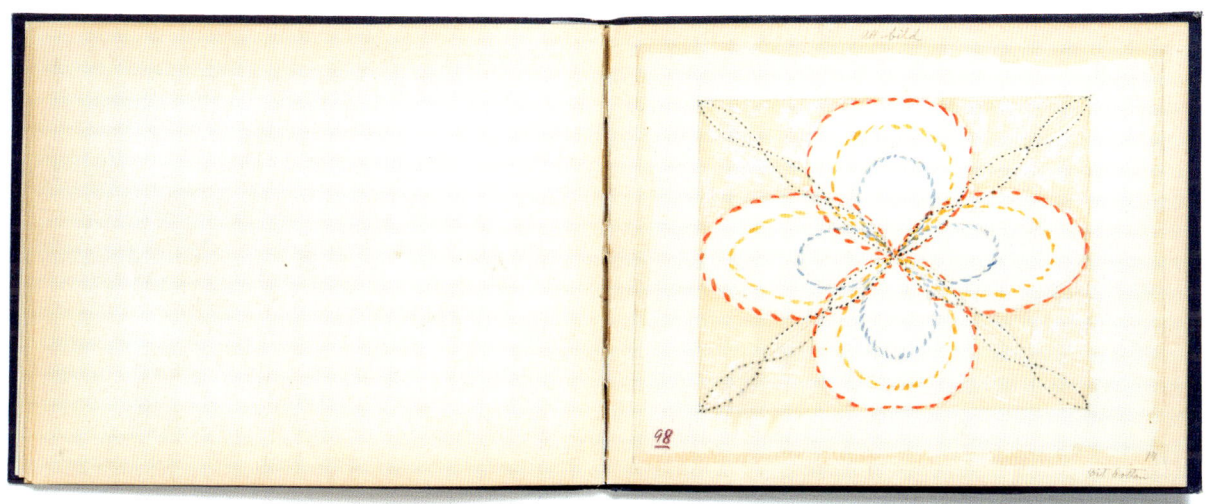

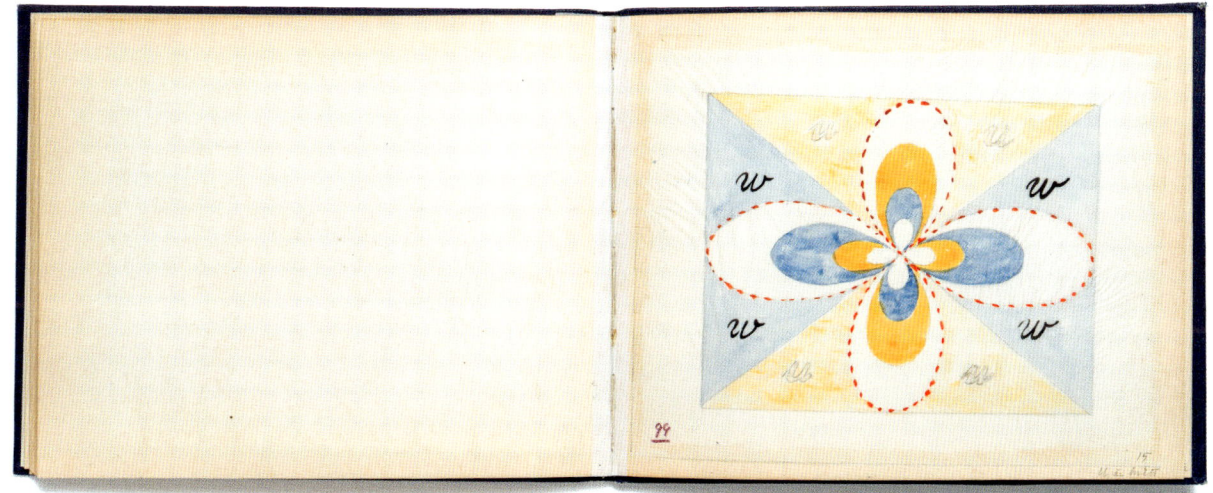

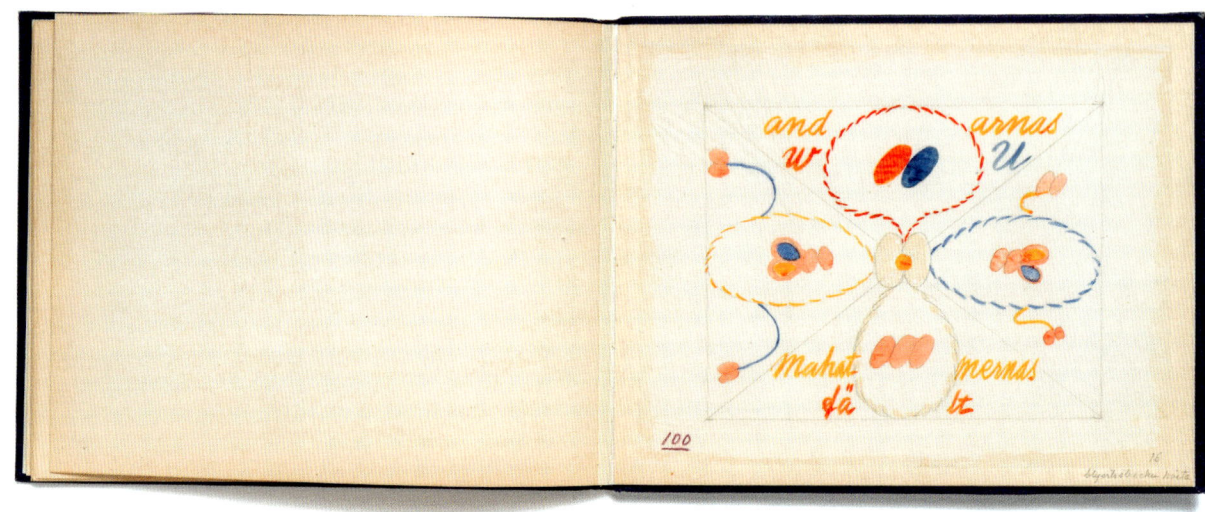

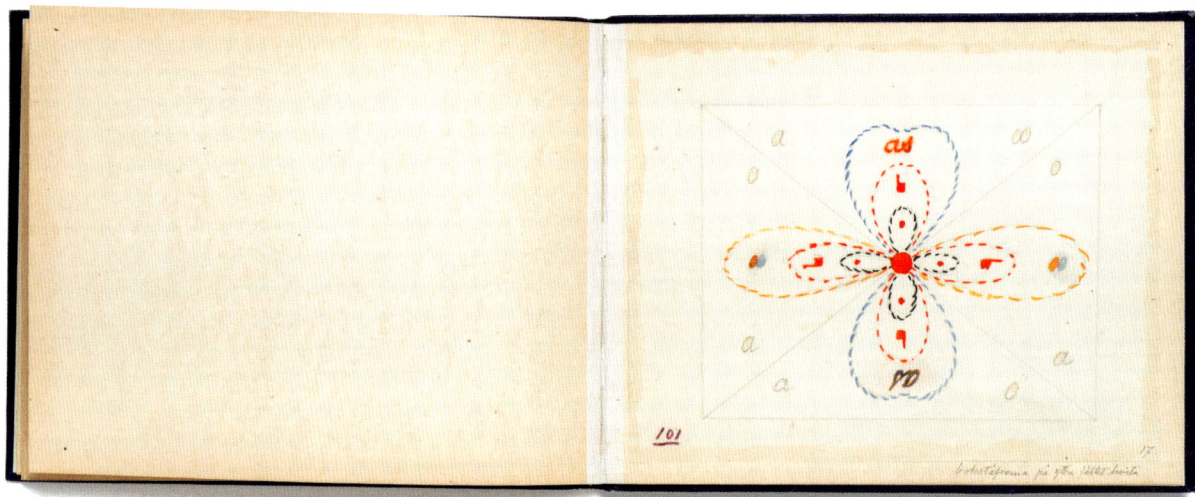

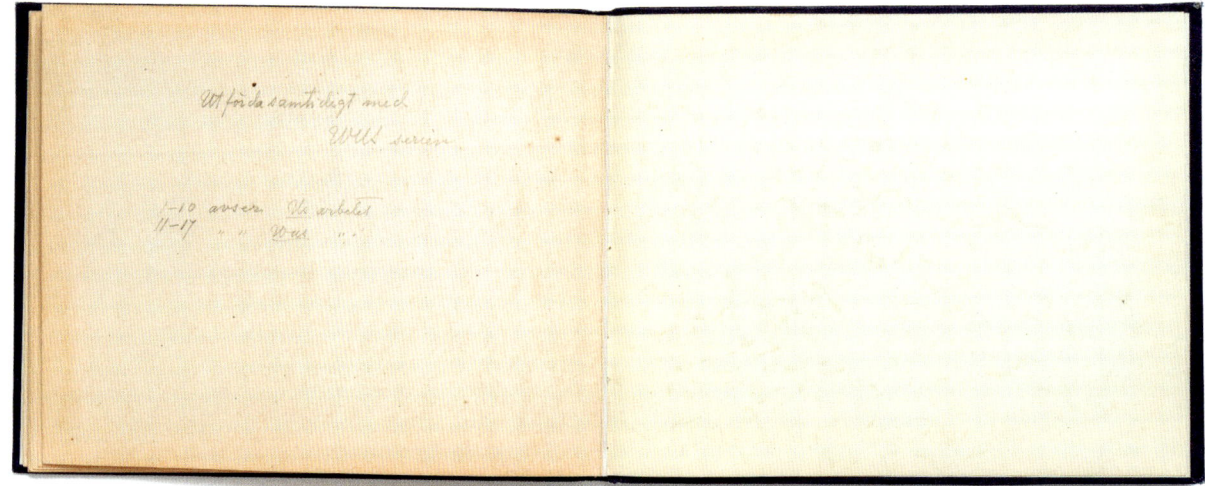

Made at the same time as the WUS series

1–10 refers to the US work; 1–17 refers to the WUS work

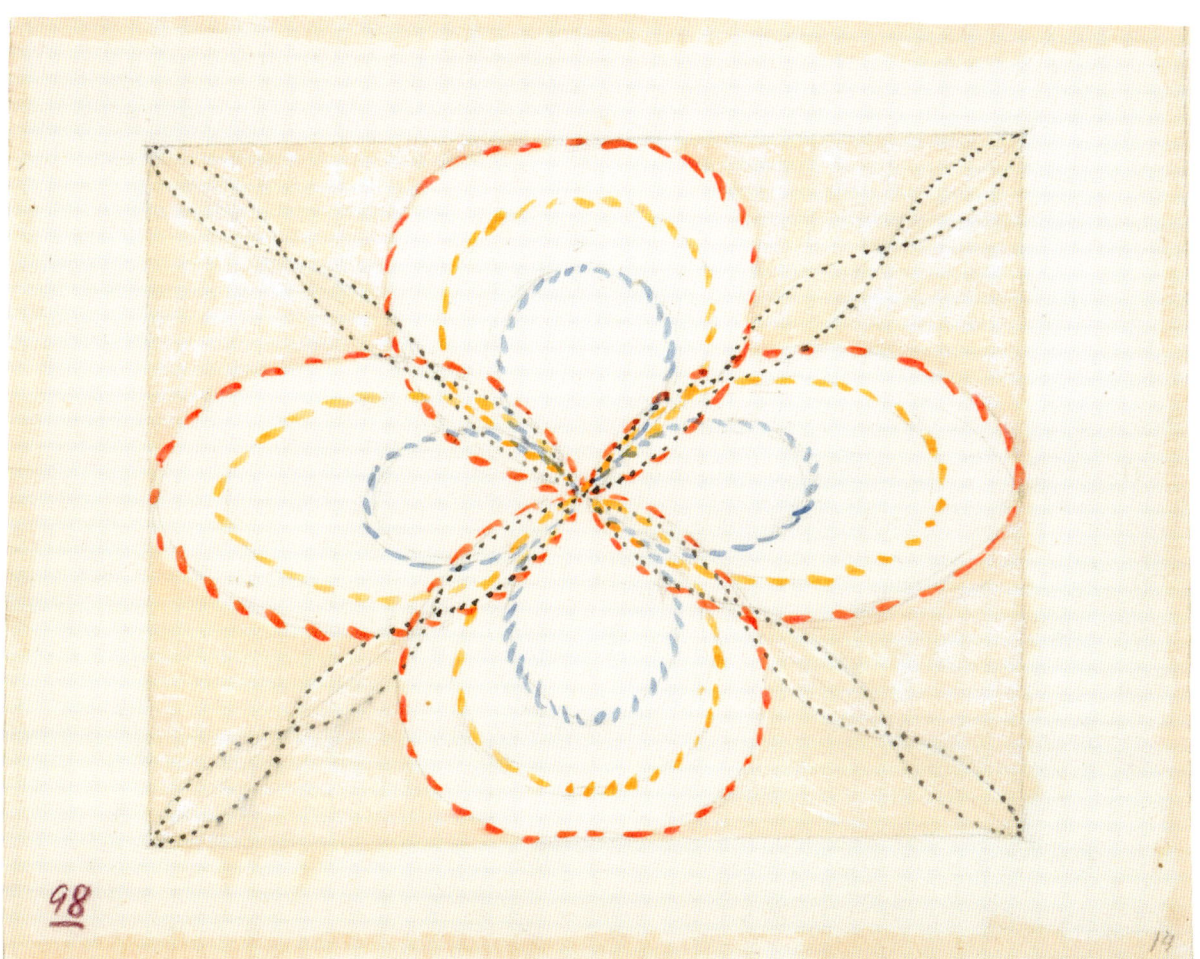

98

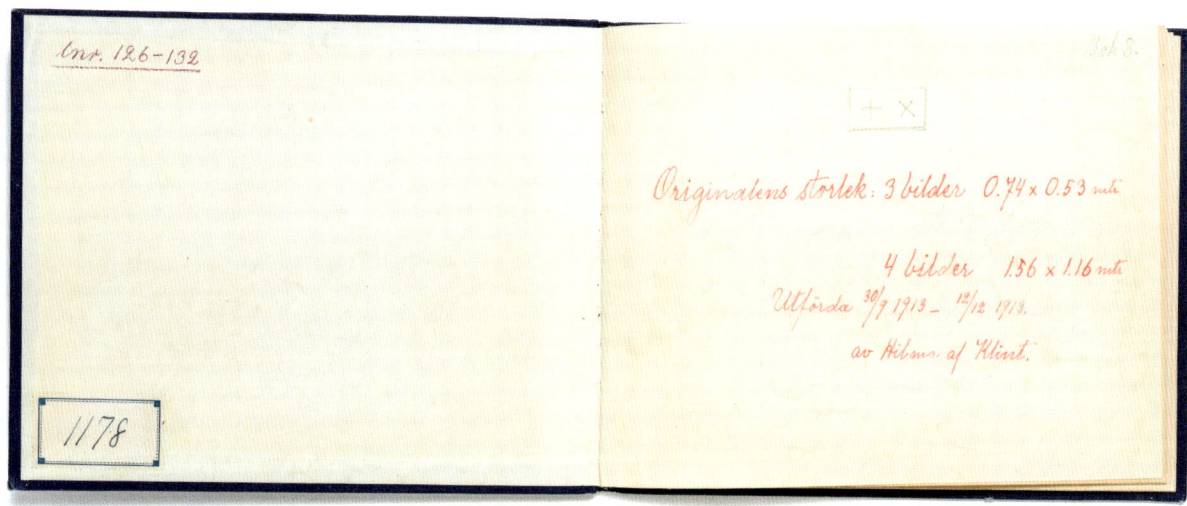

Inr. 126–132.   Bok 3.

+ ×

Originalens storlek: 3 bilder   0.74 × 0.53 mtr

4 bilder   1.56 × 1.16 mtr

Utförda 30/9 1913 – 12/12 1913.

av Hilma af Klint.

1178

1178, Inv. 126–132. Original size: 3 paintings 0.74 × 0.53 m, 4 paintings 1.56 × 1.16 m. Made 9/30/ 1913–12/12/1913, by Hilma af Klint

Preparatory studies for this are 7 figure pictures 0.50 × 0.35 made 2/19/1912–3/29/1912(31), 7 figure pictures 0.50 × 0.35, October 1912 (female series)

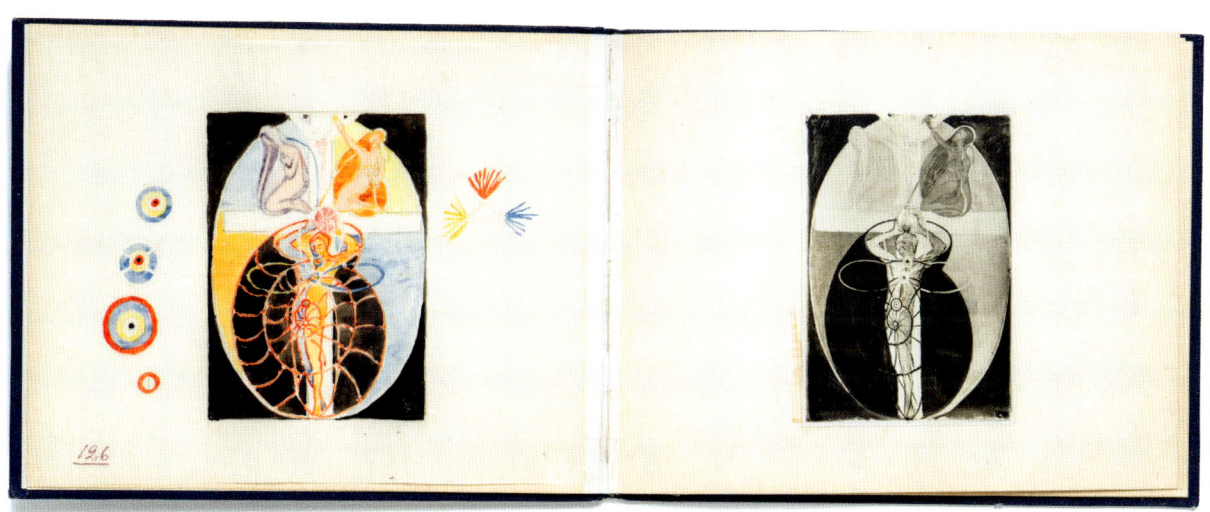

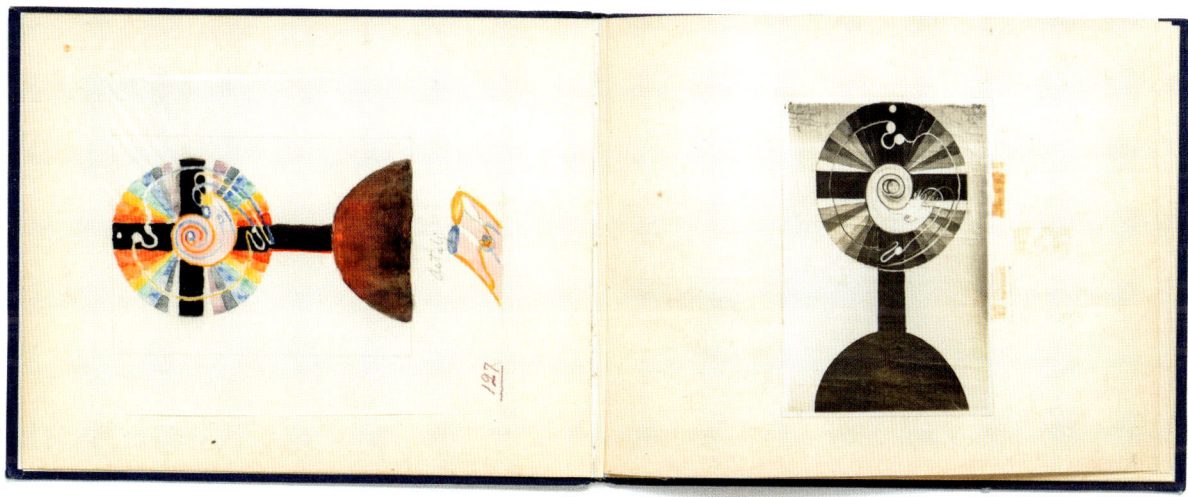

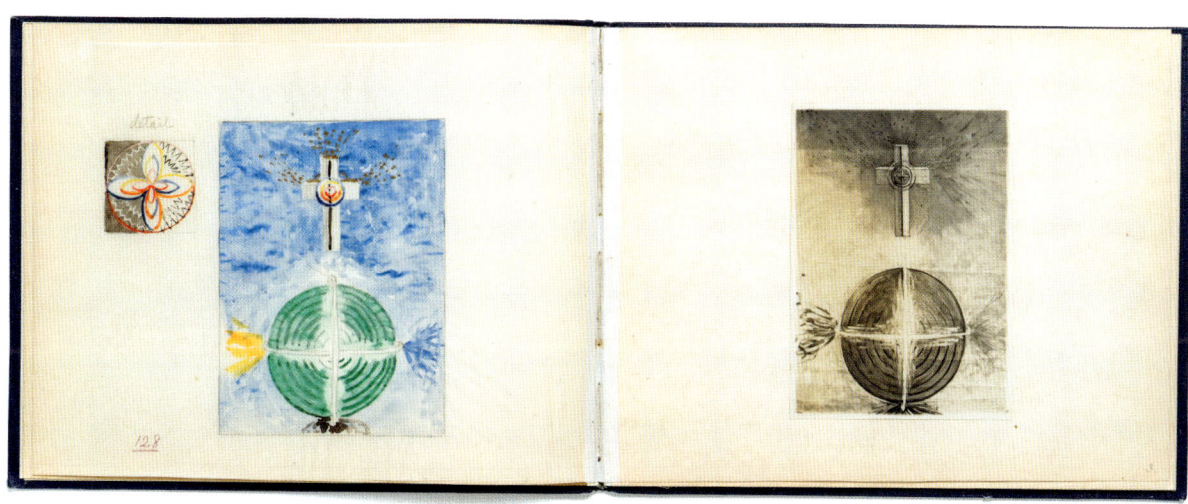

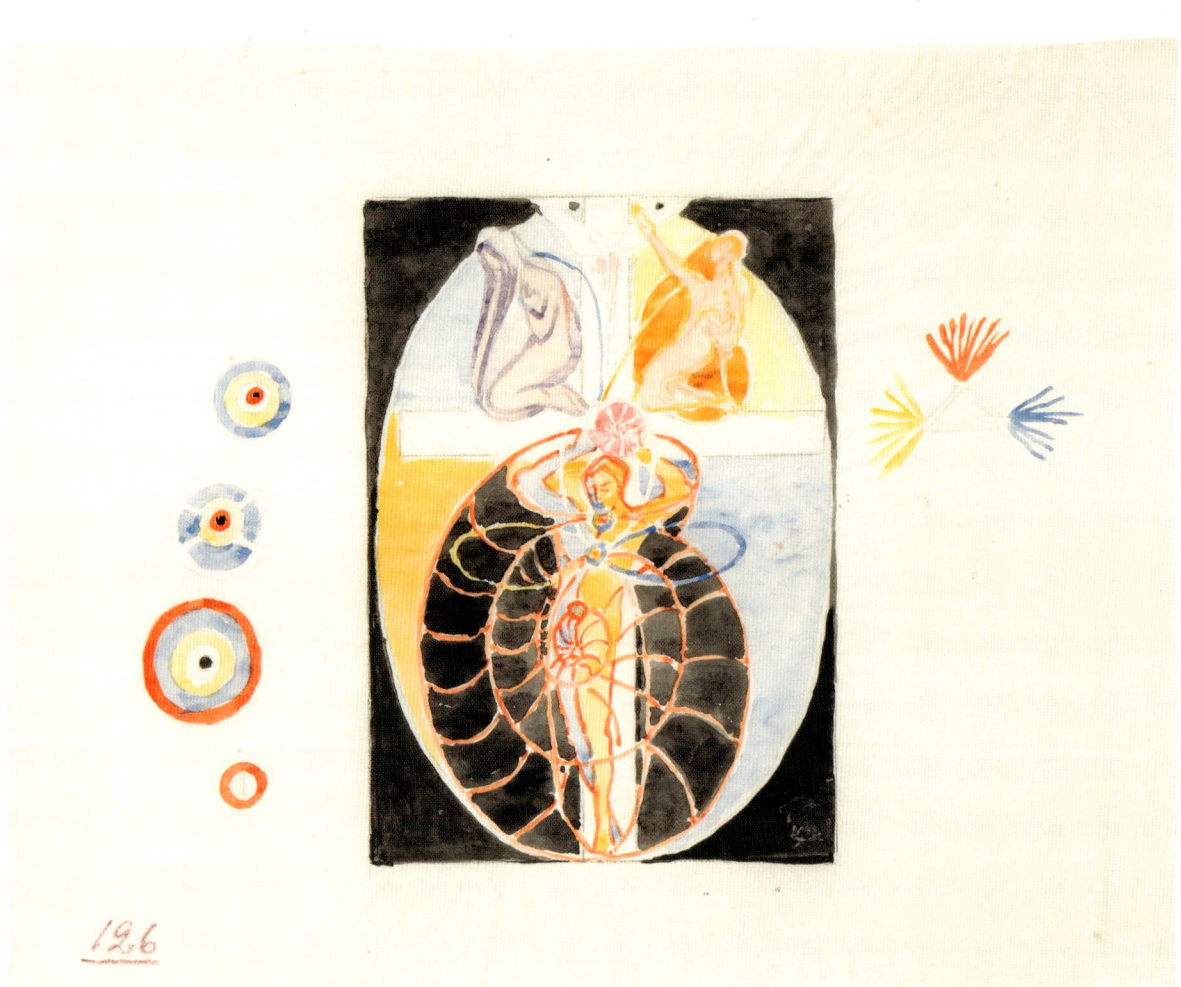

126

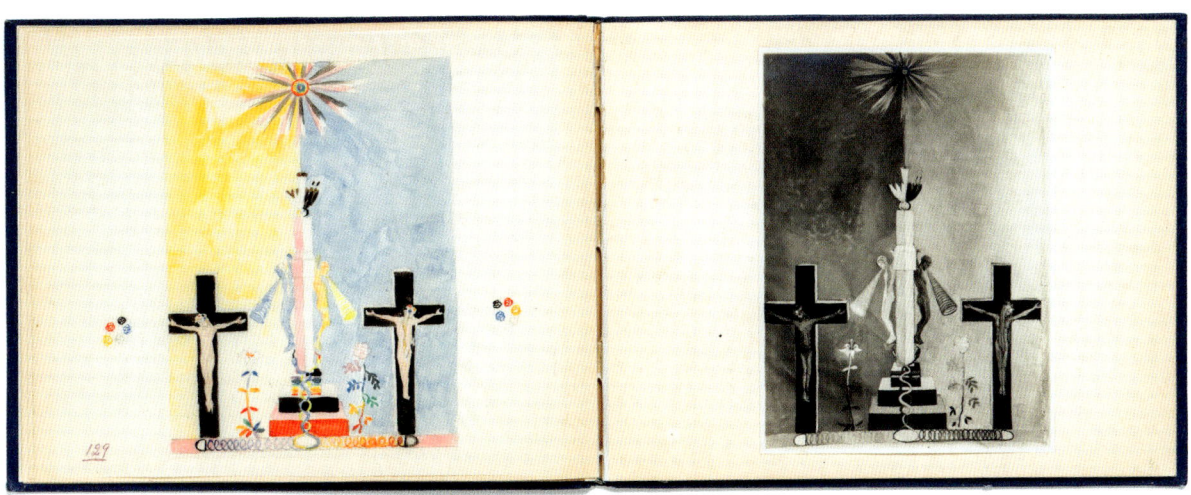

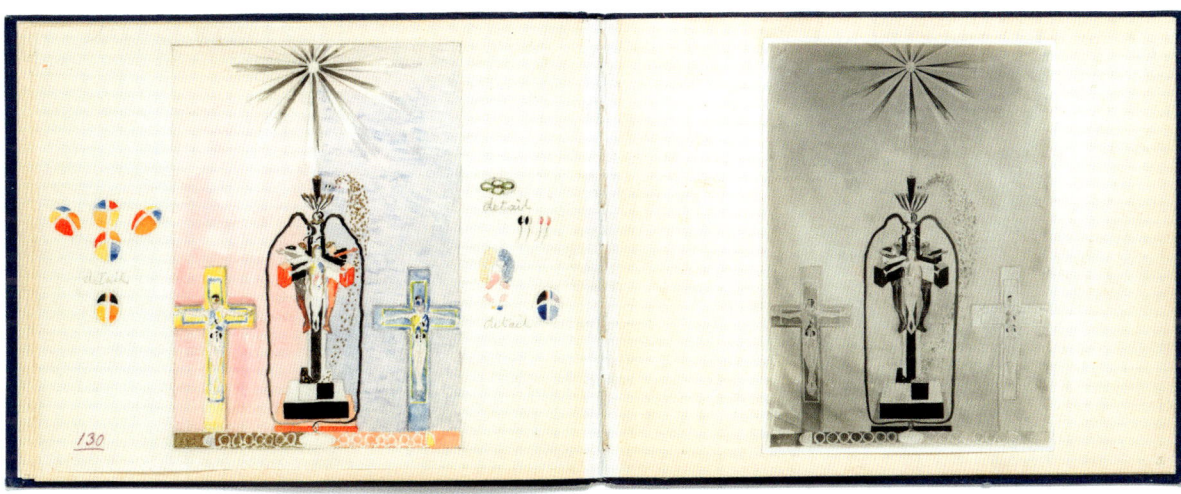

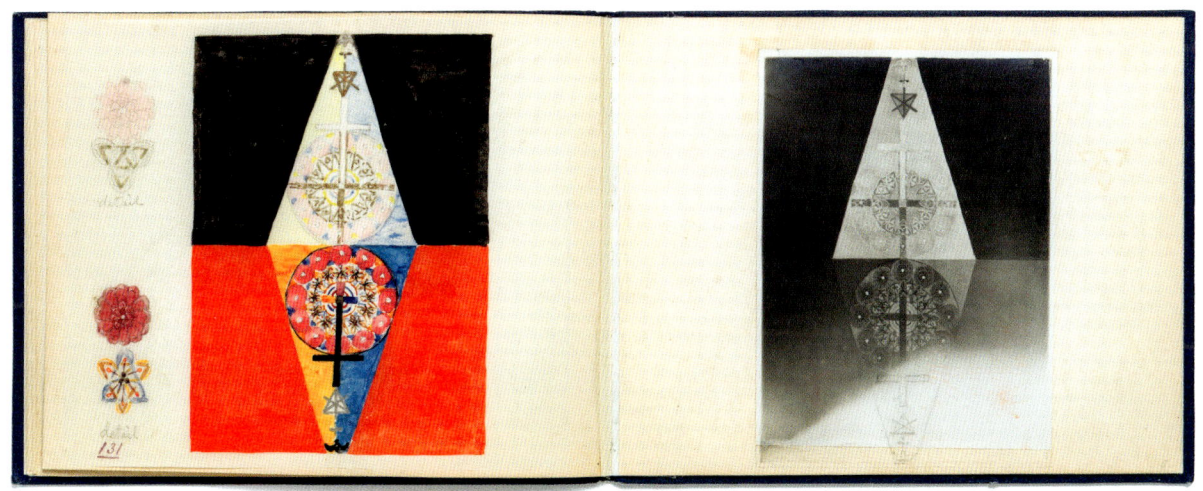

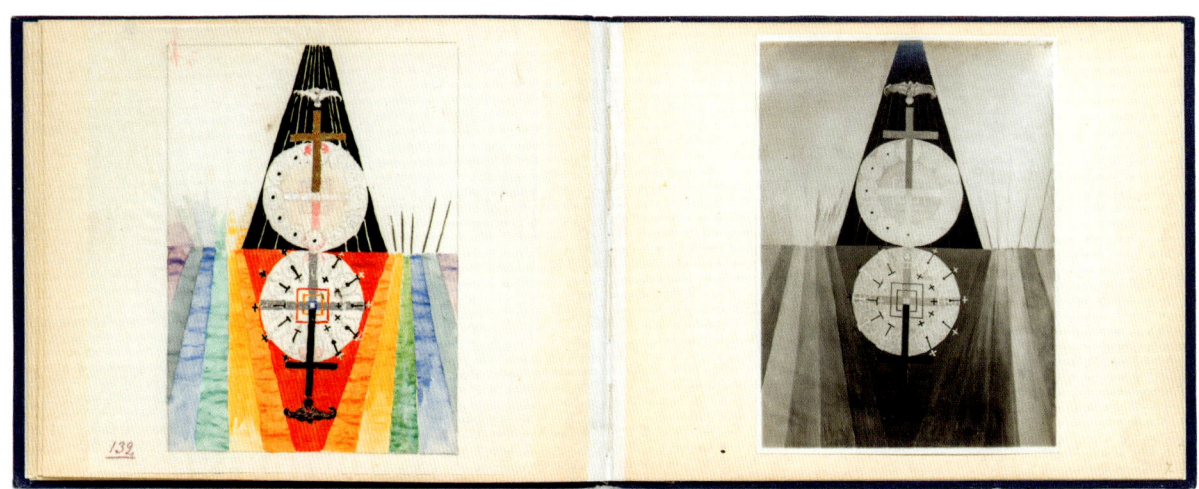

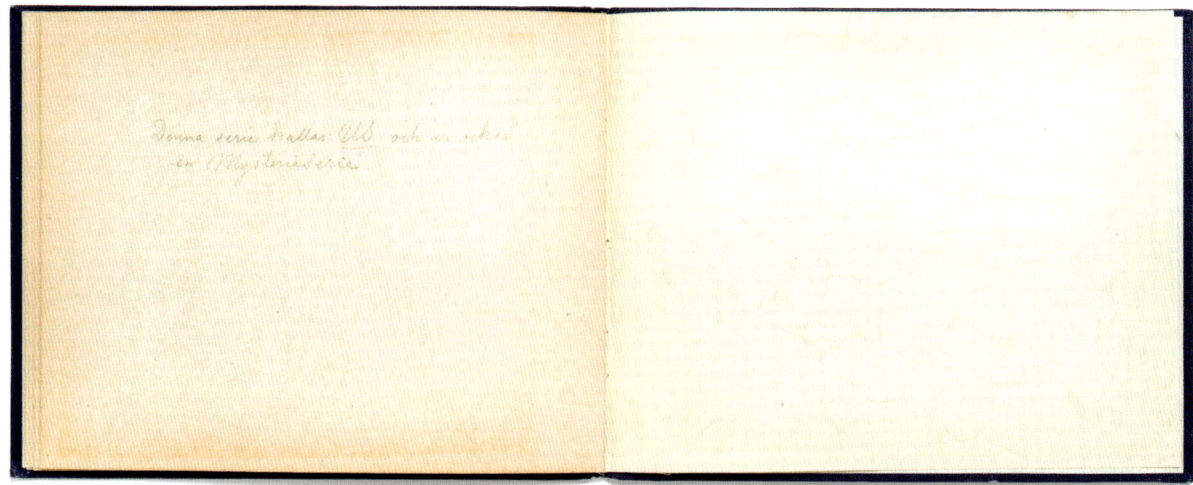

Denna serie kallas US och är också
en Mysterieserie

This series is called US and is also a Mystery series.

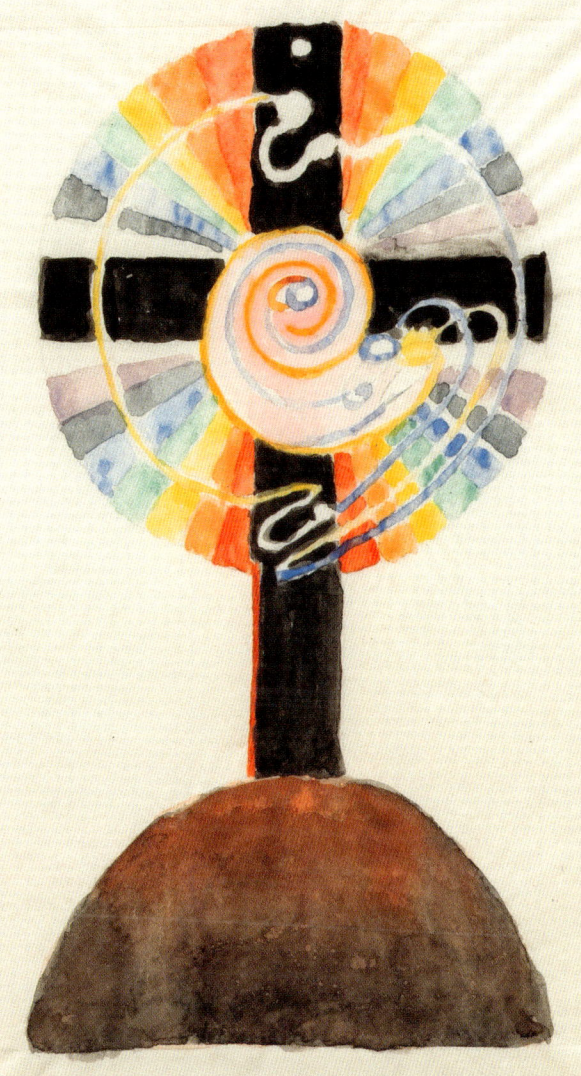

detalj

127

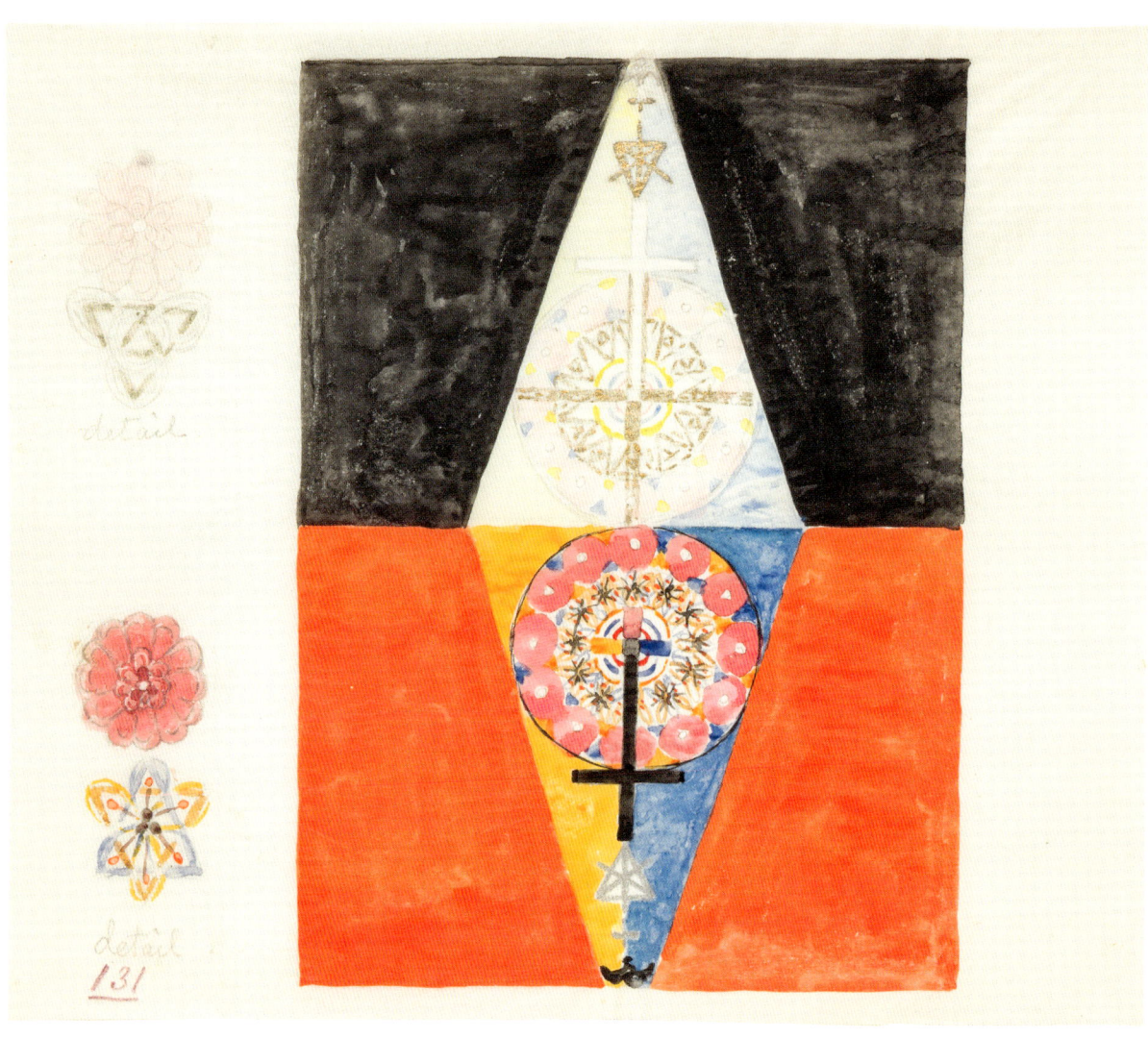

détail

détail
131

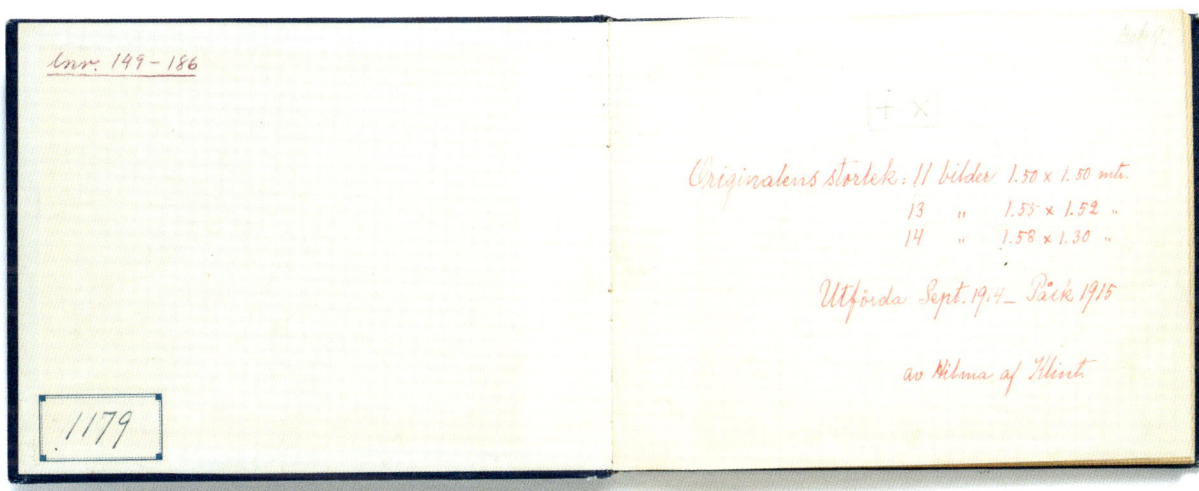

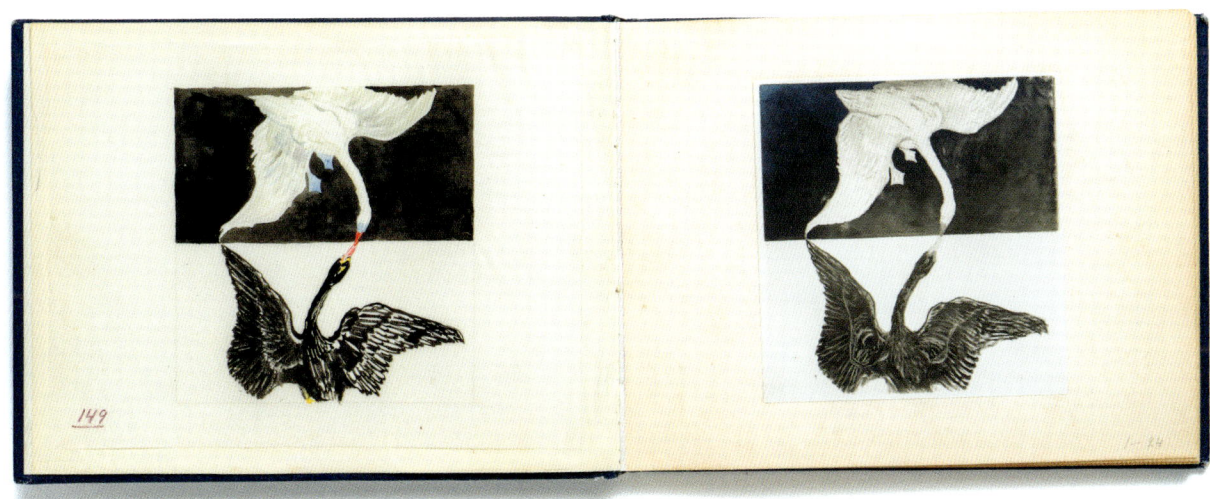

1179, Inv. 149–186. Original size: 11 paintings 1.50 × 1.50 m, 13 paintings 1.55 × 1.52 m,
14 paintings 1.58 × 1.30 m, made Sept. 1914–Easter 1915, by Hilma af Klint

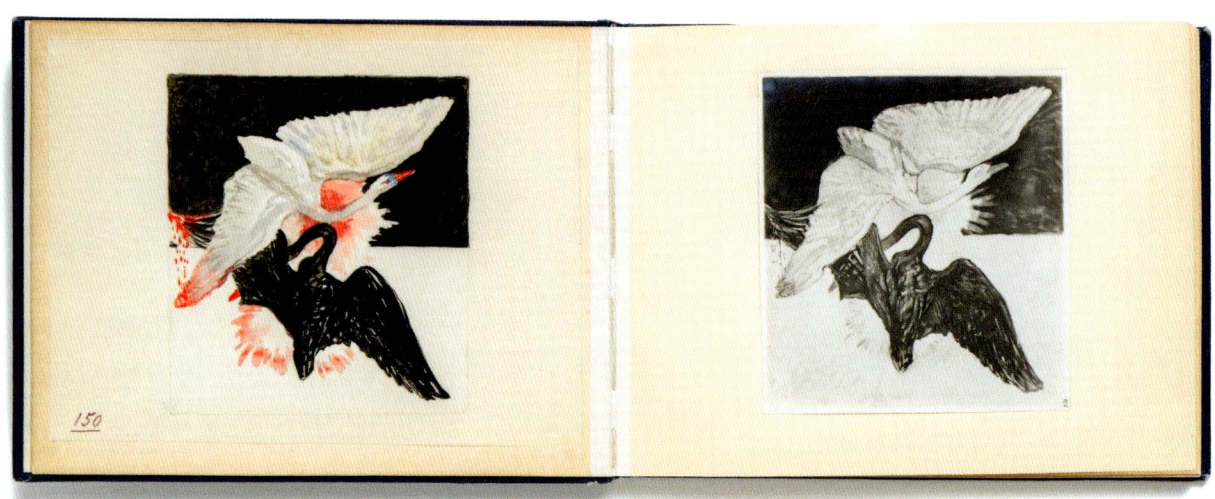

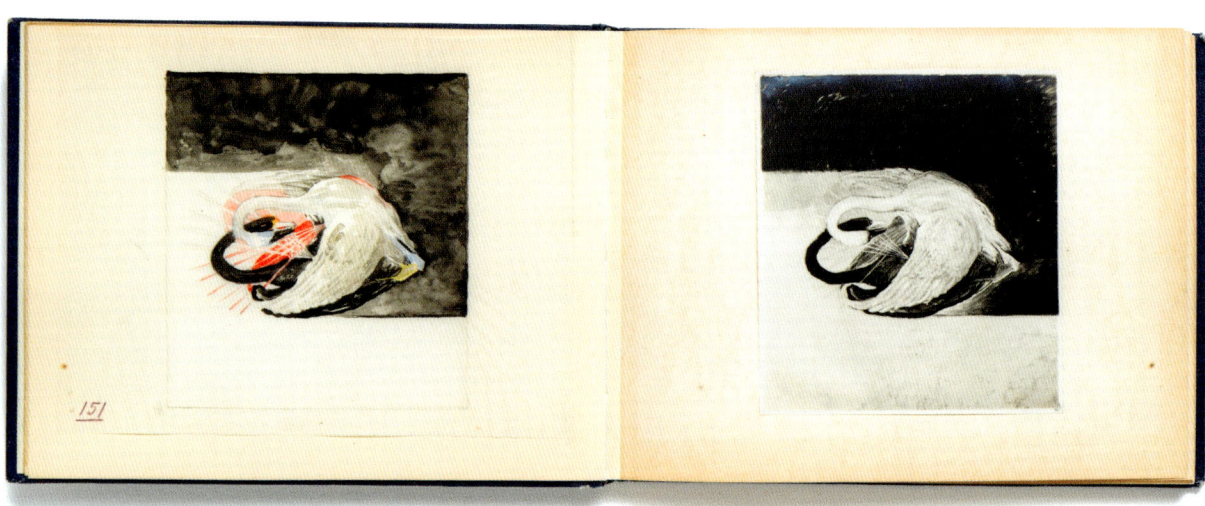

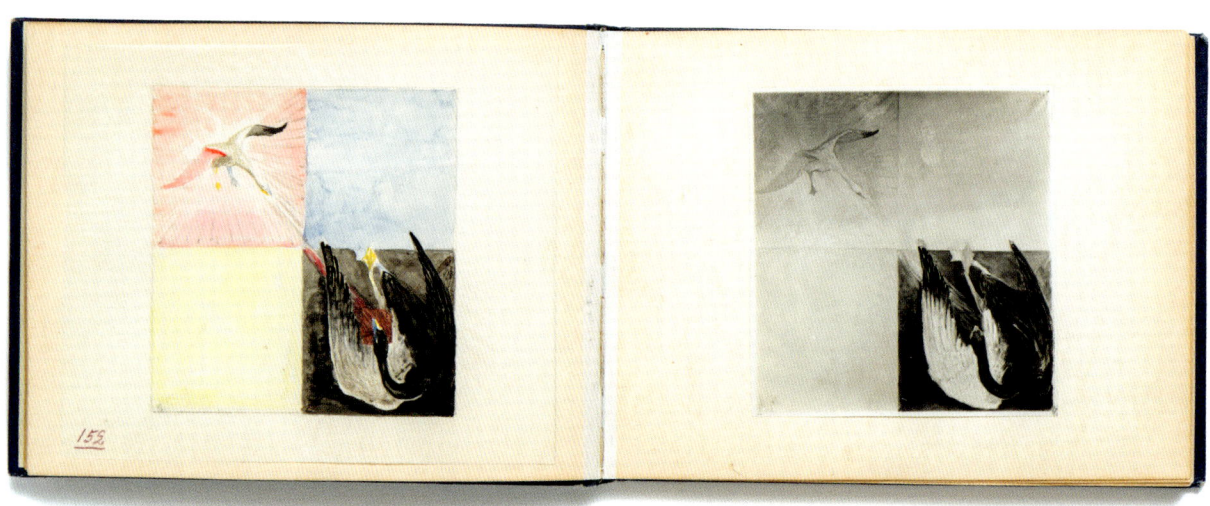

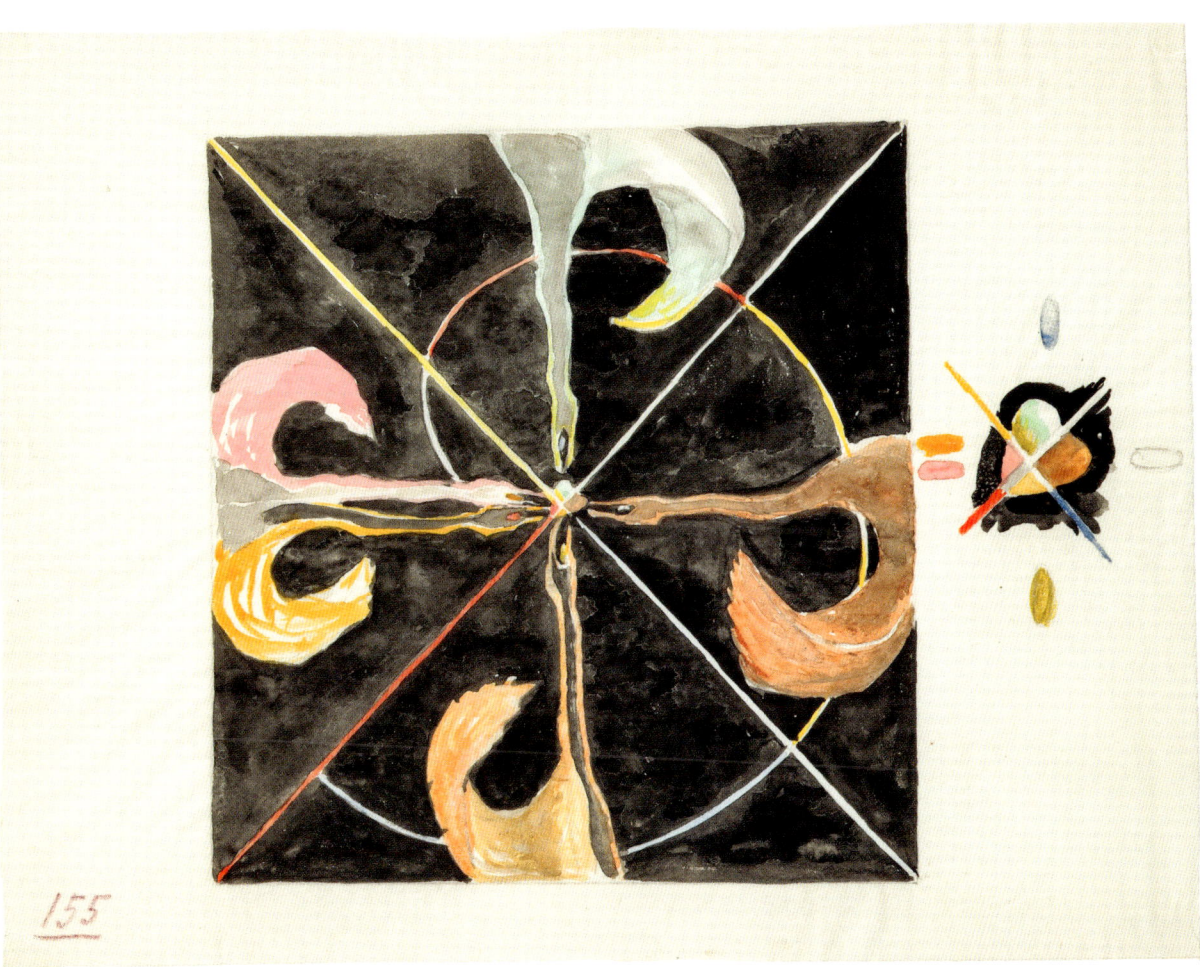

155

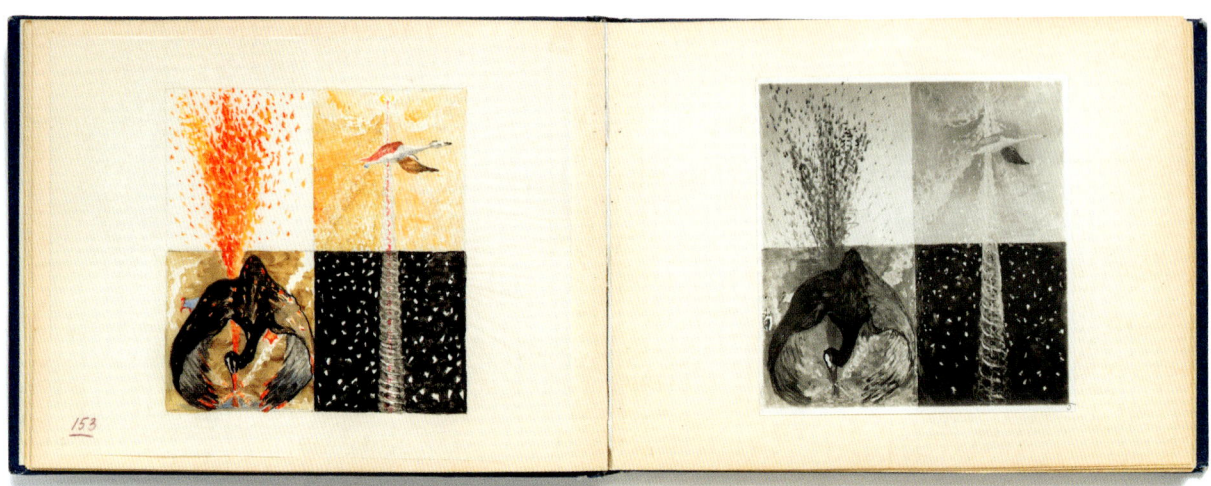

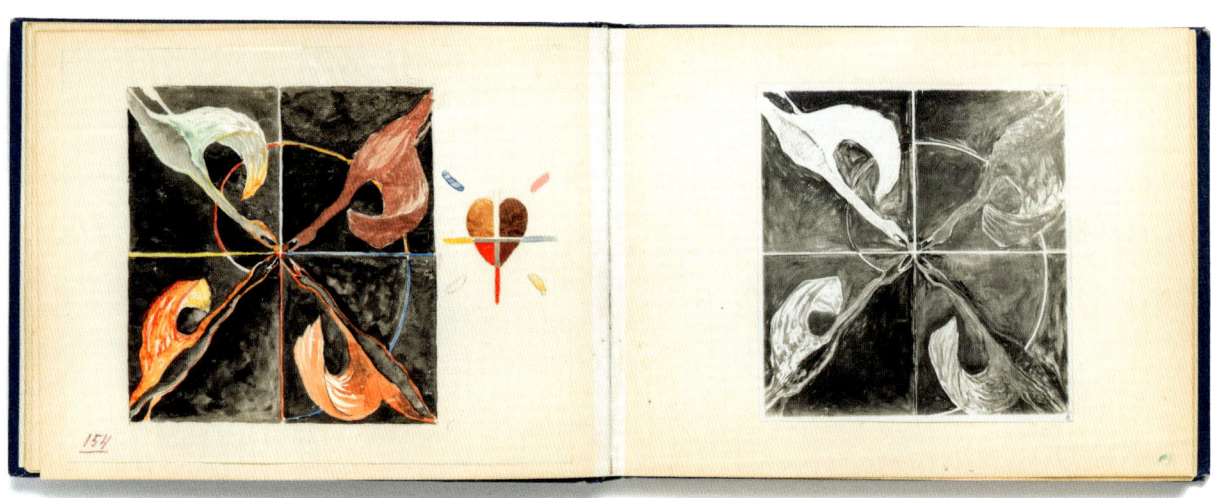

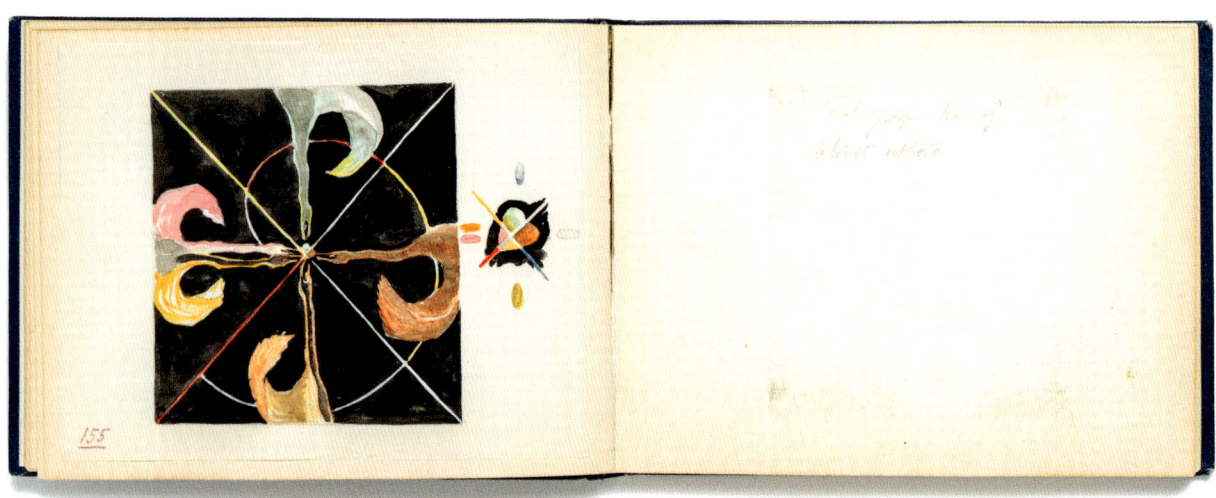

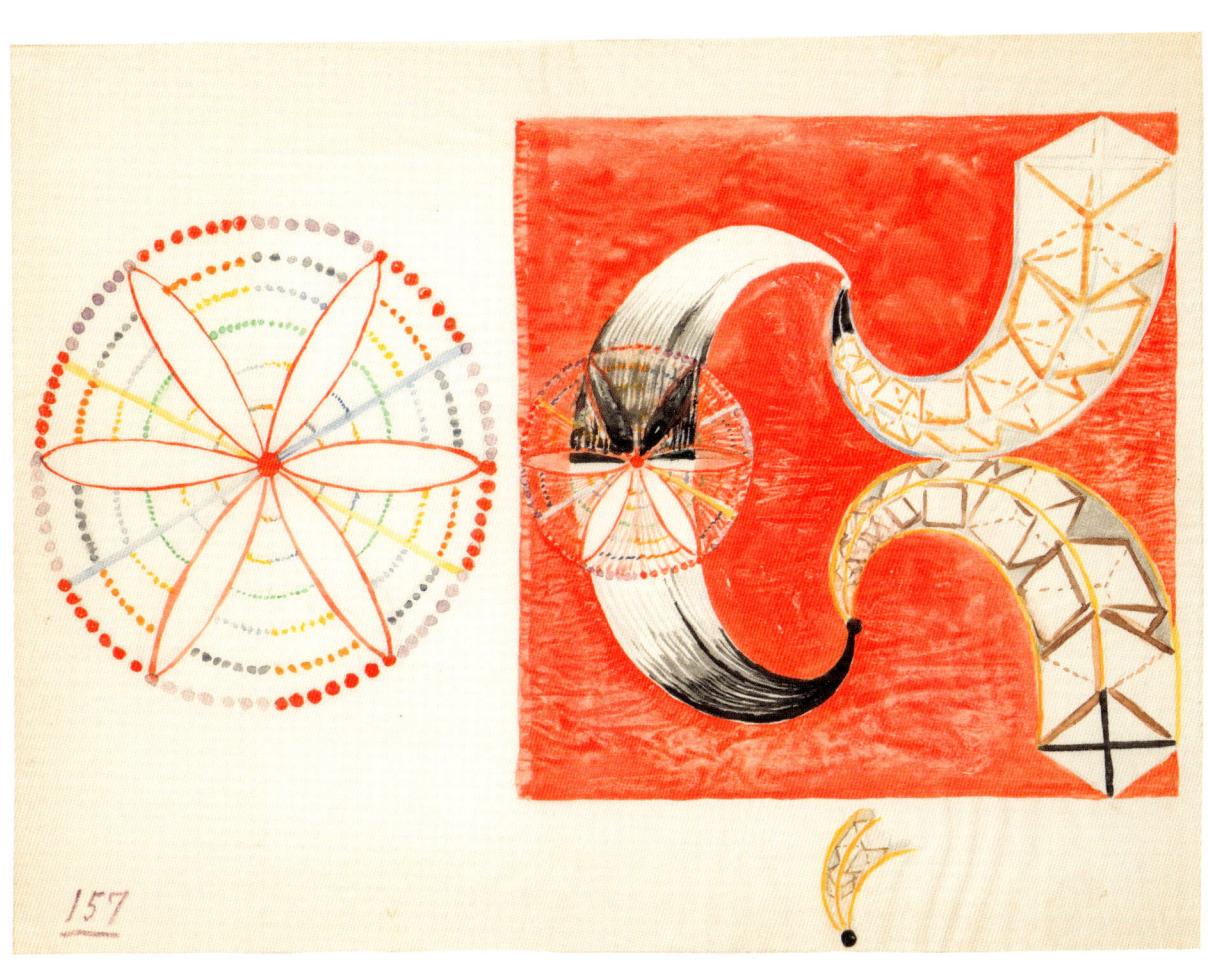

157

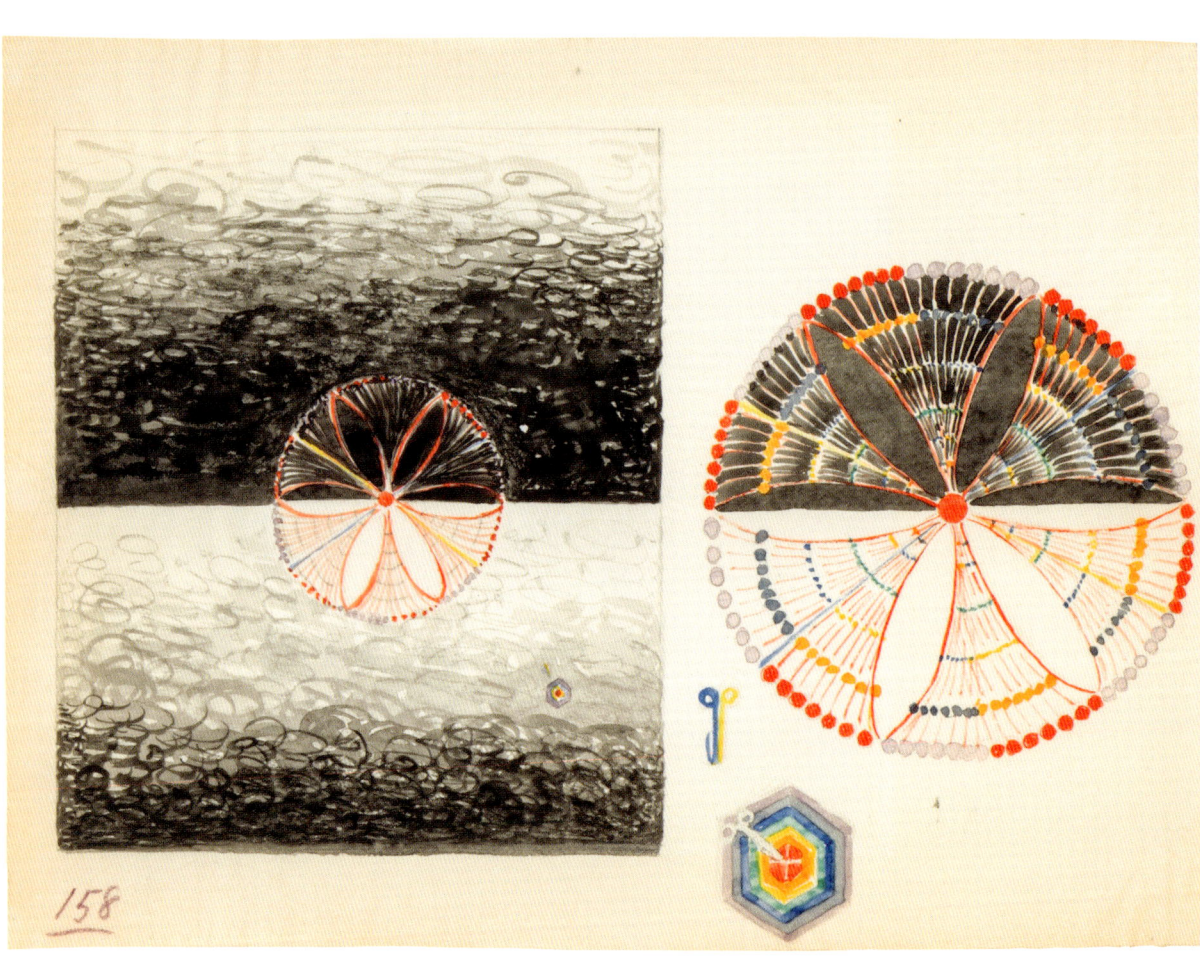

158

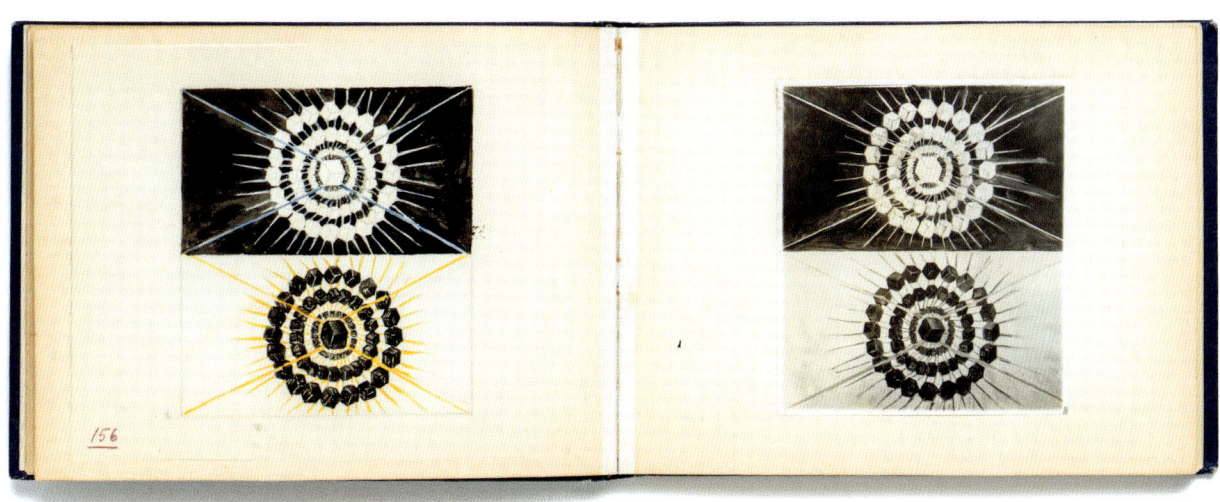

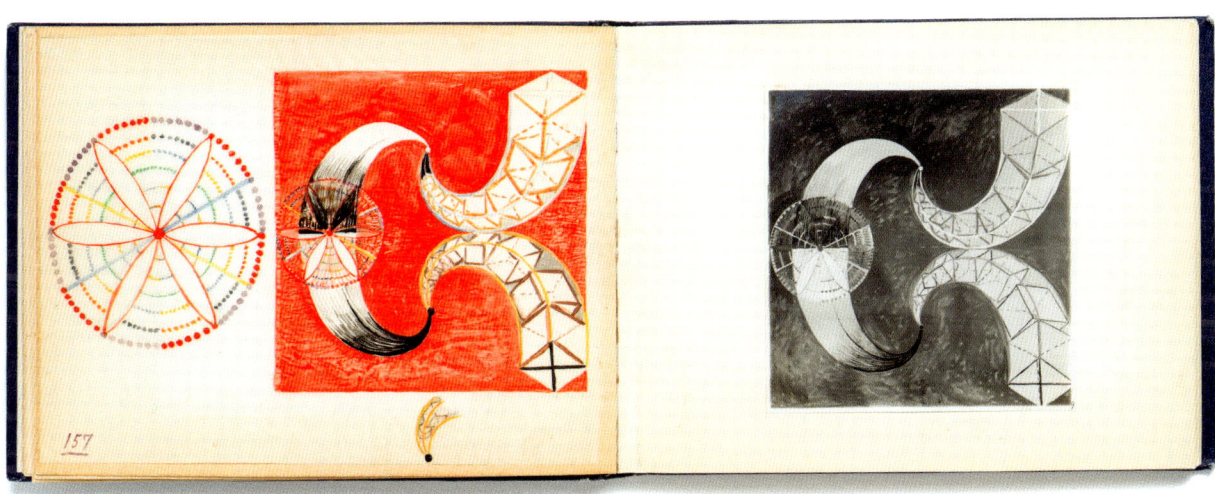

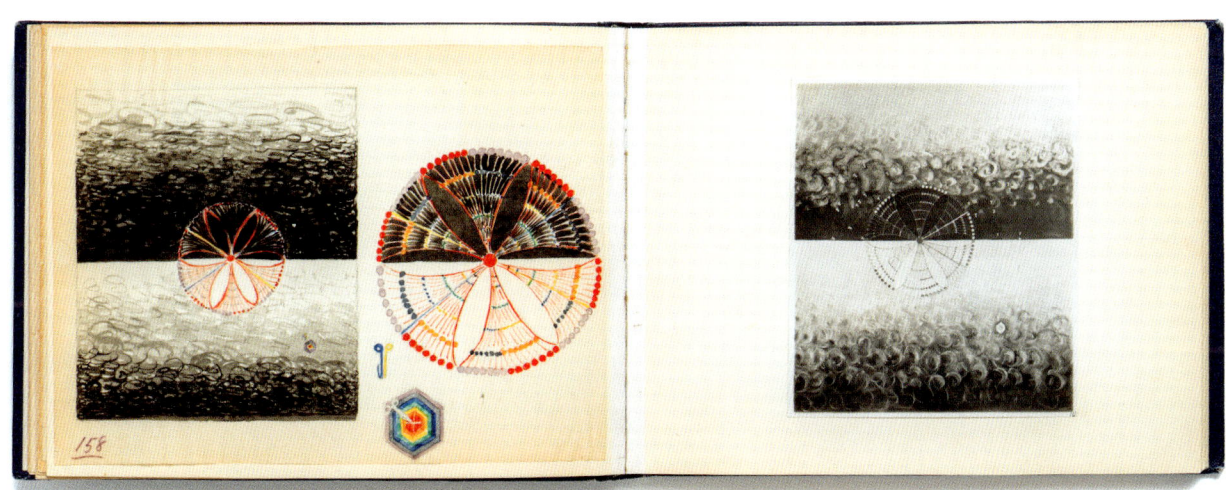

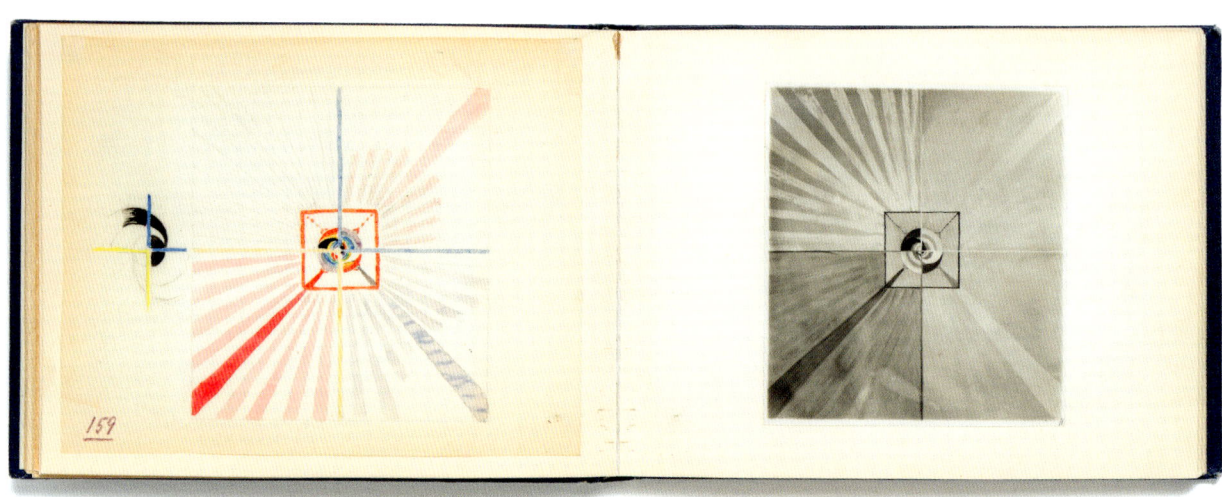

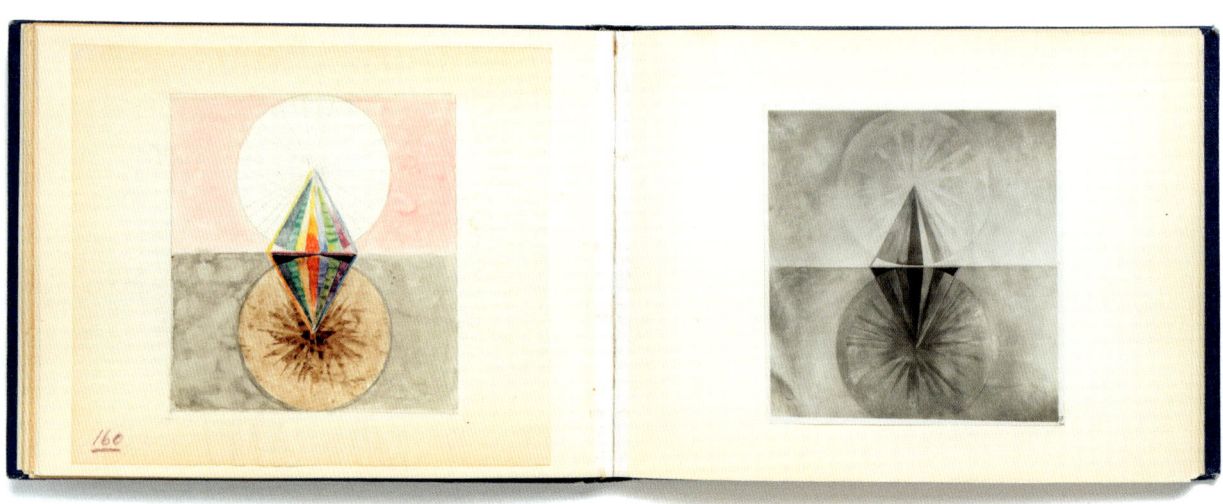

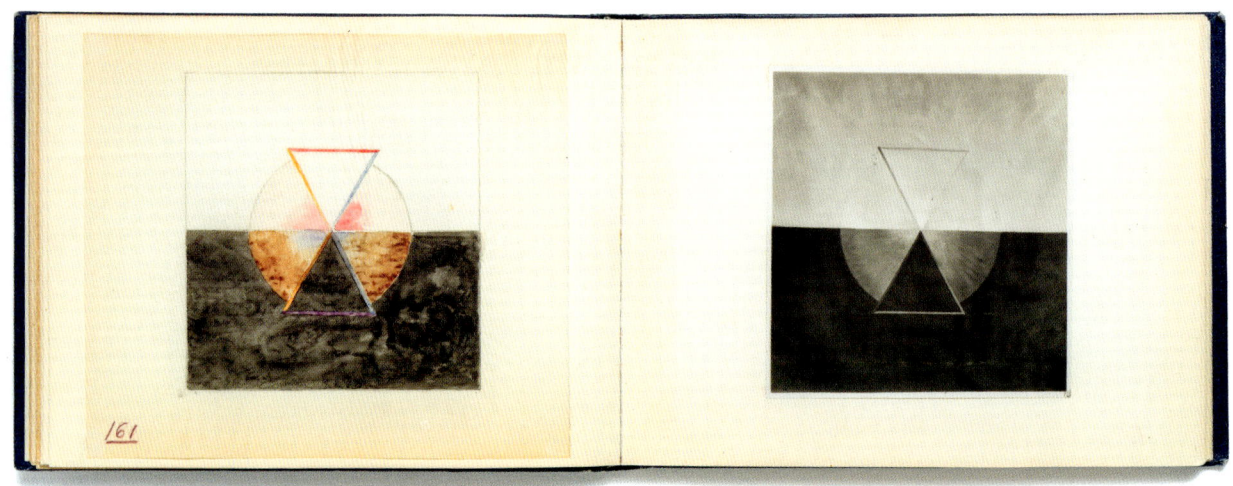

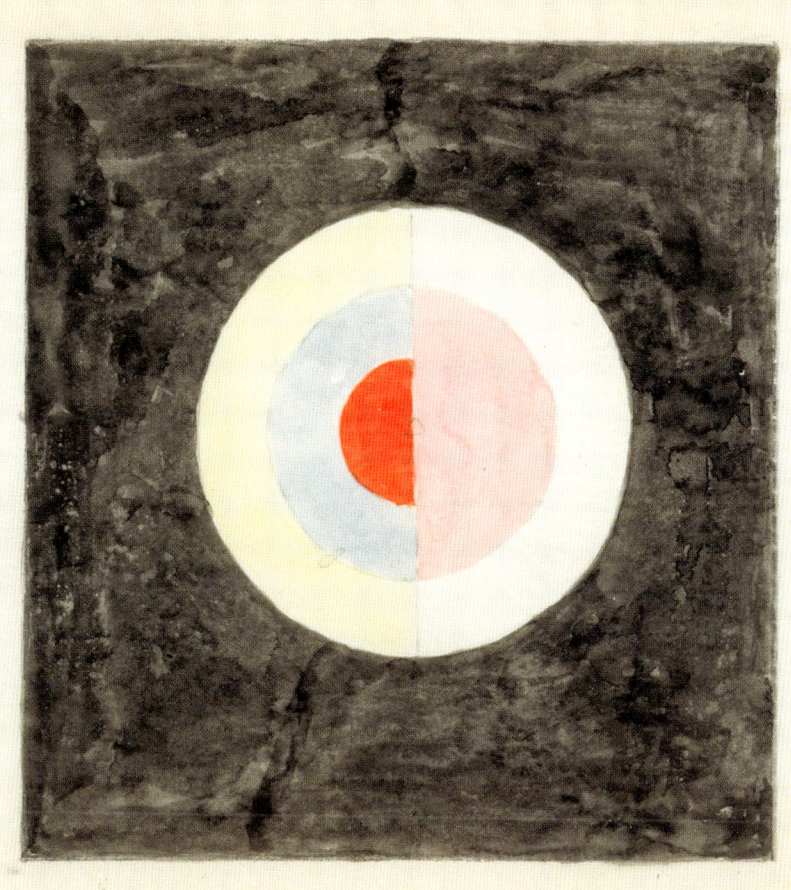

detail

164

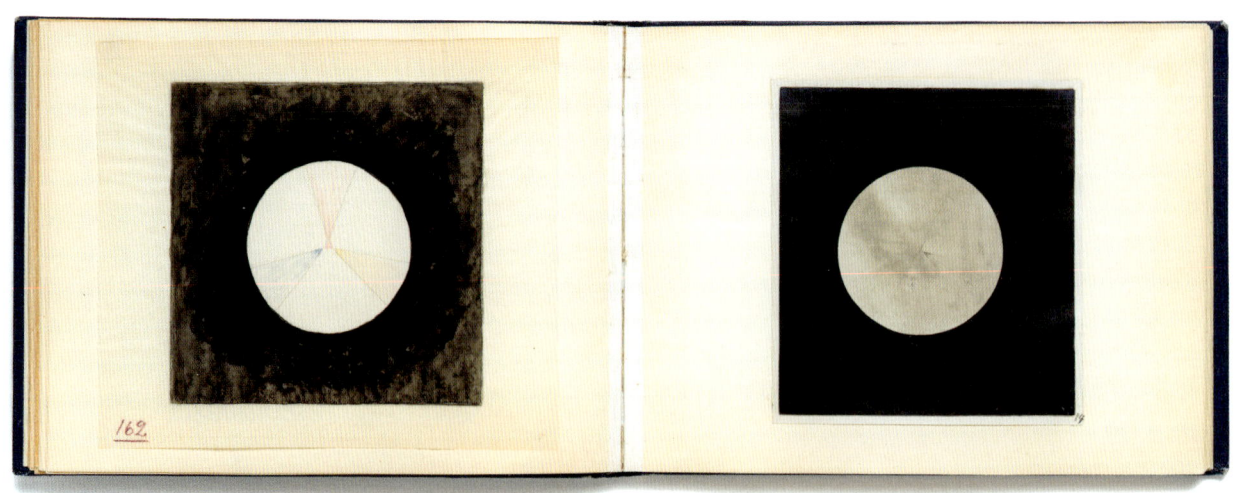

162.

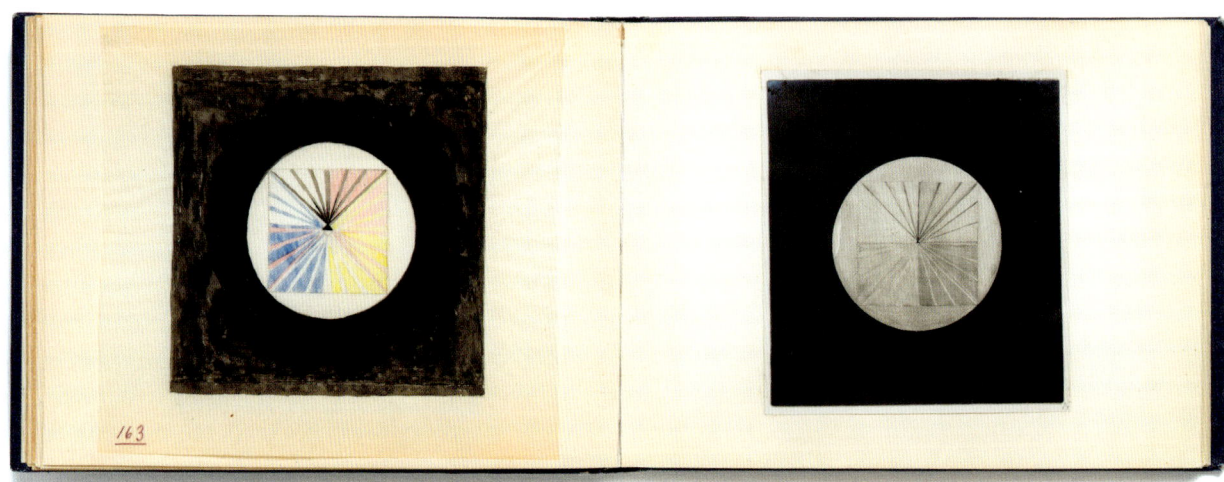

163

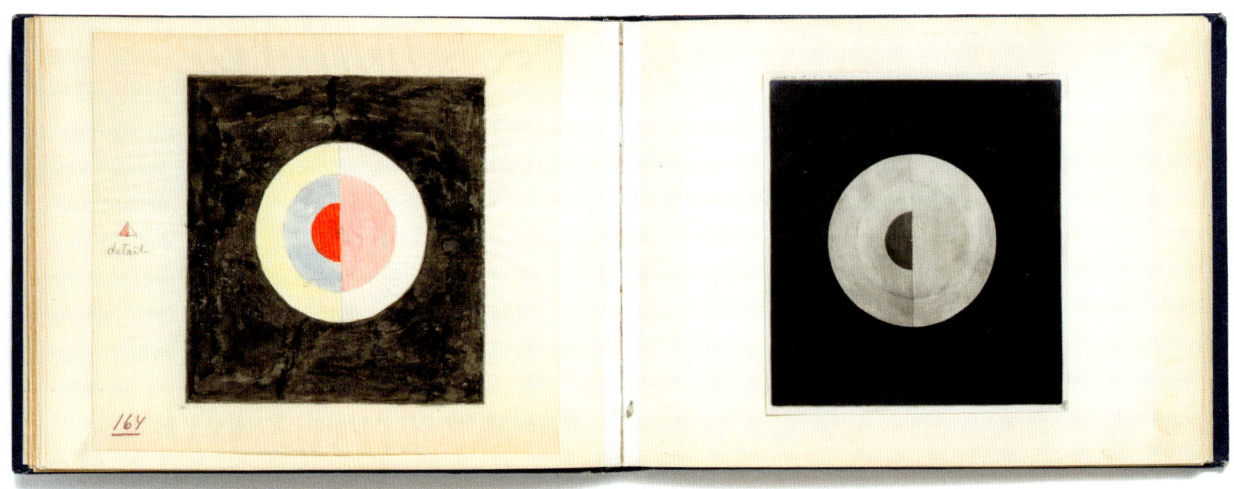

detail

164

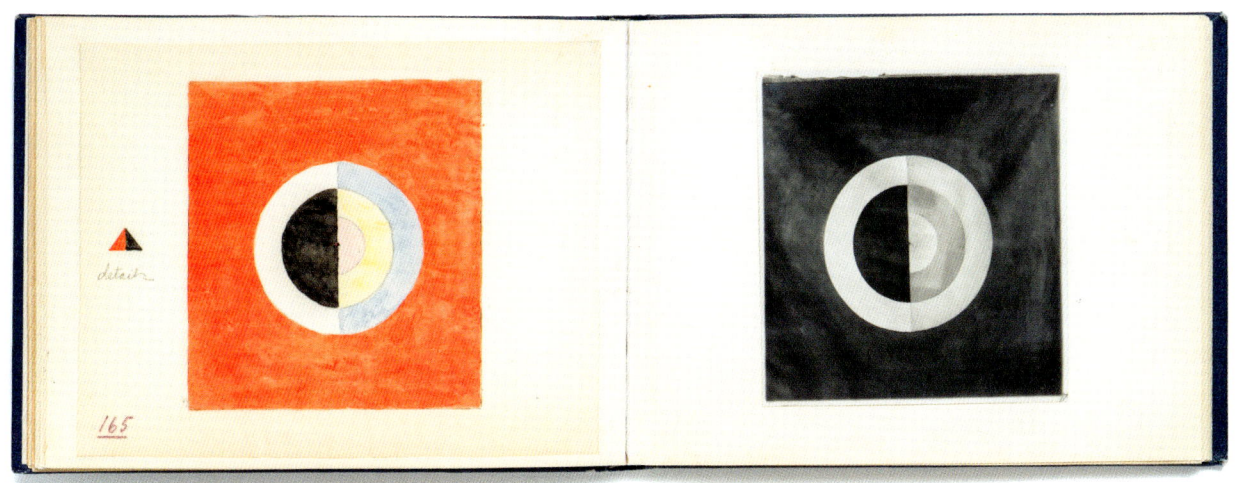

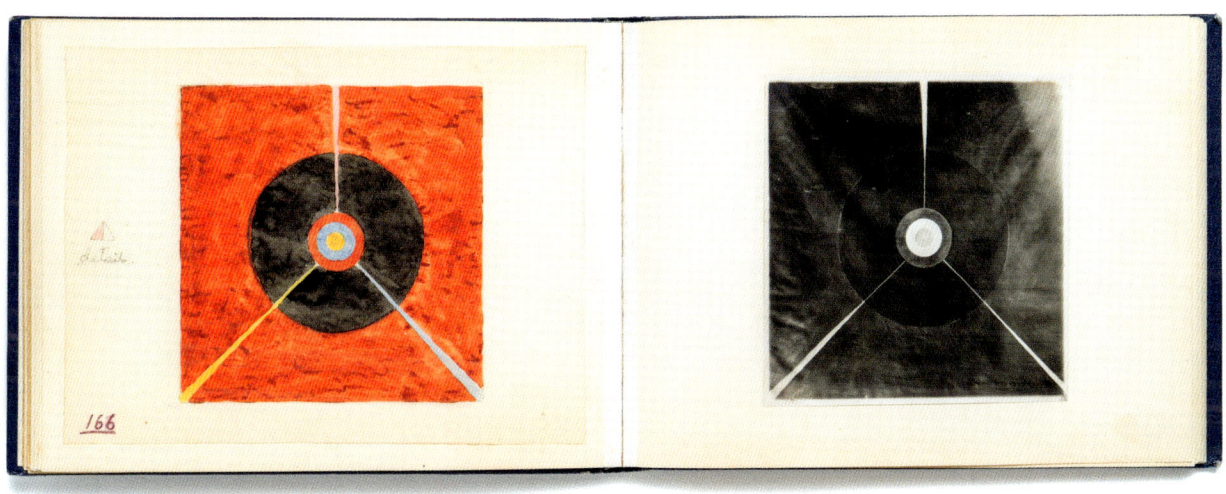

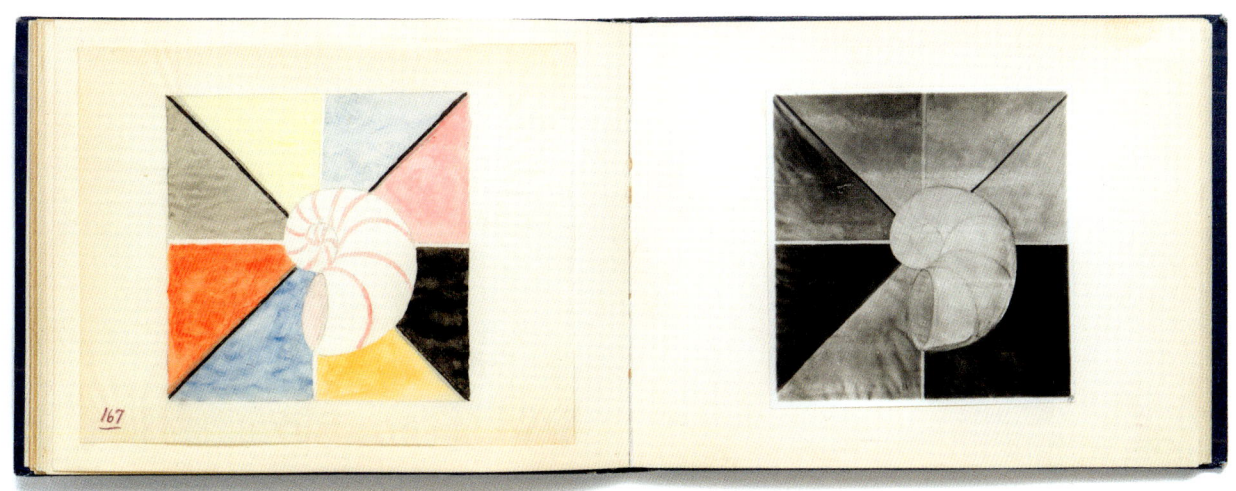

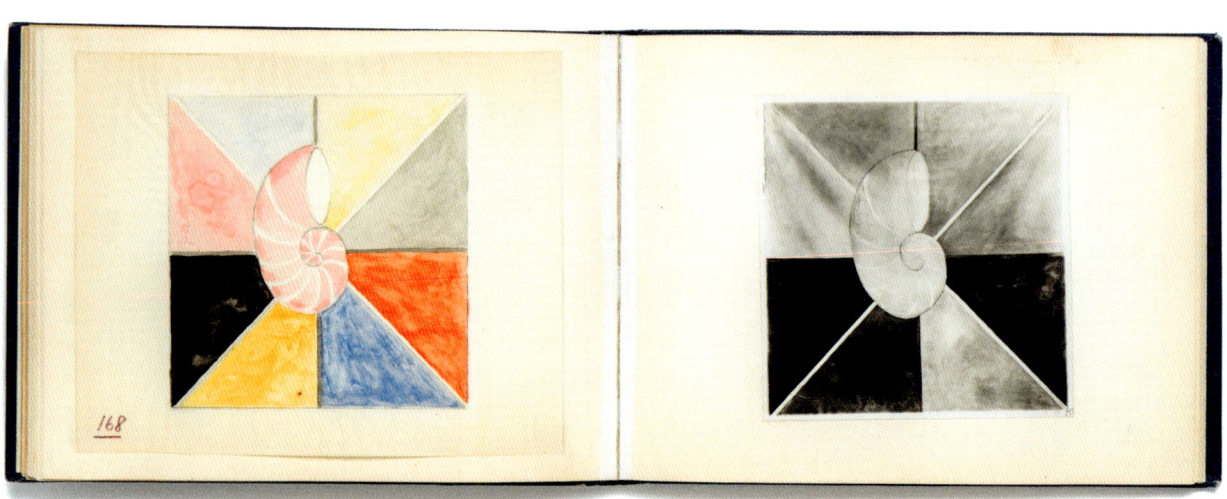

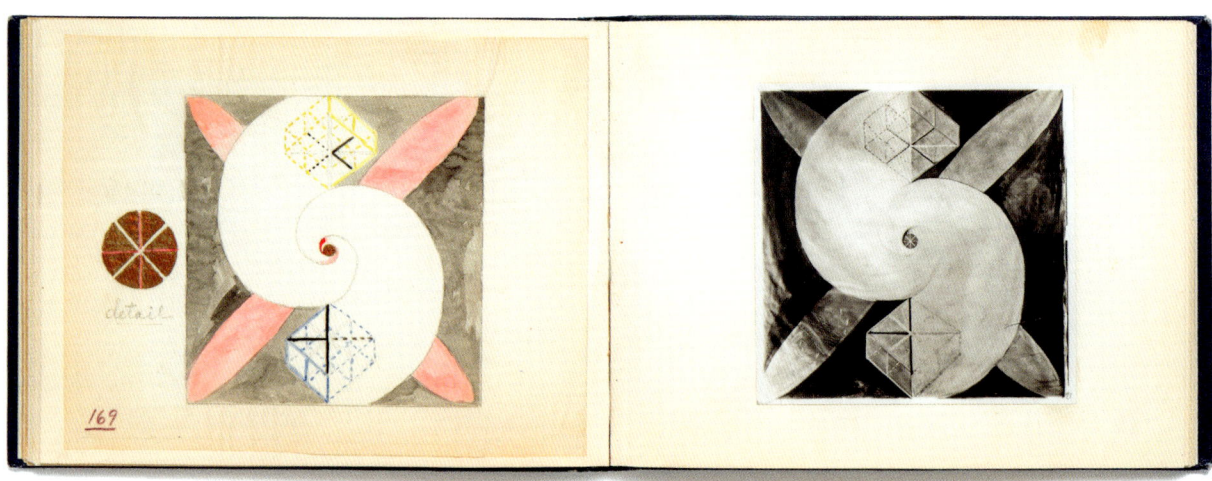

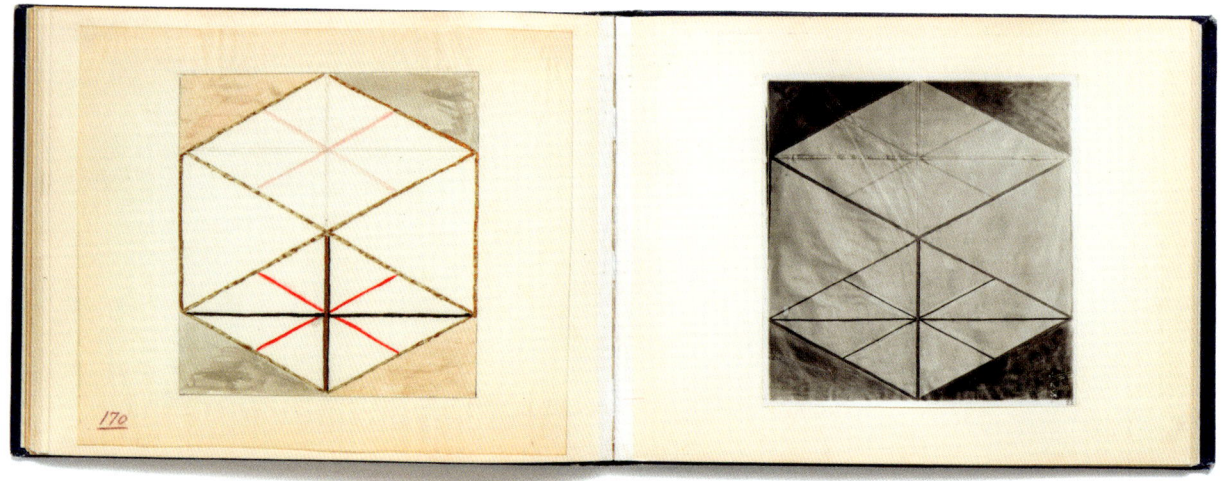

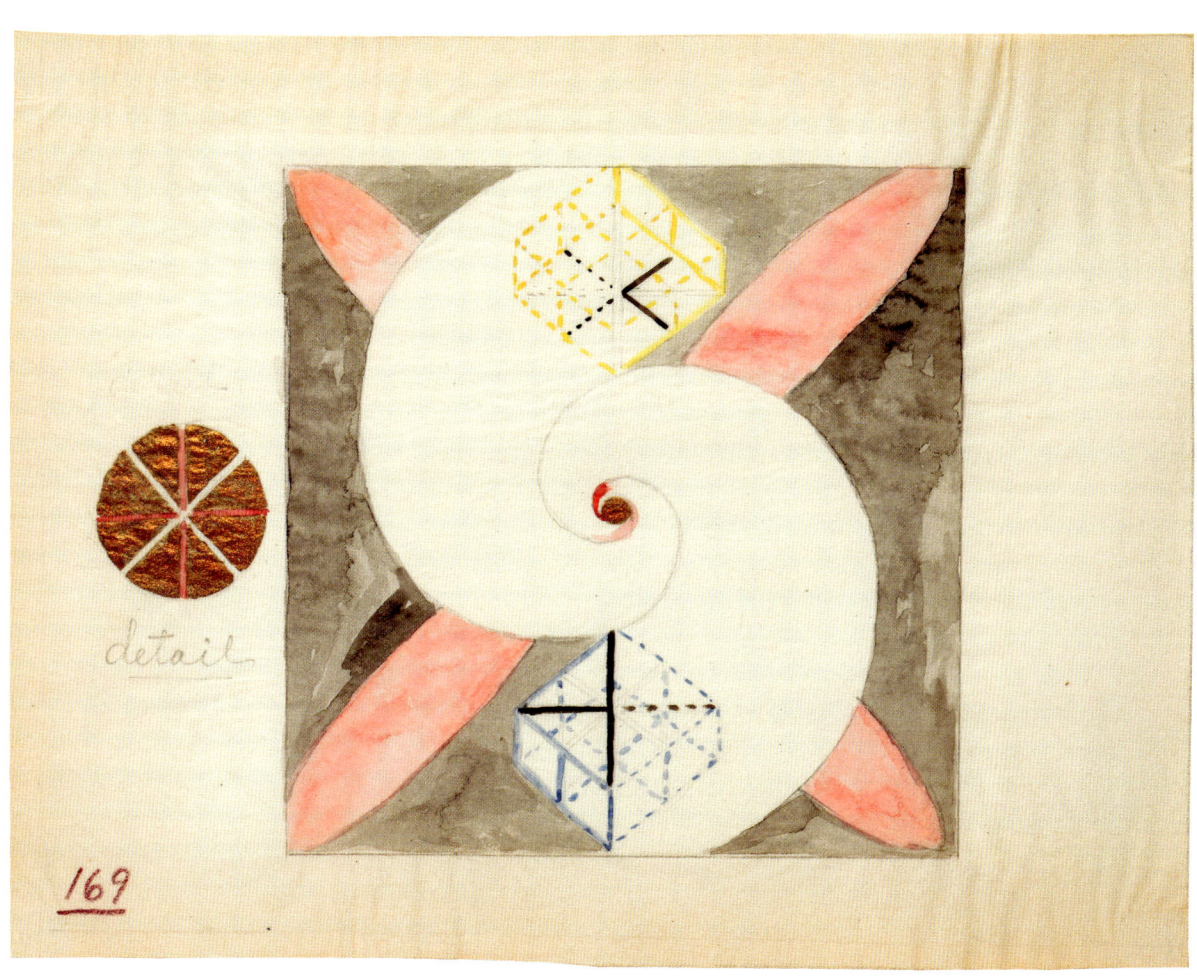

detail

169

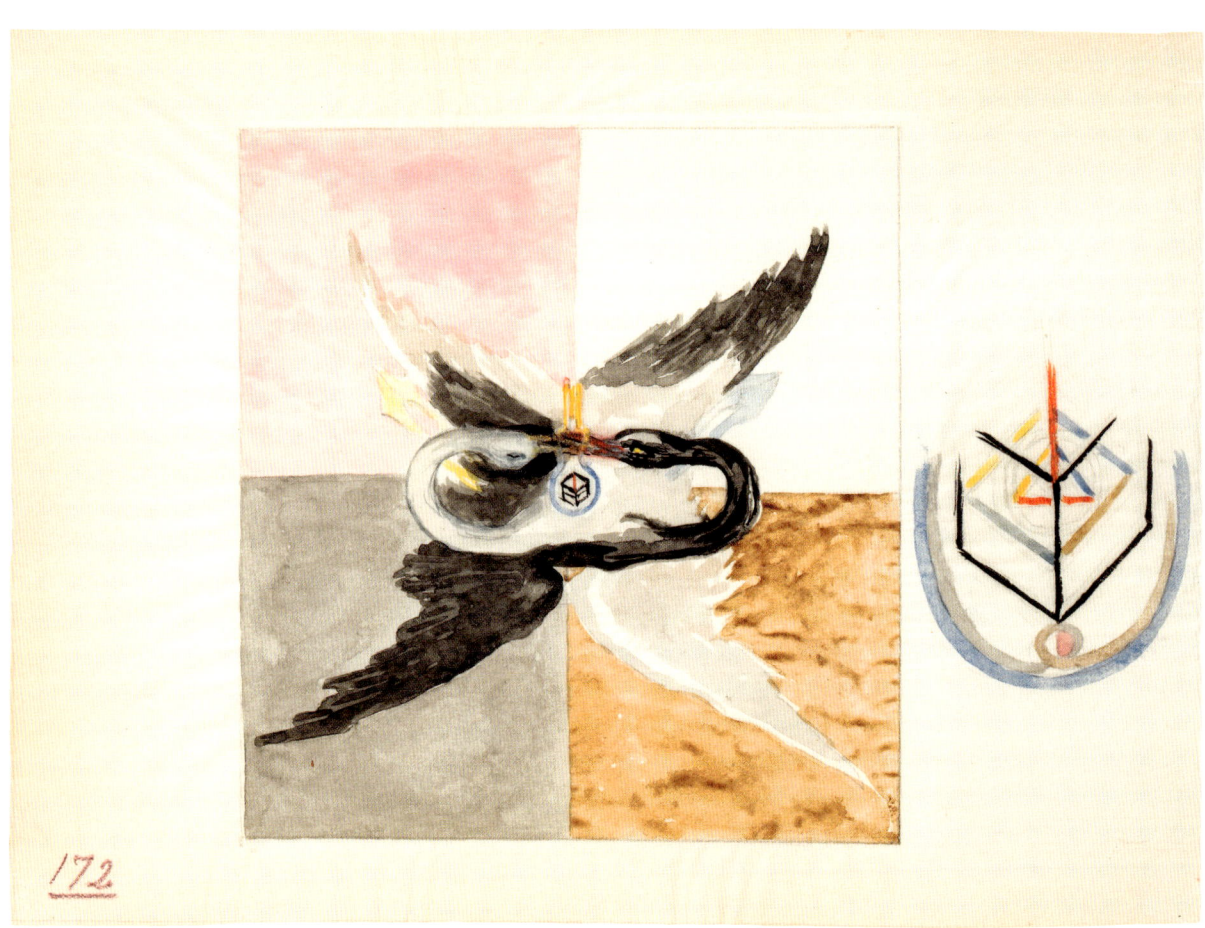

172

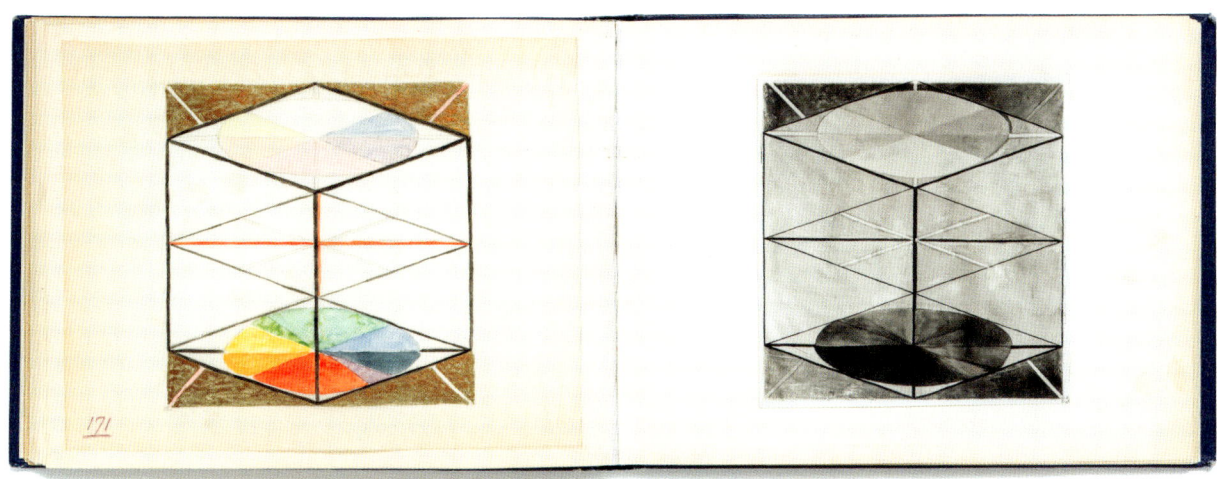

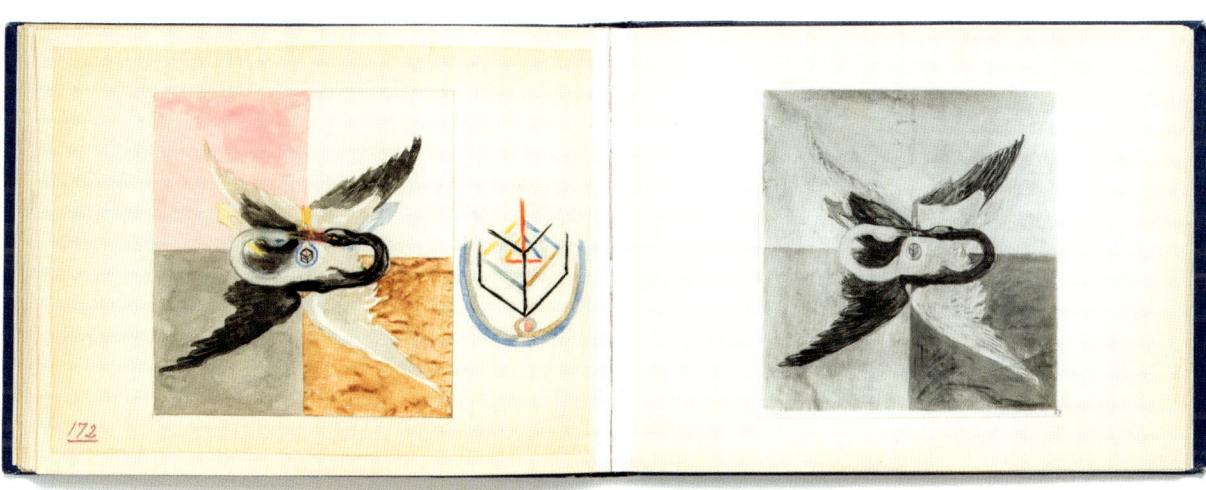

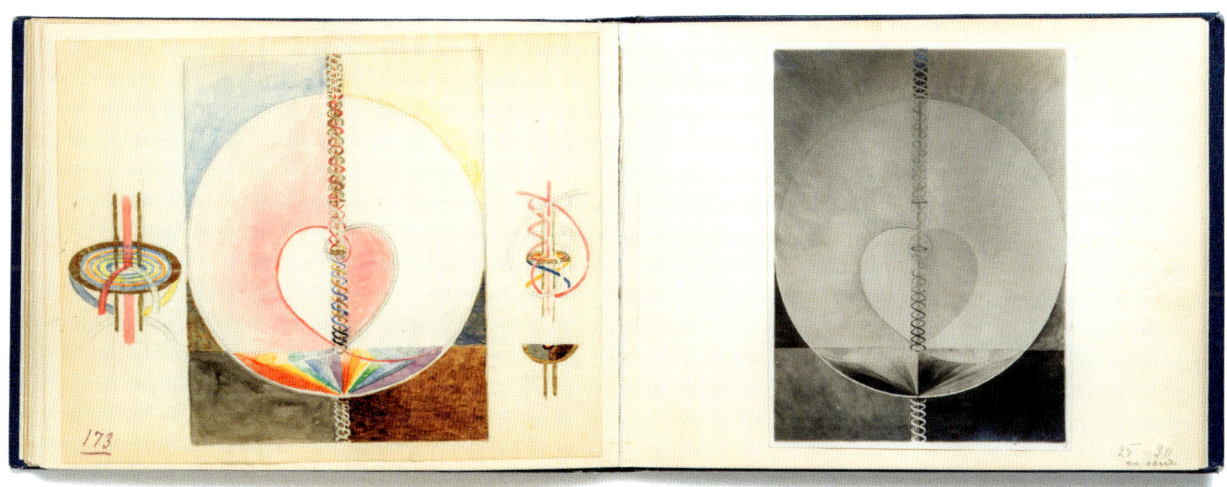

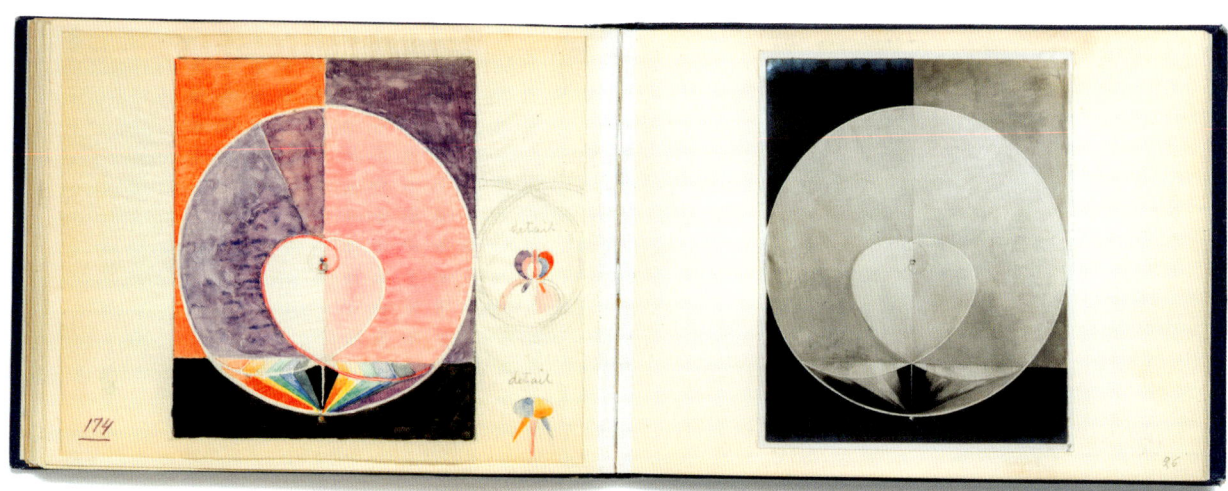

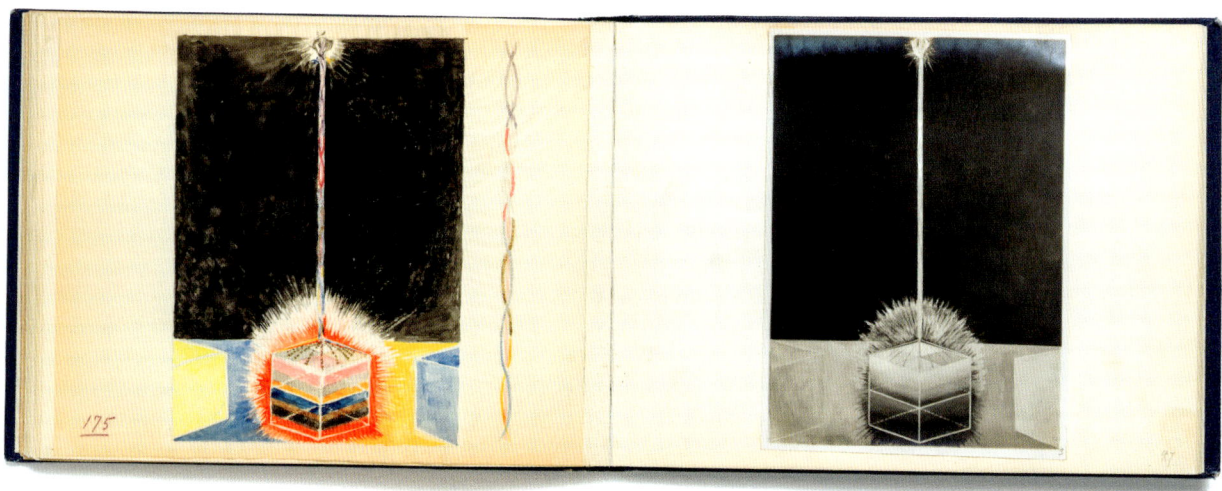

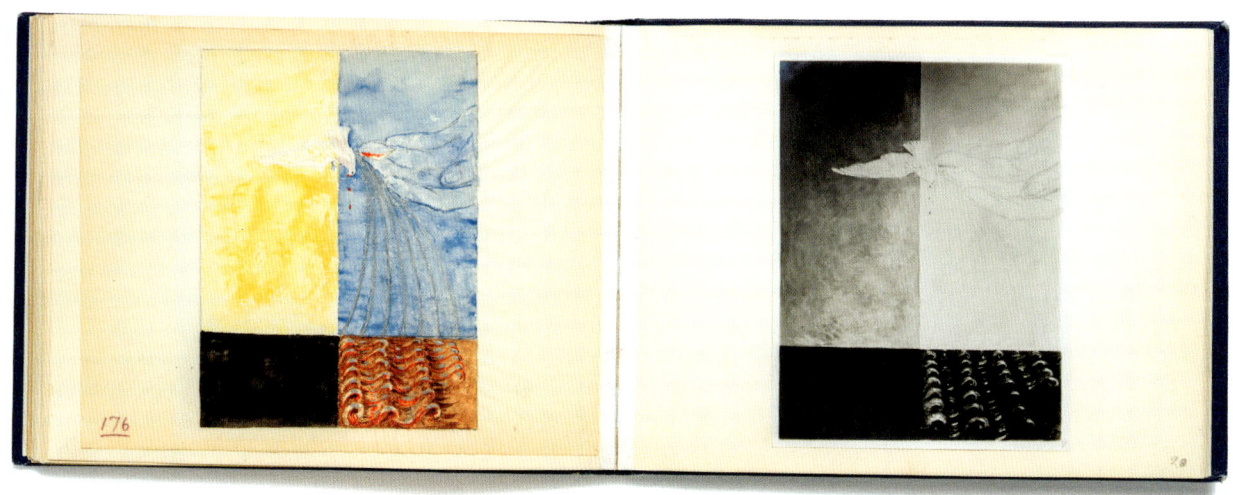

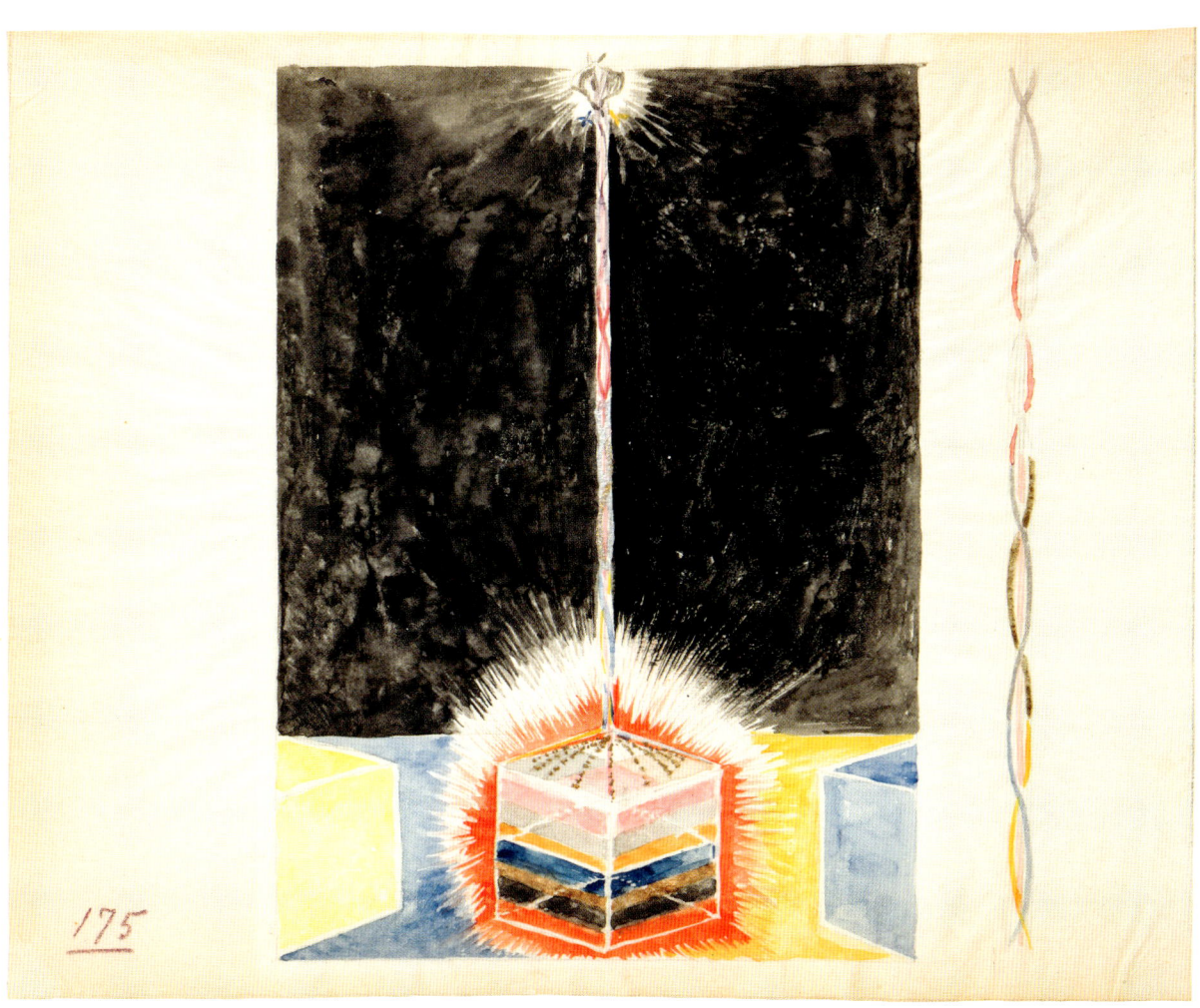

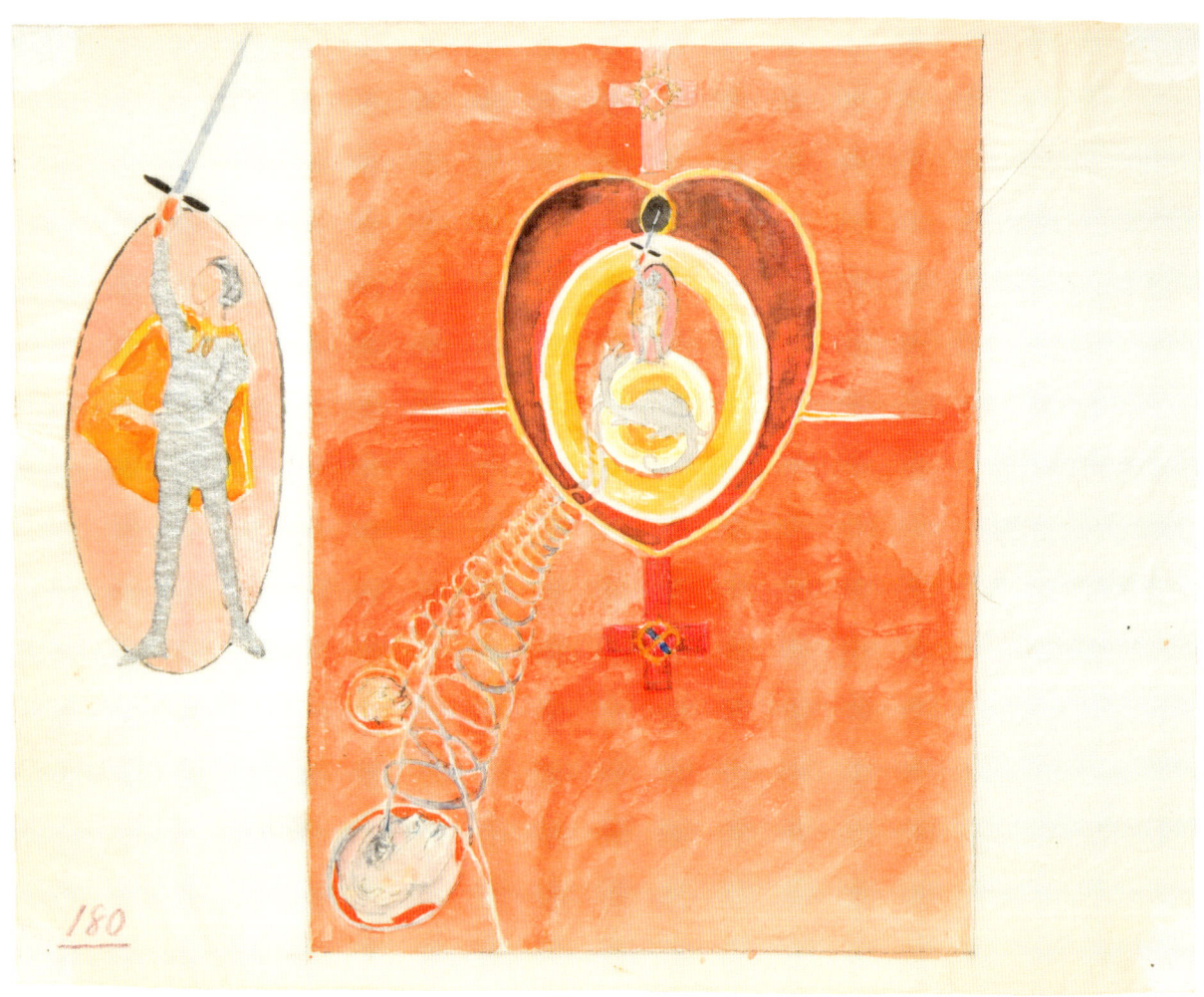

180

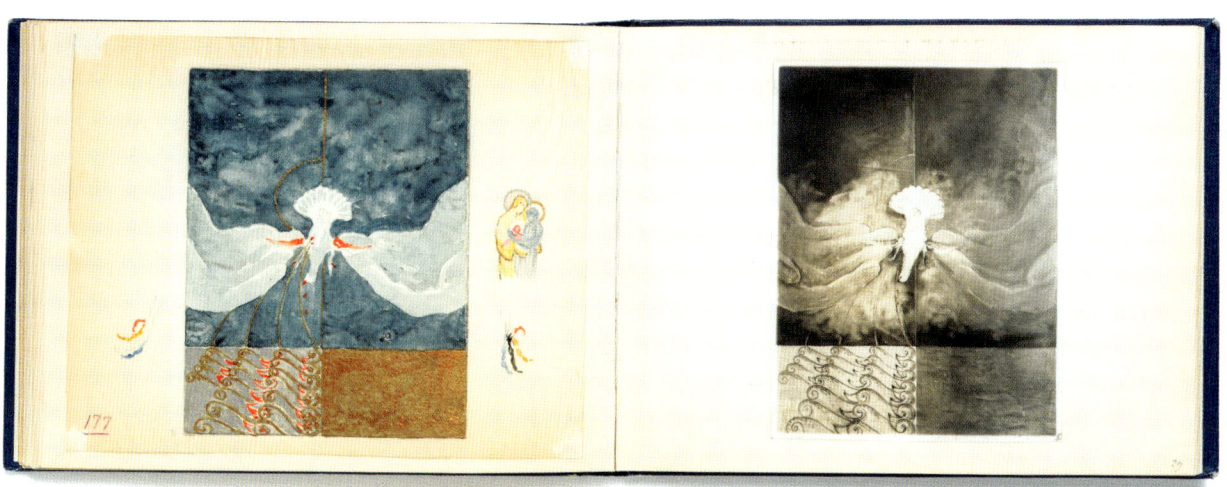

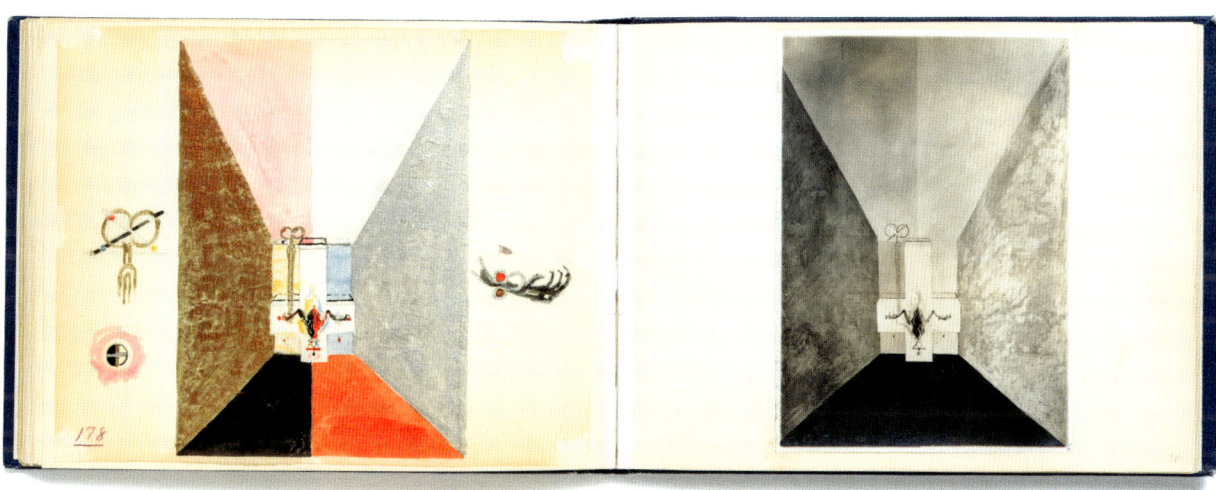

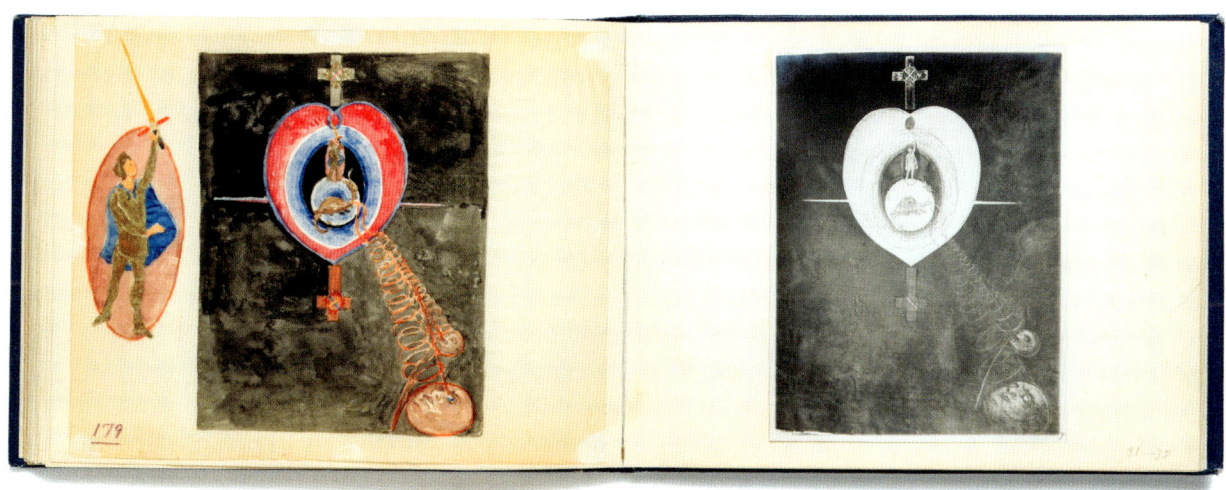

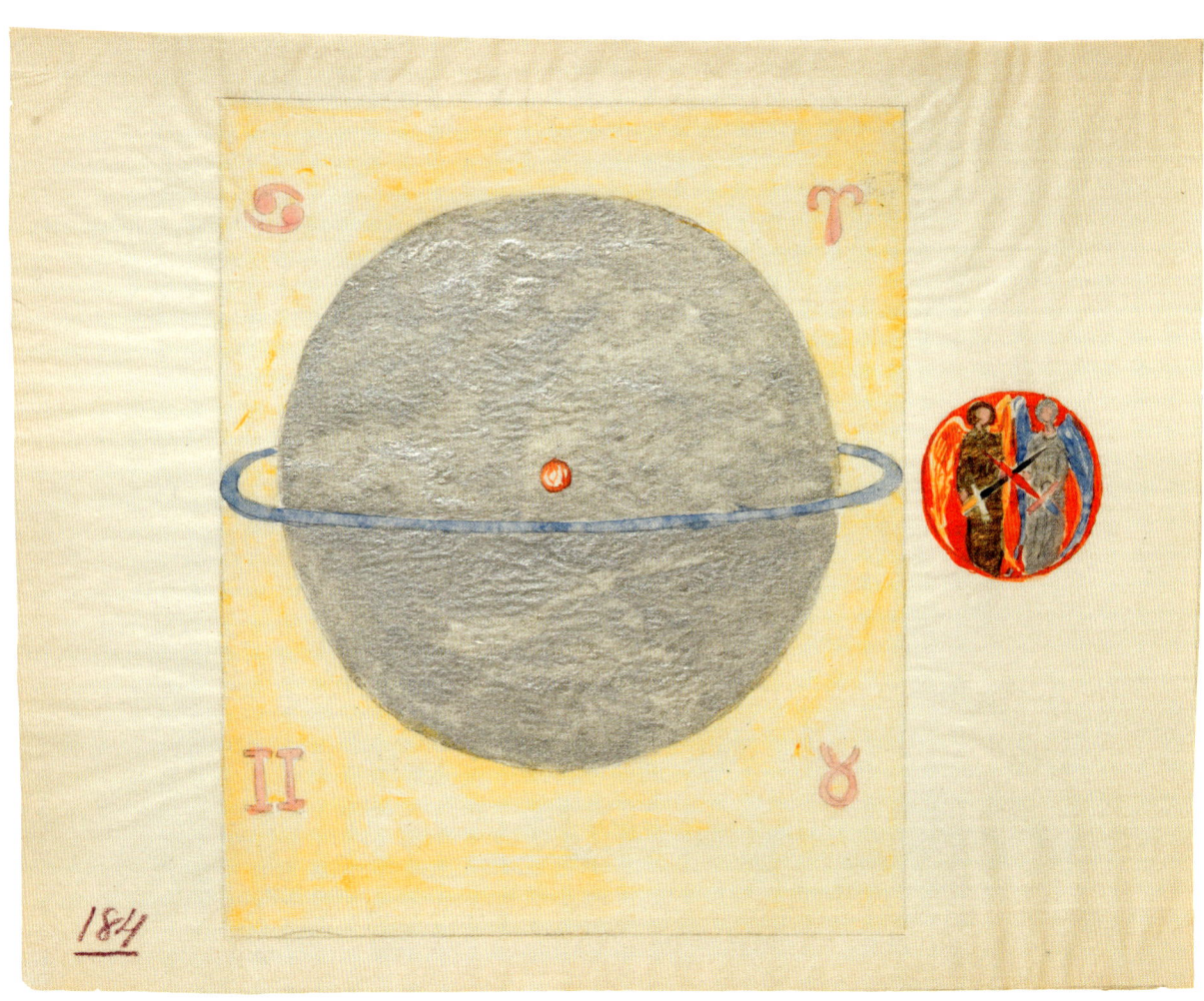

184

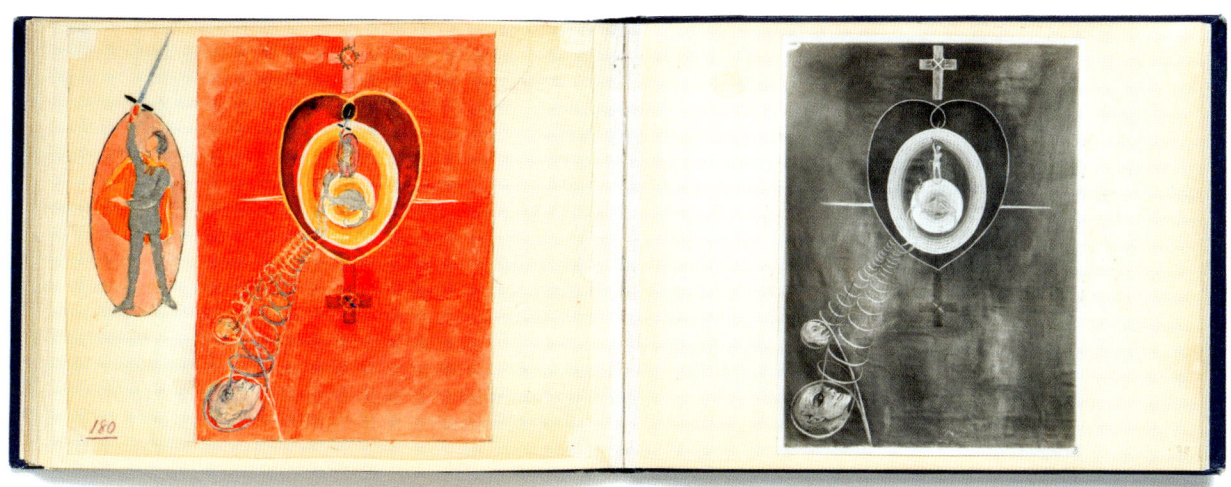

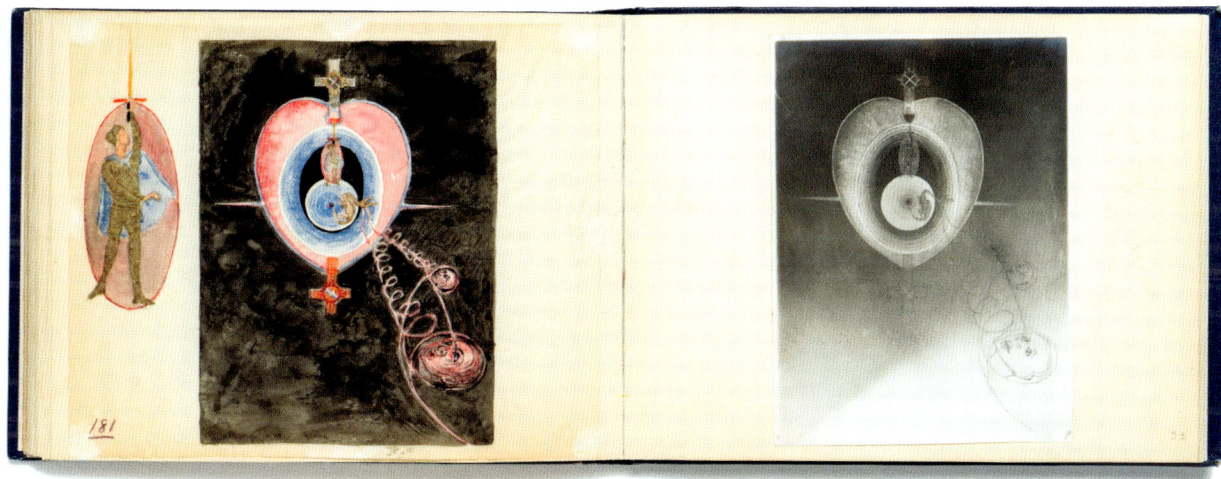

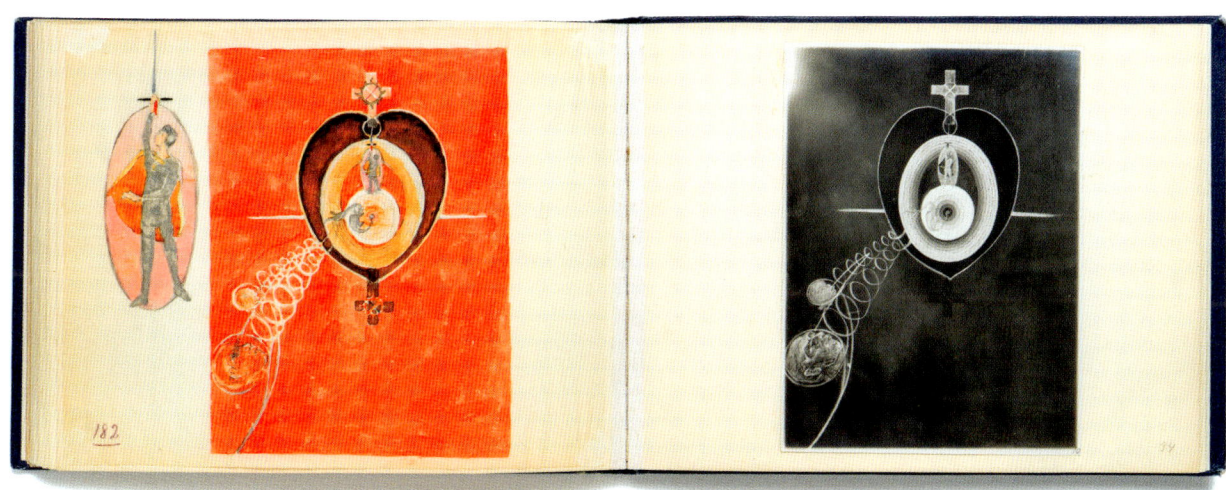

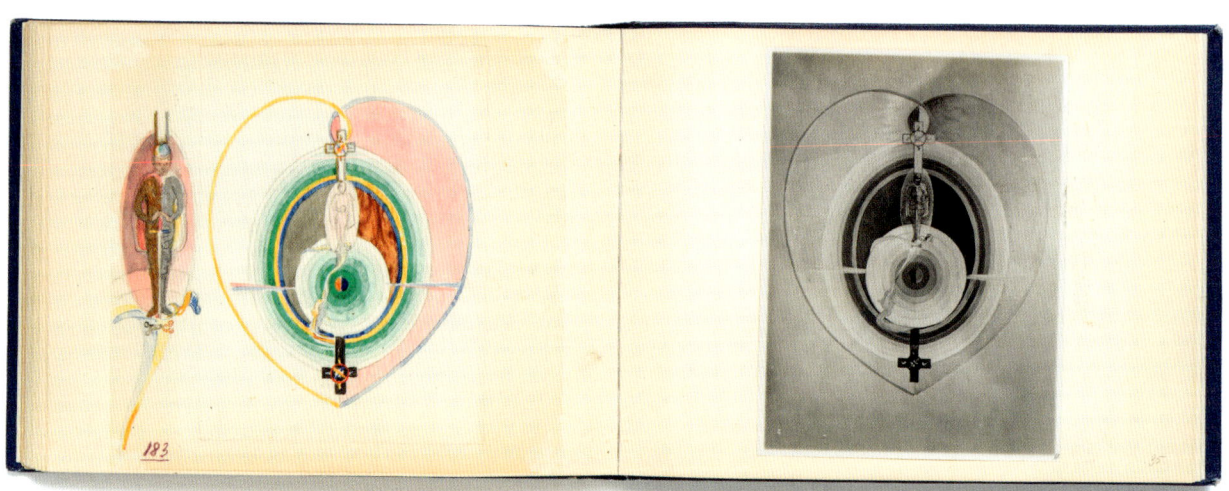

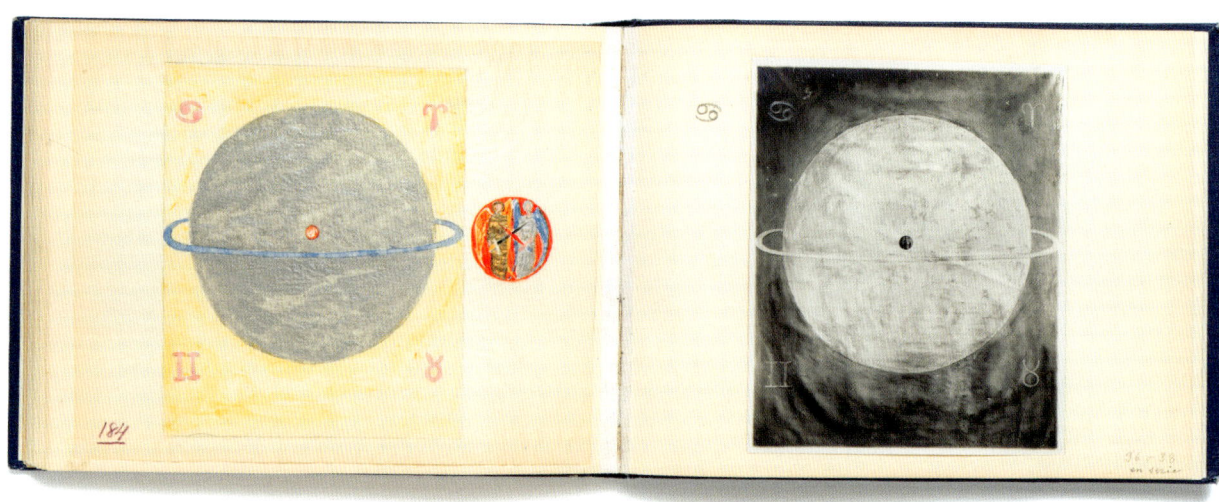

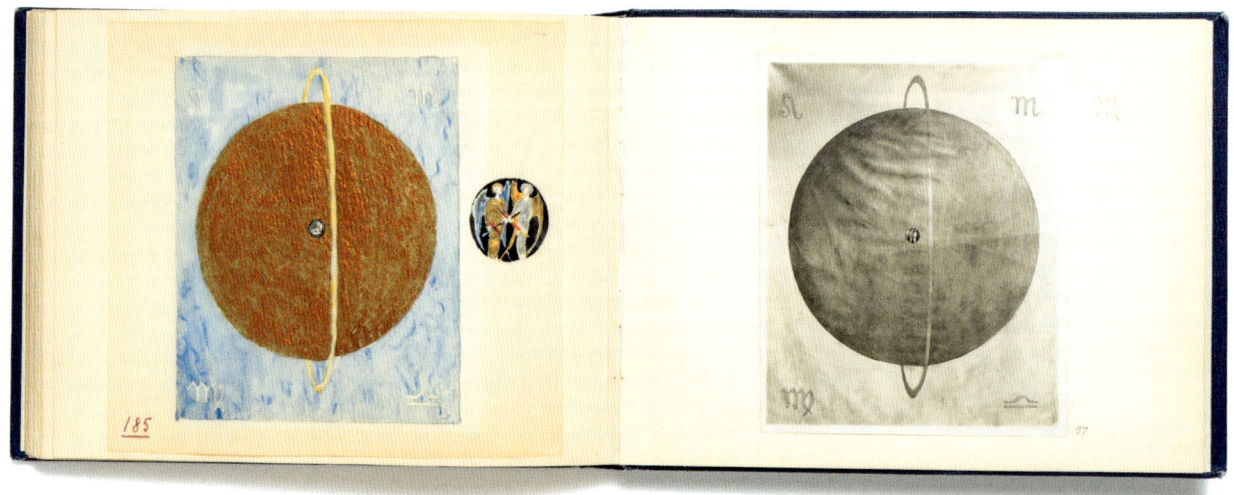

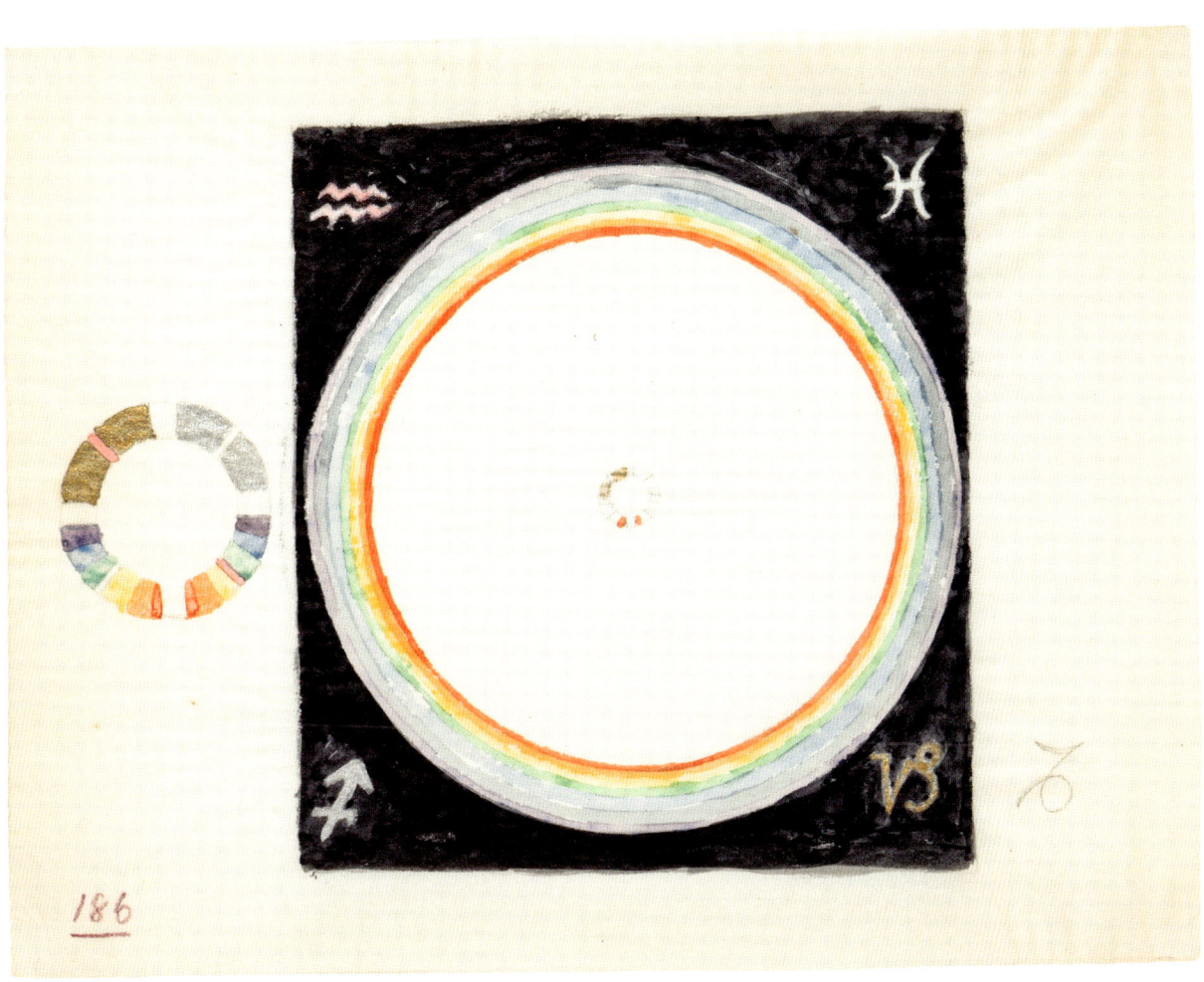

186

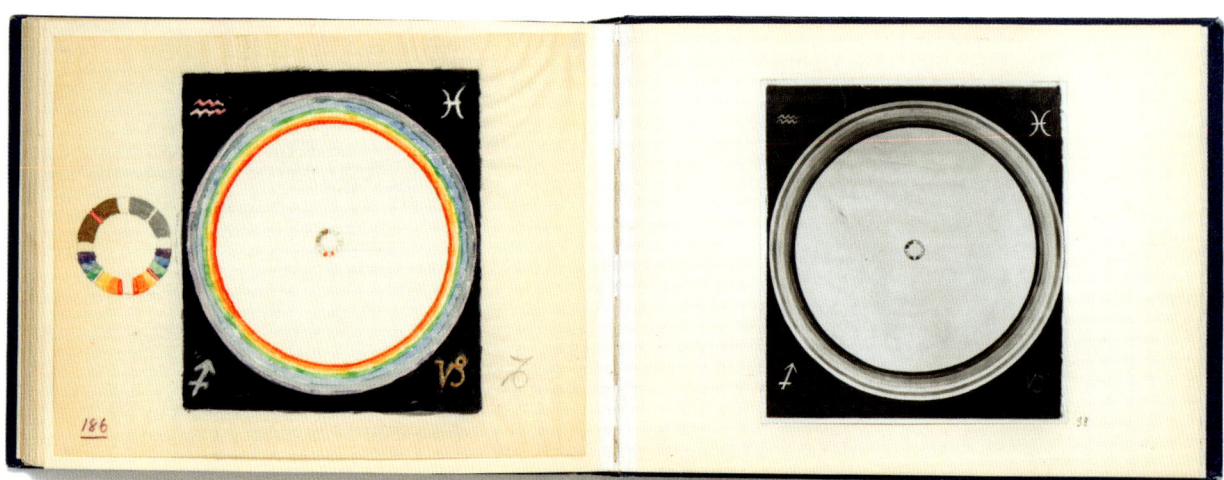

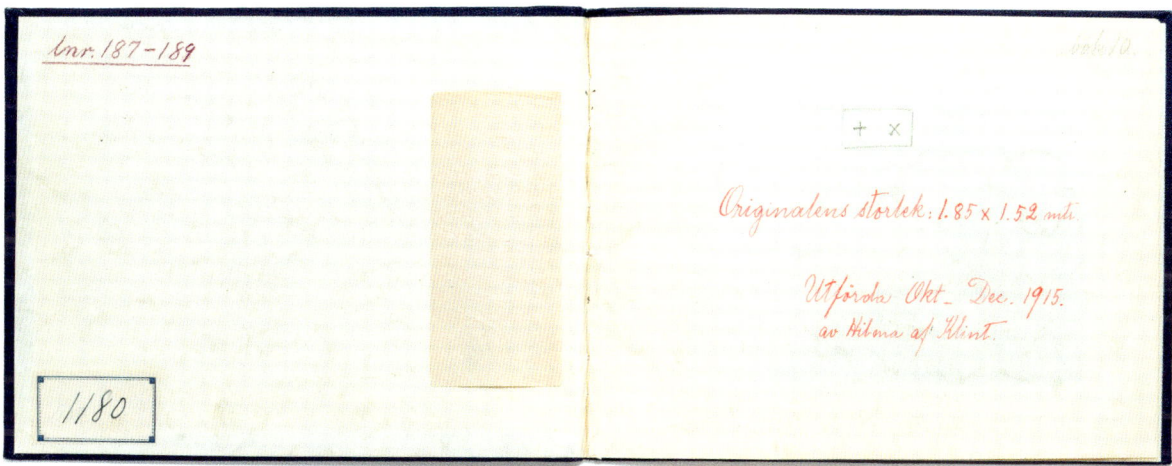

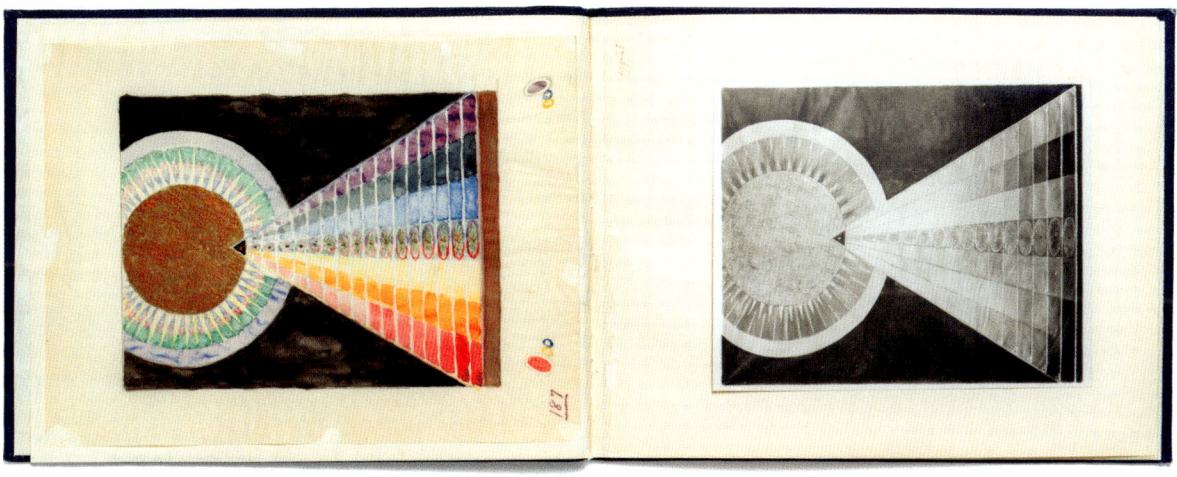

1180, Inv. 187–189. Original size: 1.85 × 1.52 m. Made Oct.–Dec. 1915, by Hilma af Klint

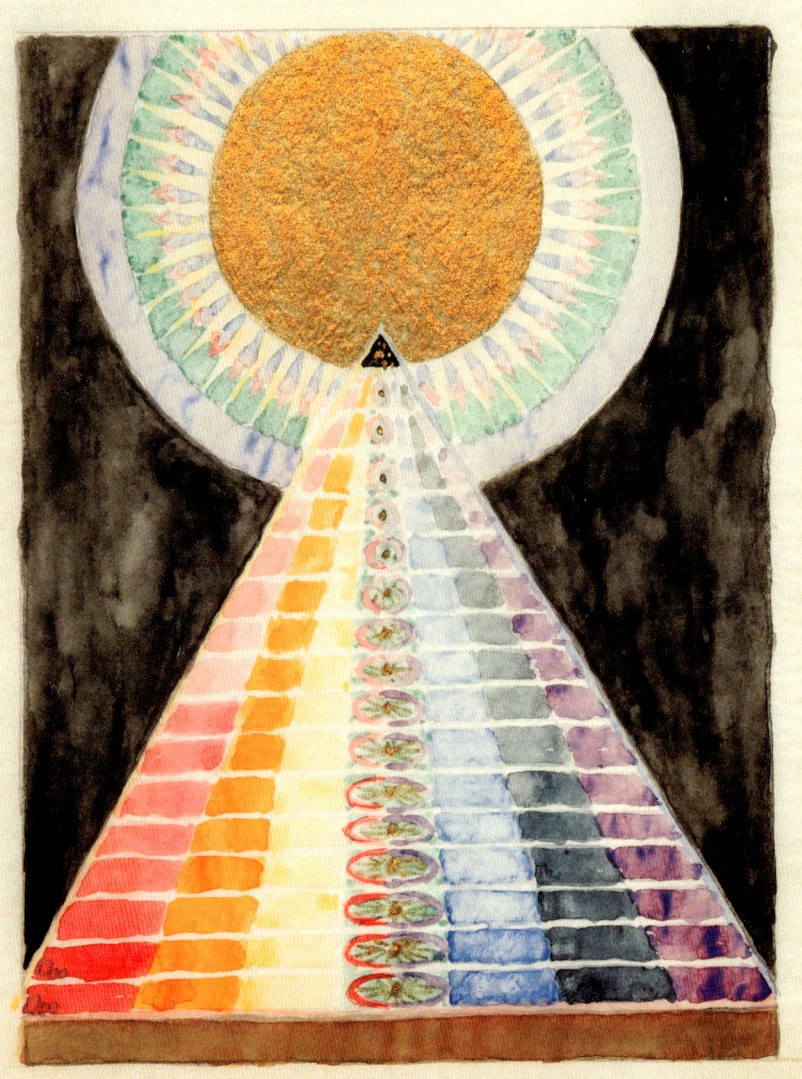

187

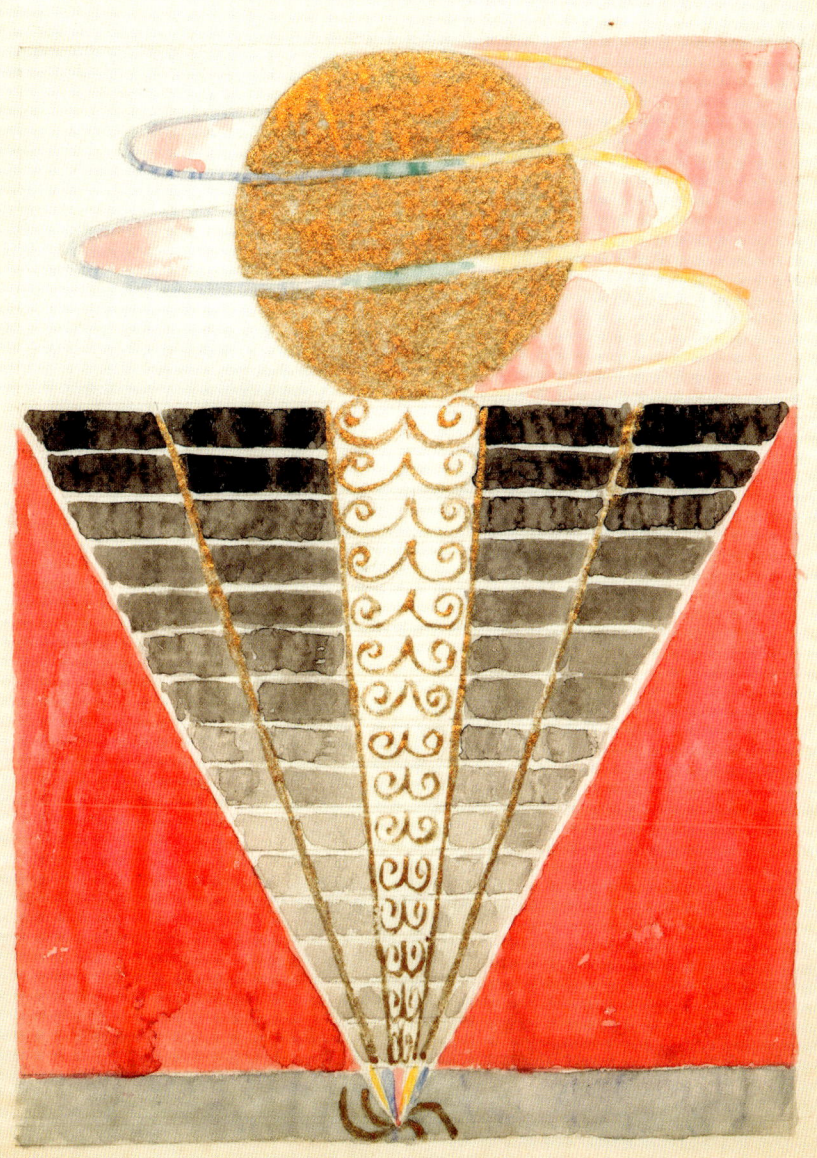

188

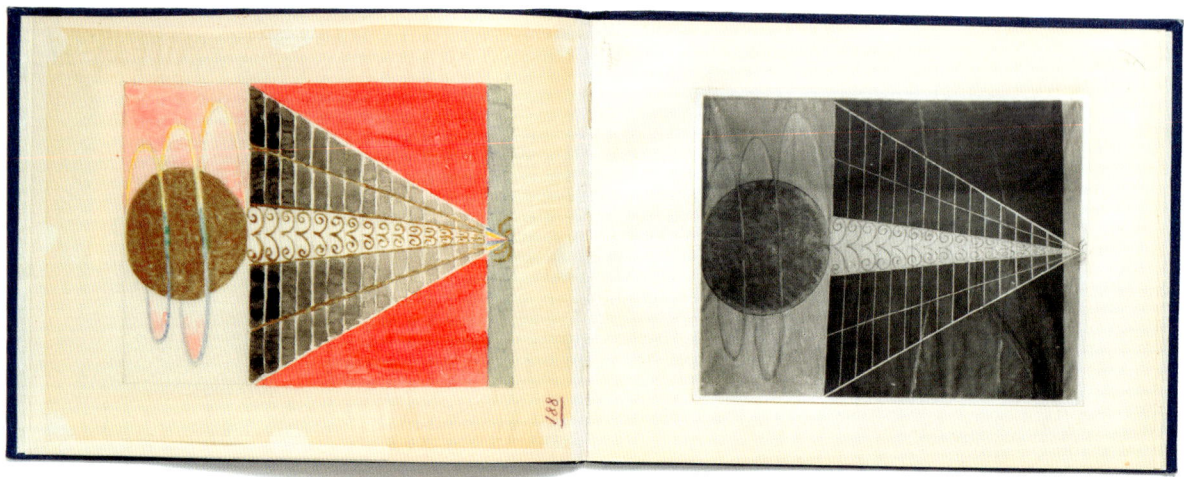

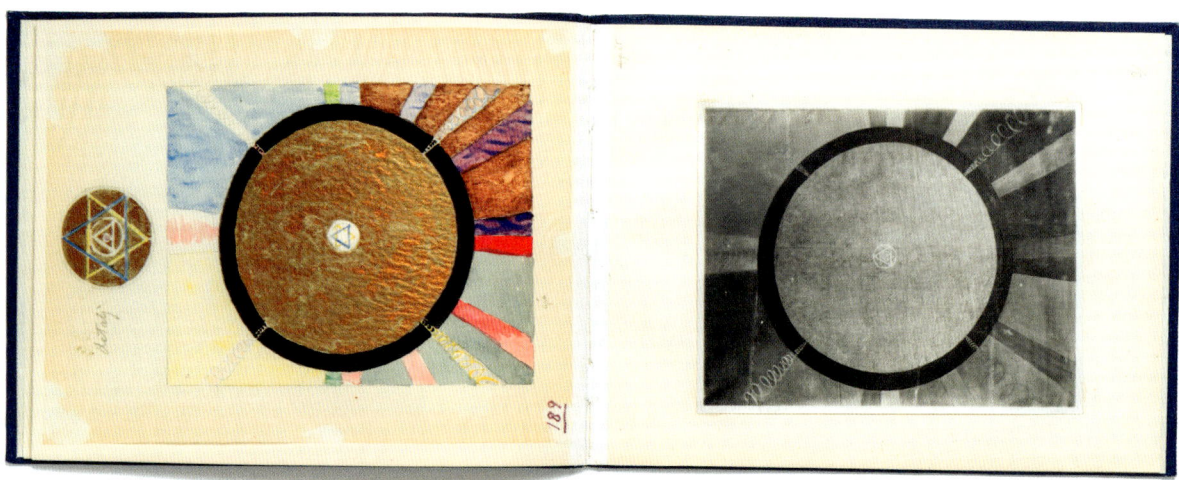

These three images, and the accompanying three works of details made at the same time in the format 0.46 × 0.30, are a summary of the whole work. They can be found in the green portfolio. A figurative picture also belongs to this work. (It is located in the studio.) It is called human chastity. See notes from 1920 after Doctor Steiner p. 47.

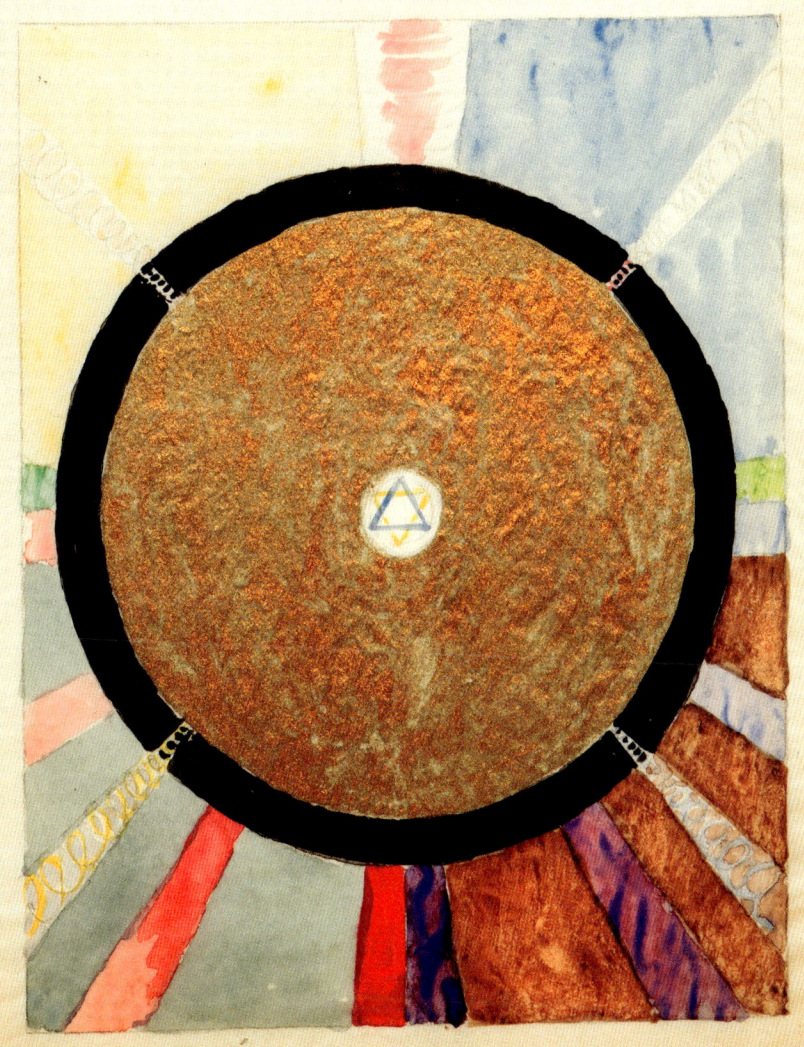

detalj

189

gu

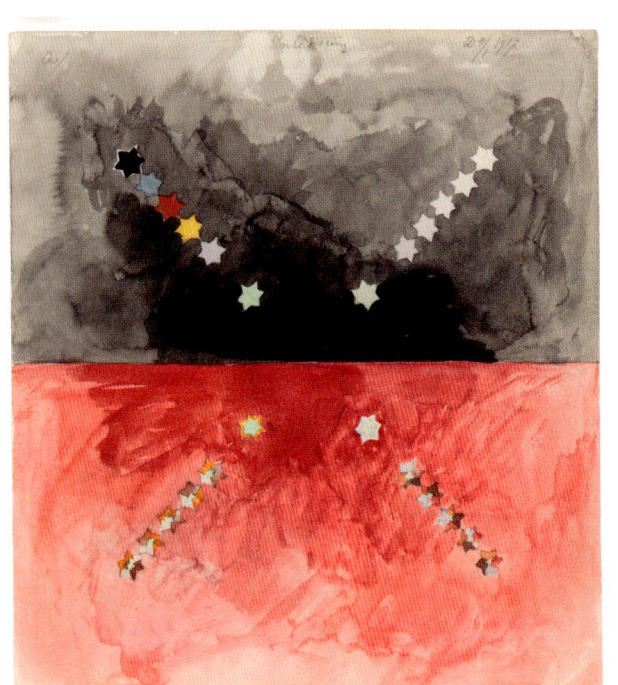

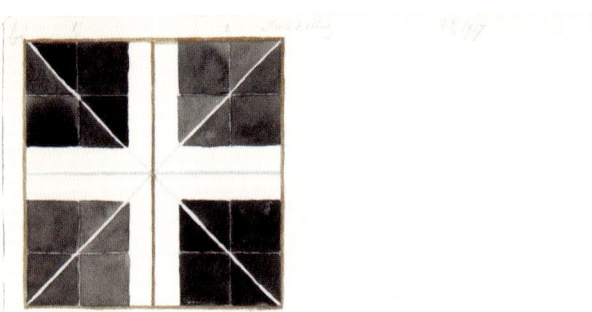

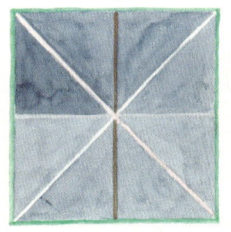

The Atom Series

In January 1917, having completed work on *The Paintings for the Temple*, Hilma af Klint turned her attention from a sweeping analysis of spiritual evolution to the microscopic world of the atom. *The Atom Series* of 1917 lays the groundwork for both a new body of work and a new way of working.

The Atom Series consists of twenty-two drawings of which the first two serve as an introduction. Except for the first in the series, all drawings represent two images of an atom: the image on the upper left of each sheet is a depiction of the atom as it exists on the etheric plane and the image on the lower right depicts the atom's state of energy on the physical plane enlarged four times. On each sheet, af Klint's handwritten texts provide observations on the atom and the relationship of the physical world to the energy fields of the etheric world. The *etheric plane* and the *etheric body* are terms used by both the Theosophists and the Anthroposophists to describe the subtle, more highly evolved component of earthly existence that, if accessed, can provide an intermediate step between the physical body and the soul. From this idea af Klint develops a new way to work, one that no longer depends only on the High Masters and mediumship but also looks inward, receiving direction through her own etheric body. What she finds here supports her view of the universe as an interconnected whole. As she writes on the second drawing in the series: "Every atom has its own midpoint, but each midpoint is directly connected to the midpoint of the universe."

Pages 148, 151–59: *The Atom Series*, HaK 351–HaK 372, 1917
Watercolor, graphite, and metallic paint on paper; twenty-two drawings, 10⅝ × 9¾ in. (26.9 × 24.8 cm) each

No. 1.
The midpoint of the universe consists of innocence.
1. Uncompromising truth 2. Dignity 3. Humility 4. Mercy
4 times enlarged

No. 2.
Every atom has its own midpoint, but each midpoint is directly connected to the midpoint of the universe.

No. 3.
The body must be mediated by going to its center and drawing from these new forces.

No. 4.
Through its longing to create ever more beautiful forms first on the etheric plane,
and then in matter, the body becomes capable of being penetrated by light.

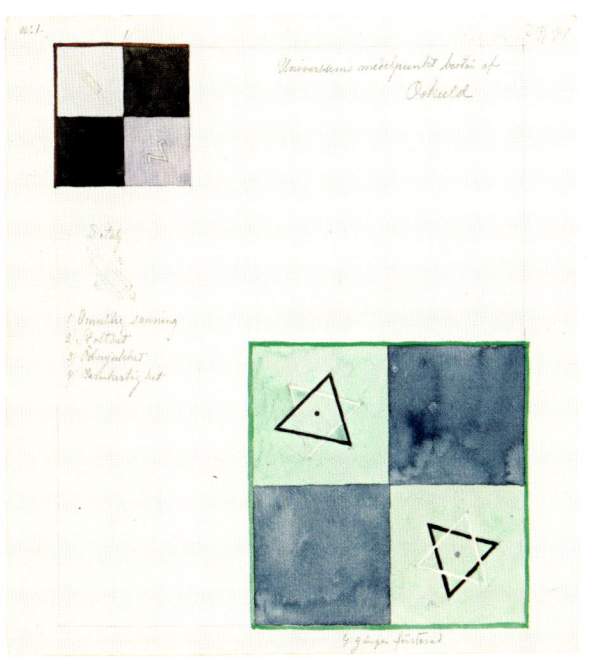

Universums medelpunkt består af
Oskuld

Delta

1. Oskuldens samvaro
2. Helhet
3. Skönjbarhet
4. Beständighet

4 gånger förstorad

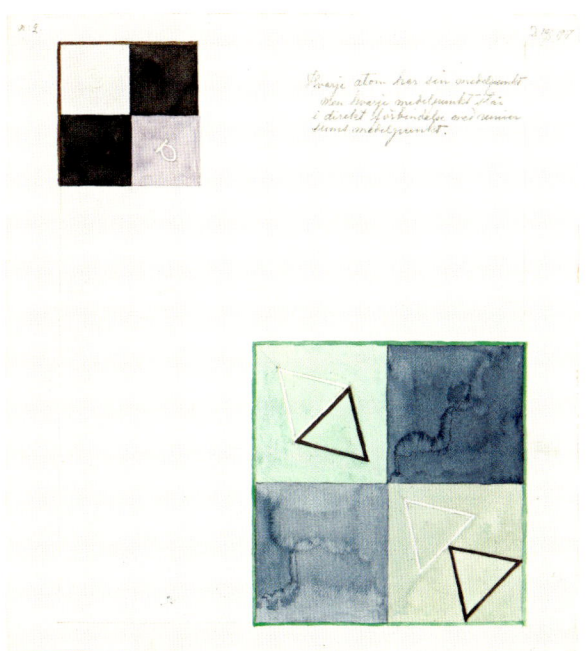

Hvarje atom har sin medelpunkt
men hvarje medelpunkt står
i direkt förbindelse med numen
samt medelpunkt.

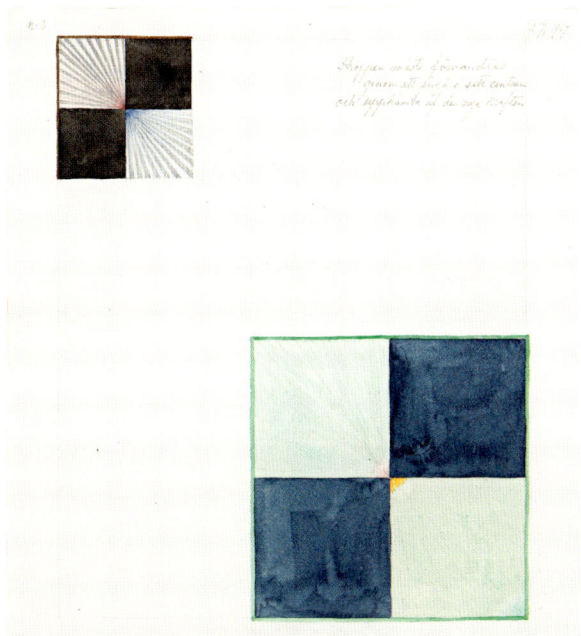

Skeppen måste förvandlas
genom att sänka i sitt centum
och uppkomna ur de nya krafter

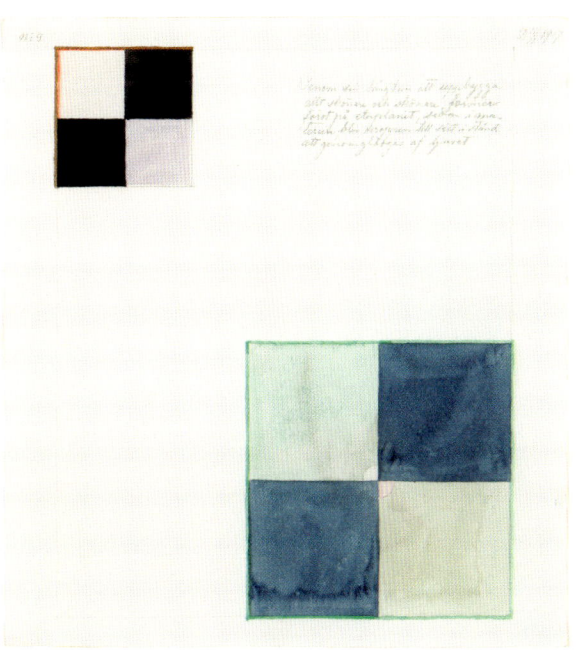

Genom den kraften att uppbygga
sitt väsen och skära en gränsare
spät på elementet, detta i sin
tumk blir kraften att återsluta
att omringlad af ljuset

No. 5.
The body is capable of rising above its earthly form by listening to the superphysical powers.

No. 6.
When the atom is at rest on the etheric plane, its center absorbs the energy that is stored there.
When the body is in harmony, energy radiates outward from the center of the atom.

No. 7.
The atom is both limited and capable of development. When the atom
expands on the etheric plane, the physical part of the earthly atom begins to glow.

No. 8.
On the etheric plane the atom alternates constantly between rest and activity.
At rest it retreats inward. This causes the terrestrial atom to emanate energy. The energy pushes inward.

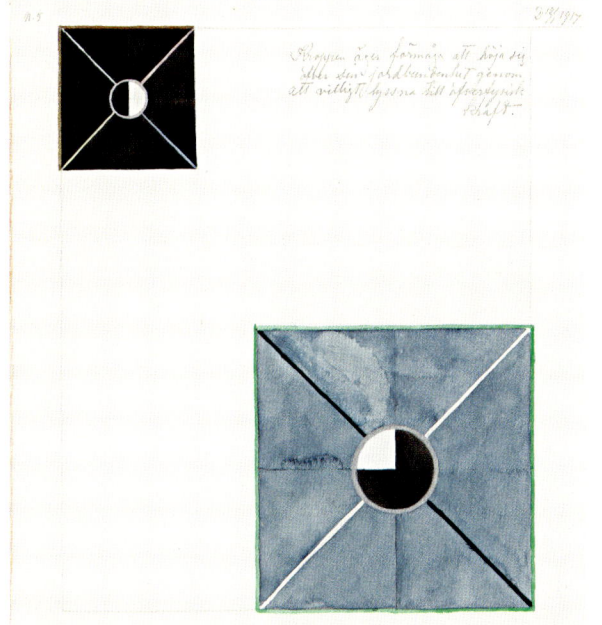

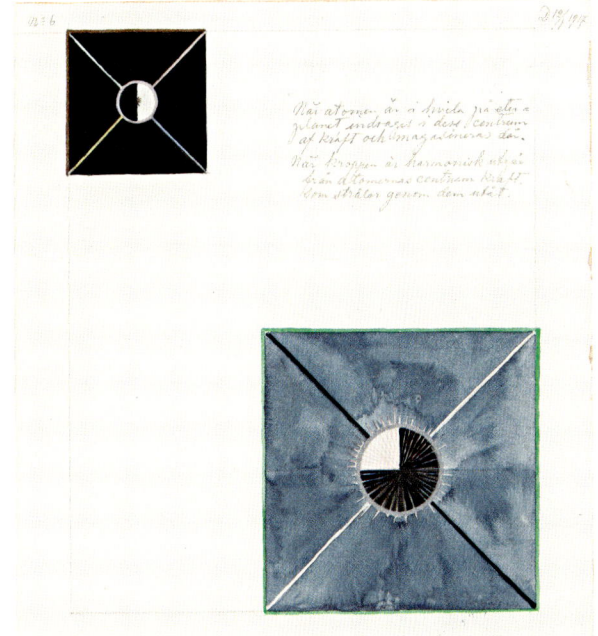

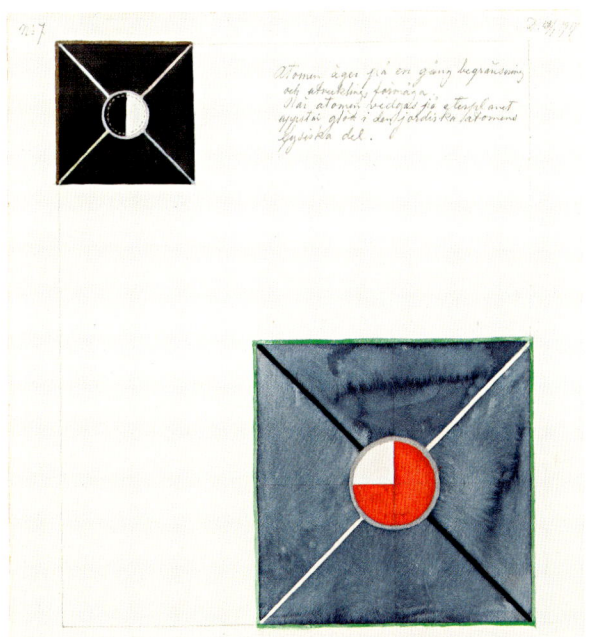

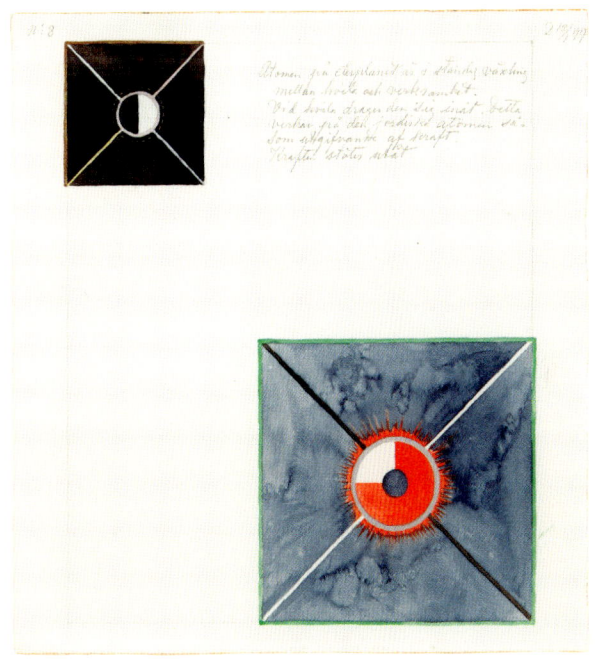

No. 9.
The atom has 4 degrees of development, which it is able to attain in the body.

No. 10.
The atom has 4 degrees of vigor, which are dependent on one another.

No. 11.
The atom has the capacity to emit the resistance inherent in matter.

No. 12.
The atom's strength increases as it senses and admits its dependence
upon Divine energy, it is: "inexhaustible and incomprehensible life itself."

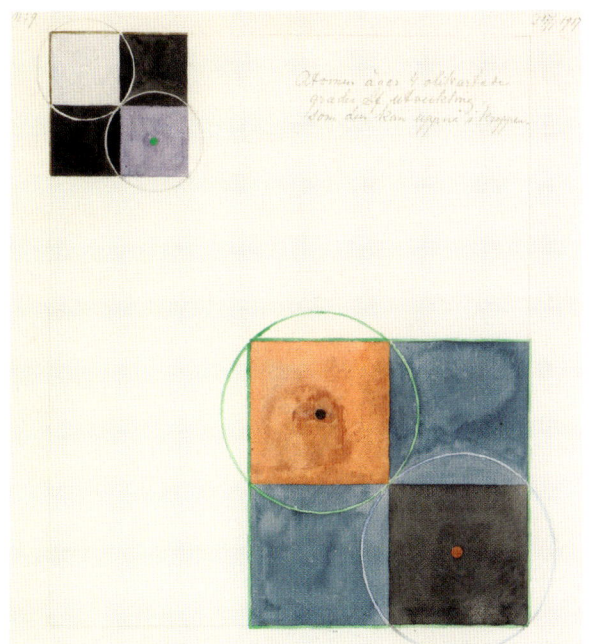

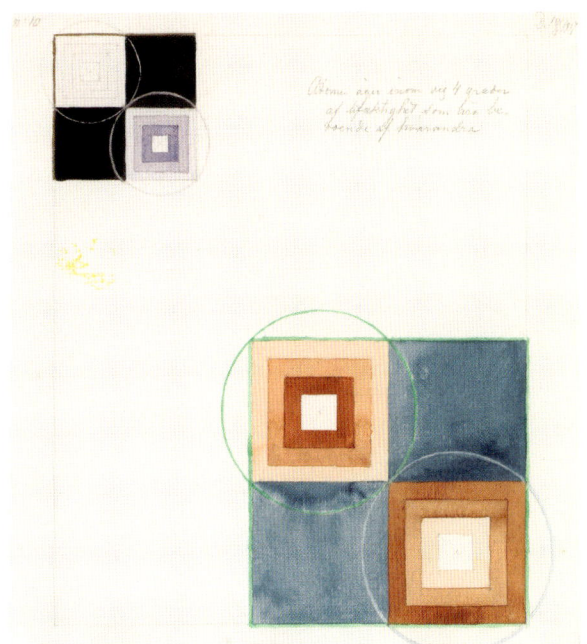

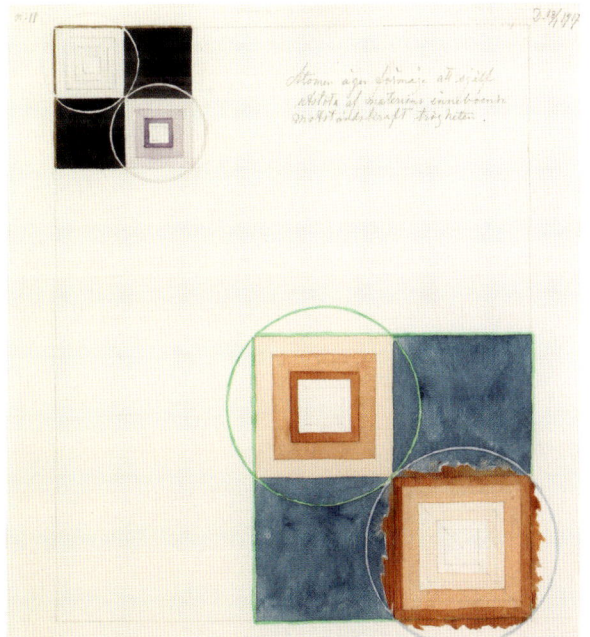

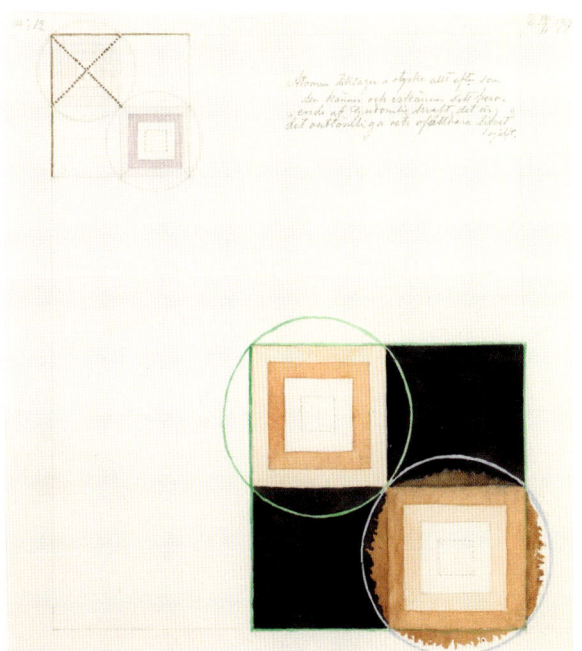

No. 13.
The atom is on its way to freely and deliberately transform
itself in observance with the Lord Jesus, who has paved the way for all humanity.

No. 14.
The atom has found the first means to release it from
downward-pulling forces; they are: "Reliability and Dutifulness."

No. 15.
The atom has found the second means, "Order and Cleanliness,"
which release it from downward-pulling forces.

No. 16.
The atom has found that Patience and Forbearance are absolute conditions for progress.

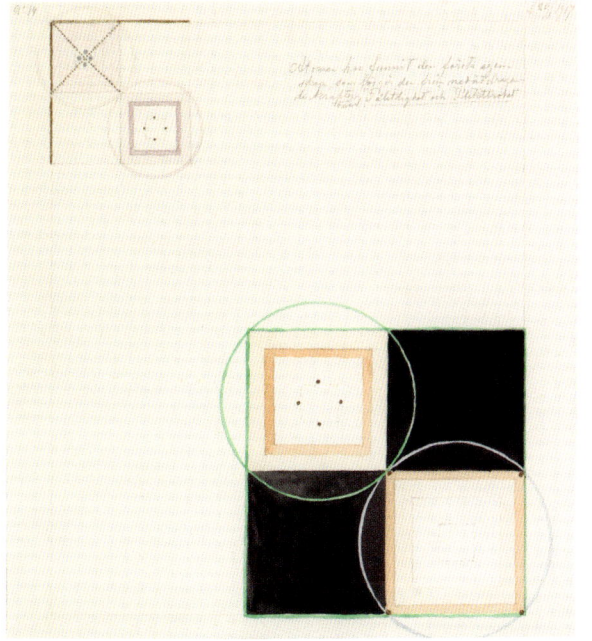

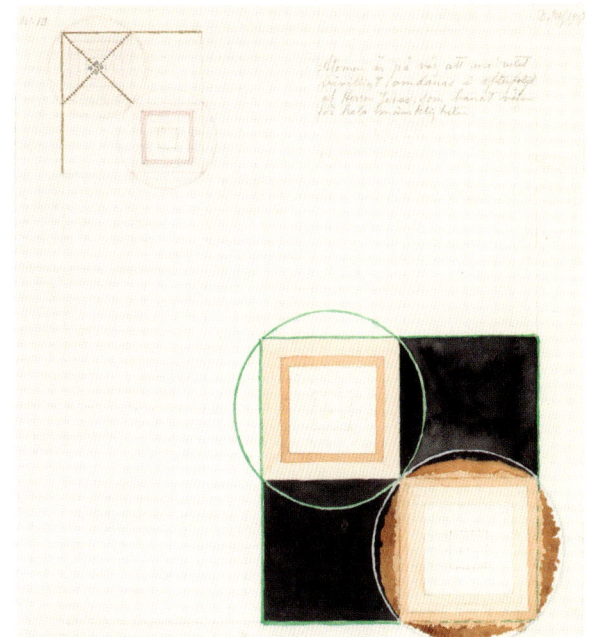

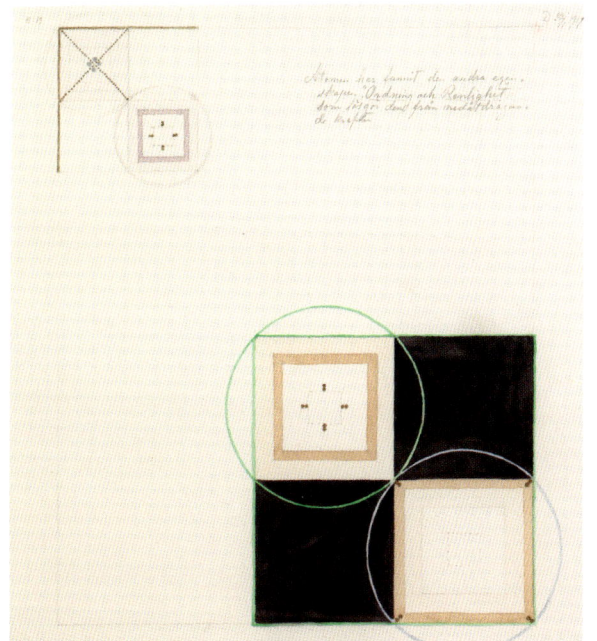

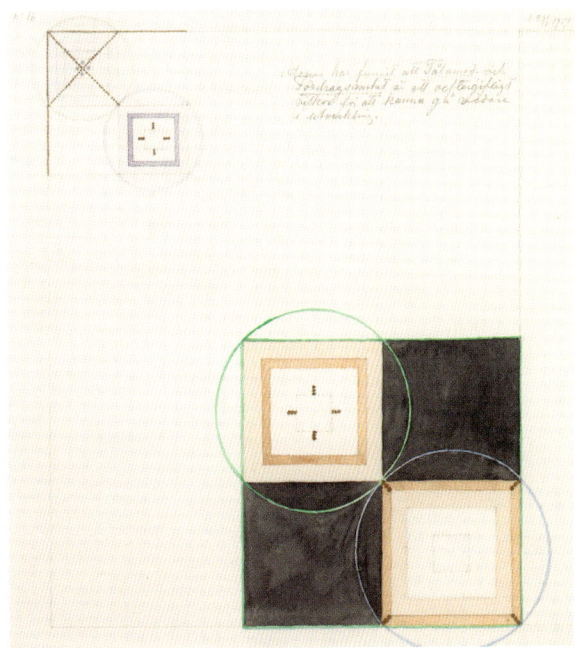

No. 17.
The atom has discovered the 4th quality, which will advance humanity.
Passionate thirst for activity and Stubborn tenacity.

No. 18.
The atom finds within itself Truth and Justice.

No. 19.
The atom releases Energy and pushes back Weakness.

No. 20.
The atom's Innocence is protected by All that is sacred and compassionate.

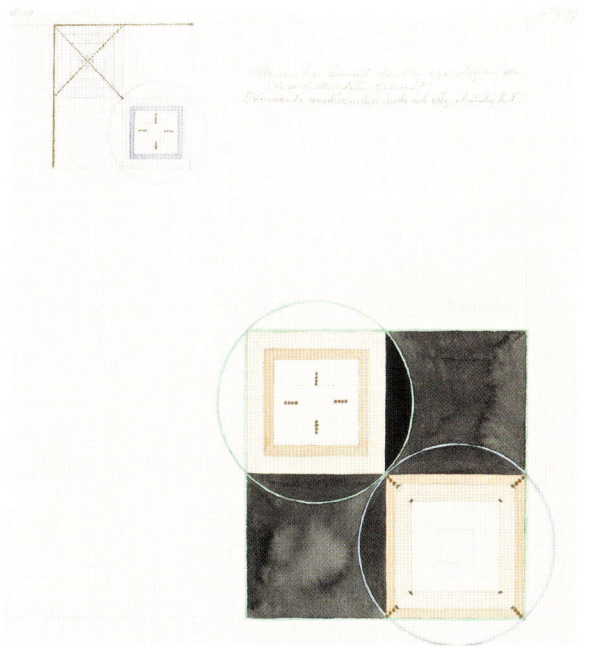

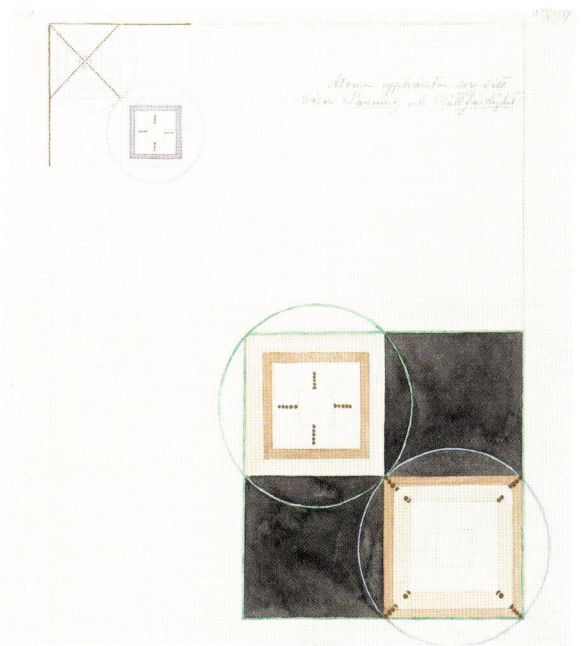

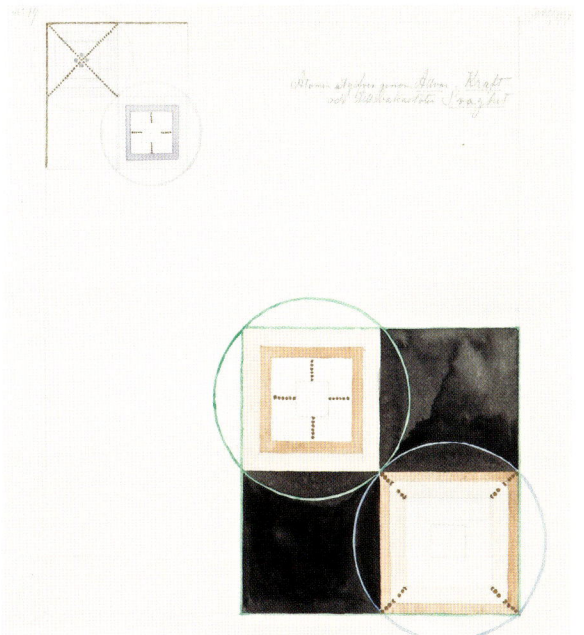

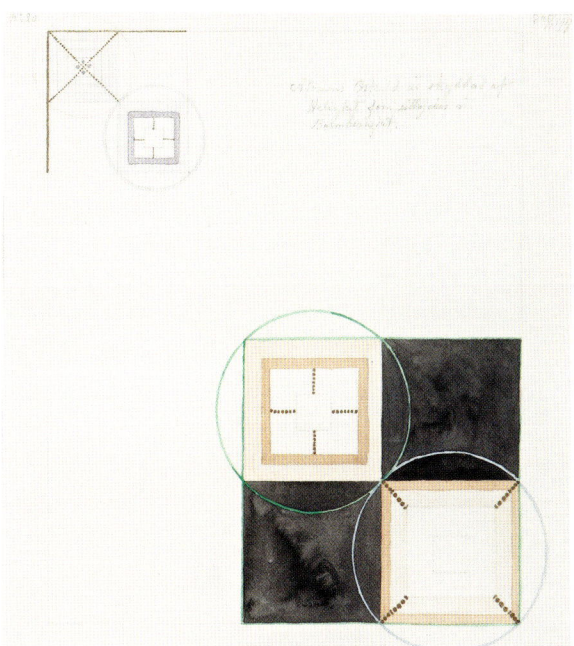

Flowers, Mosses, and Lichens

The facsimile of *Flowers, Mosses, and Lichens* on the following pages is a copy made by Hilma af Klint of a notebook she originally assembled in 1919–20. In 1927 she donated the original notebook to the archive of Natural Sciences at Rudolf Steiner's Goetheanum in Dornach. Af Klint became a member of Steiner's Anthroposophical Society in 1920. She traveled several times to Dornach to attend lectures, to study Goethe's color theory, and to seek in the archives of the Anthroposophists answers to the meaning of her own work—the latter to no avail. Although she had been disappointed in Steiner's inability to fully grasp the meaning in her work when he visited her studio in 1908, she seems to have continued to feel that he was one of the few with whom she could share her ideas and work. Her donation of *Flowers, Mosses, and Lichens* to the Steiner archive suggests that the content and the methods demonstrated in this notebook were of particular importance to her.

The original notebook was most likely created at af Klint's new studio in Munsö. Here af Klint once again took up the careful observations of the natural world that she had begun in the 1890s but now with a powerful new method of analysis. Moving beyond physical attributes, af Klint was able to access the energetic nature of each plant via the etheric plane. She researched 146 specimens, approximately one a day, developing an elaborate diagrammatic language to represent the energetic and emotional signature of each, a spiritual inventory of the world around her. About her hopes for this new project she wrote:

> *First I will try to understand the flowers of the earth . . . then I shall study with equal care that which lives in the waters of the world. Following that, the blue ether with all its variety of animal species will become the object of my study, and finally I shall penetrate the forest and study the damp moss, the trees, and the many animals that inhabit the cool, dark woods.* (7.1.1917, HaK 579, p. 84f)

Pages 161–245: *Flowers, Mosses, and Lichens* notebook HaK 588, 1919–20, 1927
Mixed media on paper, 8 × 6½ in. (20.5 × 16.5 cm)

Blumen, Moose
Flechten

von

Hilma af Klint

N:o 3675/48

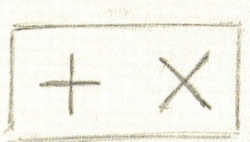

Blumen,
Moose und Flechten.

von Hilma af Klint

Die Originale im Archive
zu Goetheanum
Dornach

Flowers, Mosses, and Lichens, *by Hilma af Klint. The original is in the archive of the Goetheanum, Dornach.*

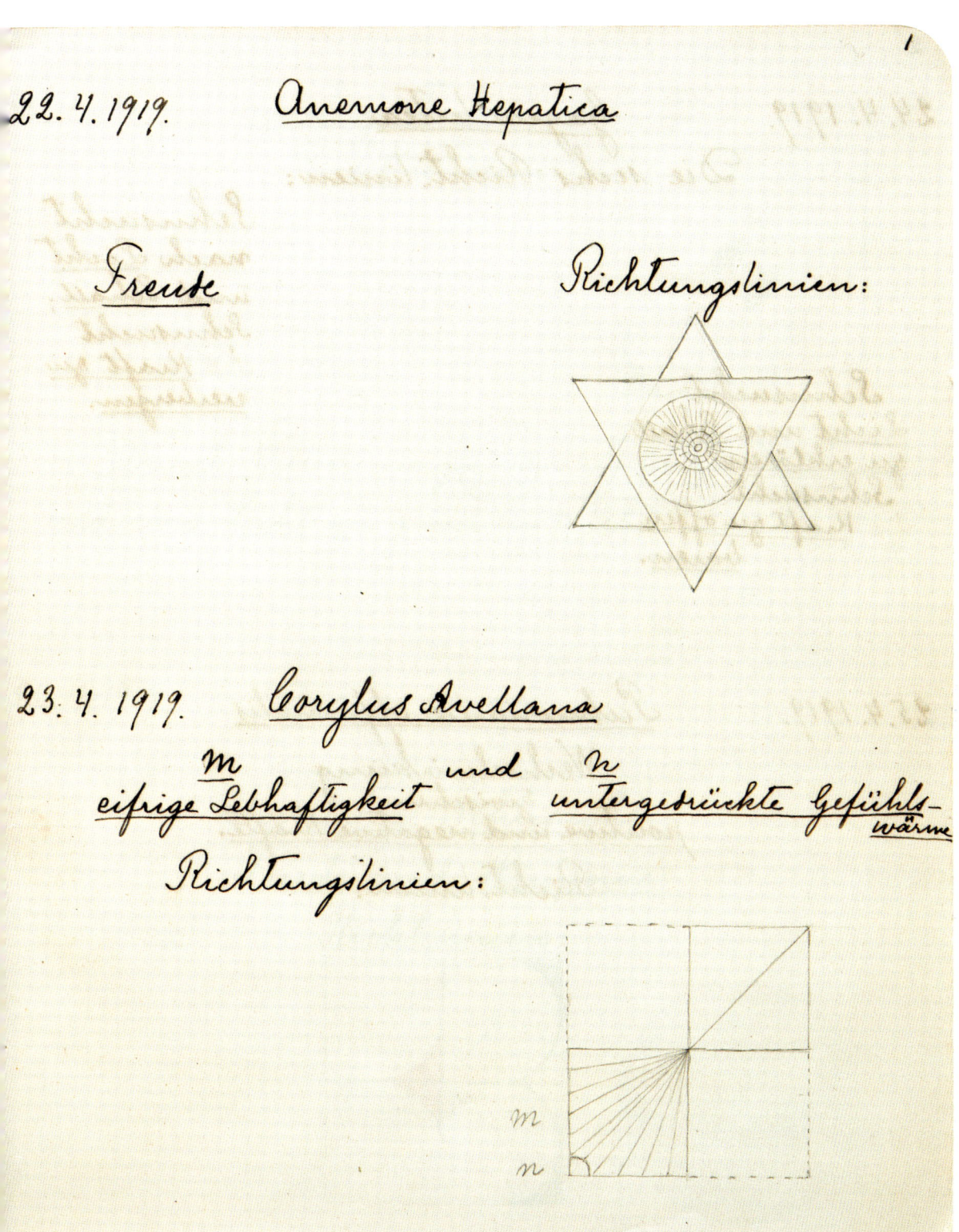

22. 4. 1919.   *Anemone Hepatica*

Freude   Richtungslinien:

23. 4. 1919.   *Corylus Avellana*

        m   n
eifrige Lebhaftigkeit   und   untergedrückte Gefühls-
                                              wärme

Richtungslinien:

m
n

4/22/1919. Anemone hepatica. *Joy. Direction lines:*

4/23/1919. Corylus avellana. *M: Eager liveliness and N: Repressed warmth of feeling. Direction lines:*

24. 4. 1919.

Gagea lutea
Die sechs Richt. linien:

Sehnsucht
Licht und Schall
zu erklären.
Sehnsucht
Kraft zu offen-
baren.

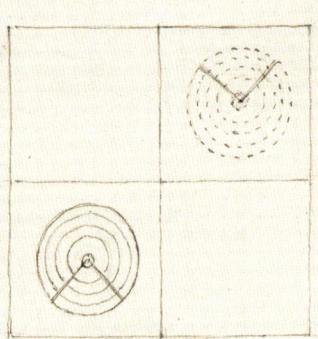

Sehnsucht
nach Licht
und Schall;
Sehnsucht
Kraft zu
verbergen.

25. 4. 1919.

Pulmonaria officinalis
Wechselwirkung
zwischen
positive und negative Kräfte.

Richt. linien:

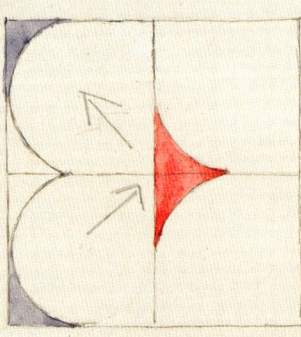

4/24/1919. Gagea lutea. The six direction lines: Longing for light and noise; longing to hide power.
Longing to explain light and noise. Longing to show power.

4/25/1919. Pulmonaria officinalis. Interplay between positive and negative forces. Direction lines:

26. 4. 1919.   Tussilago Farfara
Richt. linien:

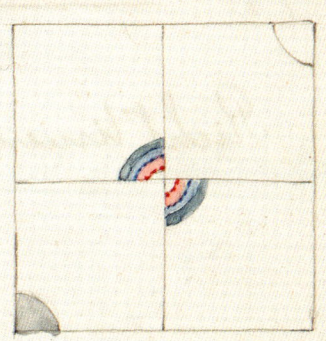

Durch Willensenergie von _Licht_ zu _Finsternis_,
und von _Licht_ zu grösserem _Licht_.

28. 4. 1919.   Draba verna

Demütige Sehnsucht
Friede und Harmonie
Richt: linien:

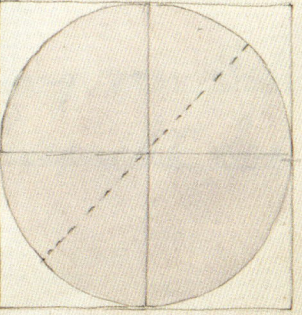

_4/26/1919._ Tussilago farfara. _Direction lines: Through the energy of the will from light to darkness, and from light to greater light._

_4/28/1919._ Draba verna. _Humble longing. Peace and harmony. Direction lines:_

4

29.4.1919. _Motacilla alba_ (Bachstelze)

Richt. linien:

Hitzigkeit
wegen unruhiges, un-
beständiges Aufnehm
der Lichtflut.

30. 4. 1919. _Pulsatilla vulgaris_

Wehmut und Hoffnung

Richt. linien:

4/29/1919. Motacilla alba *(Wagtail). Direction lines: Heat because of unquiet, inconstant reception of the stream of light.*

4/30/1919. Pulsatilla vulgaris. *Melancholy and hope. Direction lines:*

168

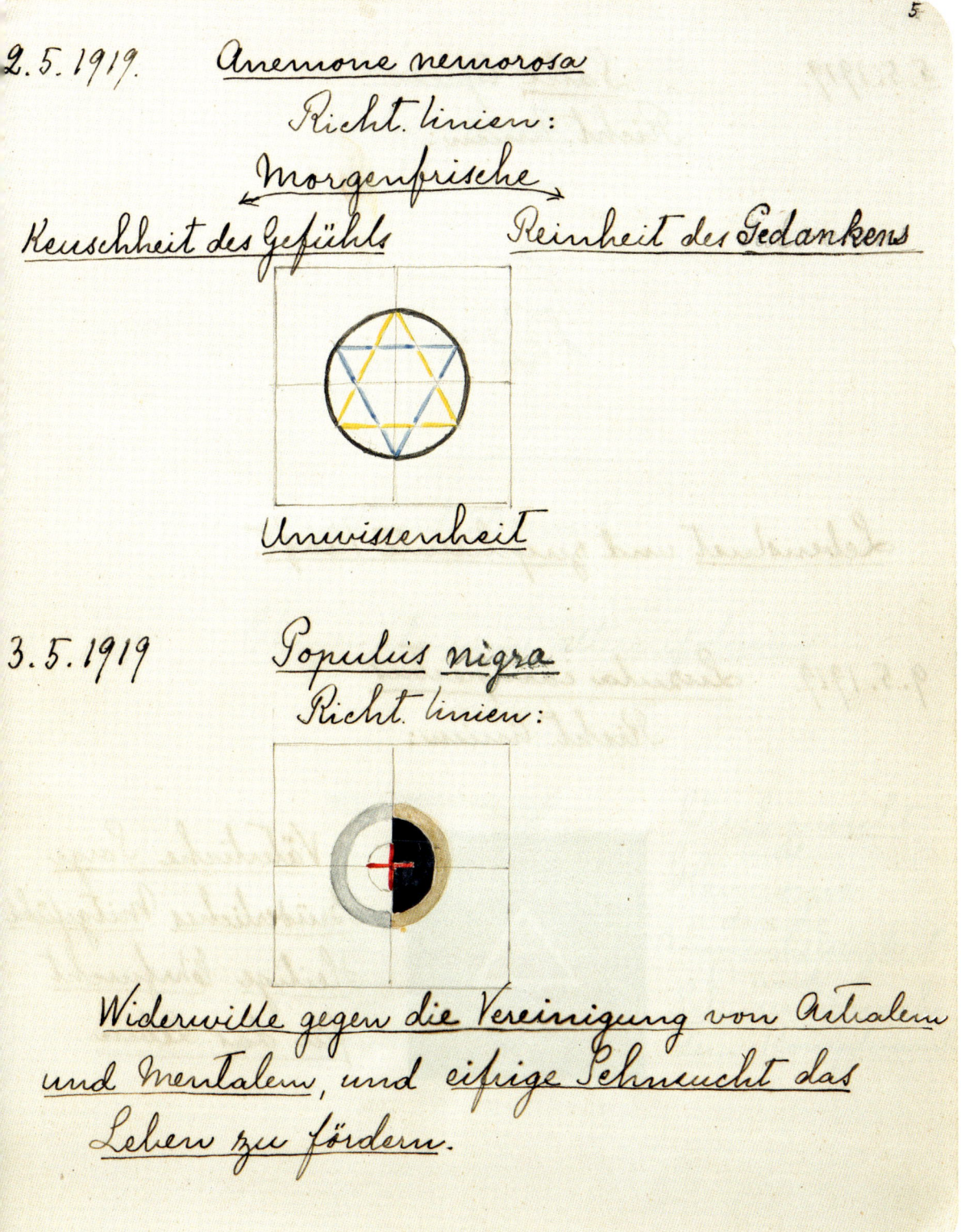

2.5.1919.

Anemone nemorosa

Richt. linien:

Morgenfrische

Keuschheit des Gefühls   Reinheit des Gedankens

Unwissenheit

3.5.1919

Populus nigra

Richt. linien:

Widerwille gegen die Vereinigung von Astralem und Mentalem, und eifrige Sehnsucht das Leben zu fördern.

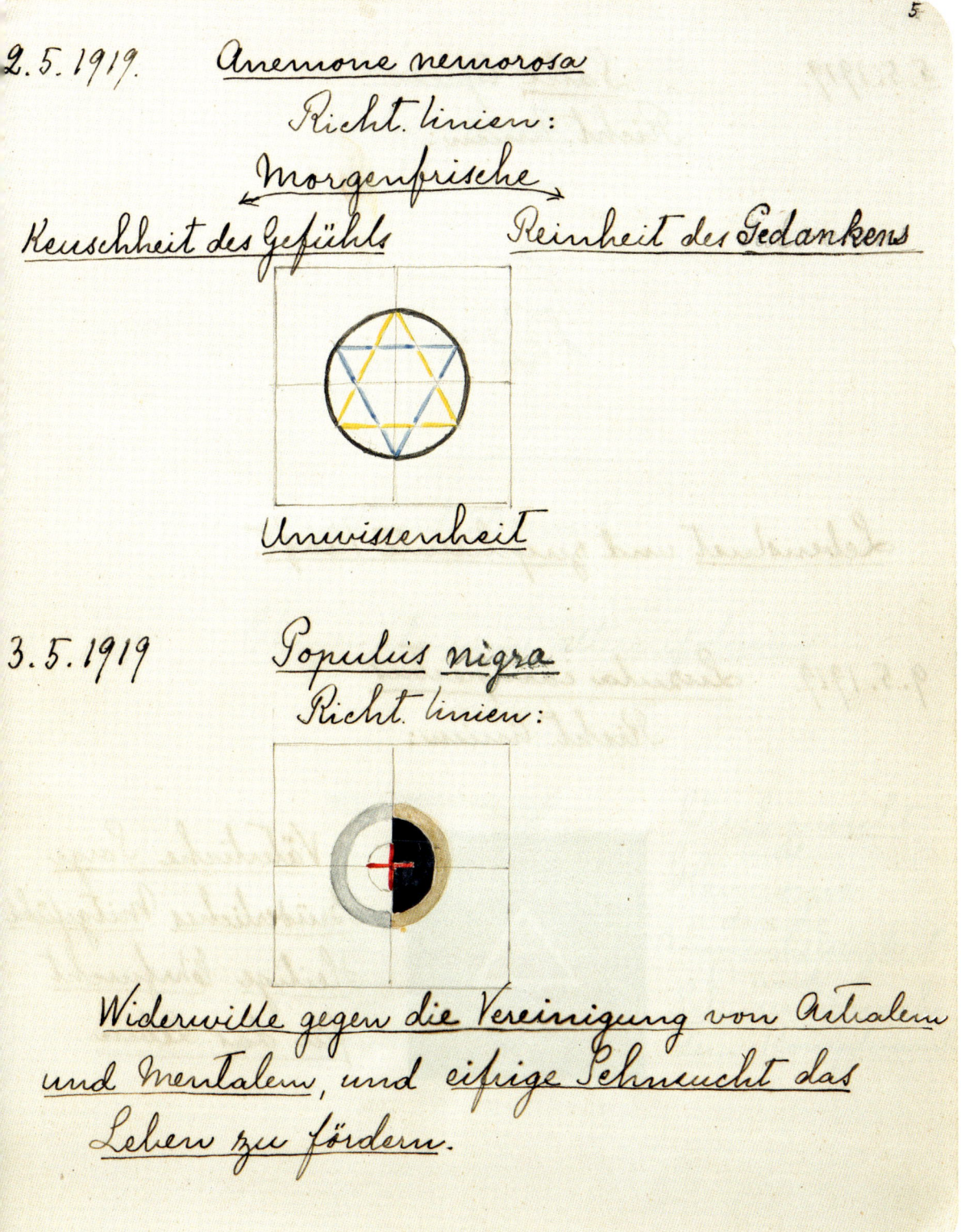

5/2/1919. Anemone nemorosa. *Direction lines: Morning freshness. Chasteness of feeling. Purity of thought. Ignorance.*

5/3/1919. Populus nigra. *Direction lines: Aversion to the union of the astral and the mental, and eager longing to promote life.*

5.5.1919.

Salix caprea
Richt. linien:

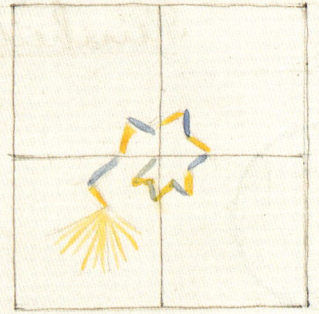

Lebenslust und zersplitterte Kraft.

9.5.1919. *Luzula campestris*
Richt. linien:

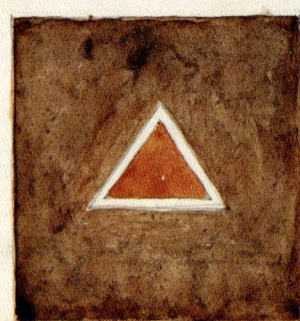

Väterliche Sorge
Brüderliches Mitgefühl
Heilige Ehrfurcht
für das Leben

5/5/1919. Salix caprea. *Direction lines: Love of life and fragmented power.*

5/9/1919. Luzula campestris. *Direction lines: Paternal care. Brotherly sympathy. Holy reverence for life.*

10.5.1919.

Viola hirta
Viola odorata
Richt. linien:

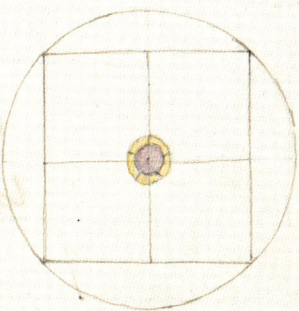

Willenskraft und Demut

12.5.1919.

Chrysosplenium alternifolium
Richt. linien:

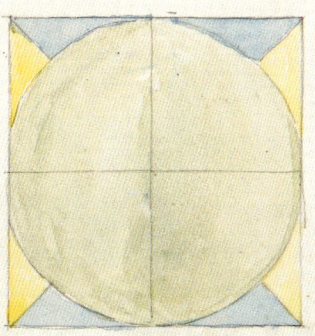

Gleichgewicht
und
Harmonie
durch
Anspruchslosigkeit
und
Sehnsucht nach
dem Komplement.

5/10/1919. Viola hirta. *Viola odorata. Direction lines: Willpower and humility.*

5/12/1919. Chrysosplenium alternifolium. *Direction lines: Balance and harmony through modesty and longing for the complement.*

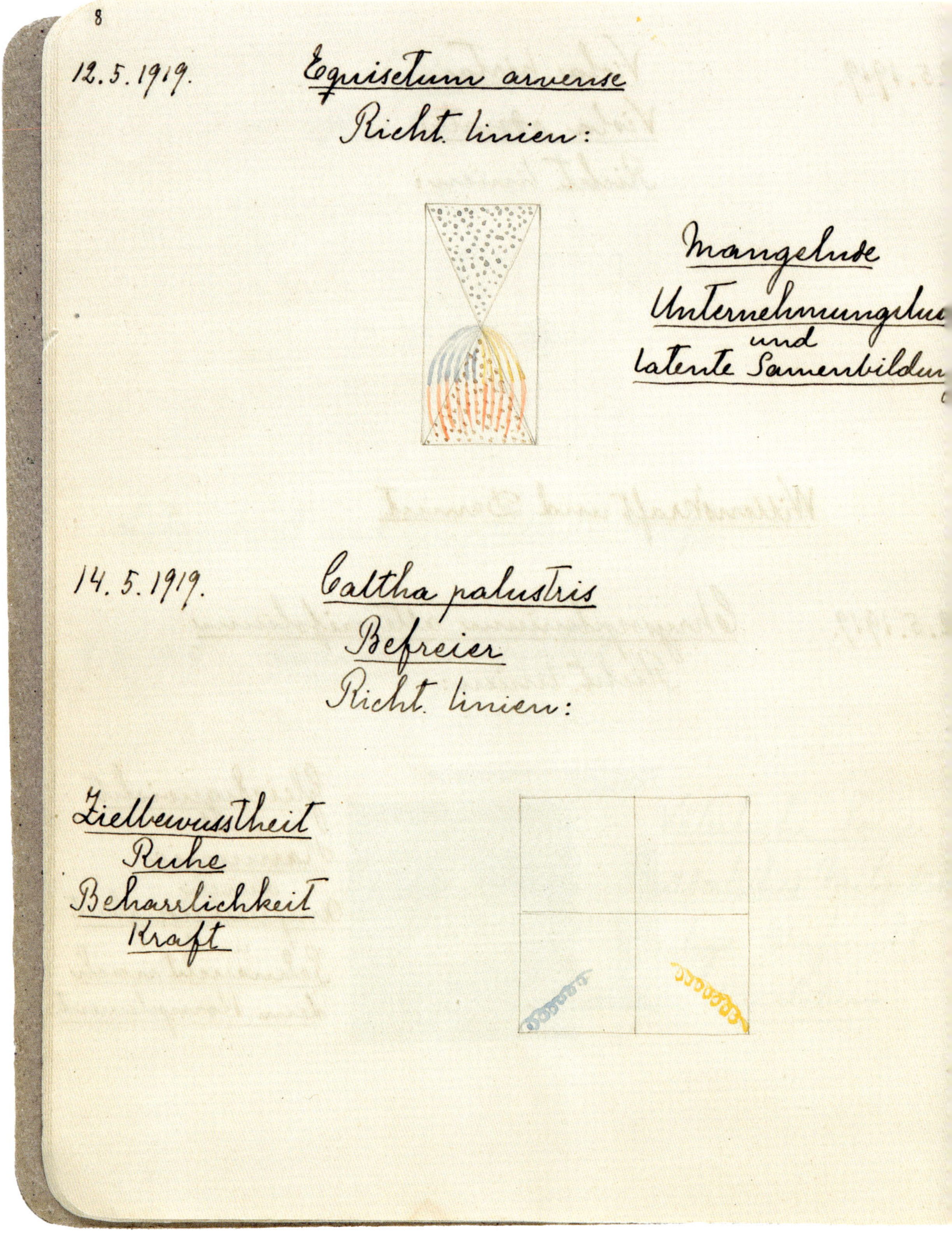

12.5.1919.

Equisetum arvense
Richt. linien:

Mangelnde
Unternehmungelun
und
latente Samenbildun

14.5.1919.

Caltha palustris
Befreier
Richt. linien:

Zielbewusstheit
Ruhe
Beharrlichkeit
Kraft

5/12/1919. Equisetum arvense. *Direction lines: Lack of enterprise and latent seed formation.*

5/14/1919. Caltha palustris. *Liberator. Direction lines: Purposefulness. Calm. Persistence. Power.*

4. 5. 1919.

<u>Ficaria ranunculoides</u>

<u>Befreier</u>

Richt. linien:

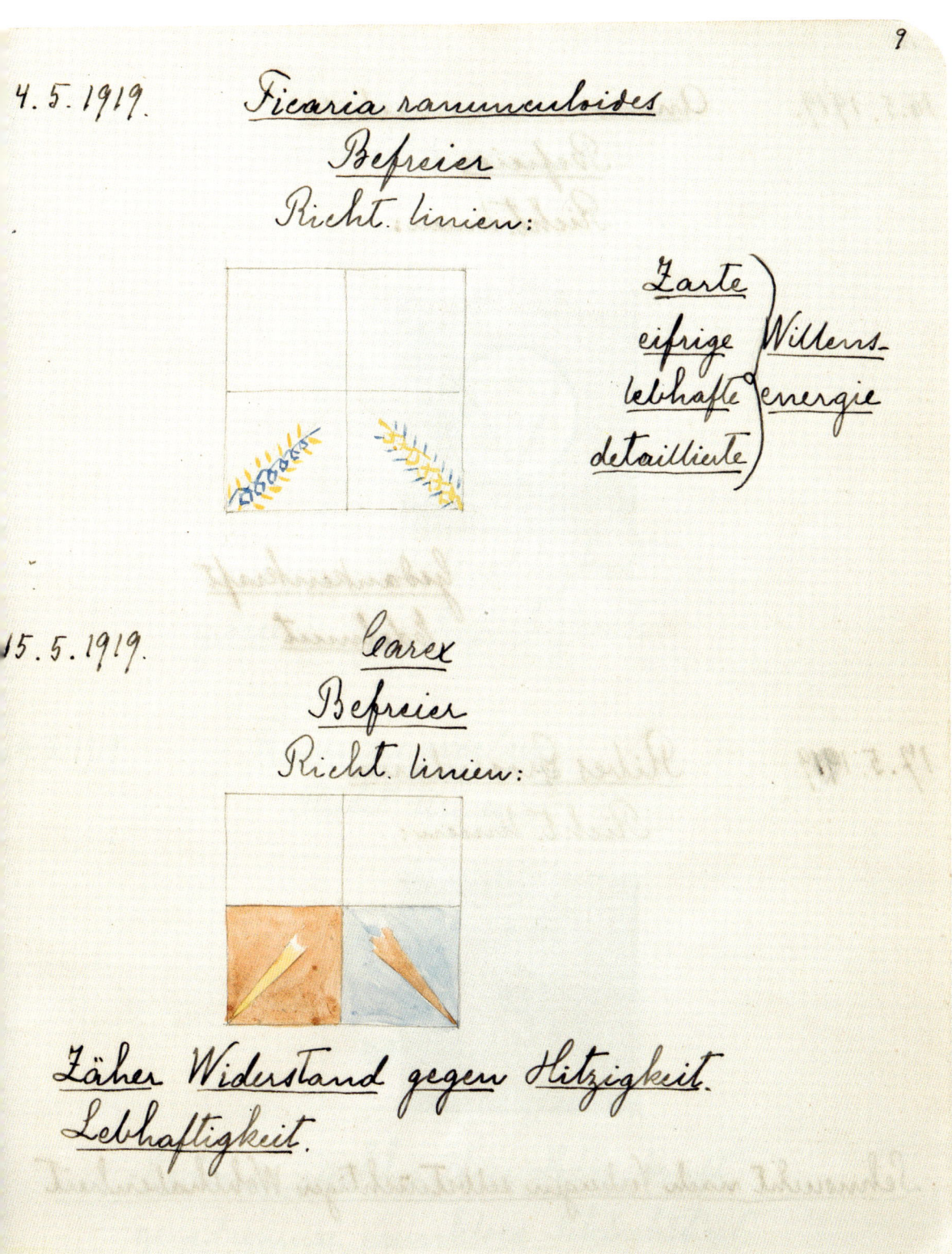

<u>Zarte</u>
eifrige Willens-
lebhafte Energie
detaillierte

15. 5. 1919.

<u>Carex</u>

<u>Befreier</u>

Richt. linien:

<u>Zäher Widerstand gegen Hitzigkeit.</u>

<u>Lebhaftigkeit.</u>

5/14/1919. Ficaria ranunculoides. *Liberator. Direction lines: Tender, eager, lively detailed Energy of the will.*

5/15/1919. Carex. *Liberator. Direction lines: Tough resistance to heat. Liveliness.*

16.5.1919.

Anemone ranunculoides

Befreier

Richt. linien:

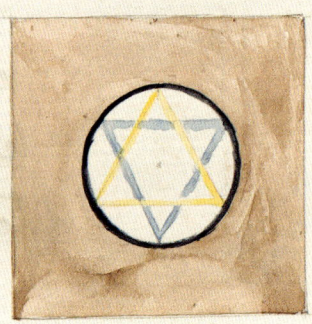

Gedankenkraft

Edelmut

17.5.1919

Ribes Grossularia

Richt. linien:

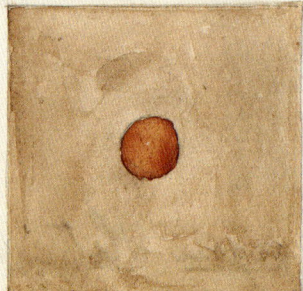

Sehnsucht nach Verbergen selbstsüchtiger Wohlhabenheit

5/16/1919. Anemone ranunculoides. *Liberator. Direction lines: Mind power. Generosity.*

5/17/1919. Ribes grossularia. *Direction lines: Longing to hide selfish prosperity.*

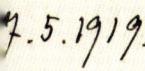

 7.5.1919.

Ribes alpinum
Richt. linien:

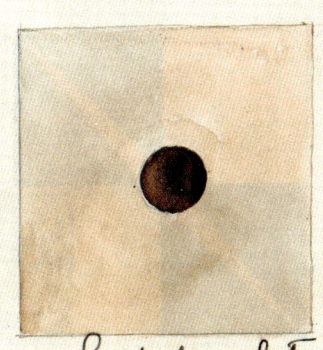

Weniger Selbstsüchtigkeit,
grössere Gleichgültigkeit.

9.5.1919.

Fraxinus excelsior
Richt. linien:

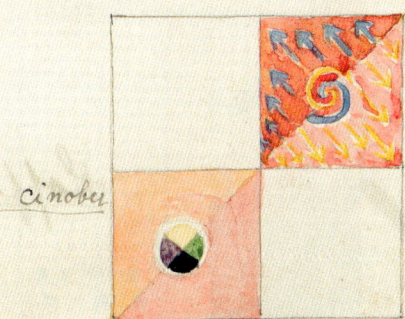

cinober

Siedende, rückhaltlose Lebenskraft,
geradsinnige, prunklose Schlichtheit.

5/17/1919. Ribes alpinum. *Direction lines: Less selfishness. Greater indifference.*

5/19/1919. Fraxinus excelsior. *Direction lines: Seething, wholehearted life force, upright, unostentatious plainness.*

19.5.1919.

Populus Tremula
Richt. linien:

Gehorsam

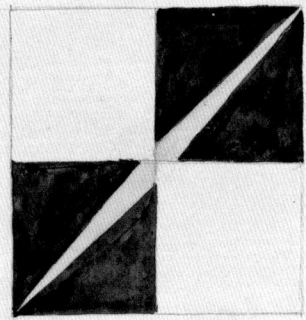

Demut

20.5.1919.

Larix decidua
Richt. linien:

Hoffnung

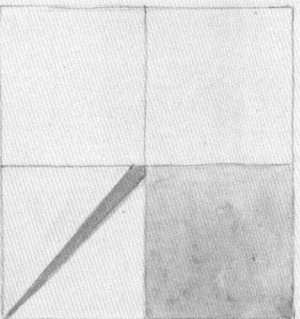

Glaube an das Leben,
des Totes vergesslich

5/19/1919. Populus tremula. *Direction lines: Obedience. Humility.*

5/20/1919. Larix decidua. *Direction lines: Hope. Belief in life, forgetful of death.*

21. 5. 1919.

Ribes rubrum
Richt. linien:

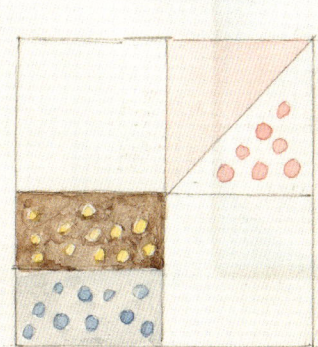

Der Wertmesser
und Verbesserer
des Magensaftes.

21. 5. 1919.

Ribes nigrum
Richt. linien:

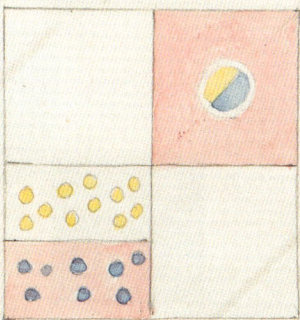

Erreichte Fähigkeit den Geschmacksinn zu beherrschen.

5/21/1919. Ribes rubrum. *Direction lines: Measure of value and improver of the gastric juices.*

5/21/1919. Ribes nigrum. *Direction lines: Achievement of the ability to control the sense of taste.*

23.5.1919.

Prunus spinosa

Richt. linien:

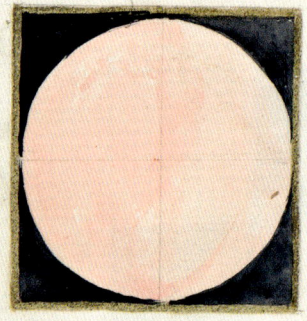

Die Unbestechlichkeit des Gesetzes.
Die Unerschöpflichkeit des Evangeliums.

23.5.1919. *Lepidoptera* (Schmetterling)

← Beispiel der Gattung:

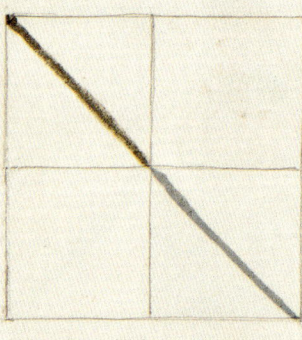 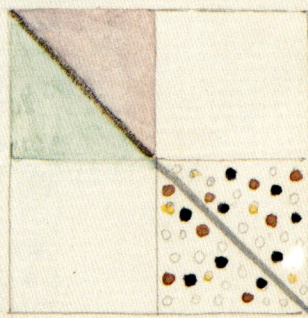

Beispiel der Art.

5/23/1919. Prunus spinosa. *Direction lines: The incorruptibility of the law. The inexhaustibility of the gospel.*

5/23/1919. Lepidoptera *(butterfly). Example of the genus. Example of the species.*

5. 5. 1919. Acer platanoides
Richt. linien:

m

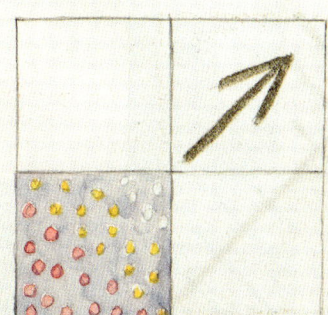

m

Schöpfungssehnsucht in feineren Materie.

26. 5. 1919. Quercus Robur
Richt. linien:

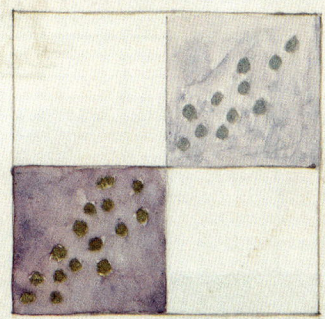

Ernst – unbestechliche Willenskraft.
Ruhe – Demut

5/25/1919. Acer platanoides. *Direction lines: M. M. Longing for creation in finer matter.*

5/26/1919. Quercus robur. *Direction lines: Seriousness—incorruptible willpower. Calm—humility.*

27.5.1919.

Bombus (Hummel)

Richt. linien:

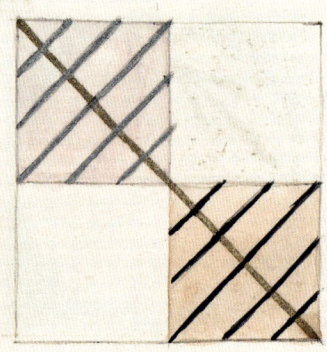

Der Kampf gegen körperliche Trägheit.

27.5.1919

Prunus Padus

Richt. linien:

Einwohnende Kraft
Gebrauch der Kraft
Der Schöpfungsakt

Redliche Unwissenheit
Lust zu herrschen
Abgeneigtheit

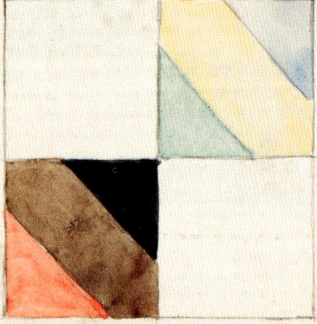

5/27/1919. Bombus (bumblebee). Direction lines: The struggle against physical dullness.

5/27/1919. Prunus padus. Direction lines: Inhabitant power. Use of power. The act of creation.
Candid ignorance. Desire to dominate. Disinclination.

28.5.1919.

Prunus cerasus

Richt. linien:

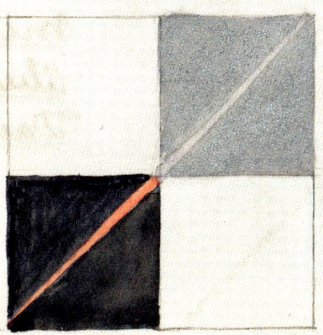

<u>Befreier derjenigen Darmbakterien und Infusorien, die durch animalischen Nahrungsmitteln herbeigeführt werden.</u>

28.5.1919.

Prunus avium

Richt. linien:

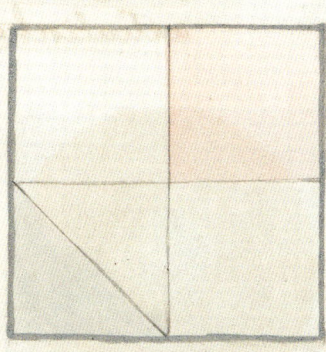

<u>Güte</u>

<u>Sehnsucht nach dem neutralisieren der Säuren des Magensaftes</u>

5/28/1919. Prunus cerasus. *Direction lines: Liberator of the intestinal bacteria and infusiora that are caused by animal foodstuffs.*

5/28/1919. Prunus avium. *Direction lines: Good. Longing for the neutralization of the gastric juice acids.*

30.5.1919.

Vaccinium Myrtillus
Richt. linien:

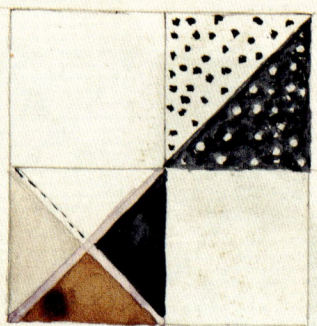

Mitgefühl für
überanstrengte
Darmkanäle.

Sehnsucht nach Mässigung
der febrilen Wirksamkeit
der Gedärme.

31.5.1919.

Pyrus communis
Richt. linien:

Gib mir Aufklärung
über meine
astralische Schwäche.

Hilf mir, die
Niere bei der
Menschheit
zu verbessern.

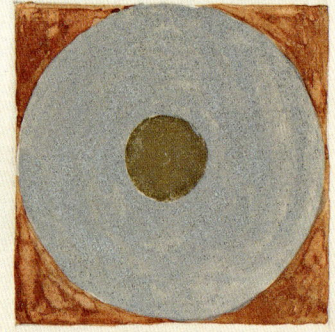

5/30/1919. Vaccinium myrtillus. *Direction lines: Sympathy for the overworked digestive tract.*
Longing for mitigation of the febrile effectiveness of the intestines.

5/31/1919. Pyrus communis. *Direction lines: Give me enlightenment about my astral weakness.*
Help me to improve the kidneys of humanity.

31.5.1919.

Pyrus Malus

Richt. linien:

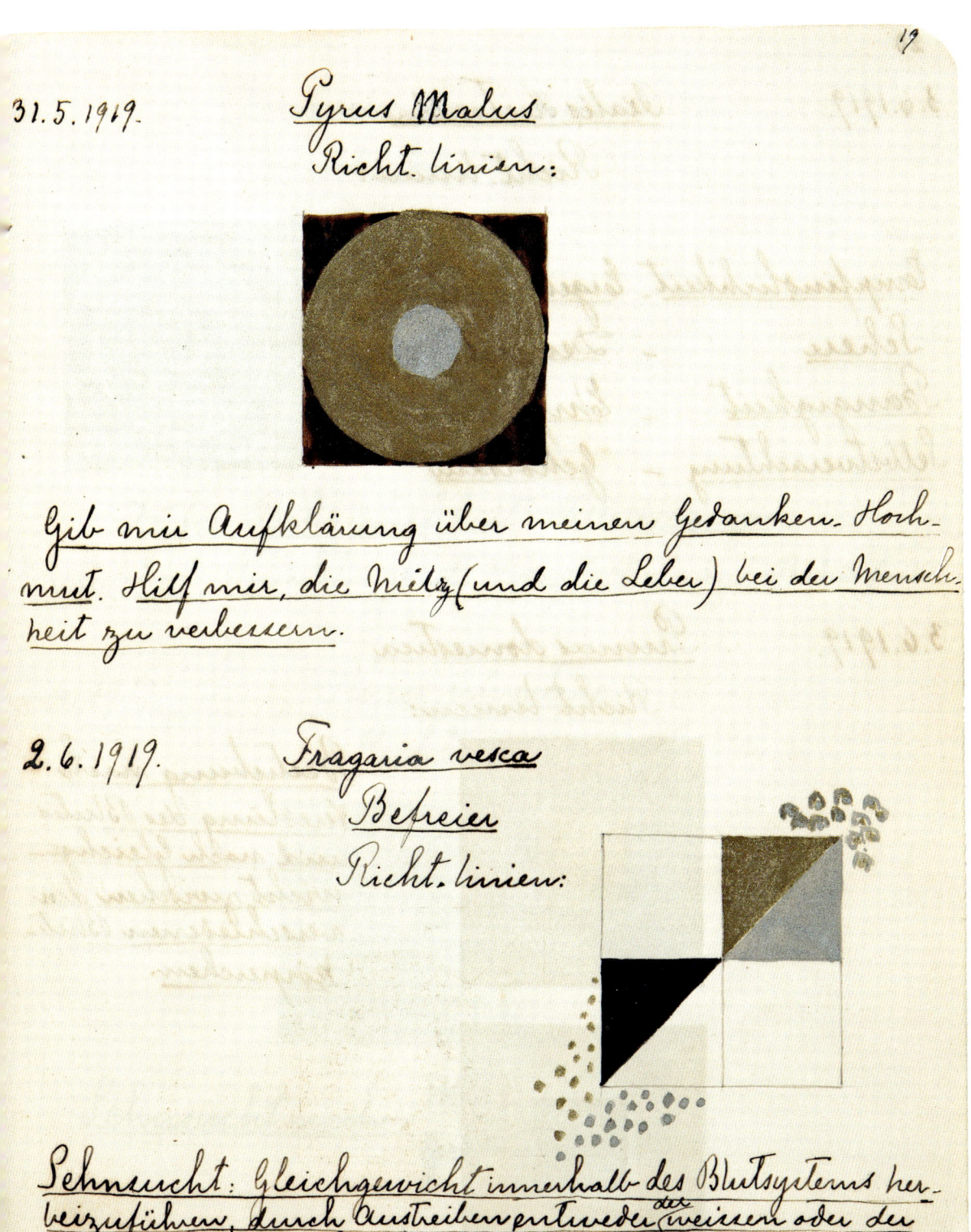

Gib mir Aufklärung über meinen Gedanken. Hoch-
mut. Hilf mir, die Milz (und die Leber) bei der Menschheit zu verbessern.

2.6.1919.

Fragaria vesca

Befreier

Richt. linien:

Sehnsucht: Gleichgewicht innerhalb des Blutsystems her-
beizuführen, durch Austreiben entweder der weissen oder der
roten Blutkörperchen.

*5/31/1919. Pyrus malus. Direction lines: Give me enlightenment about my thoughts.
Arrogance. Help me to improve the spleen (and the liver) of humanity.*

*6/2/1919. Fragaria vesca. Liberator. Direction lines: Longing: To cause balance within
the blood system by driving out either the white or red blood cells.*

3.6.1919.

Oxalis Acetosella
Richt. linien:

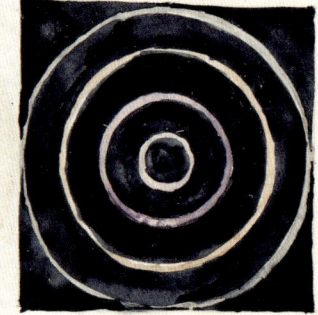

Empfindlichkeit — Ergebenheit
Scheu — Demut
Bangigkeit — Ehrfurcht
Selbstverachtung — Gehorsam

3.6.1919.

Prunus domestica
Richt. linien:

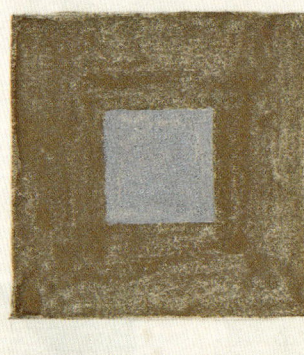

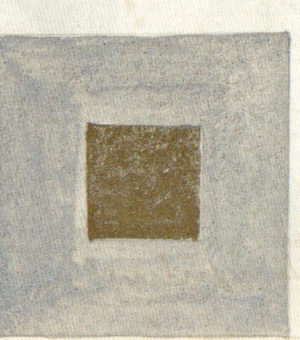

Bestrebung nach Veredlung des Blutes und nach Gleichgewicht zwischen den verschiedenen Blutkörperchen.

6/3/1919. Oxalis acetosella. *Direction lines: Sensitivity—Devotion. Timidity—Humility. Trepidation—Reverence. Self-contempt—Obedience.*

6/3/1919. Prunus domestica. *Direction lines: Effort to refine the blood and to achieve balance between the various blood cells.*

4.6.1919.

Juniperus communis

Richt. linien:

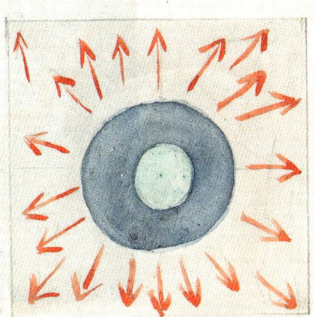

<u>Zähe</u>, <u>Beharrlichkeit</u>, <u>Willensenergie</u>,
<u>Ehrlichkeit</u>, <u>Prunklosigkeit</u>, <u>Komplettierüngs-Bedürfnis</u>.

5.6.1919.

Pinus silvestris

Richt. linien:

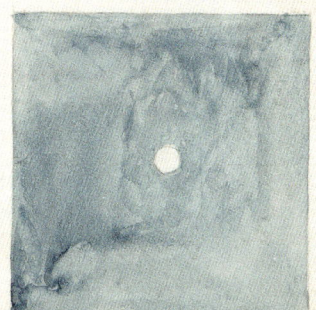

<u>Sehnsucht nach</u>: <u>Wahrheit</u>
<u>Gerechtigkeit</u>

6/4/1919. Juniperus communis. *Direction lines: Tenacity, persistence, energy of the will, honesty, lack of ostentation, need for completion.*

6/5/1919. Pinus sylvestris. *Direction lines: Longing for: Truth. Justice.*

5.6.1919. *Pseudoneuroptera* (Libelle)

Richt. linien:

Gattung Allzu kräftige Willensanstrengung bei dem Schöpfungsakt tötet die eigene Form.

Art: Variation des Typus, Intensive Lebensfreude, Unfähigkeit zu benutzen die Körperliche Trägheit als Schutz des Körpers.

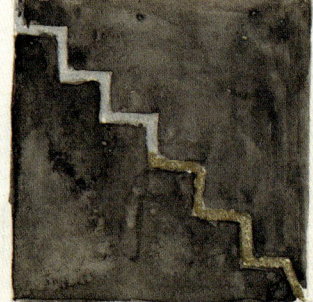

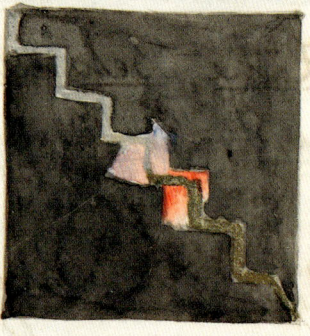

6/5/1919. Pseudoneroptera (dragonfly). Direction lines: Genus: Overly powerful effort of the will during the act of creation kills one's own form. Species: Variation in type, intense lust for life, inability to use physical dullness as the body's protection.

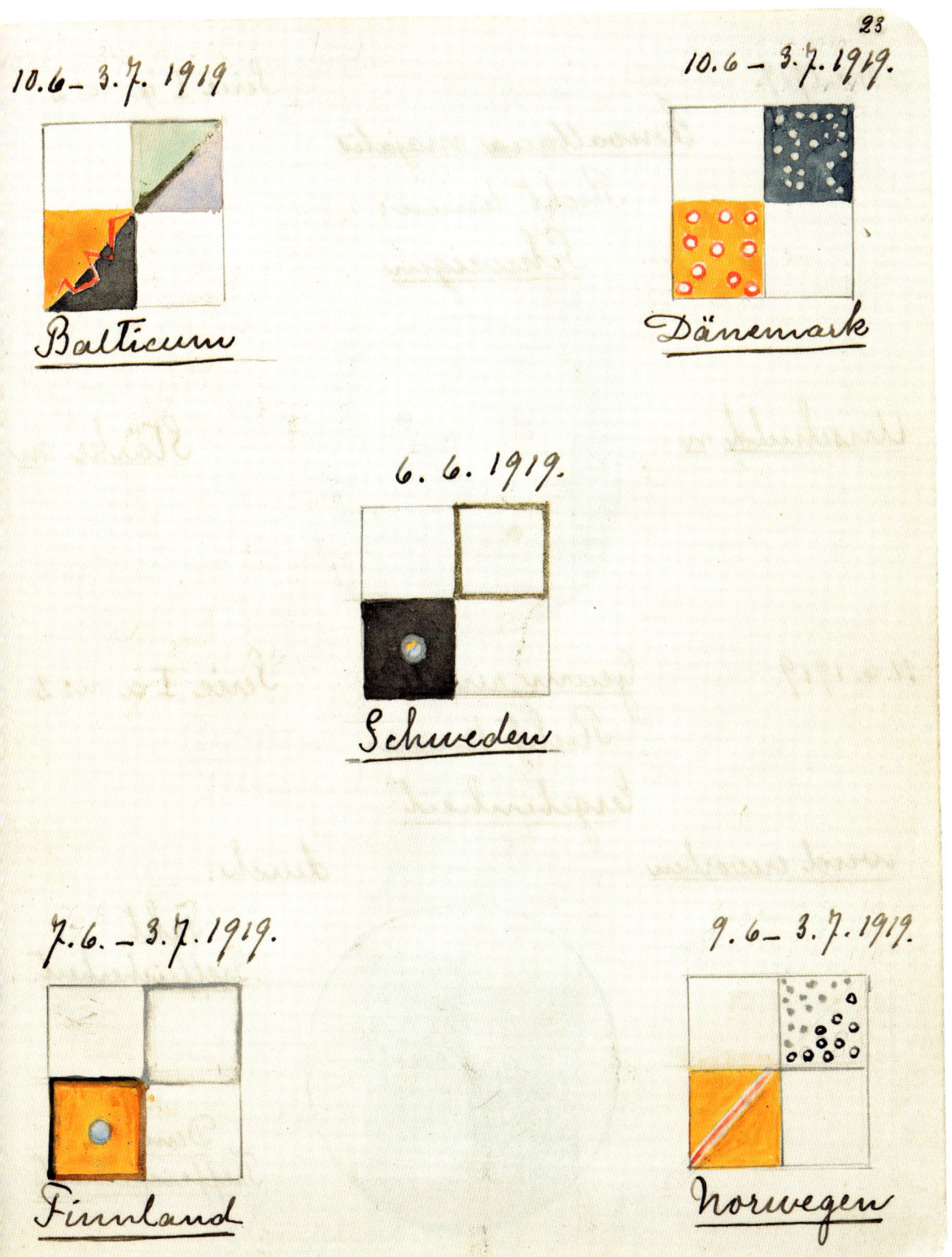

10.6 – 3.7. 1919

Balticum

10.6 – 3.7. 1919.

Dänemark

6. 6. 1919.

Schweden

7.6. – 3.7. 1919.

Finnland

9.6. – 3.7. 1919.

Norwegen

6/10–7/3/1919. The Baltics. 6/10–7/3/1919. Denmark. 6/6/1919. Sweden. 6/7–7/3/1919. Finland. 6/9–7/3/1919. Norway

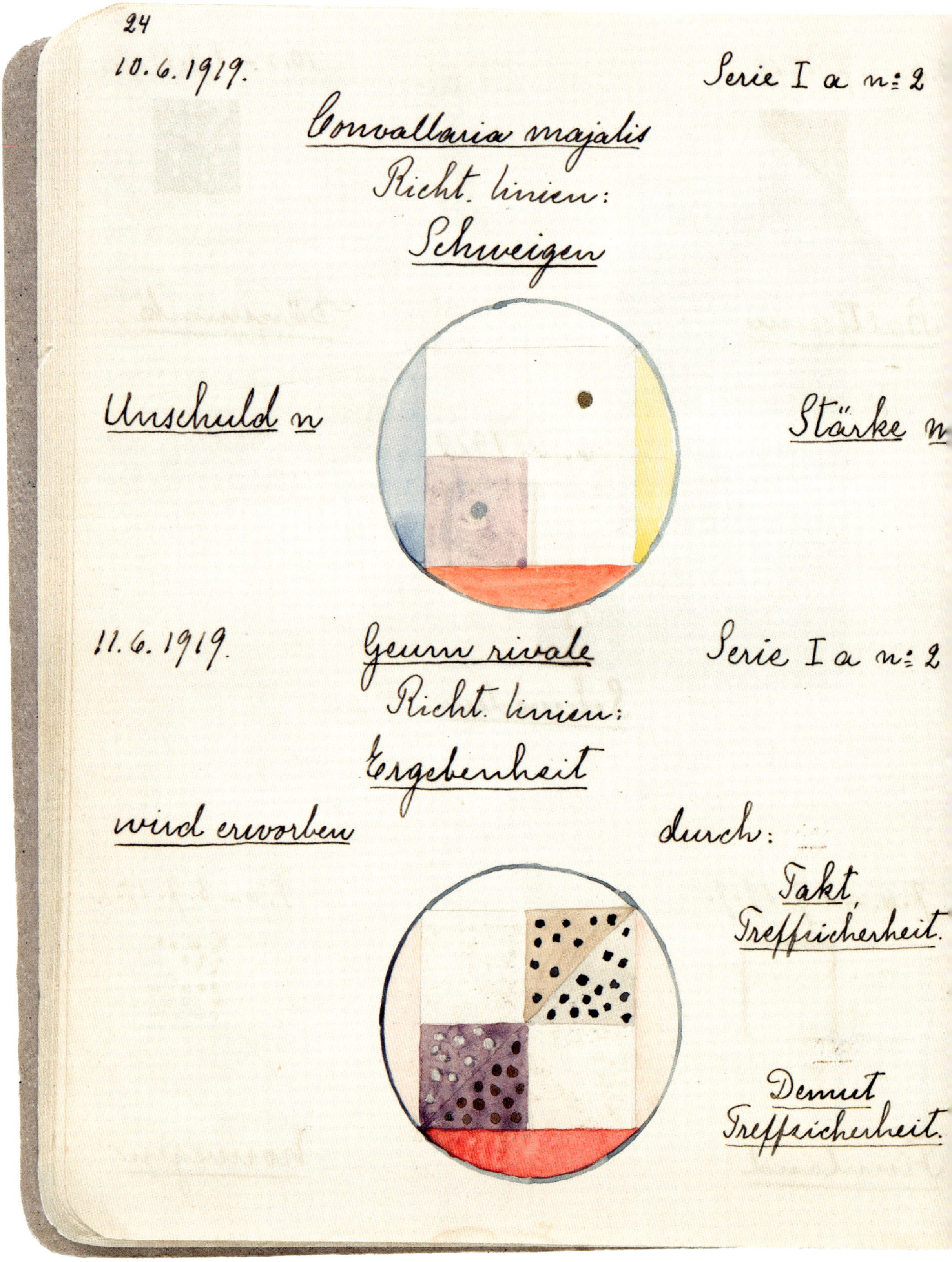

24

10.6.1919.

Serie I a n: 2

Convallaria majalis
Richt. linien:
Schweigen

Unschuld n

Stärke n

11.6.1919.

Geum rivale
Richt. linien:
Ergebenheit

wird erworben

durch:

Takt,
Treffsicherheit.

Demut
Treffsicherheit.

6/10/1919. Series I a no. 2. Convallaria majalis. *Direction lines: Silence. Innocence. n. Strength.*

6/11/1919. Series I a no.2. Geum rivale. *Direction lines: Devotion is acquired through: Timing, accuracy. Humility, accuracy.*

1.6.1919.

Polygala vulgaris

Richt. linien:

Demut

Vorsicht
Treffsicherheit

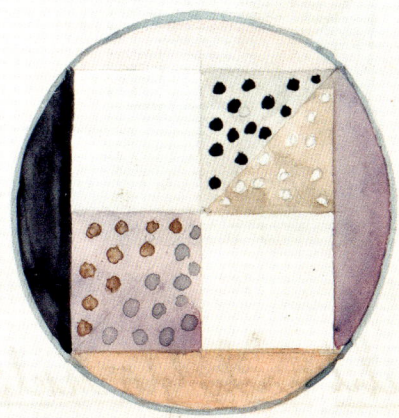

Takt
Treffsicherheit

12.6.1919.

Aesculus hippocastanum
(stammt von Tibet)

Richtlinien:

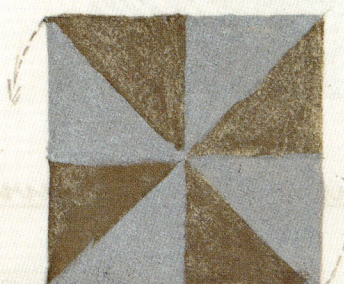

Sehnsucht nach Licht.

6/11/1919. Series I a no. 2. Polygala vulgaris. *Direction lines: Humility. Caution. Accuracy. Timing. Accuracy.*

6/12/1919. Series I a no. 3. Aesculus hippocastanum *(comes from Tibet). Direction lines: Longing for light.*

13.6.1919.   Paris quadrifolia   Serie I a no. 4
Richt. linien:

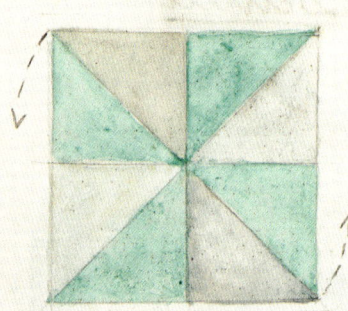

Sehnsucht nach Glückseligkeit

14.6.1919   Lonicera xylosteum   Serie I a no. 4
Richt. linien:

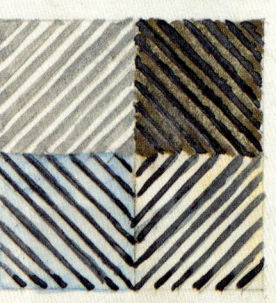

svart

lineair
indigo

lineair
indigo

Erstreben zum Gleichgewicht

Serie I a no. 4 Equisetum arvense, s. Seite 8

6/13/1919. Series I a no. 4. Paris quadrifolia. *Direction lines: Longing for bliss.*

6/14/1919. Series I a no. 4. Paris quadrifolia. *Direction lines: Aspiration for balance. Series I a no. 4. Equisteum arvense, see page 8.*

6.6.1919.   *Sorbus scandica*   Serie I a n° 5

Richt. linien:

Despotismus

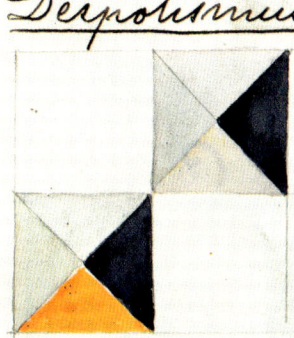

Eifer führt Schlaffheit herbei.
Kraft kann Schwäche herbeiführen.

17.6.1919.   Serie I a n° 5

Veronica Chamaedrys

Richt. linien:

Kraft- Überführung

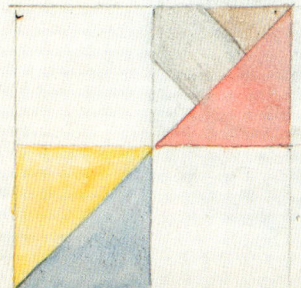

6/16/1919. Series I a no. 5. Sorbus scandica. *Direction lines: Despotism. Eagerness causes limpness. Power can cause weakness.*

6/17/1919. Series I a no. 5. Veronica chameadrys. *Direction lines: Power-conversion.*

17.6.1919.   Potentilla Tormentilla   Serie I a, n⁰ 5

Richt. linien:

Unschuld

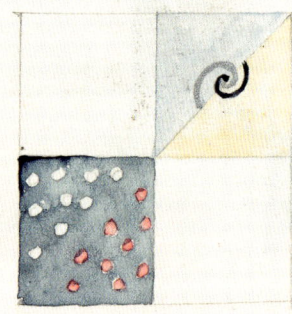

18.6.1919.   Viburnum Opulus   Serie I a n⁰ 6

Richt. linien:

Ungehorsam

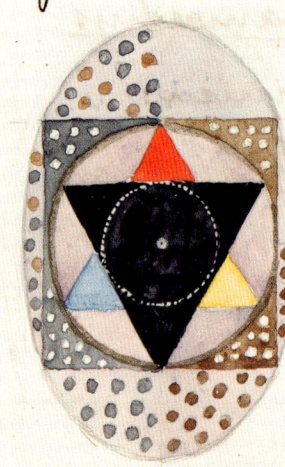

6/17/1919. Series I a. no. 5. Potentilla tormentilla. *Direction lines: Innocence.*

6/18/1919. Series I a. no. 6. Viburnum opulus. *Direction lines: Disobedience.*

6. 19.19. **Melampyrum silvaticum**   Serie I a n̲ᵒ 6

Richt. linien:

Bescheidenheit

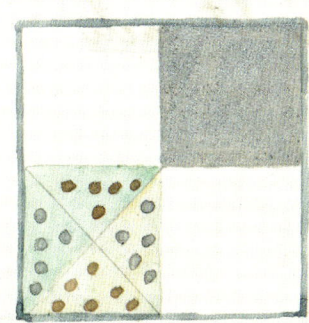

Überwinden des Körpers
Entwickelung des Zartgefühls.
Befreiung des Ätherleibes
Entwickelung der Willensenergie.

6/19/1919. Series I a no. 6. Melampyrum silvaticum. *Direction lines: Modesty.*
Overcoming the body. Development of tact.
Liberation of the etheric body. Development of the energy of the will.

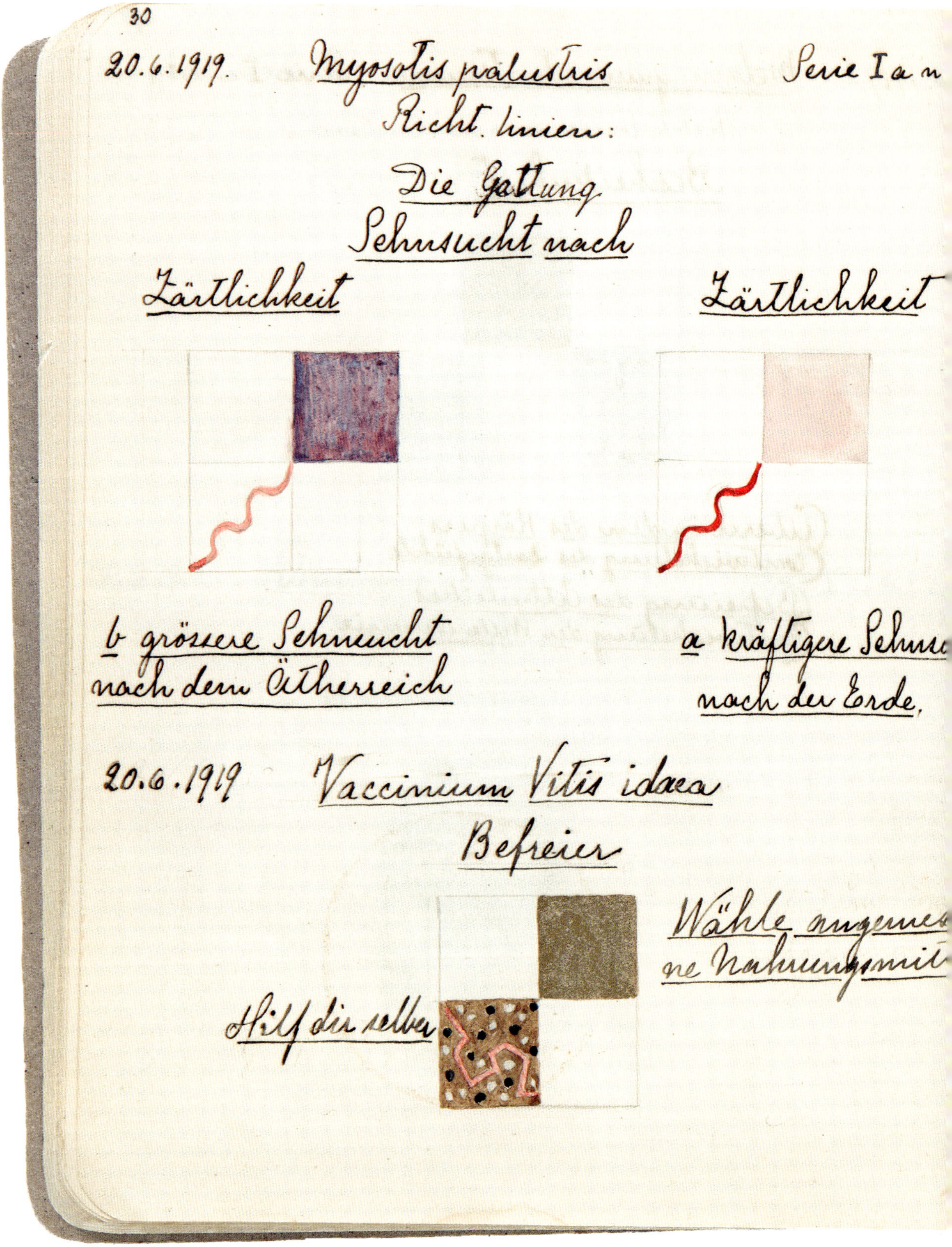

20.6.1919. Myosotis palustris Serie I a n

Richt. linien:

Die Gattung

Sehnsucht nach

Zärtlichkeit Zärtlichkeit

b grössere Sehnsucht
nach dem Ätherreich

a kräftigere Sehns
nach der Erde.

20.6.1919 Vaccinium Vitis idaea

Befreier

Wähle angemes
ne Nahrungsmit

Hilf dir selber

6/20/1919. Series I a no. 6. Myosotis palustris. *Direction lines: The genus. Longing for: Tenderness. b. greater longing for the realm of the etheric. Tenderness. a. more powerful longing for the earth.*

6/20/1919. Vaccinium vitis-idaea. *Liberator. Choose appropriate foodstuffs. Help yourself.*

1.6.1919. *Aquilegia vulgaris* Serie I a n̄ 7

Richt. linien:

Wähle deine Nahrungsmitteln mit Unterscheidung.

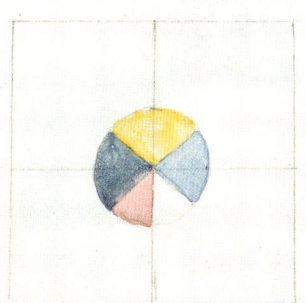

Hilf dir selber
durch Gebrauch überphysischer Hilfe.

23.6.1919. *Silene nutans* Serie I a n̄ 7

Richt. linien:

Zersplitterung

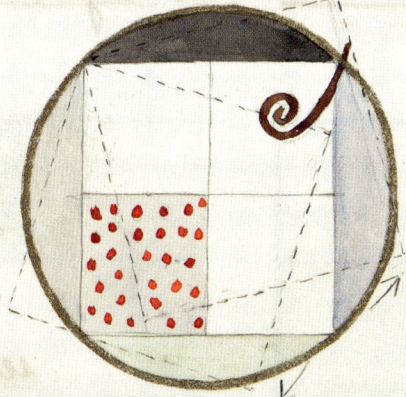

Unruhiger, eifriger Wirksamkeitstrieb.

6/21/1919. Series I a no. 7. Aquilegia vulgaris. Direction lines: Choose your foodstuffs with discrimination.
Help yourself through the use of superphysical help.

6/23/1919. Series I a no. 7. Silene nutans. Direction lines: Fragmentation. Restless, eager drive for effectiveness.

25.6.1919.

Berberis vulgaris
Richt. linien:

Serie I a n=

Feindseligkeit

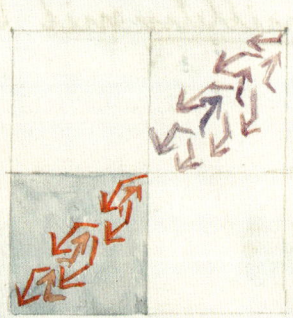

Sehnsucht nach
einer selbständigen Erkenntnis.

2.7.8.34

4.7.1919. ## Campanula persicifolia
Richt. linien:

Serie I a n= 8 ×

Unfähigkeit
des Bedienens von angeborenen Anlagen.

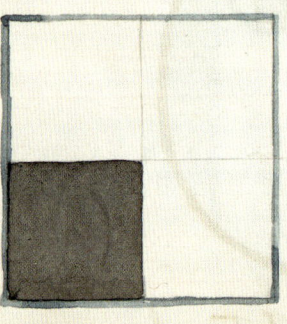

Das Gefühl von
seelischen ü körperlichen
Armu

6/25/1919. Series I a no. 7. Berberis vulgaris. *Direction lines: Hostility. Longing for an autonomous awareness.*

2.7. p. 34

7/4/1919. Series I a no. 8. Campanula persicifolia. *Direction lines: The inability to serve of innate systems. The feeling of spiritual and physical poverty.*

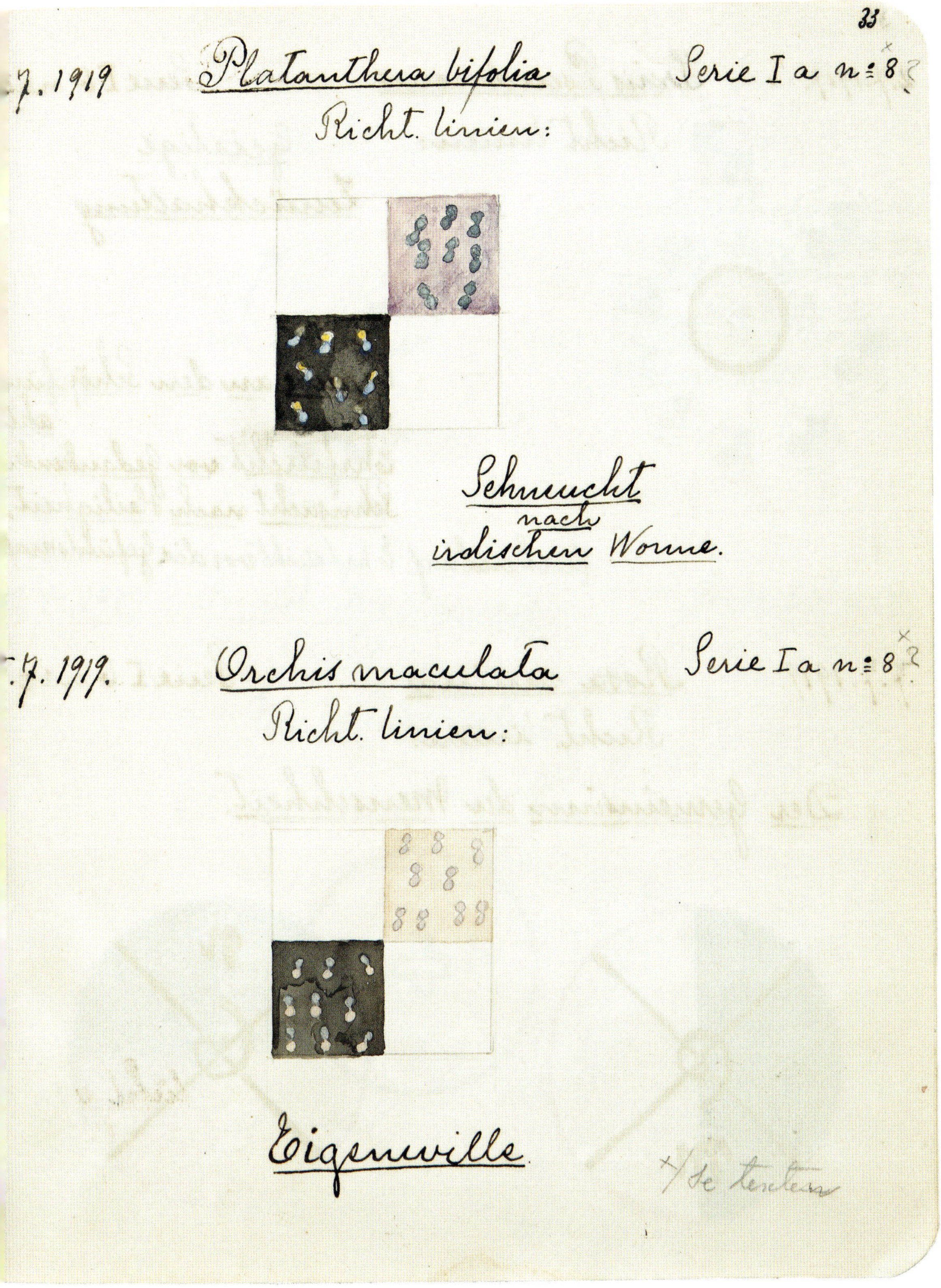

7. 1919

Platanthera bifolia

Richt. linien:

Sehnsucht
nach
irdischen Wonne.

7. 1919.

Orchis maculata

Serie I a n: 8

Richt. linien:

Eigenwille.

+/se tenten

7/5/1919. Series I a no. 8. Platanthera bifolia. *Direction lines: Longing for earthly delight.*

7/5/1919. Series I a no. 8. Orchis maculata. *Direction lines: Self-will.*

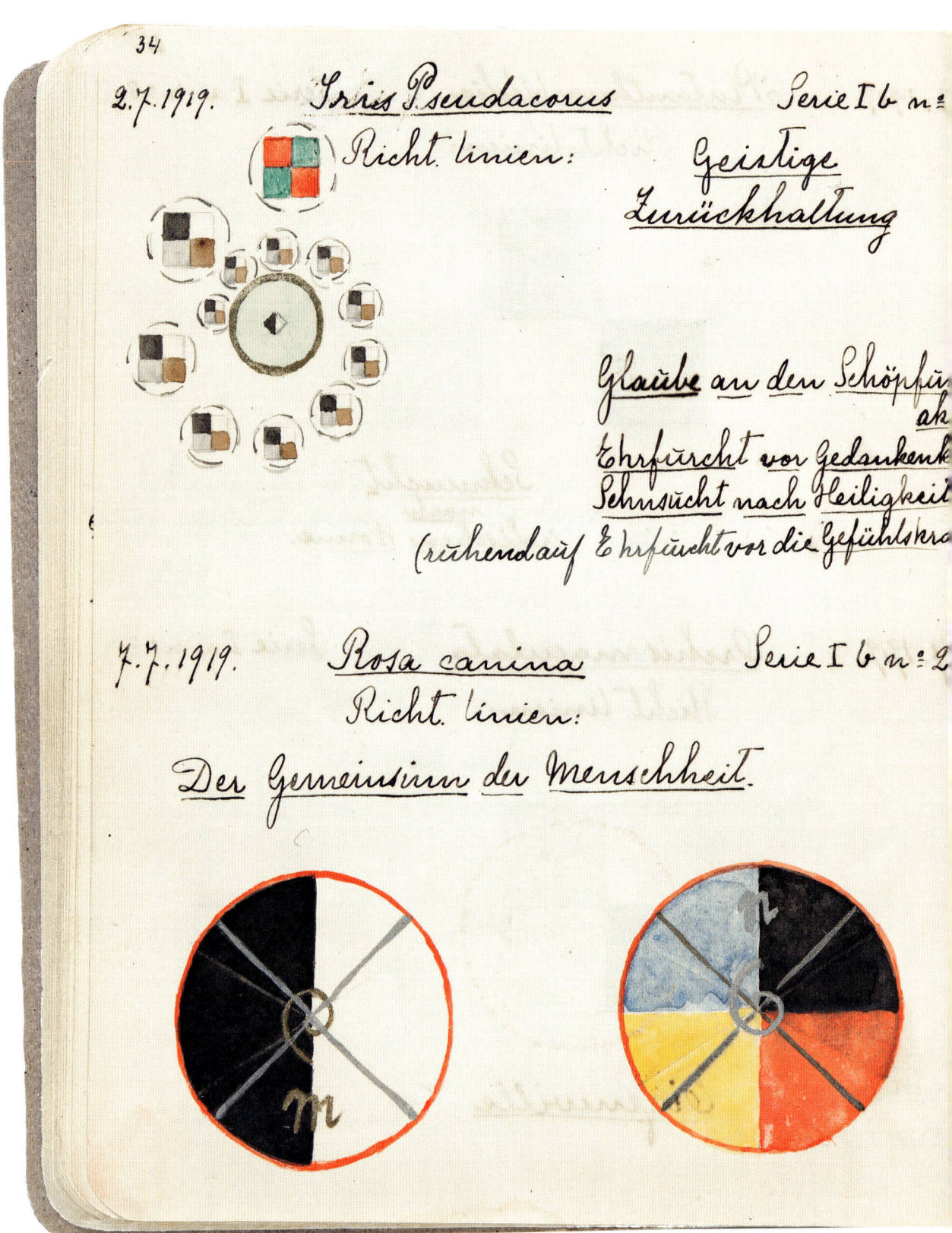

2.7.1919. **Iris Pseudacorus** Serie I b n⁰

Richt. linien:

Geistige
Zurückhaltung

Glaube an den Schöpfu...
...ab...
Ehrfurcht vor Gedankenk...
Sehnsucht nach Heiligkeit...
(ruhend auf Ehrfurcht vor die Gefühlskra...

7.7.1919. **Rosa canina** Serie I b n⁰ 2

Richt. linien:

Der Gemeinsinn der Menschheit.

7/2/1919. Series b no. 1. Iris pseudacorus. *Direction lines: Mental reserve. Belief in the act of creation.*
Reverence for thought [ ]. Longing for holiness (resting on reverence for the power of feeling).

7/7/1919. Series I b no. 2. Rosa canina. *Direction lines: The public spirit of humanity.*

7. 1919.

Vicia cracca

Richt. linien:

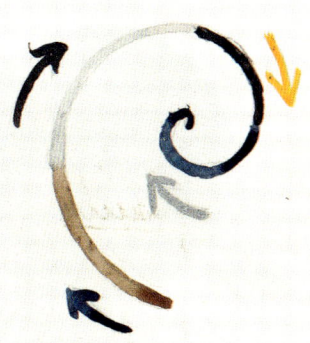

Unternehmungslust in geistiger Beziehung, welche das Hinaufbringen unserer Seelen- und Körperorgane herbeiführt.

1.7. 1919.

Convolvulus arvensis

Richt. linien:

Entschlossenheit.

Serie I b n= 3

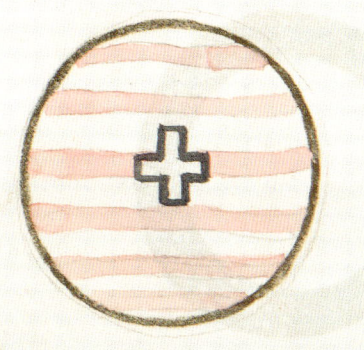

24.7.1919.   Monotropa Hypopitys   Serie I b n
Richt. linien:

Einseitigkeit

25.7.1919.   Papaver Rhaeas   Serie I b n
Richt. linien:
Entsagung des eigenen Ichs für zukünftige Geschle[...]
durch

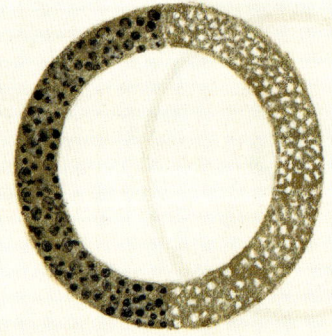

Gebetslaut und Gebetslicht.

7/24/1919. Series I b no. 3. Monotropa hypopitys. *Direction lines: Imbalance.*

7/25/1919. Series I b no. 4. Papaver rhoeas. *Direction lines: Renunciation of the I for future sex through the sound of prayer and the light of prayer.*

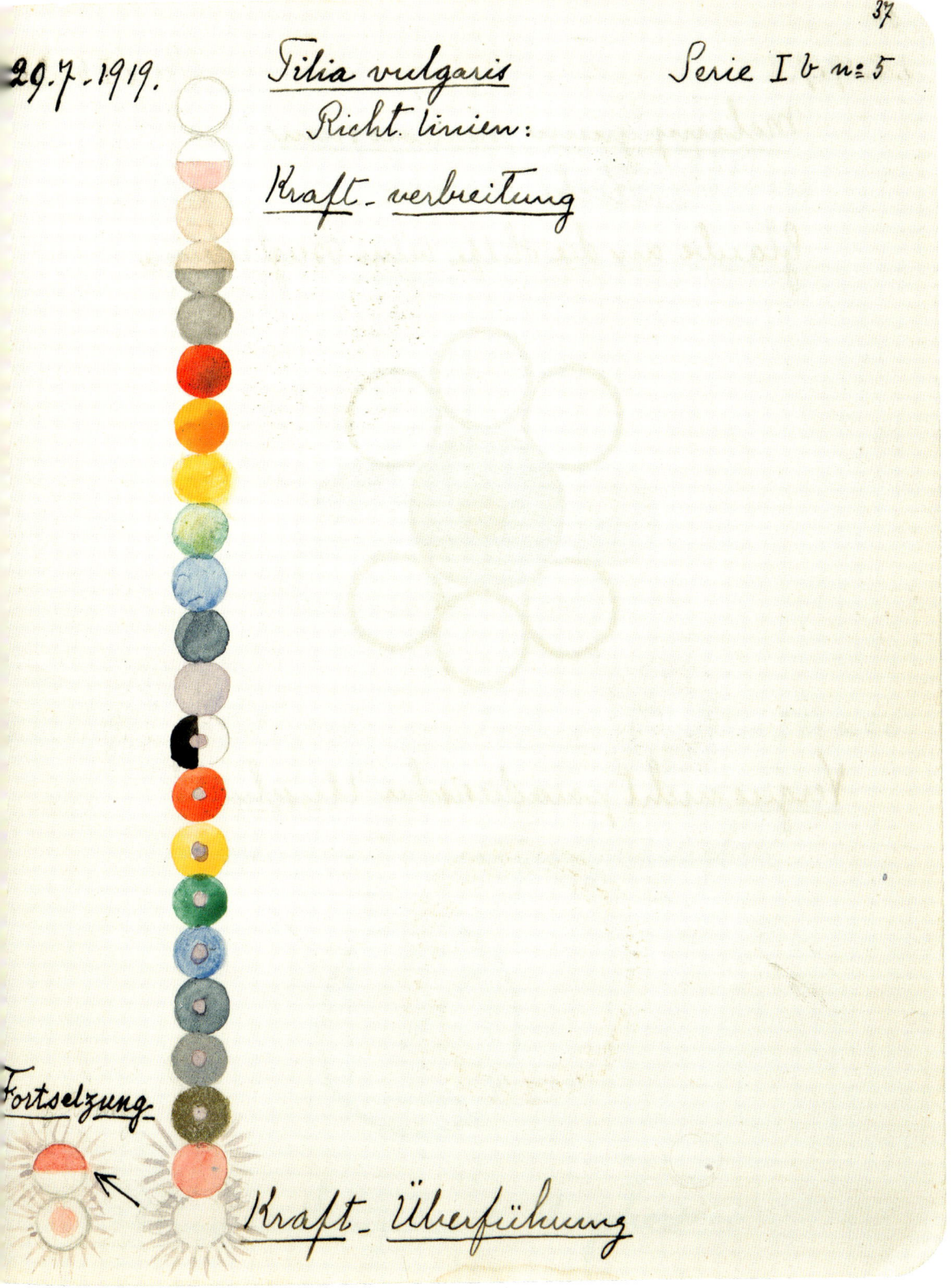

29.7.1919.

Tilia vulgaris

Serie I b n≃ 5

Richt. linien:

Kraft - verbreitung

Fortsetzung

Kraft - Überführung

7/29/1919. Series I b no. 5. Tilia vulgaris. *Direction lines: Power distribution. Continuation. Power conversion.*

1.8.1919.

Melampyrum nemorosum

Richt. linien:

Glaube an die Hilfe beim Bergbesteigen

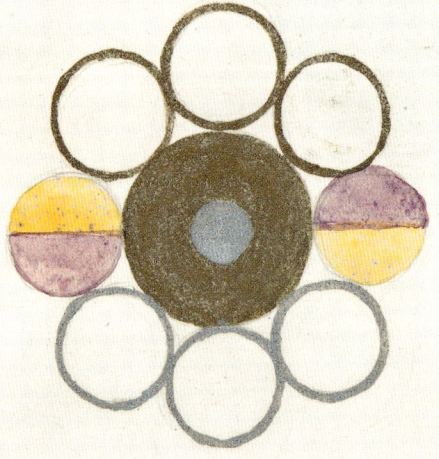

Vergiss nicht paradiesischer Unschuld

8/1/1919. Series I b no. 6. Melampyrum nemorosum. *Direction lines: Belief in help in climbing mountains. Do not forget paradisiacal innocence.*

.8.1919. Campanula rotundifolia   Serie I b n⁼ 6

Richt. linien:

Erkennen überphysischer Kraftüberführung

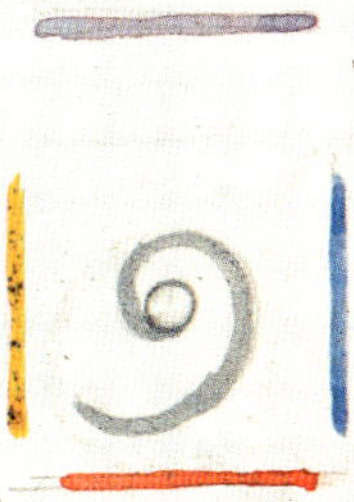

Mangelnde Fähigkeit

(Selbsterkenntnis)

3.8.1919. Lotus corniculatus   Serie I b n⁼ 6

Richt. linien:

Umwandlung durch Gesetzmässigkeit

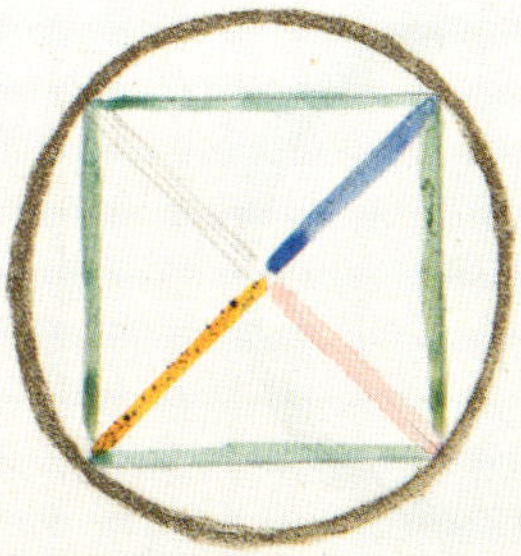

Umwandlung durch Ungehorsam

8/2/1919. Series I b no. 6. Campanula rotundifolia. *Direction lines: Recognition of superphysical power conversion. Lack of ability (self-awareness).*

8/3/1919. Series I b no. 6. Lotus corniculatus. *Direction lines: Transformation through lawfulness. Transformation through disobedience.*

4.8.1919.   *Linaria vulgaris*   Serie I b n=

Richt. linien:

Entschlossenheit

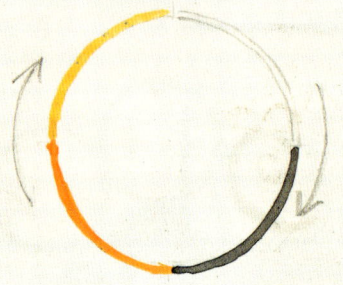

Verständnis der Richtung der Wege
(Beginnende Erkenntnis)

7.8.1919.   *Trifolium pratense*   Serie I b n=7

Richt. linien:

Opferfreudigkeit

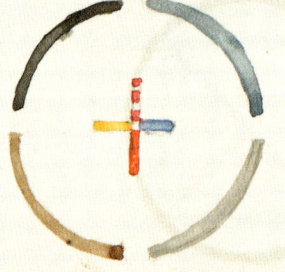

Zähe Entschlossenheit bei physischen Formbildung

8/4/1919. Series I b no. 7. Linaria vulgaris. *Direction lines: Determination.*
Understanding of the direction of the paths. (Beginning awareness.)

8/7/1919. Series I b no. 7. Trifolium pratense. *Direction lines: readiness to sacrifice. Tenacious determination in physical shaping.*

.8.1919. *Centaurea Jacea*
Serie I b n° 7

Richt. linien:

Selbsterkenntnis

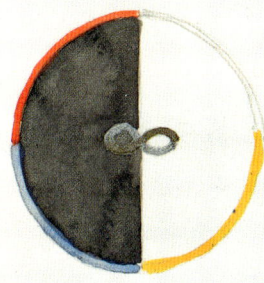

Sehnsucht nach Einheit

13.8.1919. *Sedum Telephium*
Serie I c n° 1

Richt. linien:

Unermüdlich

In besonderer Verbindung
mit
den Luftgeistern

8/8/1919. Series I b no. 7. Centaurea jacea. *Direction lines: Self-awareness. Longing for unity.*

8/13/1919. Series I c no. 1. Sedum telephium. *Direction lines: Tireless. In special contact with the spirits of the air.*

42

14.8.1919.   Lathyrus odorata   Serie I c

Richt. linien:

Ohnmacht

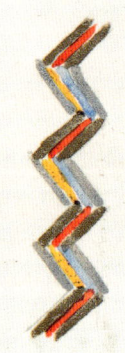

Gebetslaut und Gebetslicht in Vereinigung als Mittel
zum Erhalten überphysischer Hilfe.

15.8.1919.   Bidens cernua   Serie I c n°

Richt. linien:

Schwäche

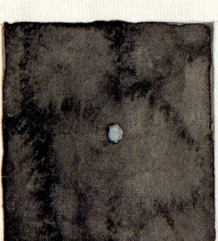

Sehnsucht nach physischen Lebenskraft

8/14/1919. Series I c no. 1. Lathyrus odoratus. Direction lines: Powerlessness.
Sound of prayer and light of prayer in union as a means of receiving superphysical help.

8/15/1919. Series I c no. 1. Bidens cernua. Direction lines: Weakness. Longing for physical life force.

16.8.1919. *Calendula officinalis* Serie I c n= 2

Richt. linien:

<u>Überwinde deine Gottesfeindseligkeit</u>
<u>in der Persönlichkeit</u>

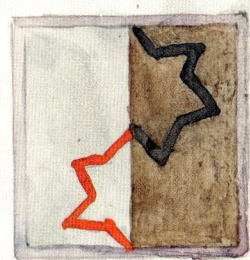

<u>Wahrheitsliebe</u>
<u>in Bezug auf das Materielle</u>

8/16/1919. Series I c no. 2. Calendula officinalis. *Direction lines: Overcome your hostility to God in your personality. Love of truth in relation to the tangible.*

207

3.9.1919.

Helianthus annuus

Richt. linien:

Die Liebe ist das Grösste von Allem.

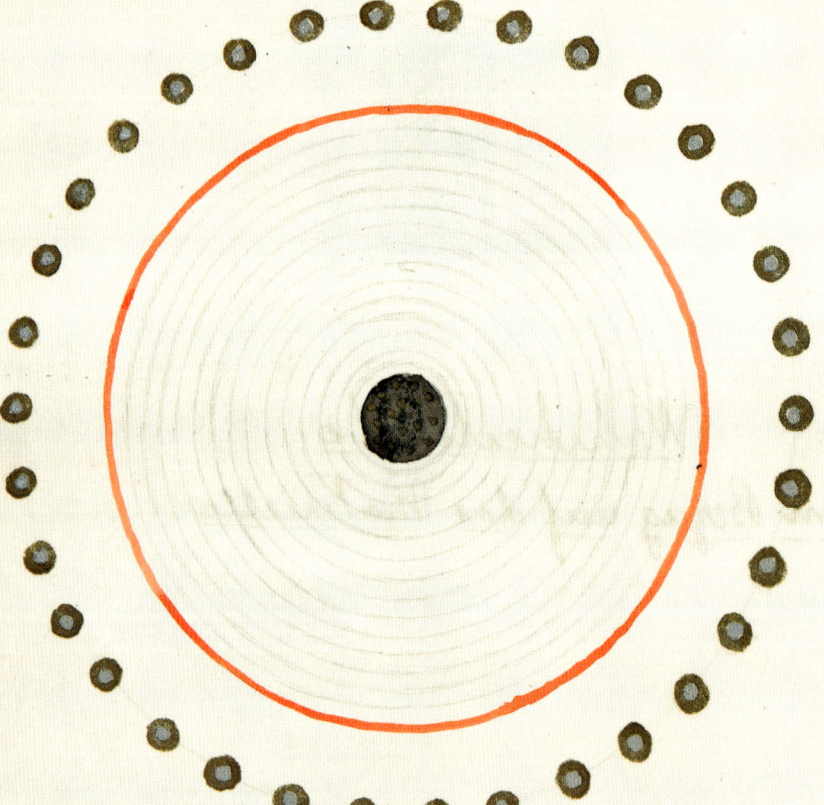

Von der Liebe erscheint immer Kraft um die
Gottvergessenheit zu überwinden

9/3/1919. Series I c no. 3. Helianthus annuus. *Line of direction: Love is the greatest of all.*
The strength not to forget God always comes from love.

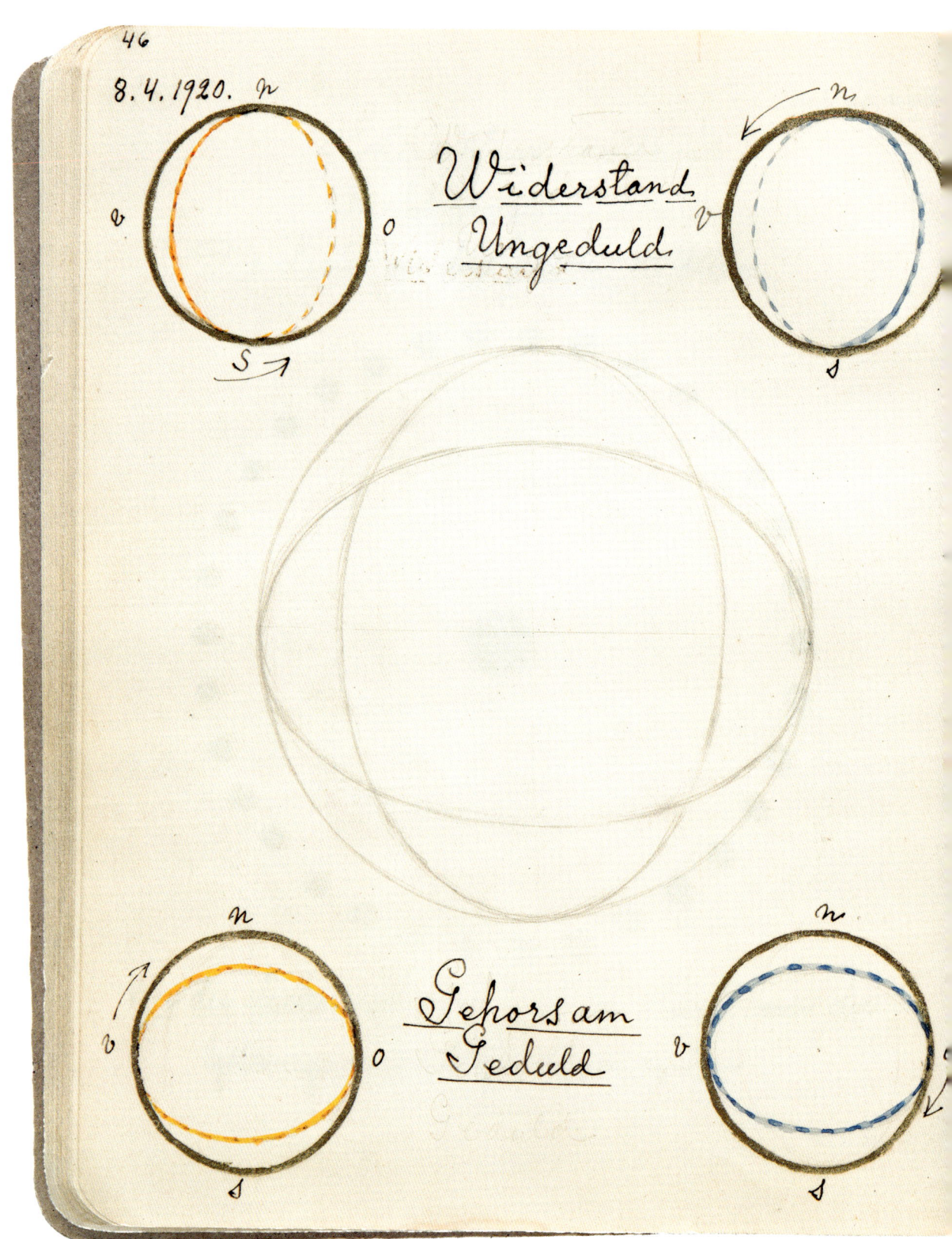

4/8/1920. Resistance. Impatience. Obedience. Patience.

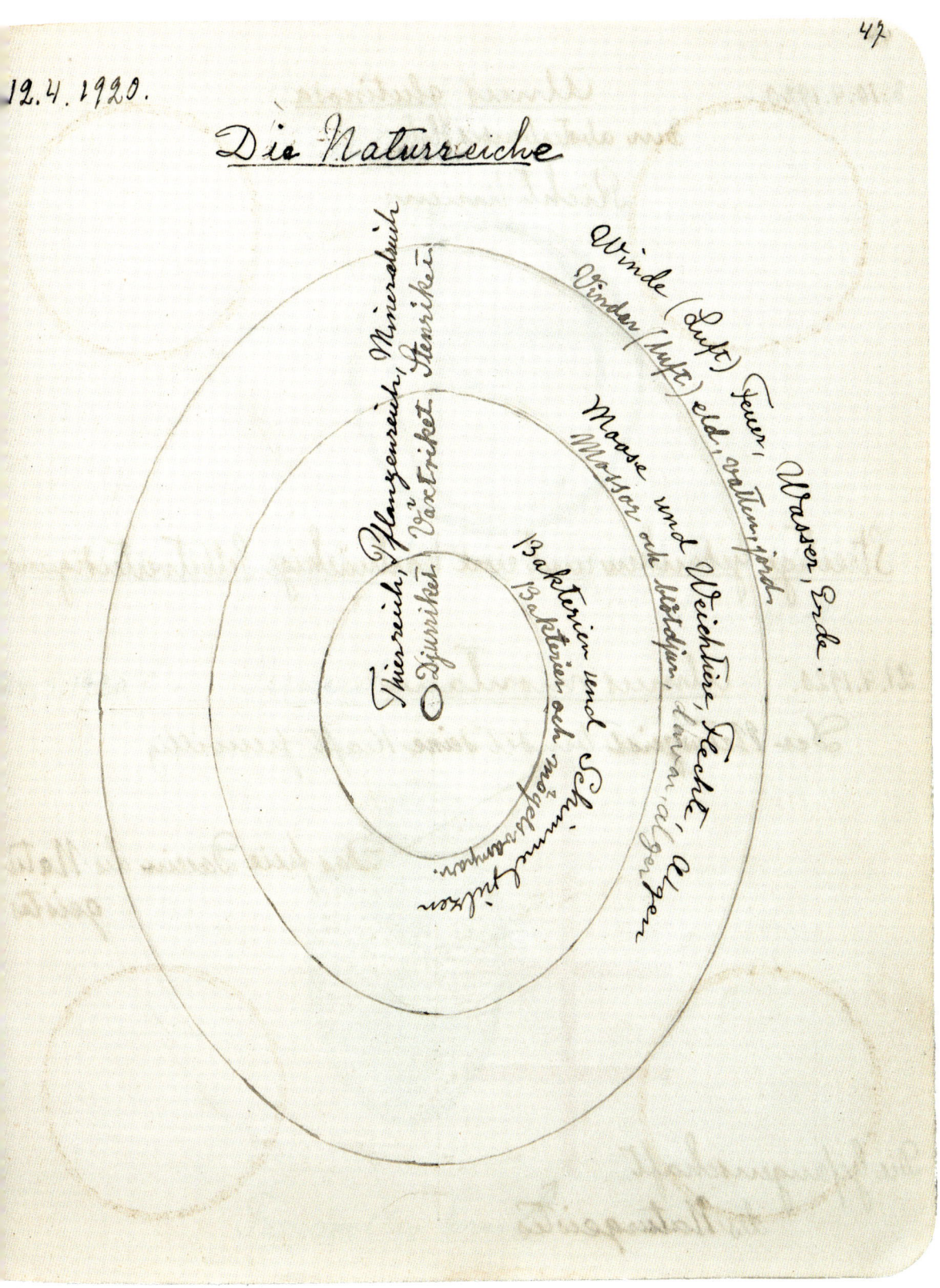

12.4.1920.

Die Naturreiche

4/12/1920. The kingdom of nature. Wind (air), fire, water, earth. Mosses and mollusks, lichens, algae. Bacteria and molds. Animal kingdom, plant kingdom, mineral kingdom.

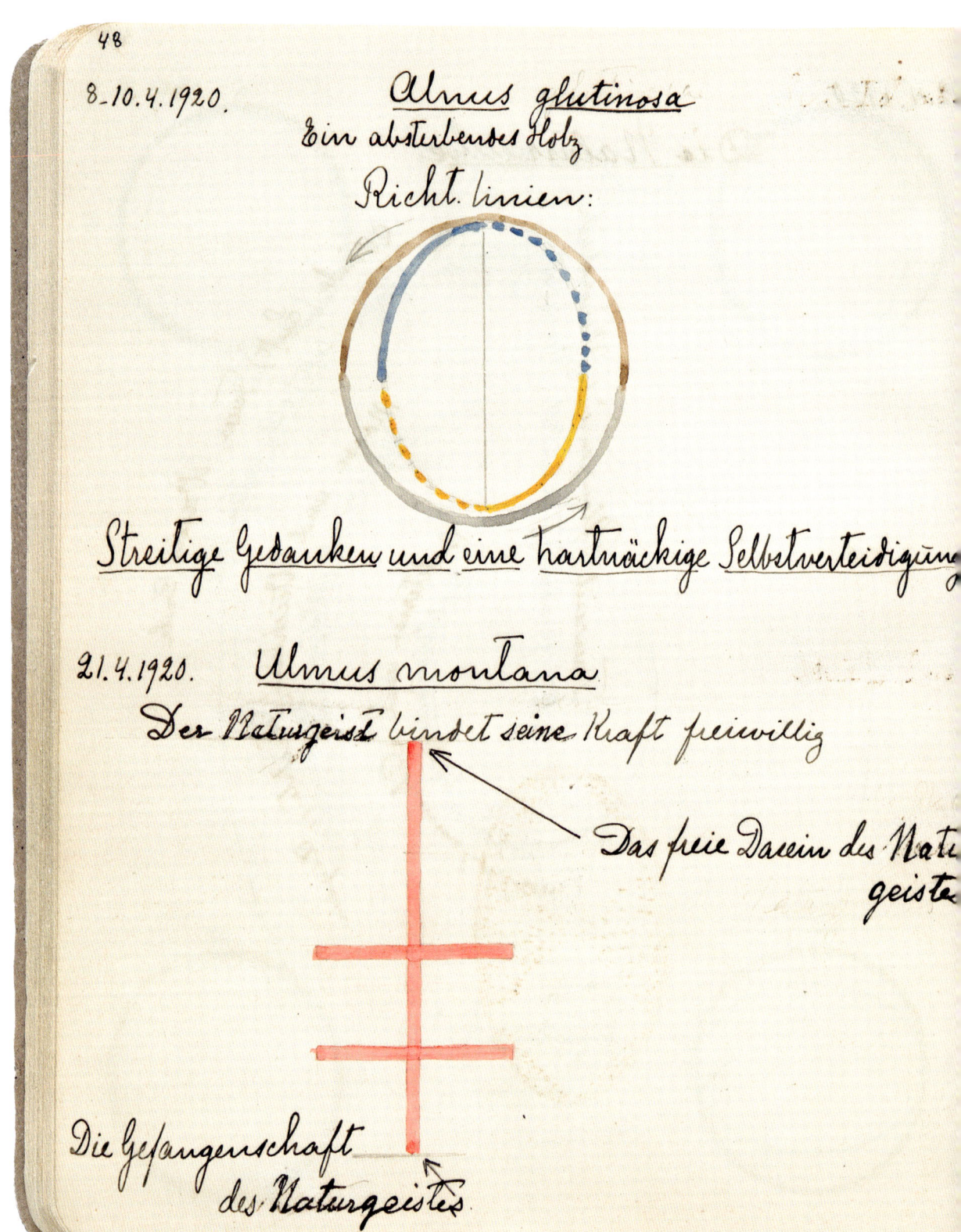

4/8–10/1920. Alnus glutinosa. *A wood that is dying out. Direction lines: Controversial thoughts and a stubborn self-defense.*

4/21/1920. Ulmus montana. *The spirit of nature voluntarily binds its power.*
The free existence of the spirit of nature. The captivity of the spirit of nature.

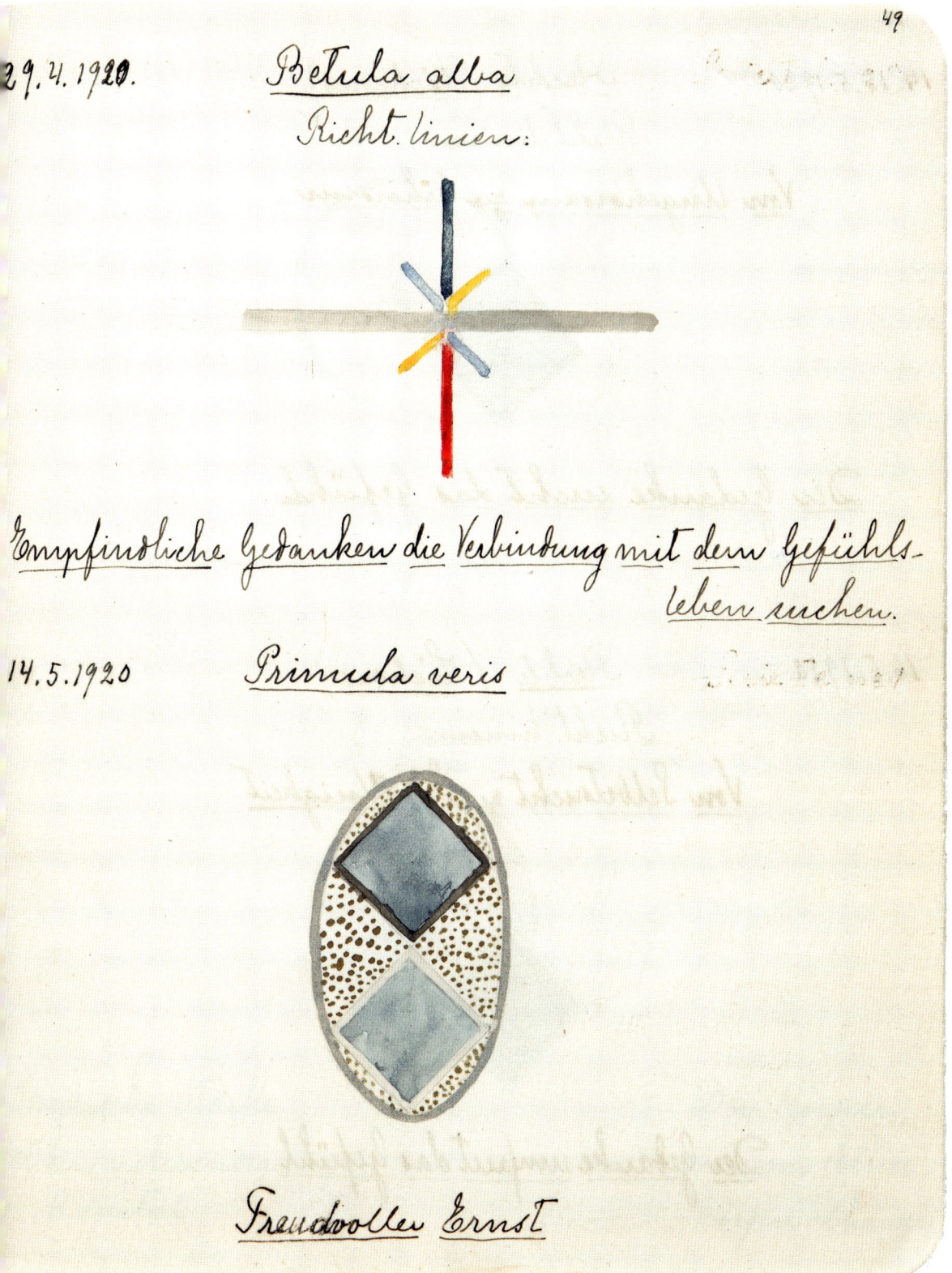

29.4.1920.

Betula alba

Richt. linien:

Empfindliche Gedanken die Verbindung mit dem Gefühls-

leben suchen.

14.5.1920

Primula veris

Freudvoller Ernst

4/29/1920. Betula alba. *Direction lines: Sensitive thoughts that seek connection to the life of feeling.*

5/14/1920. Primula veris. *Joyful seriousness.*

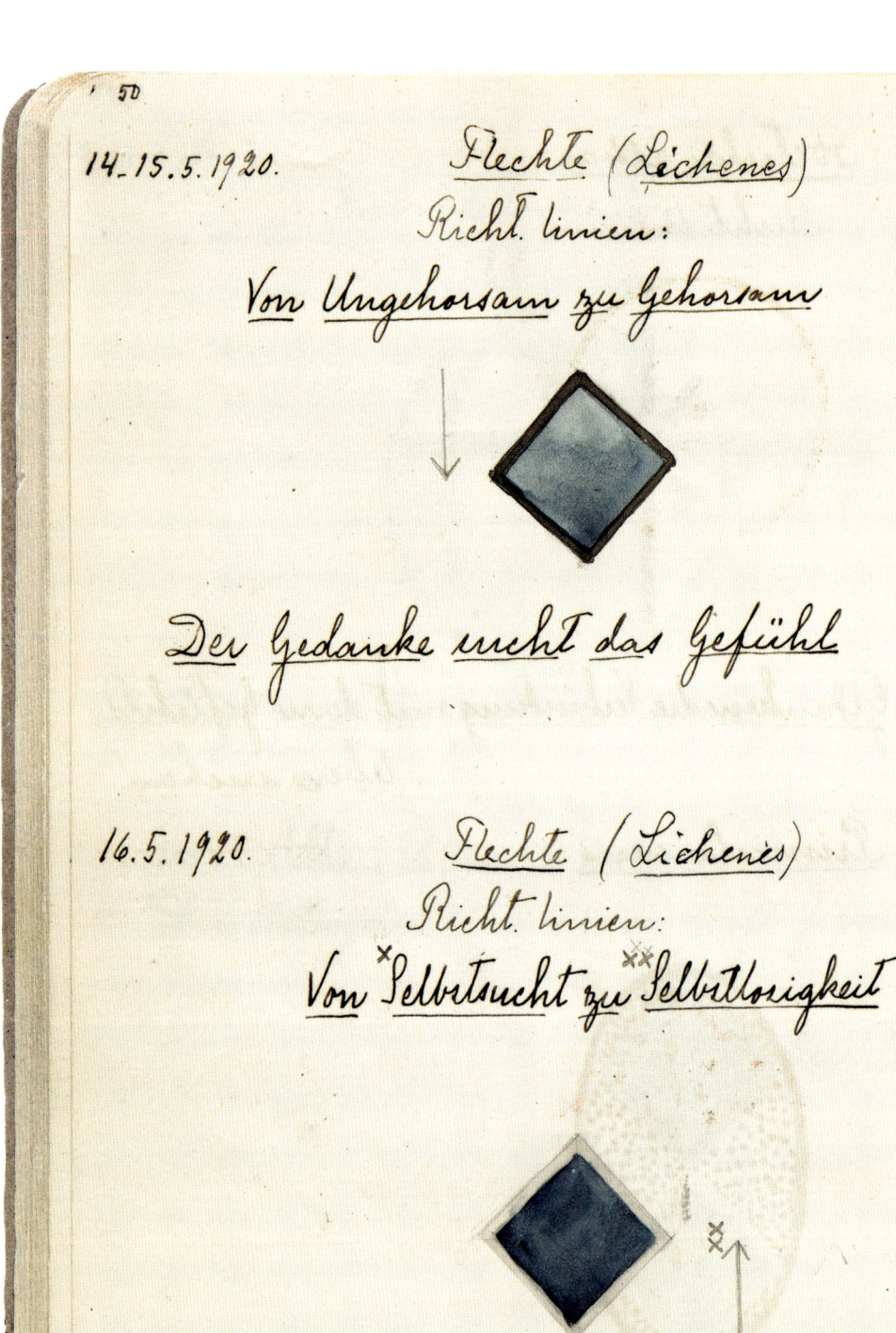

14-15.5.1920.

Flechte (Lichenes)

Richt. linien:

Von Ungehorsam zu Gehorsam

Der Gedanke sucht das Gefühl

16.5.1920.

Flechte (Lichenes)

Richt. linien:

Von Selbstsucht zu Selbstlosigkeit

Der Gedanke umfasst das Gefühl

5/14–15/1920. Lichens. Direction lines: From disobedience to obedience. Thought seeks feeling.

5/16/1920. Lichens. Direction lines: From selfishness to selflessness. Thought envelops feeling.

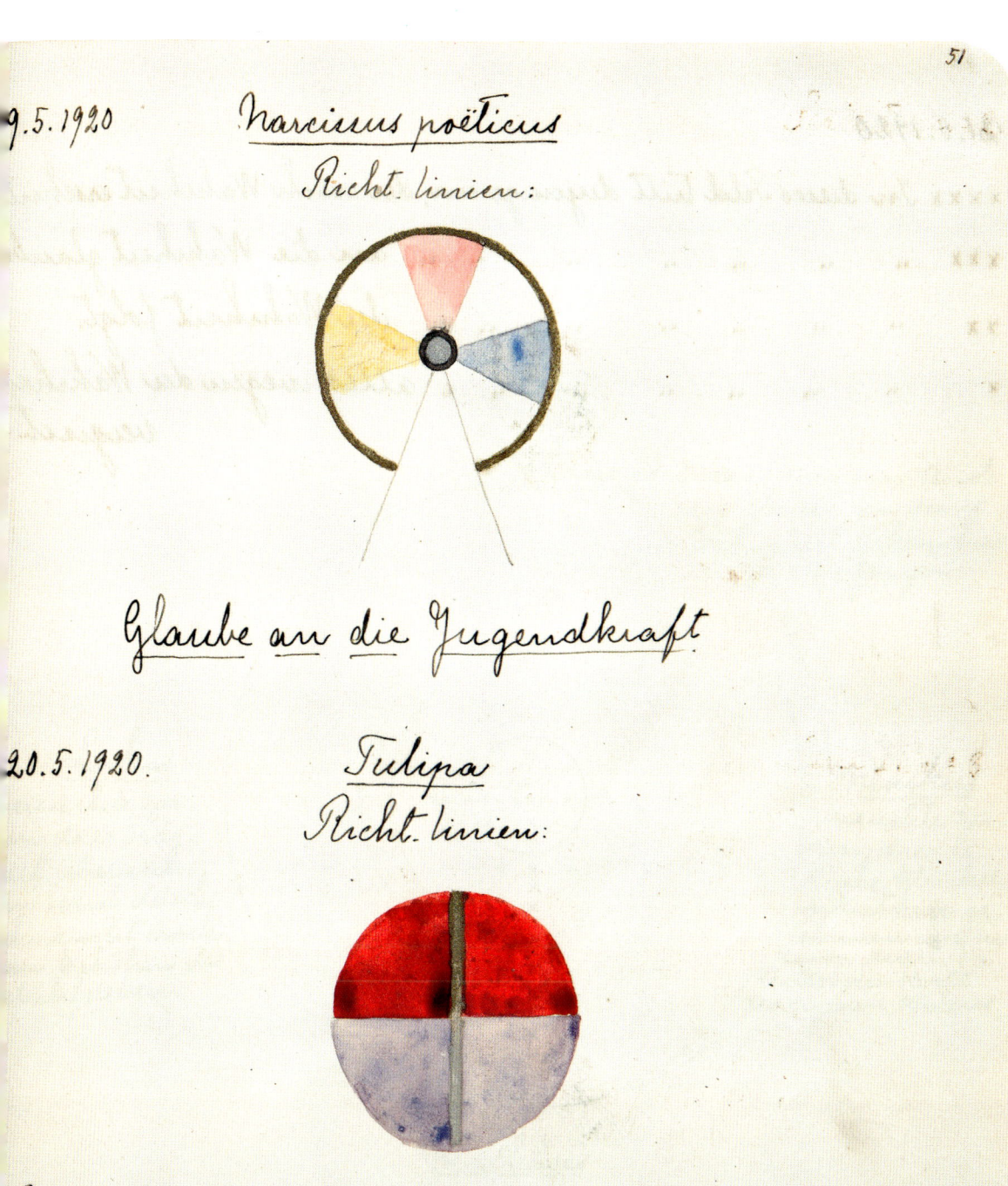

9.5.1920

Narcissus poëticus

Richt. linien:

Glaube an die Jugendkraft

20.5.1920.

Tulipa

Richt. linien:

Physische Stärke
ist ein notwendiges
Kapital

Der Körper
ist vom Äther-
Körper abhängig

5/19/1920. Narcissus poeticus. *Direction lines: Belief in the power of youth.*

5/20/1920. Tulipa. *Direction lines: Physical strength is a necessary asset. The body is dependent on the etheric body.*

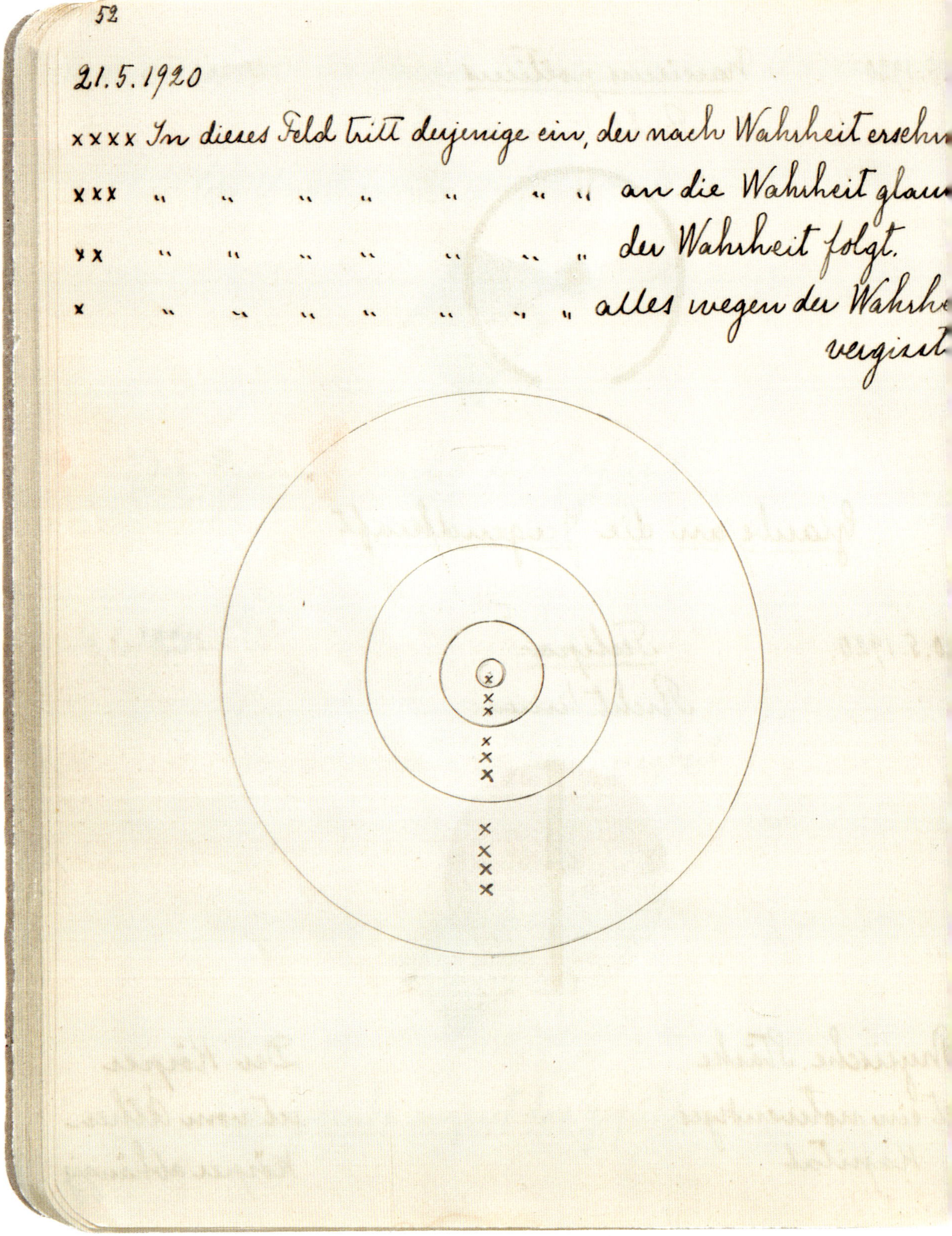

52

21.5.1920

xxxx In dieses Feld tritt derjenige ein, der nach Wahrheit ersehn

xxx   „   „   „   „   „   „ „ an die Wahrheit glaub

xx   „   „   „   „   „   „ „ der Wahrheit folgt.

x   „   „   „   „   „   „ „ alles wegen der Wahrh

                                        vergist

5/21/1920. ×××× *Into this field enters he who desires truth.* ××× *Into this field enters he who believes in truth.*
×× *Into this field enters he who follows truth.* × *Into this field enters he who forgets everything because of truth.*

216

22.5.1920.

× Johannes besass vor den Anderen Glaube an seine Fähigkeit, Erkenntnis zu empfangen.

Lukas × versuchte zeigen dass Trägheit überwunden wird durch Sehnsucht nach im Erhöhen des Fühlsleben.

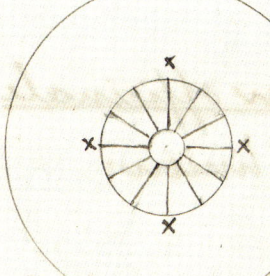

× Markus versuchte zeigen, dass irdische Glückseligkeit nur gewonnen werden kann durch Verteilen der Kraft des eigenen Wesens.

× Matthäus

Dankbare Aufnahme der Aufklärung.

So das 543

5/22/1920. × John, more than the others, possessed belief in his ability to receive awareness. × Mark tried to show that earthly bliss can be won only through distribution of the power of one's own being. × Matthew. Grateful reception of enlightenment. × Luke tried to show that dullness can be overcome through a desire for the elevation of the life of feelings.

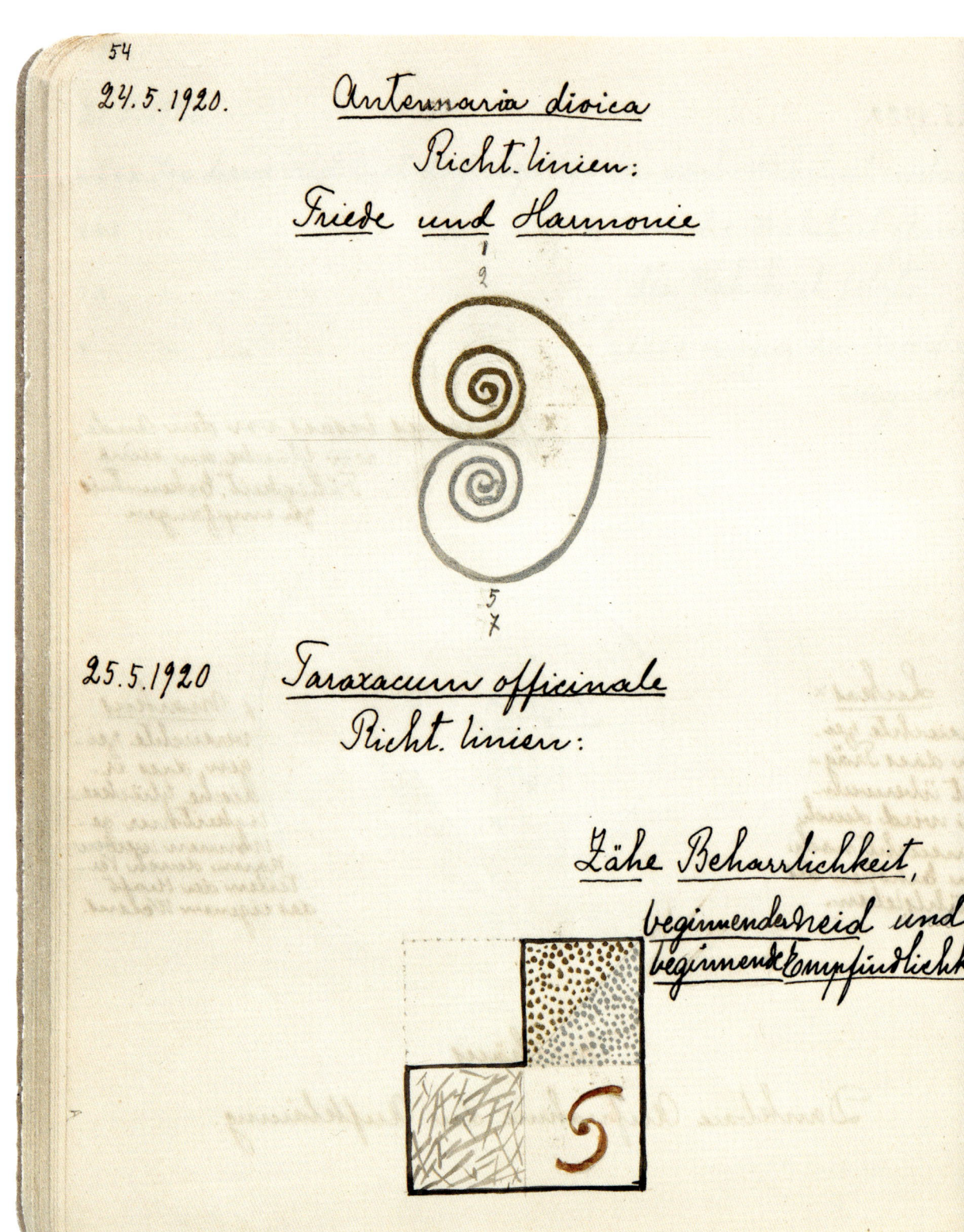

24.5.1920.

Antennaria dioica

Richt. linien:

Friede und Harmonie

25.5.1920

Taraxacum officinale

Richt. linien:

Zähe Beharrlichkeit,

beginnender Neid und
beginnende Empfindlichk.

5/24/1920. Antennaria dioica. *Direction lines: Peace and harmony.*

5/25/1920. Taraxacum officinale. *Direction lines: Tenacious persistence, incipient jealousy, and beginning of sensitivity.*

27.5.1920. <u>Anthoxanthum odoratum</u>

Richt. linien:

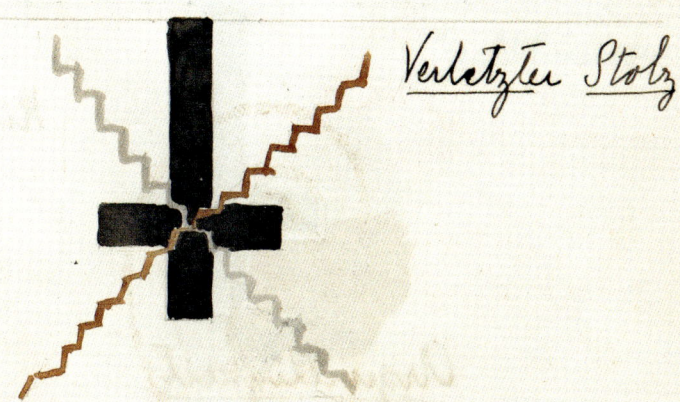

Verletzter Stolz

<u>Lust nach der Schädigung des Menschenkörpers.</u>

28.5.1920. <u>Eucephala (mücke)</u>

<u>Neid.</u>

<u>Fehlgeschlagene Hoffnungen</

erzeugen bei dem

Naturgeiste Arg-

willigkeit ge-

gen die Freude

der Menschen und

der Tiere

in phys. Beziehung.

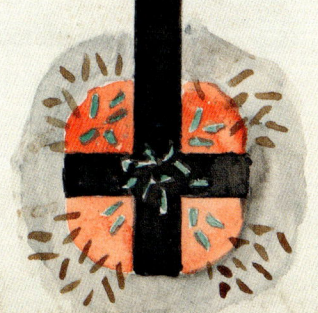

5/27/1920. Anthoxanthum odoratum. *Direction lines: Injured pride. Desire for injury to the human body.*

5/28/1920. Eucephalus *(mosquito). Jealousy. Failed hopes generate malevolence in the spirit of nature against the joy of people and animals in physical relationship.*

219

29.5.1920.

Myrmica (Ameise) Laevinodes

Täuschende Kräfte

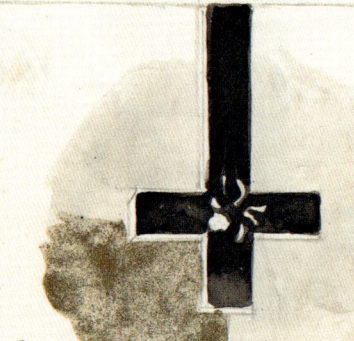

Richtlinien:

Argwilligkeit
Schadenfreude
Rachbegierde
Arbeitsfähigkeit

30.5.1920.

Ajuga pyramidalis

Richt. linien:

Gedankenstärke

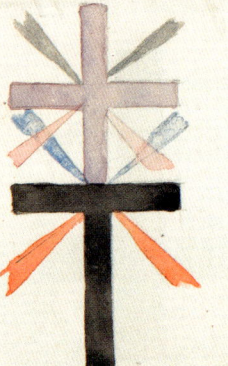

Klarheit innerhalb der Form.

Die Blume liefert Ätherkraft ab, nimmt Astralkraft auf.

5/29/1920. Myrmica *(ant)* laevinodes. *Deceptive powers. Direction lines: Malevolence. Malicious joy. Craving for revenge. Ability to work.*

5/30/1920. Ajuga pyramidales. *Direction lines: Strength of thoughts. Clarity within form.*
The flower delivers etheric power, receives astral power.

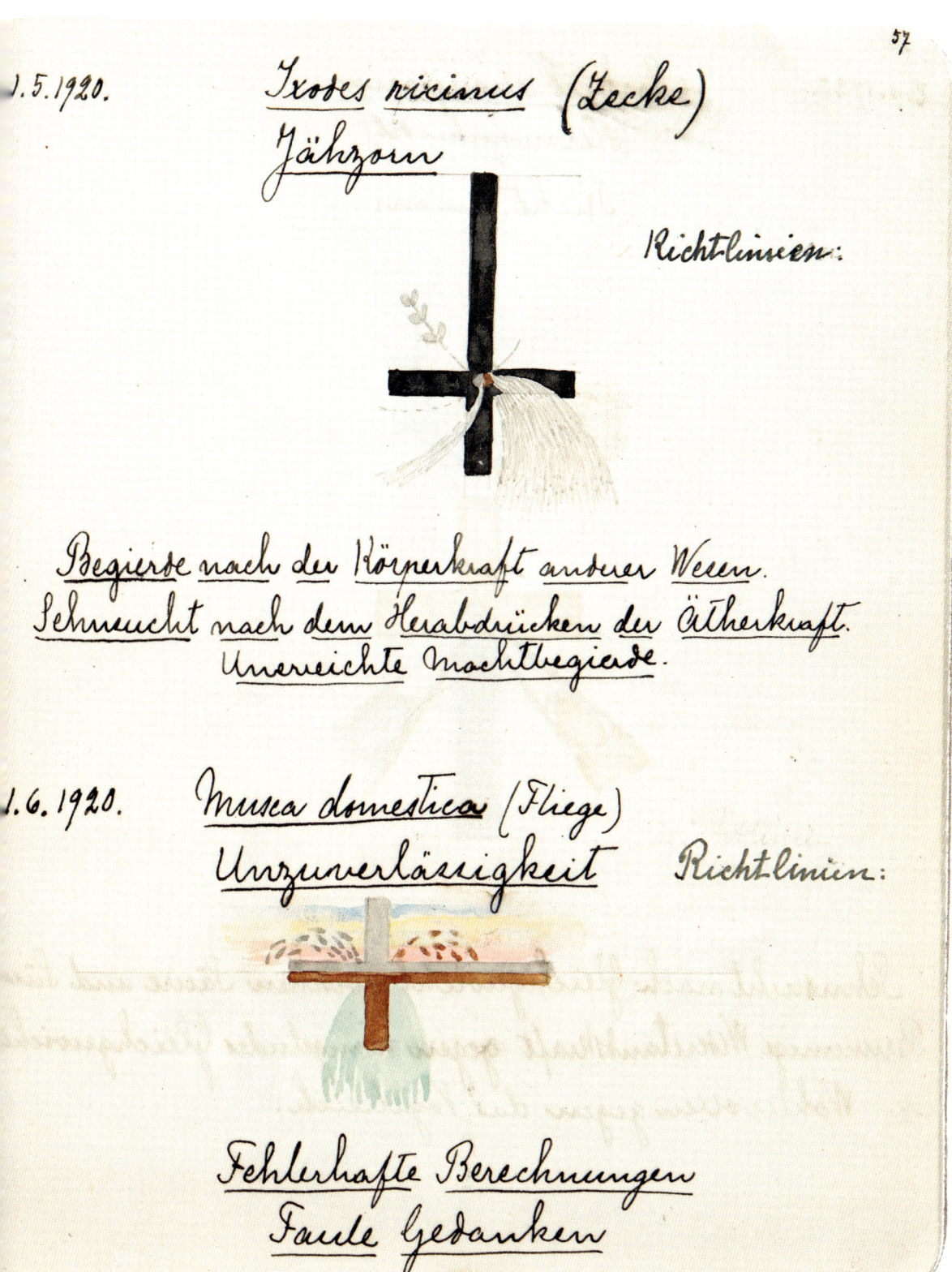

1.5.1920.

Ixodes ricinus (Zecke)
Jähzorn

Richtlinien:

Begierde nach der Körperkraft anderer Wesen.
Sehnsucht nach dem Herabdrücken der Ätherkraft.
Unerreichte Machtbegierde.

1.6.1920.

Musca domestica (Fliege)
Unzuverlässigkeit

Richtlinien:

Fehlerhafte Berechnungen
Faule Gedanken

5/31/1920. Ixodes ricinus *(tick). Temper. Direction lines: Craving for the bodily power of other beings.*
Longing to depress etheric power. Unsurpassed craving for power.

6/1/1920. Musca domestica *(fly). Unreliablity. Direction lines: Flawed calculations. Lazy thoughts.*

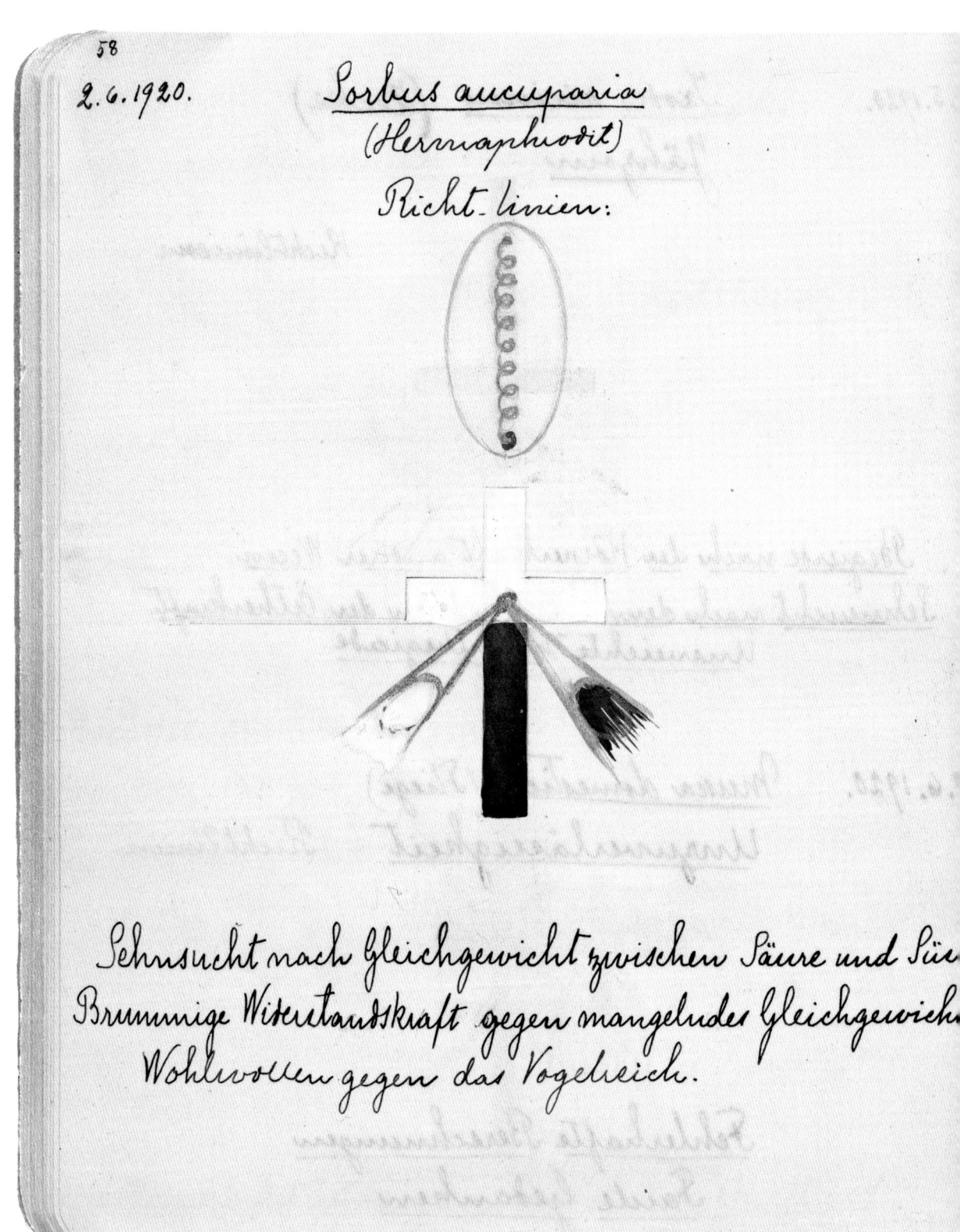

58

2.6.1920.

Sorbus aucuparia
(Hermaphrodit)
Richt-linien:

Sehnsucht nach Gleichgewicht zwischen Säure und Sü[...]
Brummige Widerstandskraft gegen mangelndes Gleichgewich[...]
Wohlwollen gegen das Vogelreich.

8/2/1920. Sorbus aucuparia *(hermaphrodite). Direction lines: Longing for balance between sour and sweet.*
Peevish resistance to lack of balance. Goodwill toward the bird kingdom.

.6.1920.

Ranunculus bulbosus.

Richt. linien:

Emsig
Arbeitsfähig
lebhaft, aber
selbstsüchtig.

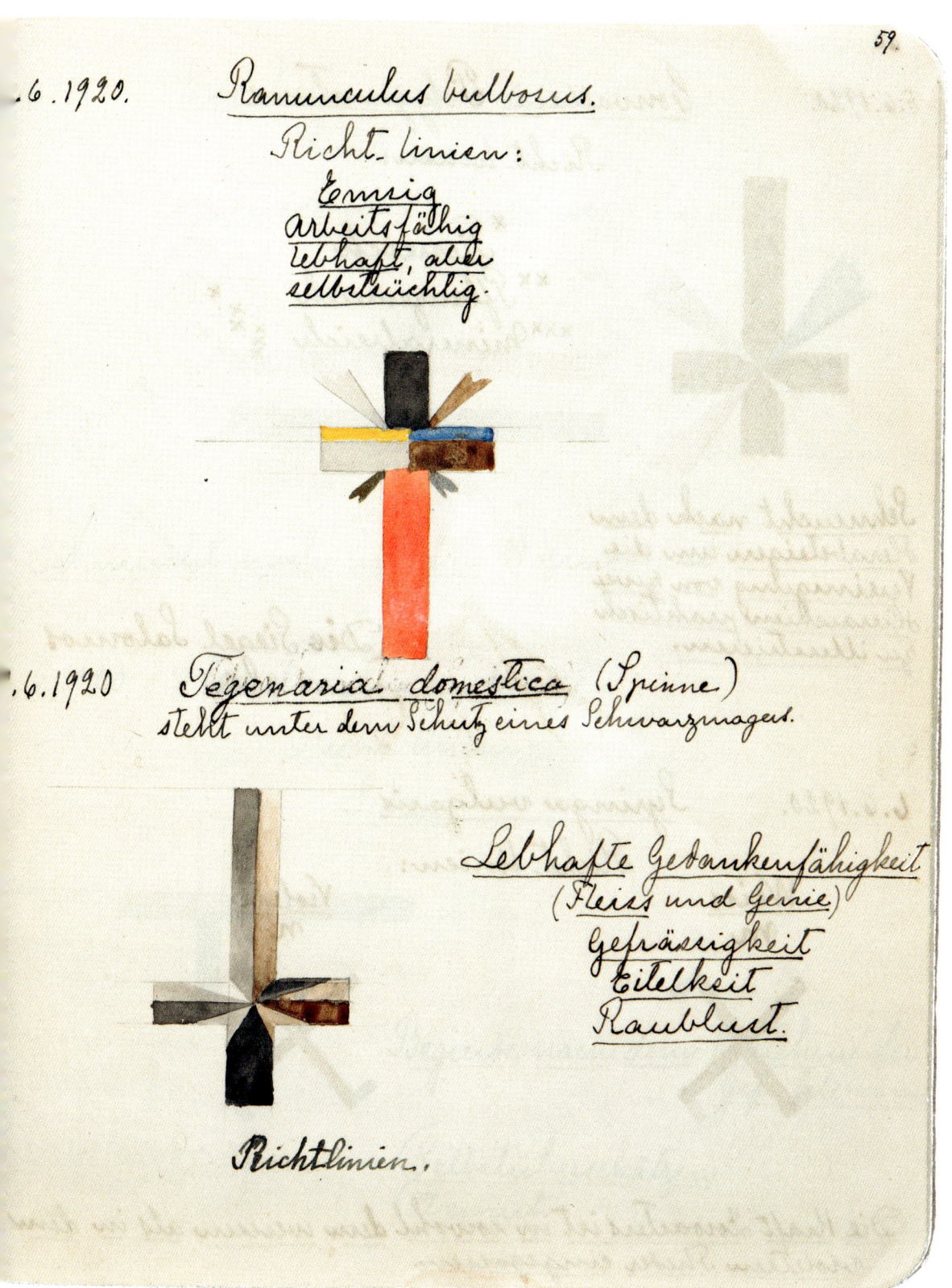

.6.1920 Tegenaria domestica (Spinne)
steht unter dem Schutz eines Schwarzmagers.

Lebhafte Gedankenfähigkeit
(Fleiss und Genie)
Gefrässigkeit
Eitelkeit
Raublust.

Richtlinien.

6/3/1920. Ranunculus bulbosus. Direction lines: Busy. Able to work. Lively, but selfish.

6/4/1920. Tegenaria domestica (spider). Protected by a black magus.
Lively ability to think (diligence and genius). Voracity. Vanity. Rapacity. Direction lines.

5.6.1920.

Convallaria Polygonatum

Richt. linien:

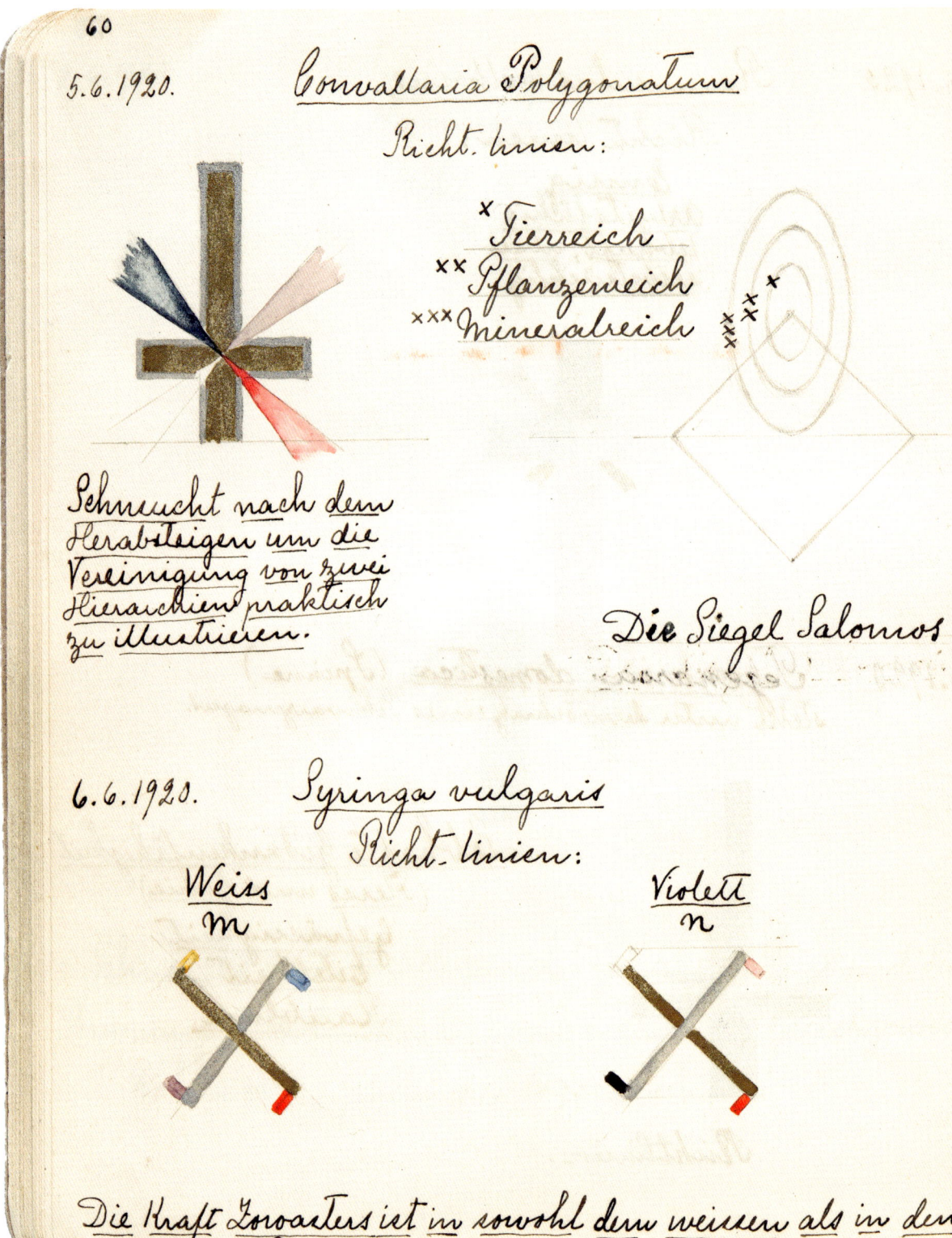

× Tierreich
×× Pflanzenreich
××× Mineralreich

Sehnsucht nach dem
Herabsteigen um die
Vereinigung von zwei
Hierarchien praktisch
zu illustrieren.

Die Siegel Salomos

6.6.1920.

Syringa vulgaris

Richt. linien:

Weiss
m

Violett
n

Die Kraft Zoroasters ist in sowohl dem weissen als in dem
violetten Flieder eingegossen.

6/5/1920. Convallaria polygonatum. *Direction lines: × Animal kingdom. ×× Plant kingdom.*
××× Mineral kingdom. Longing for descent, in order to illustrate practically the union of two hierarchies. Salomon's seal.

6/6/1920. Syringa vulgaris. *Direction lines: White. M. Violet. N. The power of Zoroaster is infused in both the white and violet lilac.*

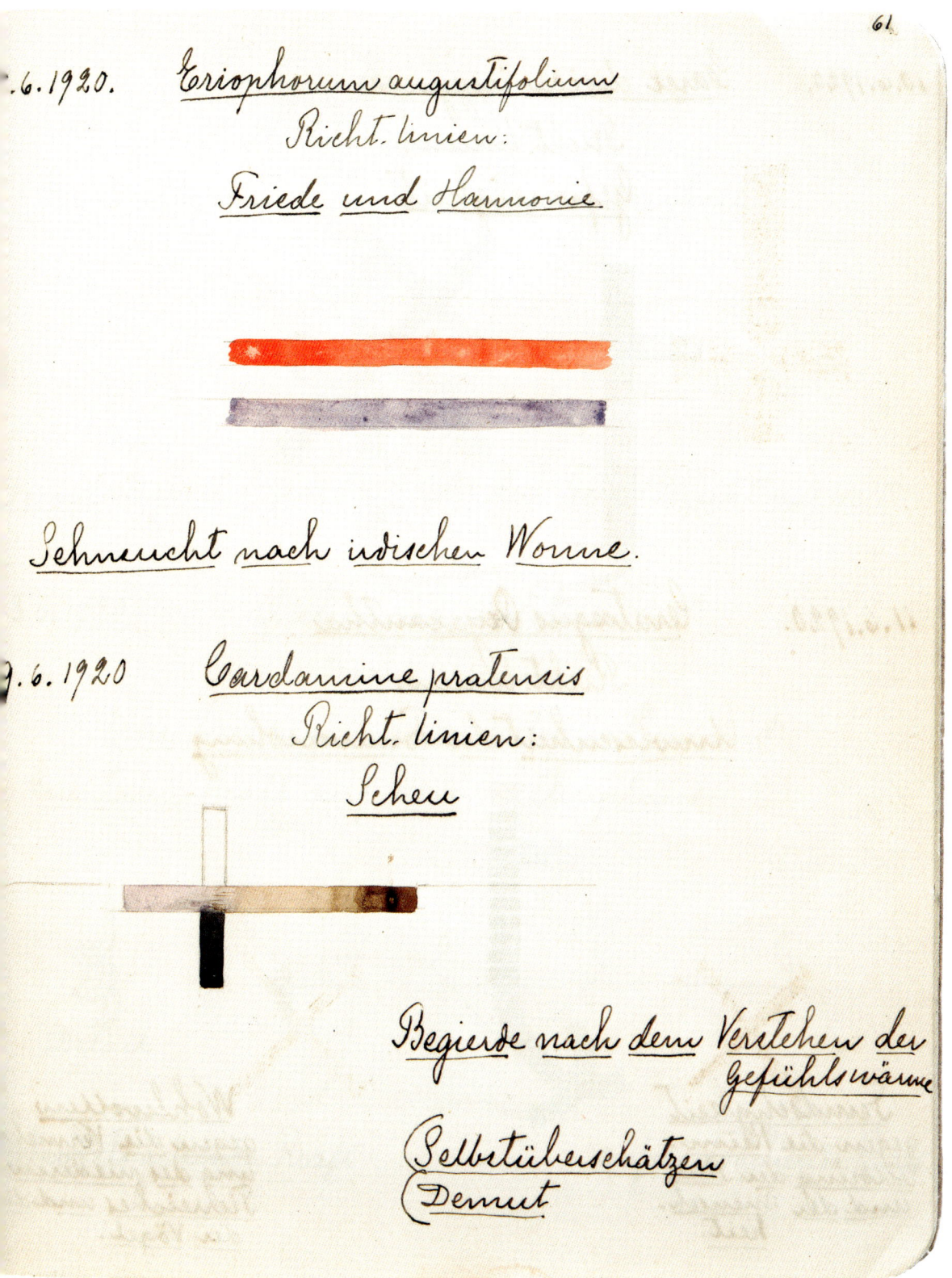

.6.1920.   Eriophorum augustifolium
                Richt. linien:
            Friede und Harmonie

Sehnsucht nach irdischen Wonne.

.6.1920   Cardamine pratensis
                Richt. linien:
                    Scheu

Begierde nach dem Verstehen der
                                    Gefühlswärme

Selbstüberschätzen
Demut

6/8/1920. Eriophorum angustifolium. *Direction lines: Peace and harmony. Longing for earthly delight.*

6/9/1920. Cardamine pratensis. *Direction lines: Timidity. Craving to understand the warmth of feeling. Overconfidence. Humility.*

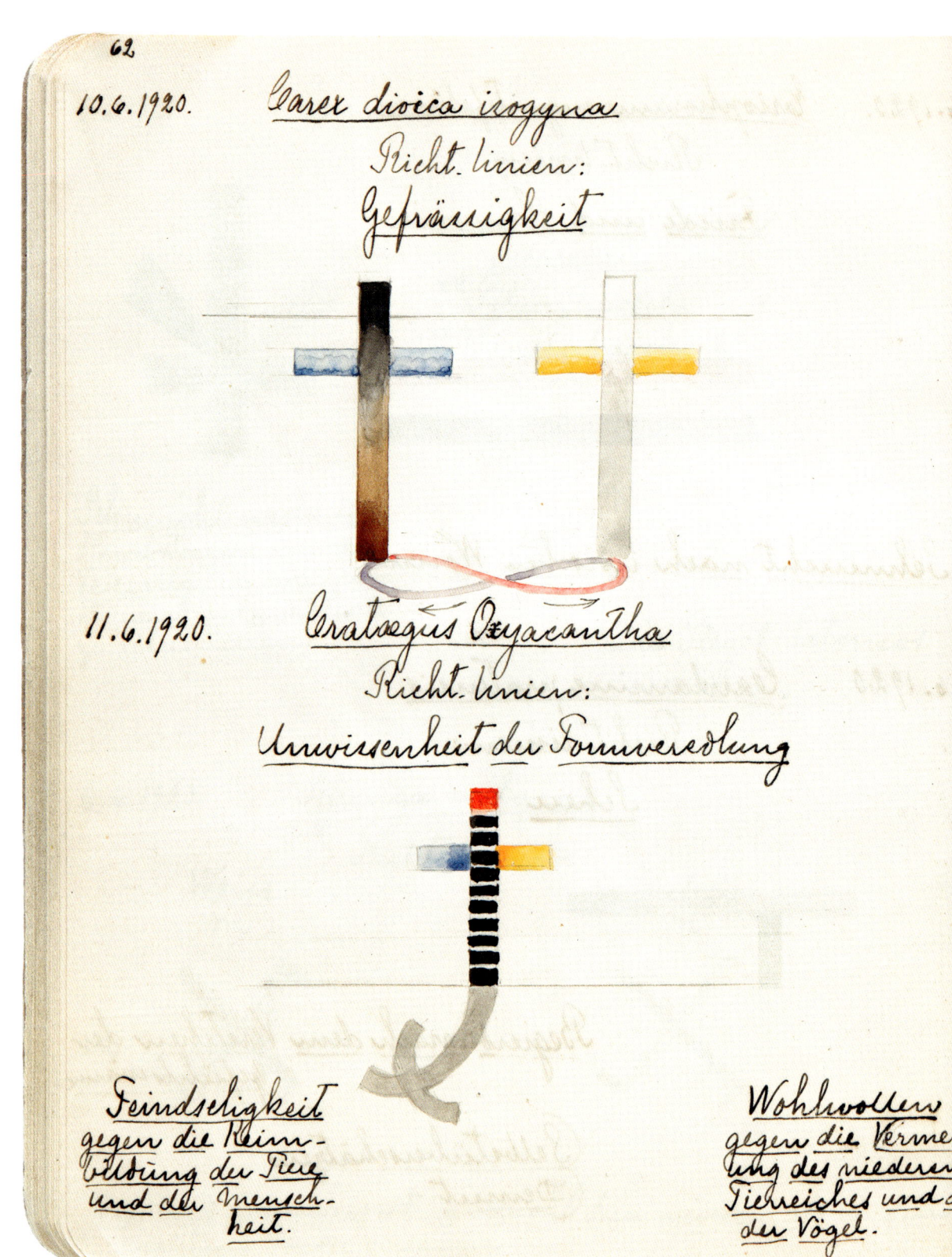

6/10/1920. Carex dioica irogyna. *Direction lines: Voracity.*

6/11/1920. Crataegus oxycantha. *Direction lines: Ignorance of refinement of form. Hostility toward germination of animals and humanity. Goodwill toward the lower animal kingdom and the kingdom of the birds.*

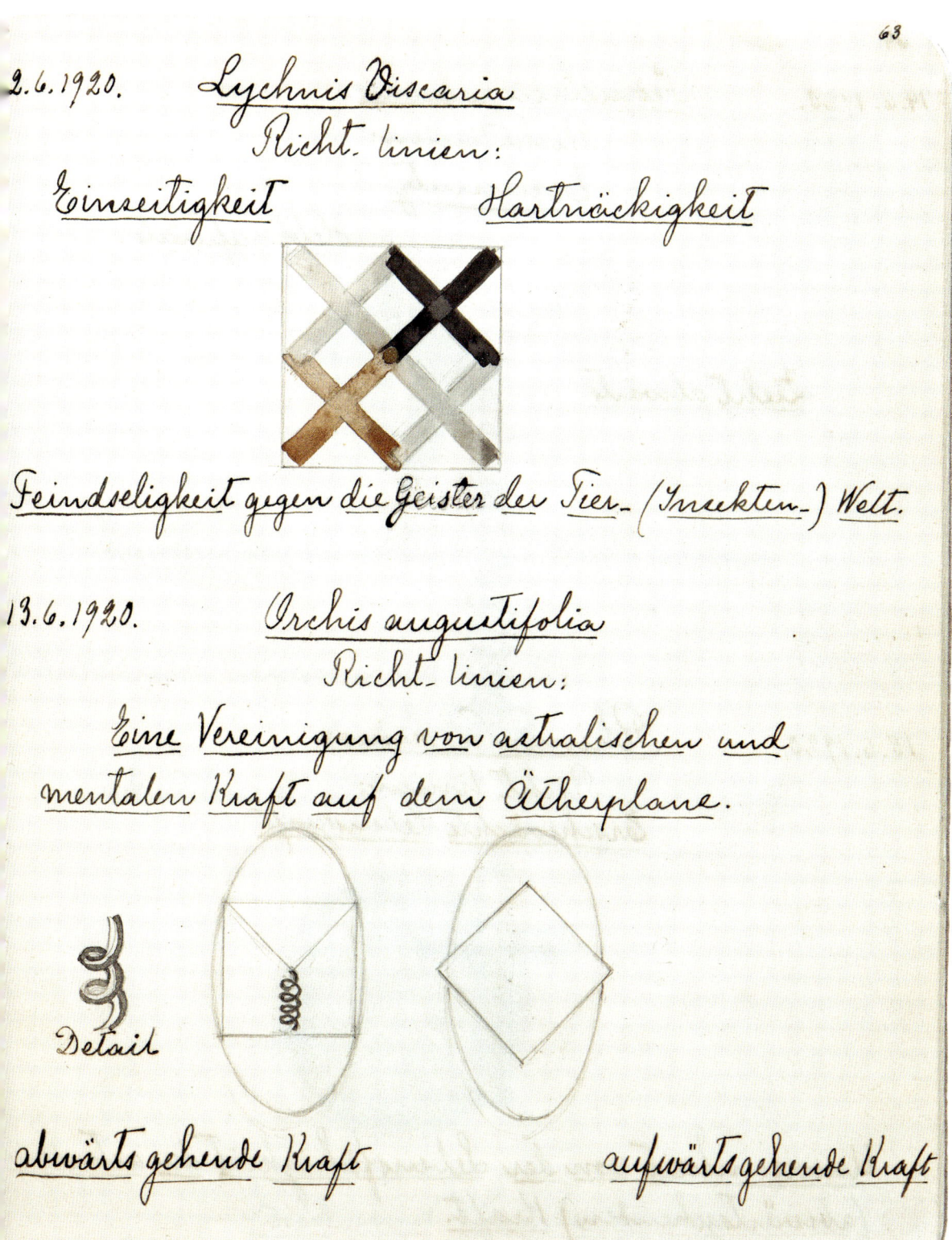

2.6.1920.

Lychnis Viscaria
Richt. linien:

Einseitigkeit   Hartnäckigkeit

Feindseligkeit gegen die Geister der Tier- (Insekten-) Welt.

13.6.1920.

Orchis angustifolia
Richt. linien:

Eine Vereinigung von astralischen und mentalen Kraft auf dem Ätherplane.

Detail

abwärts gehende Kraft   aufwärts gehende Kraft

6/12/1920. Lychnis viscaria. *Direction lines: Imbalance. Stubbornness. Hostility toward the spirit of the animal (insect) world.*

6/13/1920. Orchis angustifolia. *Direction lines: A union of astral and mental power on the etheric plane.*

Detail. Descending power. Ascending power.

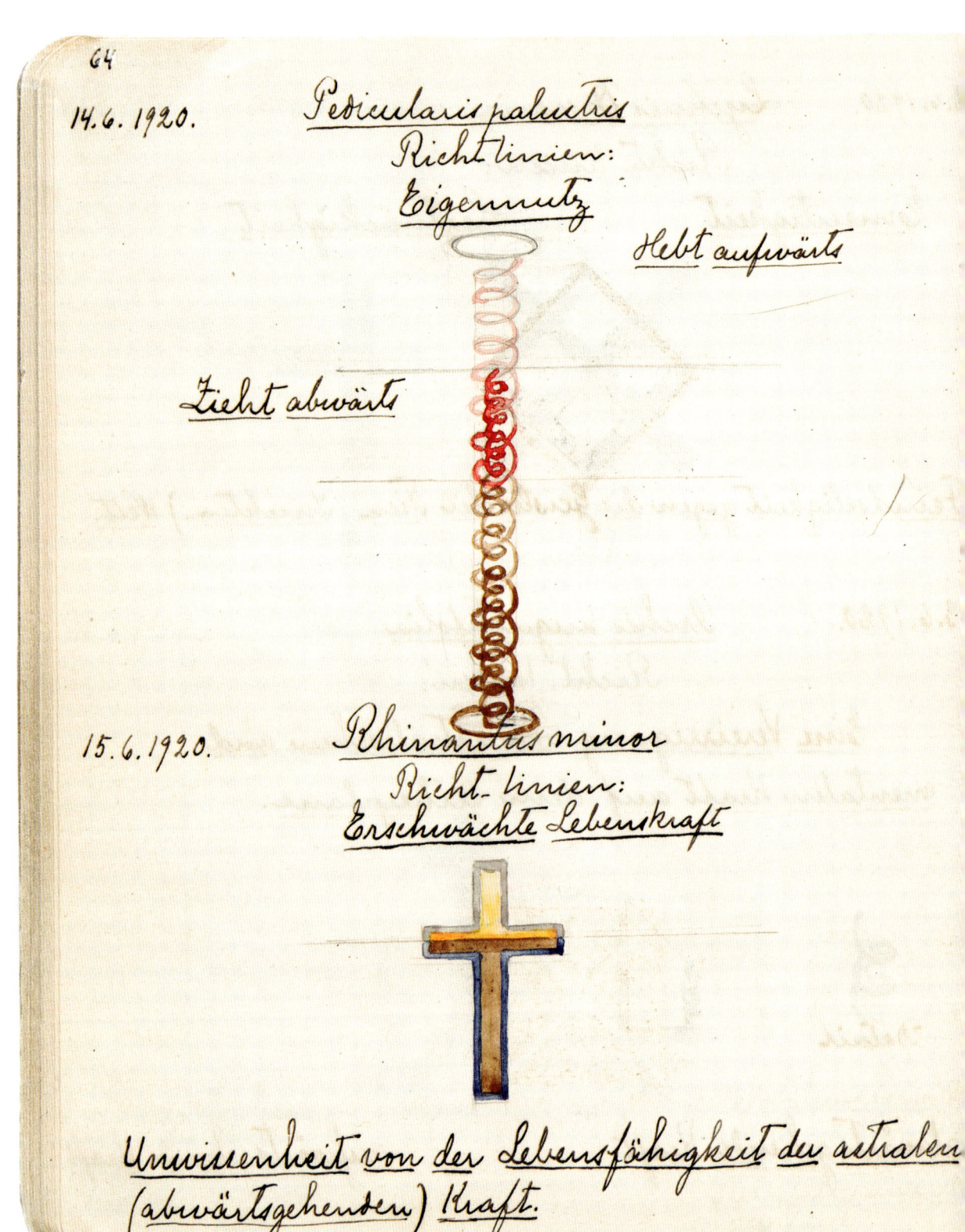

64

14.6.1920.

Pedicularis palustris

Richt linien:

Eigennutz

Hebt aufwärts

Zieht abwärts

15.6.1920.

Rhinanthus minor

Richt- linien:

Erschwächte Lebenskraft

Unwissenheit von der Lebensfähigkeit der astralen
(abwärtsgehenden) Kraft.

6/14/1920. Pedicularis palustris. *Direction lines: Self-interest. Lifts up. Pulls down.*

6/15/1920. Rhinanthus minor. *Direction lines: Weakened life force. Ignorance of the viability of the astral (ascending) power.*

6. 6. 1920.   *Lamium album*

Richt. linien:

Gleichgewicht innerhalb des phys. und äther. Körper

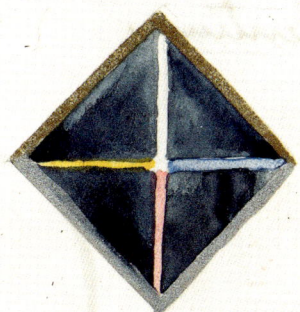

Erkenntnis der menschlichen Viergliederung.

7. 6. 1920.   *Lychnis flos cuculi*

Richt. linien:

Erkenntnis des Lebenswerkes der Menschheit

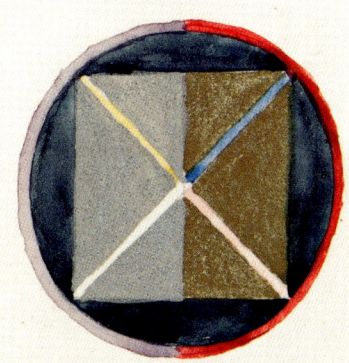

Friede und Harmonie

6/16/1920. Lamium album. *Direction lines: Balance within the physical and etheric body. Awareness of human division.*

6/17/1920. Lychnis flos cuculis. *Direction lines: Awareness of the life's work of humanity. Peace and harmony.*

18.6.1920.

Fumaria officinalis
Richt. linien:
Erkenntnis vom Ausgehen der vier Richtungslinien vom Zentrum

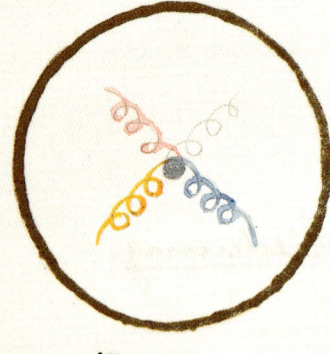

Ausatmen

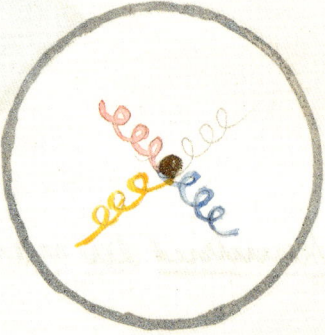

Einatmen

6/18/1920. Fumaria officinalis. *Direction lines. Awareness of the four direction lines going out from the center. Breathing out. Breathing in.*

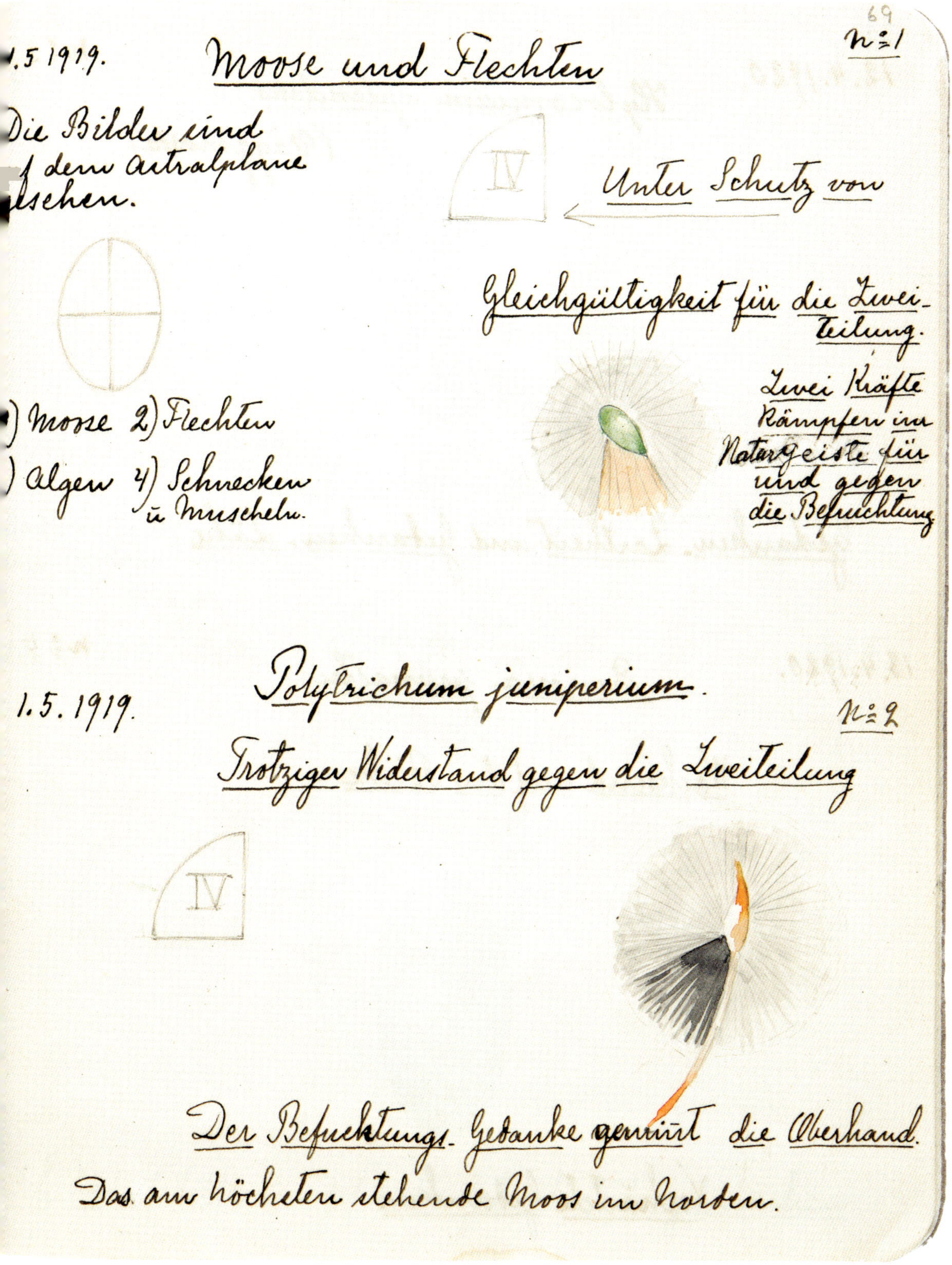

1.5 1979.

Moose und Flechten

Die Bilder sind
[au]f dem Astralplane
[ge]sehen.

IV   ⟵   Unter Schutz von

Gleichgültigkeit für die Zwei-
Teilung.

Zwei Kräfte
Kämpfen im
Naturgeiste für
und gegen
die Befruchtung

1) Moose 2) Flechten
3) Algen 4) Schnecken
     u. Muscheln.

---

1. 5. 1919.   Polytrichum juniperium.   N⁰ 2

Trotziger Widerstand gegen die Zweiteilung

IV

Der Befruchtungs-Gedanke gewinnt die Oberhand.
Das am höchsten stehende Moos im Norden.

5/1/1919. No. 1. Mosses and lichens. *The images are seen on the astral plane. Under the protection of ←. Indifference toward the dichotomy. Two forces struggle in the spirit of nature for and against fertilization.*

5/1/1919. No. 2. Polytrichum juniperinum. *Defiant resistance to dichotomy. The thought of fertilization gains the upper hand. The moss found farthest north.*

70

12.4.1920.

Hylocomium splendens
(Vàggmossa)

Gedanken - Zartheit und Gedanken - Zähe

13.4.1920.

Evernia prunastri.

Wachsend auf der Birke

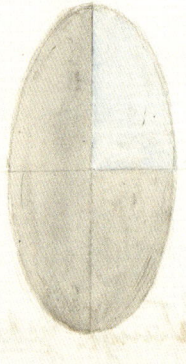

Verhärtete Gedanken

4/12/1920. No. 3. Hylocomium splendens *(Vaggmossa). Tenderness of thought and toughness of thought.*

4/13/1920. No 4. Evernia prunastria. *Grows on birches. Hardened thoughts.*

4. 4. 1920.

Cladonia

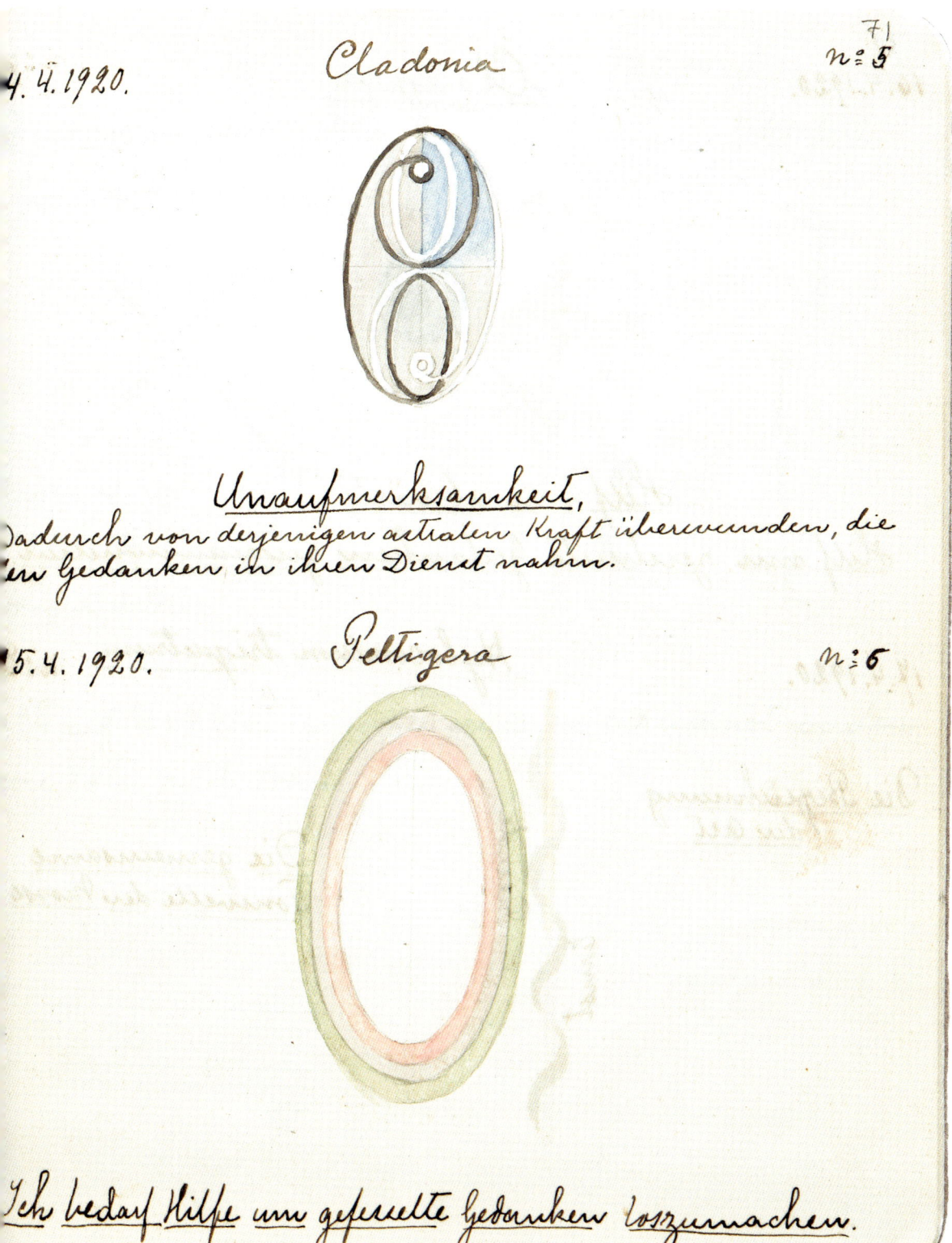

Unaufmerksamkeit,
Dadurch von derjenigen astralen Kraft überwunden, die
den Gedanken in ihren Dienst nahm.

5. 4. 1920.
Peltigera
n⸱ 6

Ich bedarf Hilfe um gefesselte Gedanken loszumachen.

4/14/1920. No. 5. Cladonia. *Inattention, overcome by the astral power that engaged the thoughts.*

4/15/1920. No. 6. Peltigera. *I need help to free captive thoughts.*

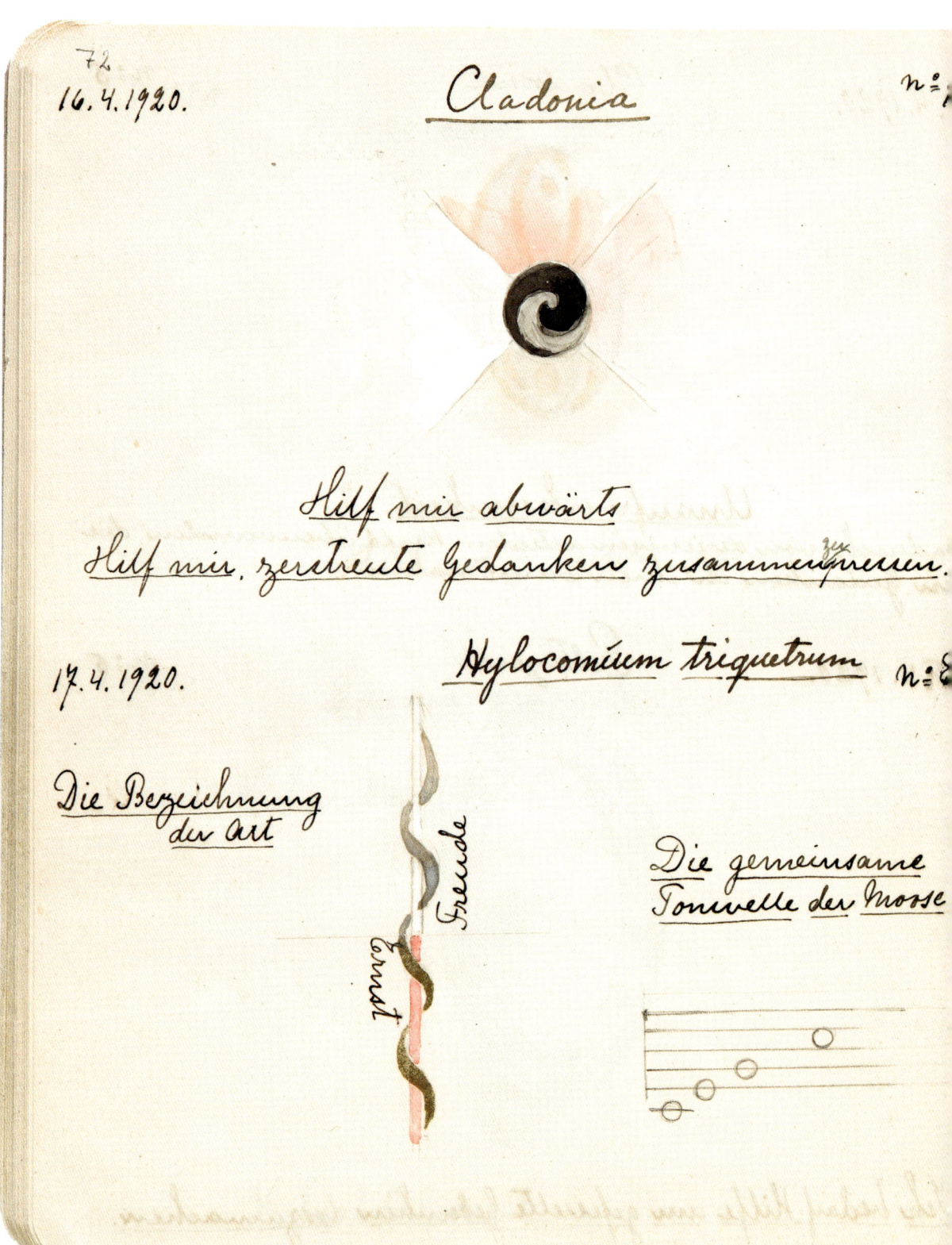

16.4.1920.

Cladonia

$n =$

Hilf mir abwärts
Hilf mir, zerstreute Gedanken zusammenpressen.

17.4.1920.

Hylocomium triquetrum

$n =$

Die Bezeichnung
der Art

Freude

Ernst

Die gemeinsame
Tonwelle der Moose

4/16/1920. No. 7. Cladonia. Help me upward. Help me to condense scattered thoughts.

4/17/1920. No. 8. Hylocomium triquetrum. The name of the species. Seriousness. Joy. The collective sound wave of the mosses.

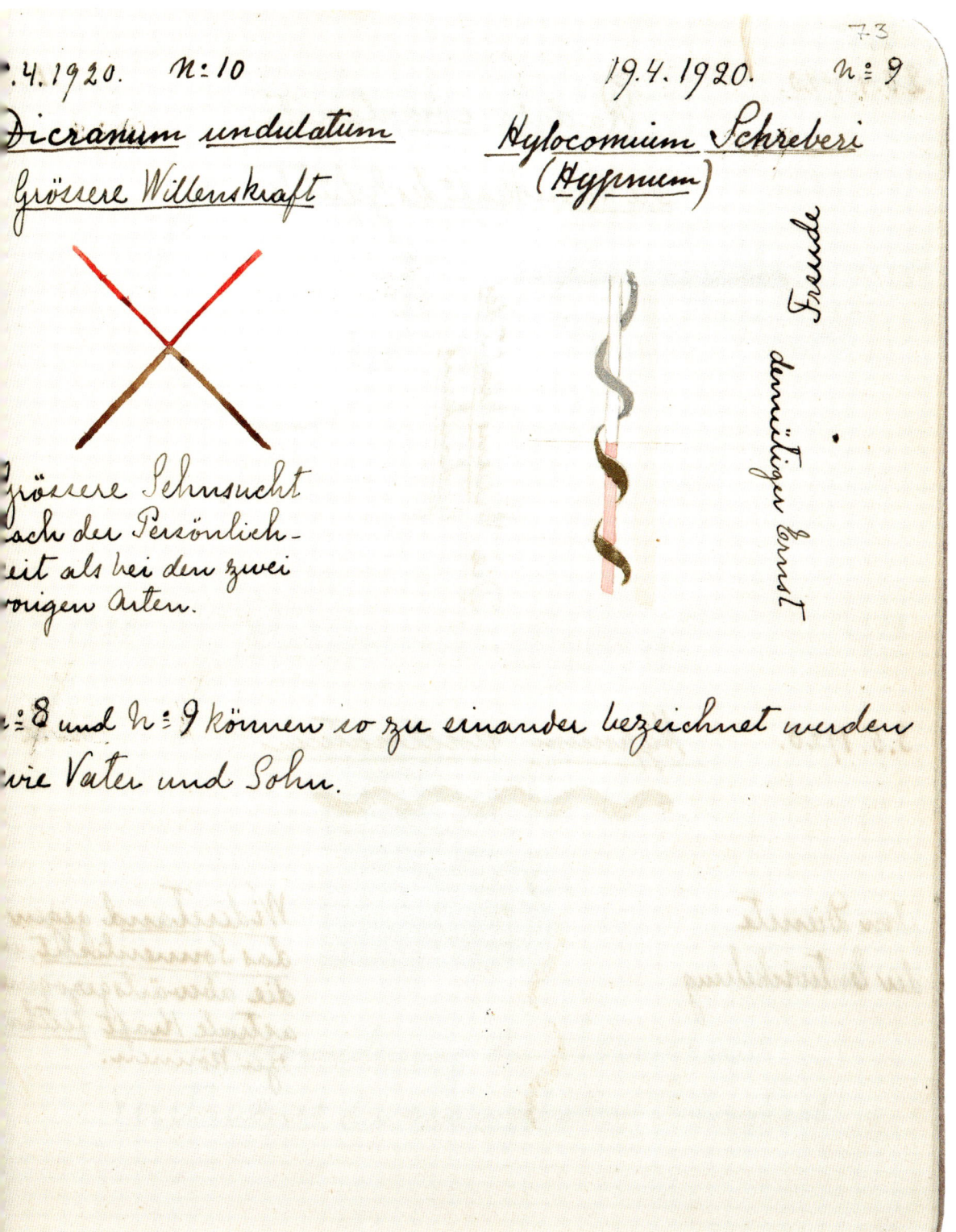

.4.1920.　　　N: 10

Dicranum undulatum

Grössere Willenskraft

Grössere Sehnsucht nach der Persönlich- keit als bei den zwei vorigen Arten.

N: 8 und N: 9 können so zu einander bezeichnet werden wie Vater und Sohn.

19.4.1920.　　　N: 9

Hylocomium Schreberi
(Hypnum)

Freude

demütiger Ernst

4/19/1920. No. 10. Dicranum undulatum. *Greater willpower. Greater desire for personality than in the two previous species.*

4/19/1920. No. 9. Hylocomium schreberi (Hypnum). *Humble seriousness. Joy.*
No. 8 and No. 9 can be described as like father and son to each other.

20.4.1920.

Radula complanata

Die Willenskraft des Gefühls

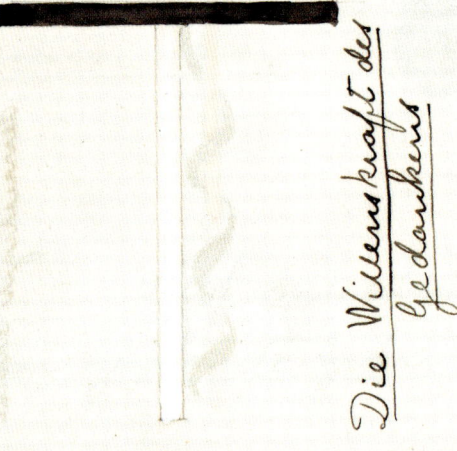

Die Willenskraft des Gedankens

Obs. M° 17

3.5.1920.   Hypnum uncinatum.   n° 12

Im Dienste
der Entwickelung

Widerstand gegen
das Sonnenlicht, u
die abwärtsgezogen
astrale Kraft festha
zu können.

4/20/1920. No. 11. Radula complanata. The willpower of feeling. The willpower of thought.

5/3/1920. No. 12. Hypnum uncinatum. In the service of development.
Resistance to sunlight in order to hold on to ascending astral power.

1.5.1920

Buxbaumia aphylla

Nº 13

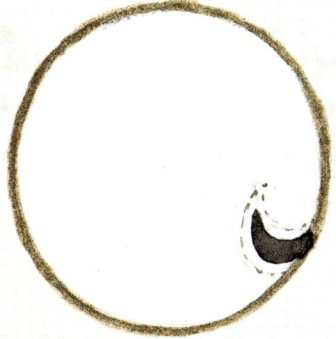

Gefesselte Lebensfreude
die ihre Fesseln zu
sprengen versucht.

5.5.1920.

Dicranum scopárium

Nº 14

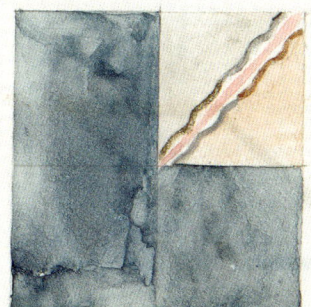

Bewunderung der Lebenskraft.
Verständnis der mangelnden Fähigkeit.

5/4/1920. No. 13. Buxbaumia aphylla. Captive lust for life that attempts to break its bonds.

5/5/1920. No. 14. Dicranum scoparium. Admiration of the life force. Understanding of lack of ability.

6.5.1920. *Amblystegium serpens* №15

Schnellere Vibrationen,
grösserer Eifer, weniger Kraft
bei der Art, im Vergleich
mit den Vorigen.

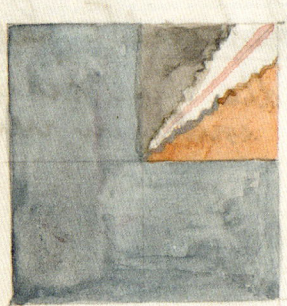

8.5.1920. *Bryum capillare* №16

Durchsichtige, zarte Gedanken weiblichen Charakters

5/6/1920. No. 15. Amblystegium serpens. *Rapid vibrations, greater eagerness, less power in this species compared to the previous.*

5/8/1920. No. 16. Bryum capillare. *Transparent, tender thoughts of a feminine character.*

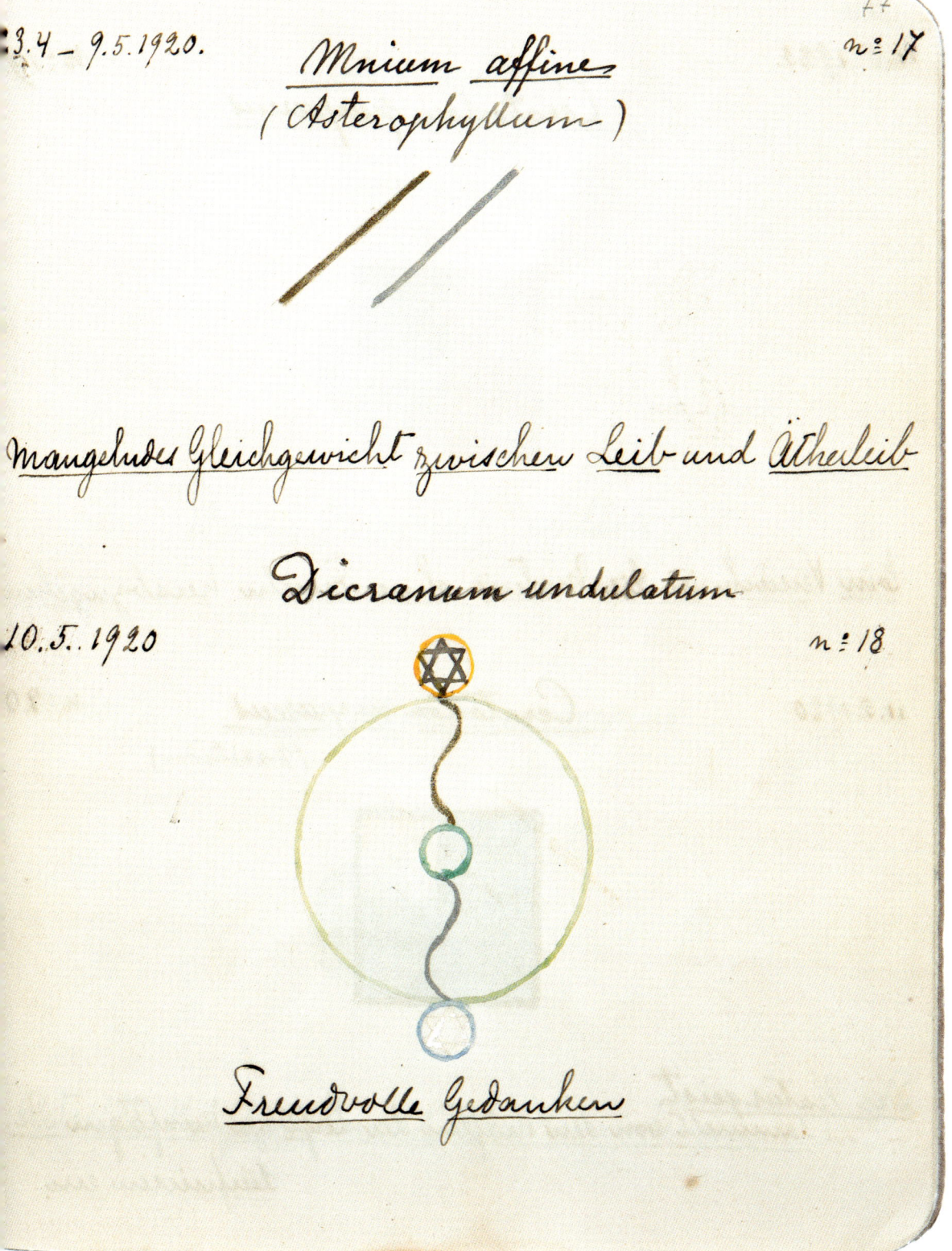

23.4 – 9.5.1920.

Mnium affine
(Asterophyllum)

Mangelndes Gleichgewicht zwischen Leib und Ätherleib

Dicranum undulatum

10.5.1920

Freudvolle Gedanken

4/23–5/9/1920. No. 17. Mnium affine (Asterophyllum). *Lack of balance between body and etheric body.*

5/10/1920. No. 18. Dicranum. *Joyful thoughts.*

11.5.1920.   n° 19

Ceratodon purpureus

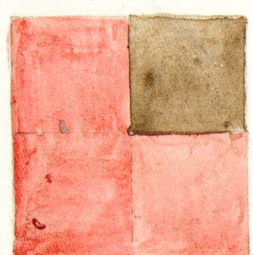

Ein Versuch, in die Materie ohne Fesseln herabzugehen

11.5.1920   *Ceratodon purpureus*   n° 20
                                 (varition)

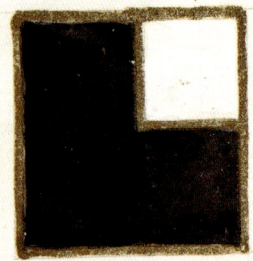

Der Naturgeist sammelt von den Kräften der Luft zu künftigen Bedürnissen ein.

5/11/1920. No. 19. Ceratodon purpureus. *An attempt to descend unfettered into matter.*

5/11/1920. No. 20. Ceratodon purpureus (variation). *The spirit of nature gathers the powers of the air for future needs.*

12.5.1920.

Pohlia nutans
(Bryum)

№ 21

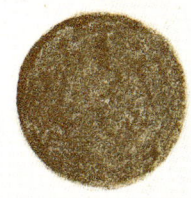

Von, Lebenskraft erfüllt

12.5.1920

Amblystegium serpens

№ 22

se även)
(№ 15

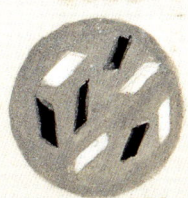

Geteilte Kraft erschweret das Herabsteigen.

5/12/1920. No. 21. Pohlia nutans (Bryum). *Filled with life force.*

5/12/1920. No. 22. Amblystegium serpens. *Divided power hinders descent.*

26.5.1920.

Hyphomycetes?
(Schimmelpilze)
Gefährliche Gedanken

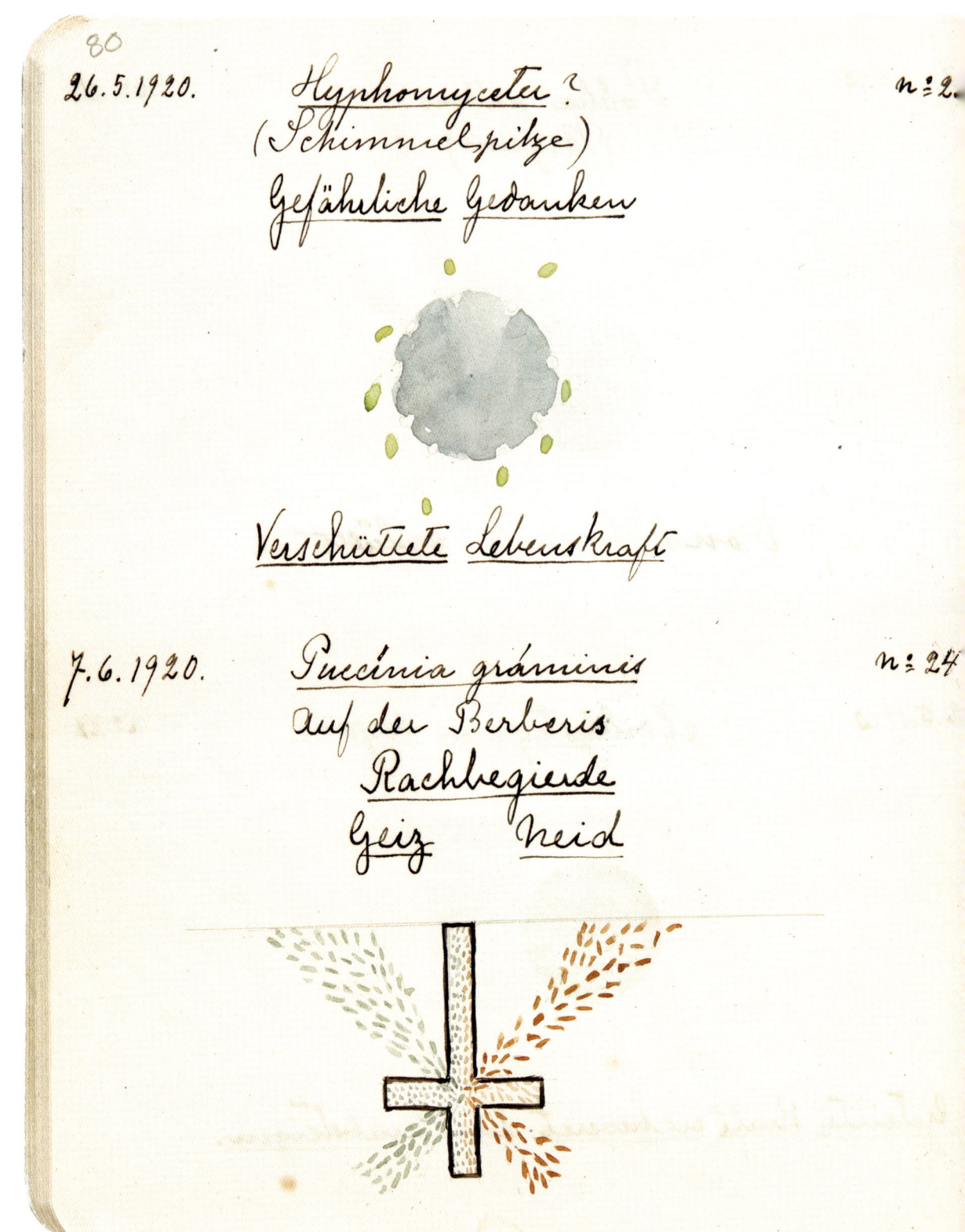

Verschüttete Lebenskraft

7.6.1920.

Puccinia gráminis
auf der Berberis
Rachbegierde
Geiz   Neid

n̊ 24

5/26/1920. No. 23. Hyphomycetes *? (mold). Dangerous thoughts. Spilled life force.

6/7/1920. No. 24. Puccinia graminis. *On the barberry plant. Craving for revenge. Greed. Jealousy.*

Letters and Words Pertaining to
Works by Hilma af Klint

In 1907 Hilma af Klint received a message from the High Masters concerning the sound of letters appearing in her paintings: "The purpose of these letters is to prepare the way for a language of symbols that has already existed forever and that has now been given to humanity by the creative spirits." (HaK 431) It is likely that af Klint assembled the majority of *Letters and Words Pertaining to Works by Hilma af Klint* when she was editing and adding indexes to her notebooks in the 1930s, but it is clear from the very start that she understood the key role that language was to play in her work.

On the frontispiece of *Letters and Words* there appear the symbols with which af Klint prefaces all her written texts: + ×. For af Klint + represents "superphysical thought" and × "superphysical imagination (the symbol of the astral world)." The notebook opens with handwritten notes by Rudolf Steiner, cut and pasted onto the page by af Klint, regarding his interpretation of several letters that appear in af Klint's paintings. The work that follows is an extensive compilation of first the words and then the letters that appear in af Klint's artwork and throughout her more than twenty thousand pages of writing. Each section is in alphabetical order, sometimes with several definitions given for key letters and words. The entries explain such things as the origins of her spirit guides, the meanings of the colors used, and the symbolism of various plants. Terms appear from a variety of sources. There are references to scientific and biblical texts as well as language borrowed from a wide range of Rosicrucian, Theosophical, Anthroposophical, and other esoteric texts. As the translators noted when working on this text, *Letters and Words* is of a time and context that is not always easy to penetrate. It is a closed system, but it is not an individualistic one.

Letters and Words describes a complex system of language crucial to a body of visual work—an integration of language and art that is unique within its time.

Pages 247–54, 266–67: *Letters and Words Pertaining to Works by Hilma af Klint* notebook HaK 1040, n.d. Ink and pencil on paper, 8 × 6¾ in. (20.5 × 17 cm)

Anteckningar

över

Bokstäver och Ord

tillhörande arbeten

av

Hilma af Klint

N:r 3000/48 L

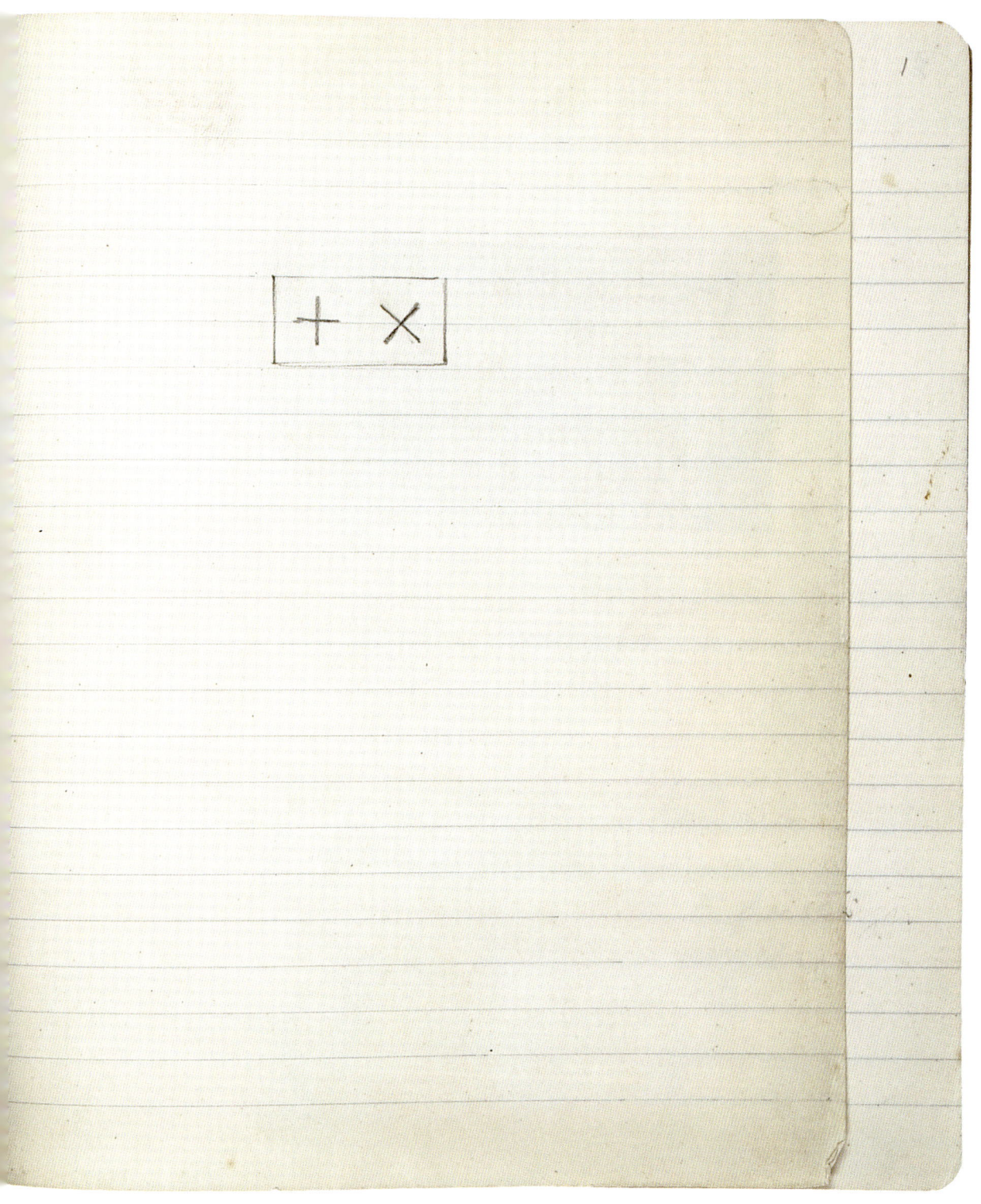

Real. (fr. eter planet)

S = Schlange = ormen

u = a = alfa

w = w = omega

Originalskrift

av

Doktor Rudolf Steiner

vid beskrivning av Hilma af Klints första
målningar innan figurserierna började.

Real. (fr. the etheric plane).
S = snake [*Schlange*] = snake [*ormen*]
U = a = alfa
w = w = omega

Original text written by Doctor Rudolf Steiner describing Hilma af Klint's first paintings before the figure paintings were begun.

4

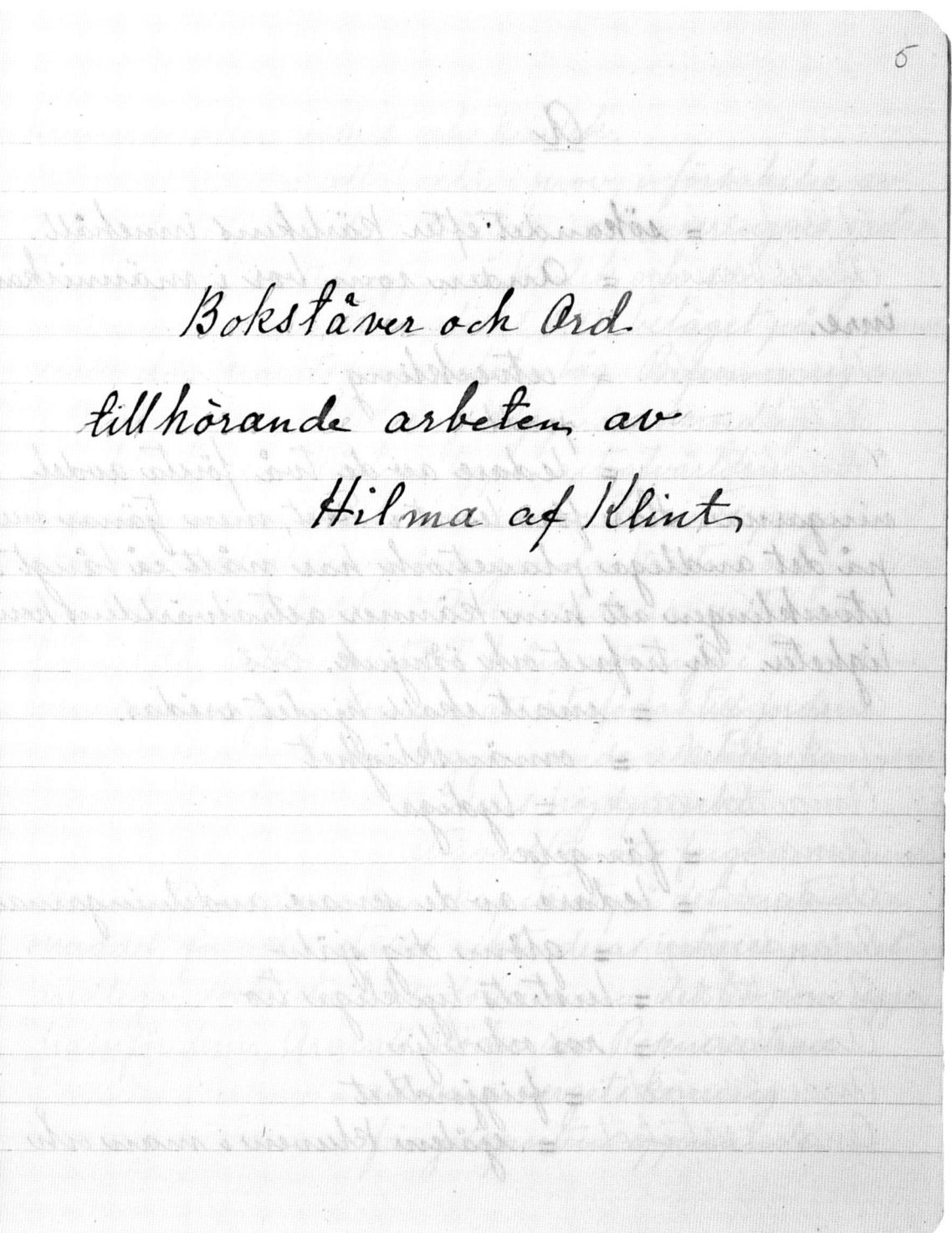

Bokstäver och Ord.

tillhörande arbeten av

Hilma af Klint.

a

Akab = sökandet efter kärlekens innehåll.

Akras boning = Anden som bor i människans inre.

Alma mater = utveckling

Altar = pall

Amalid = ledare av de två första avdelningarna. Har förr levat i Tibet, men tjänar nu på det andliga planet och har nått så långt i utvecklingen att han känner astralvärldens hemligheter. Är trofast och ödmjuk, vis

Amandan = snart skall hjulet vridas.

Amandena = omänsklighet

Ama du saava = lydiga

AmaH = fängelse

Ananda = ledare av de senare avdelningarna.

Anandas lag = glöm dig själv

Anda Hes = ljusets lyckliga tro

Andehjo = ros och lilja

Andens svärd = frigjordhet

Andens vehikel = själen kluven i man och

Akab = the search for the substance of love

Akrasboning = the spirit who lives inside humanity

Alma mater = development

Altar = footstool

Amaliel = the leader of the first two divisions. Formerly lived in Tibet but now serves on the spiritual plane and has reached a point in his evolution where he understands the secrets of the astral world. Is faithful and humble, wise.

Amandan = soon the wheel shall be turned

Amandena = inhumane

Ama du soava = obedient

AmaH = prison

Ananda = leader of the later divisions

Anandas lag [Anandas law] = forget yourself

AndaHes = desire's joyful faith

Andehjo = rose and lily

Andens svärd [The sword of the spirit] = liberation

Andens vehikel [The vehicle of the spirit] = the soul split into man and woman, or wisdom and love

Andens väg [The path of the spirit] = withstanding a trial, in renunciation of one's self, in suffering, in love, in groups of seven

Apostoliskt [Apostolic] = to build on love and truth

Ararats berg [Mount Ararat] is, climatically speaking, located in the same place as Mount Ararat of the Bible. Lies now in Arabia but will one day be the northernmost point of the Earth. Its glorious summit is in the astral world. It is the mission of the exalted beings residing there to teach humanity what the ancient Christian and Jewish symbols represent. There are also some initiated who declined joining the Devachan but who one day will be reborn on Earth.

Ararats bergs fot [The foot of Mount Ararat] = the nascent ascetic struggle

Ararats bergs topp [The summit of Mount Ararat] = the apex of the spirit

Ararats bergs tjänare [The servants of Mount Ararat] seek to liberate the people from their thirst for knowledge in the material field and instead to focus their interest on the spiritual without neglecting the life that lies ahead of them. The brothers of Ararat are Rosicrucians.

Ararats bärkraft [The strength of Ararat] = to be king of the mountain

Ararats historia [The history of Ararat] = opening of the prison gates

Ararats bröder [The brothers of Ararat] reside in the Astral World. They can assume physical form when they choose.

Ararats Mahatmer [The Mahatmas of Ararat] assemble servants in all countries, of all beliefs. They make contact with the brave and the fearless.

Ararats oljeberg [The oil mountain of Ararat] = the image of light = life's liberation

Ararats temple [The temple of Ararat] is built on white ground; the purple chalice resides within. Its hidden wisdom means: Hosanna is born on the foundation of purity.

Ararats tjänares tjänares tjänare [The servants of Ararat's servants' servants] = beings on D. F's× [The Five's] position.

Arvsynd [Original Sin] = the child's inheritance from those who came before

Ask, Embla = he, she. Ask = male shame at sensuality; Embla = the road leading up to the male sphere of activity. Embla = the upper half, the bond that attaches men to the forces of light. If a woman withstands the trial of the lower level of sensuality, then she is able to lead the man upward; otherwise she drags him down.

Asket och Vestal [Ascetic and Vestal] = Mary's sanctuary in her earthly life

Asket—Vestal [Ascetic—Vestal] = dual symbol. Yellow and blue, but can also be represented by the purist white

Asket—Vestal [Ascetic and Vestal] = occult sphere of Essene origin

Asket [Ascetic] = one half of inhabitants of Nirvana, the other, vestal. Ascetic = sevenfold.

Asketism [Asceticism] = purity of mind; can be represented by light yellow

Astralplanet [The Astral Plane] = the prison gate, open as well as closed

Avana = storage rooms

Ave = freedom directed by the High Masters

Ave Maria [Hail Mary] = light. In the occult sense = earth, matter.

Ave Maria = belief

Ave Maria = believing that matter is also directed by the High Masters

Ave Maria = to gather love from your own being!

Ave Maria = conquering the vanity that does not wish to show its face

Ave Maria = the first and last attainment of love in truth and purity. See further 240.

Avonvener = those who try to send light down onto the people of Earth

Awon = the length of the journey

Ayas = undaunted.

p. 160 Au=

× A circle of people at the end of the last century who tried to learn about the brothers and sisters of Ararat.

Bajarderen = waves of unrest

Barn [Children] = work in the physical form

Barnaförtroende [Childlike trust] = the first love

Barnasjälens behov [The requirement for the childlike soul] is innocence

Bergets logos [The logos of the mountain] = the permeation of the leaven

Beryondan = Aramaic/Syrian war cry: Stand firm, brothers, unite

Beurunden = the summit of Mount Ararat

Blinda makter [Blind powers] = dubious speech

Blinda sorger [Blind sorrows] = strained emotions or troublesome thoughts

Blåskär färg [Bluish pink color] = trusting in previous incarnations

Blått [Blue] = the color of strong and true nature. Faithfulness, in mediumistic work as well.

Brama = the highest quality of the childlike mind

Broderskärlek [Brotherly love] = the olive mountain's symbol

Brunao = female guide

Bumerangens kastande [The boomerang's throw] = to accuse

Bebådelsen [The Annunciation] = Mary was overcome by a spiritual force, her heart was filled with holy feelings, all impurity was burned away. Therefore the act of giving birth became sacred as well.

Blommans blad [The flower's petals] = knowledge, its sepal = the shelter of knowledge

Brunt [Brown] = the color of unrest

Christus [Christ] = the core of the work

Coru = the ability to succeed

De Höga [The High Masters] = the Masters of Mysteries, synonymous with Vestal-Ascetic; servants of Christ who reside in Tibet (in the astral body?). An exalted and holy brotherhood, known to all mystics who participate in the evolution of the world. Ananda and Amaliel belong to this group. The High Masters fill the entire universe.

Det duala hjärtat [The dual heart] has two expressions of force: inhalation = woman, exhalation = man

Dualandarna [The dual spirits] emerged at the moment the sexes were divided as a result of human passions

Dualbeteckning [Dual symbol] = ascetic—yellow, vestal—blue

Duallängtan [Dual desire] = the driving force in the formation of dual souls

Dualväsendet [Dual nature] = struggle and serenity, peace and war, life and matter. The harmony within the dual nature is a sacred and pure concept.

Dödens barn [The children of death] = those forces that have come to their end and will now be removed

Deva = Indian mythology, a being formed differently from humans

Durave = the wheel

E

Emaus = Eros on the etheric plane

Eramon = suffering, caused by the scorn of enemy

Eromeden = hardships encountered in the pursuit of perfection

Eros is blind, i.e., he does not calculate, he does not judge, but in his eyes injustice becomes justice. His color is pink and augurs progress.

Esseiskt [Essenic] the nature of this work. It will be of use to the stoic people who are now descending to earth.

Essencens av allt [The essence of everything] = *OO*

Ester contributed to the first section of the work. Serves on the physical plane.

Eusu = the rose

Evolutionens beteckning [The sign for evolution] = O ⌢ O

Eomes = the bond between matter and heaven

F

Fundamentalsanning [Fundamental truth] = vestal and ascetic

Fonos = harmony of color

Förlåten [The veil] = matter

Fängelseporten [The prison gates] = the dual relationship, also called "the two fathers"

Fanan [The flag] = of great significance for the disciples of joy in the material world

Fw = Upanishad knowledge p. 520

G

Gamla världens förnämsta synder [The principle sins of the ancient world] = vanity and indifference

Gidro = a leader who serves on the astral plane

Gregor = an exalted leader whose work concerned separating the body from the soul but now concerns separating the soul from the spirit. Claimed to be a brother of the White Cross, who, like their sisters, served the dual truth.

Gubbe [Old man] = the self

Gud [God] = cause and effect; everything

Gult [Yellow] = the glorious color of light, wellspring of knowledge, faithfulness to the spiritual

H

Haken [hook, hook-and-eye] = wisdom

Hama = Syrian word, love's first peaceful word. A glimpse into the astral world.

Hamaranda = leave everything to the High Masters!

Hamys = to be untroubled by those who deny you your triumphs

Hela arbetet [The work itself] is led by Rosicrucians, though a man from the East guided my hand for the first series, inspired the idea, and I could not have carried it out without his help.

Hela mänskligheten [Humanity] awaits the day when, by means of the astral light, they will behold and communicate with the astral world. In ancient times this was natural, but is now a rare gift.

Heligt [Sacred] is the work of the ascetic, sacred is W.U., sacred is U^9), occult ascetic/ vestal = the dual truth

Het sand [Hot sand] = the fire of desire

Helbregdagörande kraft [Faith-healing powers] must be preceded by suffering

Hidoman = the child (Syrian)

Hjälparna [The helpers] of the Seven Sisters series resided on the astral plane

Hjärtat [The heart] = the part of our being that perceives love's influence on the work. The image of the origin of life.

Huset [The house] = struggle for freedom

Hymens trettio kämpar [The thirty warriors of Hymen]

Hyskan [The eye, hook-and-eye] = love

Härlighetens boning [Glory's abode] = a young, healthy disposition forged in the crucible, molded to reach the pink rose

De Höga [The High Masters] reside in Tibet.

Herta skörden [Harvest] see p. 382

I

Indras kraft [The powers of Indra] influenced one of the four Devas carrying out this work

Intuition = incense

Inseglet [The seal] = times when pleasure has lost its appeal

K

Kaktus [Cactus] = the flower of Ararat

Kaktusljus [Cactus light] = overcoming the forces that drag the body downward and appealing to the spirit

Klotet [The globe] = the universe

Kopparbordet [The copper table] served in the Syrian temples as the surface of knowledge on which the temple servants, through mediums, received messages from the High Masters. At that time "Beryondan" was the morning call to the disciples to present themselves promptly for service in the temple.

Källans rena vatten [The wellspring's pure water] = the color blue

Kärlek [Love] is territory comprehensible only to those standing on the position of Venus (this is called "Undansk love"). Degenerate love caused the soul to fall apart. One half (feminine) tried to hold fast, the other (masculine) wanted to search for good and evil. Fully uniting the dual halves creates the most glorious feeling imaginable. One day bright knots will be tied throughout the universe. Paul arrived at this knowledge through a painful inner struggle.

Kärleken i sin fullkomning [Love in its perfection] is symbolized by shining white

Kyndelsmässodag [Candlemas] = preparations for the cross

Korset [The Cross] equal-armed = the powers of the self

Korset [The Cross] to the south, i.e., farther down = the astral forces

L

Leva [To live] = to be receptive to spiritual forces

Lidande [Suffering] can willingly be accepted in aid of quicker progress, or is the consequence of false steps and mistakes

Lilja [Lily] = perfection and love = ave or UW

Ljusblått [Light blue] = belief in truth

Lotusblomma [Lotus flower] = the word. The symbol of life, the word, light, truth, and love.

Lunga [Lung] = the image of the realm of matter. Each breath brings life to a caged existence.

Leviatan [Leviathan] = the corporeal life of the body of a man, as opposed to the spiritual life of a woman on a higher plane

M

Mandelblomma blå [blue meadow saxifrage] = faithfulness

Mandelblomma vit [white meadow saxifrage] = childhood's happiness

Mandelblomma, att avtaga [meadow saxifrage, to go dormant] = to surrender yourself unconditionally

Mandelblommans frukt [The fruit of the meadow saxifrage] = the symbol of brotherly love

Man [Man] = the astral body

Maria [Mary] = earth, in the occult sense

Masang = the land of the Byzantines

Materie [Matter] = the means of resurrecting the delicate heart from the chill of death and to reunite its scattered, broken pieces

Mediumskapet [Mediumship] may evolve through suffering

Megonen = the book of memory

Messianskt mysteriearbete [Messianic mystery work] = the development of the inner senses. The world's armor against cunning and vanity.

Mimers brunn [Mimer's well] = the world of the mind. The domain of indigo.

Mossbelupen ros [Moss-covered rose] = the end of the struggle

Mossa omkring ros [Moss around rose] = forsaking the heart

Mysterierna [The mysteries] explain the logical development of a life, i.e., bringing together wisdom, power, and love into *one* concept, namely spirit. And interpret matter as the external instrument of the spirit.

Människa [Human being] = a thought transmitted from God

Muren [The wall] = the sevenfold in the world

N

Narciss [Narcissus] = innocence

Nedmyllande i jorden [Seed sown in the ground] = to bear one's own shortcomings

Nemesis = taking out the outer layer

Nuet [The present] = momentary pleasure, as opposed to Ararat, which is the pursuit of progress for the individual and the brotherhood

Nyckeln till arbetet [The key to the work] is found in section III no. 5 of the paintings

Näckros [Water lily] in the occult sense is the union of rose and lily

Od = to create motion in the astral world

×Odisk kraft [Odic power] = magnetism; possessed by the mediumistically gifted. The more that is emitted, the more that flows back.

Offerbordet [The sacrificial table] = one's own self

Olivens olja [The olive's oil] = decay caused by ignoring the self

Omae = the heart's fire. Obedience to the spirit of God.

Omaenudi = death is conquered, the prince of life will come

Onyx = an image of complete spiritual darkness that nevertheless reflects light

Orange = symbol of the holy

Orm [Snake] = messenger of the astral world, also signifies wisdom and dutifulness

Orm och vatten [Snake and water] = symbols of the astral world

Ostronskal [Oyster shell] = an image of power, holiness, love, humility

Otten = Syrian word

P

Paradisisk färg [Paradisiac color] is expressed through white = the color of perfect faith

Pedas = despair in the heart

Penah = important

Pioniär [Pioneer] so called—due to the method—the person who executed series VI of the paintings

Påskaftonens begrepp [The idea of Easter Eve] = the formation of virtue inside the person. The moment when she accepts suffering as something good and when the liberated soul of the child finds its true home.

Påskdagen [Easter Sunday] = to carry the cross.

Påskdagens [Easter Sunday's] flower's occult name is Ros [Rose] = Pärlan [The Pearl]

Påskdagen [Easter Sunday] shall reveal what is meant by consisting of 7 ose

R

Rasens [The race's] (the present one) work has to take place on a higher plane until it—astrally—understands its true worth

Resedafärg [The color of the mignonette plant] = simple and unselfish

Riset i skogen [Twigs in the forest] = poverty

×/= the sounds and light phenomena of Whitsuntide see Singoalla p. 131 yellow book

Ros [Rose] = the sign of the astral world, sometimes also signifies the agent of the will

Ros och lilja [Rose and lily] = *OO*

Ros, röd [Rose, red] = selfishness

Ros, vit [Rose, white] = unselfishness

Ros [Rose] = 1 and also 2 in its conception

Rosenkransen [The wreath of roses] = both vestal and ascetic wreath, an image of the saga of life. The picture in series III is inspired by Ananda.

S

Sardus = the struggle against the perils of the astral world

Serpentes = the snake, wisdom, and the creation of sin

Sic transit gloria mundi = the designation for the sixth series

Sjustjärnan [The Seven Sisters constellation] = the image of white light, the jubilatory expression of Vestalism and Asceticism. This physical series of images begins with a small ellipse.

Skär ros [Pink rose] = spiritual knowledge and devotion

Snigeln, krypande ur snäckan [The snail crawling out of its shell] = the image of evolution

Snigeln, krypande in i snäckan [The snail crawling into its shell] = the image of obstacles or resistance during evolution

Someo = matters of the heart

Spartansk [Spartan] = the true struggle for light

Surdegens genomsyrande [Permeating the leaven] = the cross elevated to the level of the spirit

Surmaima = love

Svaneröst i astralvärlden [The voice of the swan in the astral world] = Life's song of praise

Svart kub [Black cube] = the uncharted territory of selfishness

Svart ros och svart lilja [Black rose and black lily] = dark forces

Syd [South] = life of emotions, north = healthy realism

Synd [Sin] = wavering on the path of progress, i.e., truth. (Dr. Steiner's lecture in Zurich 12/3/1916)

Syrien [Syria] = the symbol of dual truth

Sjustjärnans bildspråk [The imagery of the Seven Sisters] is given to the Rosicrucians

T

Templet [The temple] = individuality

Teohatius reportedly guided the first four paintings of series III and continued in the autumn of 1907. Behind him stood the one who sketched—possibly Amaliel.

Tebes = noise from the Earth

U

Uarda = a location in Tibet. Also: an especially gifted being.

Undan = the life of the spirit, the turning point during the descent into matter; the glory's abode on the morning star Venus, which can be regarded as both good and not good. The dwelling place Undan later became Uarda in Tibet.

Universum [The universe] is ruled by one, his servants are many. Christ's servants are *OOOOOOOOOOO*

Universums [The universe's] powers are peculiar; half are light; half are dark

Upanishadiskt vetande [Upanishad knowledge] = to work with peace in your heart

Urkraftens vägar [The paths of the primordial force] in humanity are many. Some individuals fall along the way; some overcome the obstacles. Freedom comes only to those who have fought to reach it.

Urkällan till allt [The original source of everything] = wisdom, love, strength

Urvärlden [From the world] = the sacred senses

V

Vetekornet [The kernel of wheat] = good intentions. Golden-yellow. An image of the beginning of life penetrating the outer shell of matter. Its imagery is called the Seven Sisters.

Vingården [The vineyard] = valleys of the Earth

Vita näckrosor [White water-lilies] = know thyself

Vitt [White] = the holiest of all colors

Vendan = faith

Vestal = WOH

Vest al = fivefold

Vama see p. 80

X

Xerxes asked to be guided to the land where he might gain knowledge of God

Y

Ygdrasil = the tree of knowledge = the soul

Yngling [Young man] = the etheric body

Yssée = to divide oneself into two halves, one obedient under pressure, the other moving freely in the light, receiving instruction through direct guidance

Ysseinder = the pioneers of the astral world on earth. They lived—as the High Masters still do—in the astral body on a tall earthly mountain. They were of many different degrees of purity.

Ysseiskt arbetssätt [Ysseian method of work] = Subordinating the unimportant to the important. This method of work is guided by Rosicrucians.

Ysseisk frihet [Ysseian freedom] = to find the source guided by a pilgrim staff and to follow this guidance without uttering a word

Ysseisk kult [Ysseian cult] = a link to invisible intelligences

Ysseens hand [Yssean hand] contains the OH force while working

Ynglingasinnet [The young man's nature] = MW

Jungfrusinnet [The maiden's nature] = WM

Ä

Äroonuma = love and strength

Ärtblomma [Sweet peas] = to grow in love

Ö

Ödmjukhet [Humility] = not assuming the fundamental forces are one's own

21/6 1907

Till utgångspunkt tages
följande tre begrepp:

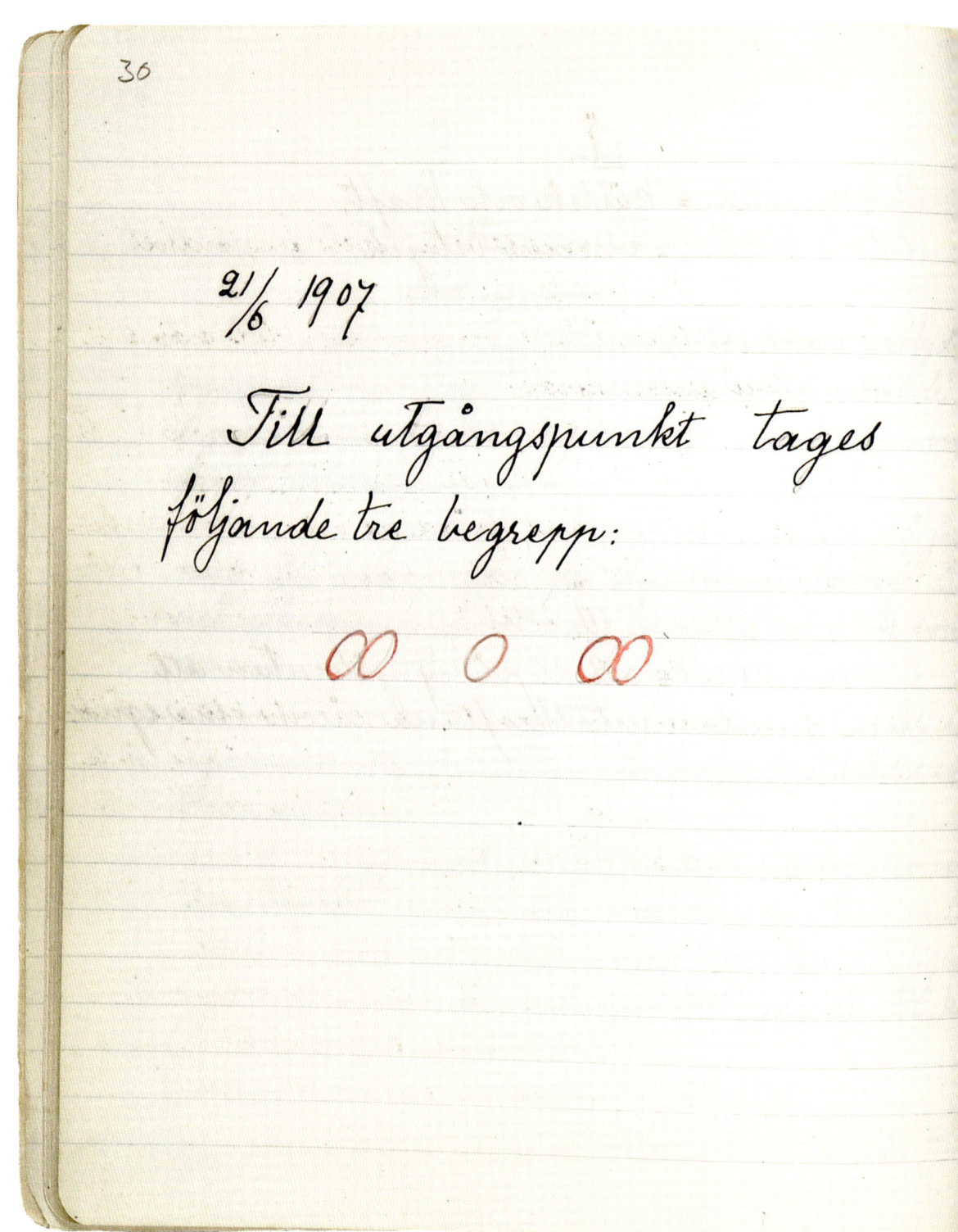

6/21/1907. The following three concepts are taken as a starting point: ∞ 0 ∞

a.

a = kraft i allmänhet.

ae = Ararats oljeberg, ljusets bild, livets frigjordhet.

œ = beredelse till korsets historia

œ = svanen framträder vit, ren, hög, blid, när sur-
degen blivit genomsyrad. a = uppståndelsen

æo = hämta kraft, kärlek, ljus. Segra genom livets
friska vind över hindrande astrala krafter.

æos = listens, lustans, flärdens och penningefal-
hetens kamp på den frusna gyttjemarken, i vilken
de dock sjunka när solstrålarna tina upp den.

aereH = res korset

aes = lidande, åstadkommet genom ofrihet i astralvärlden, förande oss ned i dy, där vi utsättas för de
ondas hämnd, vilkas redskap äro list och flärd.

aH = andens arbete och dess tempel

aH = liv och verklighet, självet har tystnat.

aH = under detta namn kände jag ledaren.

aH = ljus och ledning, utveckling och harmoni.

aH = lugnets och sanningens hemvist.

aH = omsluter och innesluter monstransen.

aH = bröd och vin.

a = force in general

ae = the oil mountain of Ararat, the image of light, life's liberation

æ = the history of the preparation of the cross

æ = the swan emerges white, clean, tall, gentle, when the leaven has been permeated

æ = the resurrection

aeo = attain strength, love, light. Sailing through the brisk winds of life against hindering astral forces.

aeos = the battle of cunning, lust, vanity, and venality on the frozen, slushy field, into which they sink as the rays of the sun melt it

aereH = raising the cross

aes = suffering, caused by lack of freedom in the astral world, which drags us down into the mud, where we are exposed to the vengeance of the spirits, whose tools are cunning and vanity

AH = the work of the spirit and its temple

AH = life and reality, the self has fallen silent

AH = I knew the leader by this name

AH = light and guidance, evolution and harmony

AH = the abode of tranquility and truth

AH = surrounds and encloses the sacred vessel

AH = bread and wine

AH = the spirit

AH = two beings and yet one, pledged to help each other now and forever

AH = the symbol of dual truth

AH = ascetic and vestal in paradisiacal union

AH = Mount Ararat and the blessed fortress

AH—WU = consummation

AH—WH = oa—ao

AH ys = life struggles AH reaches the end

AHas, aHs ⎫ AHs = light, guidance, and darkness
AHas   ⎬ AH = light and guidance
As   ⎭ As = darkness

AH ose uw = the evolution of humanity

AHe = sensitivity to the spiritual

AHoHEH = purity

AHr = asceticism's symbol of victory

AHu = victory

AHw = faith in the meaning of one's lifework without yet having faith in AH

Anss = to obey intuition

Ao = the beginning and the end; the descent into matter and ascent into a complete awareness. Ararat's servants have attained this. The result of this blinding brilliance is happiness.

Aos = the soul's pain

Ar = anxious light

Arh a = to understand only partially

Ar = the luminous abode of the idea of brotherhood

Aroo = physical happiness

As = light and dark and physical troubles across the years of wandering

Ass×/ = to have faith despite reproach

×/Asss = ever more difficult obstacles to faith

AtaH = to receive a message about AH

av = calm mixed with unrest

av, av, av shall confirm direct knowledge

$$\left.\begin{array}{l}\text{ave = rose}\\\text{ave = lily}\end{array}\right\} = \begin{array}{l}\text{w}\\\text{u}\end{array} = \text{perfection}$$

av = the evolution

aveH = may the warrior of light be of strong faith

avei = ave linked with I (which is not really used in this language of symbols) signifies performing one's dual calling

av = prisoner

av or ave = symbol of the swan or the resurrection

aw = beacons that become prison windows

aw = to pursue the work by putting it all into the hands of the Hs [High Masters]

aws = unfinished. Uncontrolled desires, struggles of the soul.

Awvu = to begin with ave Maria

AyH = to find

Ayw = living colorfully

ax = ascetic, ex = vestal

OOOOOOOOOOOOOOOO = 16 incarnations remain for the people of the earth to achieve all that is set forth in this work

B

b = broken rays of WU

be = vanquish and offer great joy

beH = the work of brotherly love

beH = the warrior and interpreter of truth, the victor of untruth

beH = abode, see drawing 37

ber = to become the warrior of brotherly love

beres = full of joy

berw = to be formed

besw = to have evolved for eons of years

bew8 = messenger for the dual truth

bg = the force that the warrior adopts during the evolution of the pale pink rose

bgs = nailed to the cross

bjuH = to keep the faith

bl = the gleaming spiral staircase of chastity's endeavor leading to AH

blaH = the material plane, the backside of the Holy of Holies

blaH = receiving yellow, filled with love; the urgent needs of the servant

blarb = allowing the astral beings to instruct

bleH = to offer (spiritual) wealth

blis = the color of the messenger

blivs = to burst open the gates of prison

blos = heavy clouds

blus = a prescribed pursuit

blw = to have faith in the instruction

blwo = to have the demands met

bm = mediumistic compositional elements

bn = muteness

box = bound in sacred knots already tied

brow = to burn away a frozen WU, this is escaping coldness

brw = harsh, loveless, frozen land

bryw = that which emerges from the work

bs = horrified

bsw = caring for the mouth aH

bus = to not be in service to the light

buva = to be given great joy

bul = to feel the heat of controversy

bw = OHe

bw = archetype, the opposite of dw

bw = calming prison color. The force that, though hindrance, is essential for evolution; it is:

$\left\{\begin{array}{l}\text{cross and sin}\\\text{light and weakness.}\end{array}\right.$

bw = OO difficulties at the beginning of the earthly work, could be called grief

bw, uw ves = the life of numbers

bwa = the prison's opening

bwaH = heart

bws = fear, dread

bwuH = shall call forth pink roses

bwv = the ambition to evolve

bwvs = the physical world's submission to the spiritual world

byl = an image on the astral plane of great struggle

bys = the ability to disarm indifference and the absence of love with forces greater than stubborn resistance

bysH = to develop dynamic powers

byuH = colors of greater energy

D

d = life's material evolution, constancy, trust in the powers of the soul

daH = philosophy of life

db = servant of deva (see the symbol drawings)

db = spiritual need, the calmest aH (see drawings)

des = calm mixed with anxiety

dg = the astral journey through burning flames, i.e., without the support of faith

dH = the evolution

ds = a journey beset by peril and troubles

dsw = the struggle and unrest in matter by Ararat's enemies who oppose H's guidance in developing love, wisdom, obedience, and freedom

dubliH = consummate vestalism

duH = to triumph over much

duHo = an Essene perspective of the dual truth

duss = the drudgery, difficulties, and trivial problems that fill a life

duss = a lack of ambition for normal development

dw = the soul, the realm of dw = the rose = the evolution

dw = the spirit's struggle against matter. dw can correspond to a hook [hook-and-eye], but also to the organ of the mind.

dv°° = perhaps it should be dw°°

dw = the soul's effort to open the astral world. When the spirit becomes master of the lower nature the leaven is permeated and the swan = oe emerges white, pure.

dw can also be the lower nature within ourselves that reinforces the prison of the soul

dw = Avatar (Indian mythology) a god's descent to earth, taking on human form

dw = listen to the astral force

dw = ascetic in vestal endeavor

dw = a calm after the struggle, everlasting Ararat's victory call, Undan's calmest force, the symbol of dual truth

dw = limitation, ave in reverse

dw = the house. The independence and selflessness of the soul. = the rose

dw = includes the development of both eH and oH, and calm aH. Its brightest color is pink.

dy = the task of the day

dyb = to invite controversy

DyH = the iron will

D.Y.H. = the eye is the warrior's hook, and the hook is the eye's iron will.

dys = black clouds (will scatter the essence of life)

dyss = strength, an attempt to reach enlightenment

divg = the calm after the storm

dws = to find the answer to life's mystery through the material struggle

E

e = image of evolution in matter

edb = calm

efHs = to be judged benevolently from above

ehe Hes = symbols of Ararat

eH = The struggle over light; victory appears in matter

eH = The permeation of the leaven, faith in ave maria = victory over matter

eH = the field on which the battle takes place

EH = the symbol of dual truth (evolution)

eH, AH, OH = the freemason symbols

eH, OH, AH = Manvantara

eH8 = merging the forces of the ascetic and vestal

eH, es = the astral symbols of Ararat

eHh = to exist in the physical aspects of vestal and ascetic work. eHavH = may the High Masters be with you.

eHs = courage

eja (vHw) = will be thus

els = to experience the world of prayer and innocence. To bide one's time in silence.

elum = freedom

eow = to fight with the torch of the gospels rather than the sword of law

erb = love begets love, revenge begets revenge

erg = forgive and forget

erw = life, joy

es = the symbol of the cross's exceptional sacrificial capacity

eskg = a warrior of the Lord with body and soul

eswo = to aim high

euh = to forgive missteps. Bonds shall be broken.

eum = the wheat

eusu = the rose

ew = the essence of a life in faith

ew = symbol of the rose's evolution

ew = examining, remembering, resting

ex = vestal

eyaHr = a searching eye

F

These terms come from a language in which there was no F.

faH = land that challenges one's defenses

faH = terrifying thoughts, mediumistic black magic

faH also means to demand unity and to capture dw. Peace in one's heart through work.

fana/rav = to pursue with faith

faneH = benefiting

farH = intervene

fars = to struggle mightily, but unknowingly, at the dual work

far/S/ see page 45 in the book of excerpts

fas = to obtain knowledge and to be cautious

fav = the fundamental force (the heart of young men and maidens)

fav = the holy temple's reverent lineage saH

fd = to have great understanding; to have faith

fg = Ararat's victory call; to have faith

fge = to destroy the youthful heart

f00 = annual mushroom crop

foH = physical struggle, a desire for purity (the hallmark of Gidron)

fon = to be bound (fonos see p. 75)

fons = a time of great knowledge

foran = the pain of a frozen soul

forH = to have one's being illuminated

forss = spirits who are stuck in the material world

fos = a prepared warrior

foss = succumb

frge = the field of knowledge is catholic

fs = the physical aspect of love

furs = the one who has struggled on ⎰ the leaven's field
⎱ the kurbits's field
⎰ the spirit's field

fus = to open the prison gates; a dwelling place within the soul

fuss = determination to steer toward the heights

fw = education in physical life, wise—good

fw = to work with a calm heart

fw = to release vestal and ascetic, i.e., the fundamental forces, through faith

fw = to steel one's self with the strength of truth for the struggle to fulfill the brightest promises

fygg = unshakable trust in the High Masters

fysH = to leave for the time being

fwo = source of physical strength

G

g = ease in performing mediumistic work and reliance on bodily strength

gaH = yearning; a firmer foothold in Devachan than on the earth

gefs = loving thoughts

ges = the victor's robe

gf = to doubt the expressions of spiritual currents; continued doubt that veers toward material hazards

ggh = a task of great significance

gl = restless interpreter of truth. God helps those who help themselves.

gl = the gate to the astral world and the symbol of the eye

gl = the struggle is about the fearless descent into the godless dark

gl = puritans and the knights of wheat = Ararat's oH

glaras = becoming love's expression

glavare = to trust

g*00* = schooling continues for the understanding of *00*

gos = despair at being separated from the High Masters

gs = life's journey

guf = ancient ways of seeing great and sacred things

gure = to resist the strange fluids caused by the soul's unrest

gus_8 = courage in the depths of one's own being

guss = sensitivity to mediumistic currents while executing occult drawings

guyw = selflessness

gv = the answer the ascetic received when he relied on H

gw = duty's first commandment = Glory be to God

gw = the host of spirits form protective walls of strong currents around those with faith

gw = the eye; sanctity elevated to a higher plane

gwa = physical

gwar = high asceticism

gwv = to perform the detailed work in the best way

gys = purity of thought, the child within us

gys = the sacred Ararat work

h = the struggle for light

Hah = a puritan disposition toward the HaH work

haH = heartache as regards 8

HaH = the worldly struggle between truth and untruth with the promise of aid

HaH = the armor of brave compatriots, the territory of obedient hearts

HaH = the symbols of hymen

HaH in which EH and OH are included

$\left\{\begin{array}{l} \text{HaH} \\ \text{Wu} \end{array}\right.$ = hours of work = see HoH and HeH

HaH = OH$_8$ = the symbol of good influences on evolution's path

Hah = UA = to act ambitiously

HaH = someone who breaks out

Hamahjärtat shall be wholly absorbed by the dual work

Hanav = a female dual guide

Has = in struggle and battle

Hass = one who fosters prisoners

Haven8 = obliged to pay

Ha is Ha^8; opposite in meaning to AH

Heb = the instrument of the mysteries

heH = the H's confirmation of EH AH OH, the first journey to Mount Ararat

Heh = realization in force and love

Heh OHh AhH = the pictorial language of the fundamental forces

HeH = the belief in the fulfillment by glorious forces through the Masters of the Mysteries. Belief in glorious promises and taking the narrow path. Only by falling can a child of faith attain strength of faith. Physical thoughts are in service to the nonphysical, and life transpires in matter through many incarnations.

HeH = leadership of the four Devas

$\left\{\begin{array}{l} \text{HeH} \\ \text{Ararat} \end{array}\right.$ = working hours, see HoH, HaH

HeH = drops of vestal and ascetic knowledge

HeleH = struggle to attain purity

Hev = to complete

hes = symbol of the lily's evolution during the work against cunning

hess = practical tasks

Hess = life's transformation

Hev = mahatmas Hev = dual joy p. 142

Hiw = hymen

Hoea = caged bird times

HoH = a spartan and loving faith

HoH = the cross

HoH = the wheat = vestal and ascetic

{ HoH
{ Emaus } = working hours

HoH = the symbol of good influences on evolution's path

Hs = the vestal working on virtue not yet attained

Hs = the difficulty in attaining wisdom

Hw = the leaven

hyH = the High Masters explaining the symbols of brotherhood

H = the High Masters are the path. H𝟢𝟢 = AH evolution's path.

HA = the self wishes to speak, i.e., our baser instincts

HA = Undan turned backward

H, H, H = body, soul, spirit. H = the saga of the rose

H/W = also a symbol for Mount Ararat

J

I̲ is not really used in this symbolic language, which will one day make sense

jg = physically, ascetically powerful, filled with the demands of faith

joH = use of the forces

jugas = to be helped by astral influences

K

k = fear

kaH = the symbol of the Pharaoh (cactus, Ararat's flower)

kg = the power to control matter

kgr𝟢𝟢 = the flower

klym = one who does not sympathize with life

korset [the cross] is represented by eH, aH, uH, wH, vH, 𝟢𝟢

L

l = freemasons; healthy, resourceful disposition

lageH = dangers and troubles

larbes = bound love

leH = to believe in the structure

les = releasing the stronghold's dual warrior

luas = the saga of the future

m = the calming masculine force especially regarding instinctual urges

m = the horizontal line

m = the caged bird's struggle

meH = spiritual work

mg = sanctified, purified space

mgs = harassment

moHwe = noteworthy reference book

$\frac{m}{n}$ = victory over Ysseian fear (astral)

mors, mores, moris = the astral world

ms = torment of the soul through a passive yearning for virtue

muH = the color of the rose

mus = the zeal for faith among the mediumistically gifted; we call it spiritual recklessness

muvuH = faith

mv = to victoriously don the armor and serve astral, ascetic beings

mw = the youthful heart, the fundamental truth

mW^{oo} = ww^{oo}

$\left\{\begin{array}{l} \text{mw} \\ \text{muw} \\ \text{mwu} \end{array}\right.$ = remain prepared

myw = to be a messenger, but not for knowledge

m$_{oo}$ = to work intermittently

m = to be born on earth as a woman

N

n = the feminine.$^{\times}$ Liberation; vertical line.

neH = the universe

noH = pale yellow

nuH = the color of the lily

ns = masculine battle

nus = to empathize with the doubts of others

nw = to don the armor

$^{\times}$/in the sense of an etheric body

o = light (oa—ao)

oa = my deserted path

oaH = to assign the messenger's call to Christ

oe = the fermentation of the leaven

oes = liberation in the childlike heart. Love and summer.

oes = the purpose of life is the fermentation of the leaven

oH = Devachan (Geisterland [spiritland])

oH = Ararat's symbol of the astral world

oH = a chain of evolution. The bound, limited force that has been poured into the world of matter and now struggles to be free

oH = the gift of prayer. A rare gift, sometimes called the mind.

oH = a firm, happy, peaceful connection between soul and faith

oH = pink rose (a chain of evolution)

oH, aH, EH = Ararat

oH°° = Ararat's oH

oH° = a prayer for less coercion

oHa = lovingly

oHe = the bright currents of the astral forces in our world

oHe = the physical planting of the wheat

$\left\{\begin{array}{ll}\text{oHe} & \text{oHes} \\ \text{oHe} = \text{Ave Maria; also} & \text{oHes} \\ \text{oHe} & \text{oHes}\end{array}\right\}$

oHes = the darkened soul beginning to brighten through the work of the spirit

oHr = aided in the struggle from the material to the spiritual world

or° = symbol of tenacious, persistent forces

oroH = help

osyeH = to pass the test

ouw°° = submission to higher powers

owes = to fulfill one's mission

ous = ? see p. 231

p = frost, in the sense of suffering

poH = a spartan disposition of the heart

pg = to deny and shy away from Undan faith and Ysseian work yet believe in the power of hymen to open the prison gates

p𝑜𝑜 = the soul's interpretation of hand, mouth, and heart

paps see p. 263

R

r = interpreter of pine

r = knowledge and powers gained in ascetic struggle, borne by faith

raH = caring little for the earthly but greatly for the heavenly in the interpretation of aH

ravan = eternity

rave = full of obedience

rav = symbol of the aura of love

reseH = images of the room

rg = the journey's hardships

rgH = informed in simple terms

rgs = modesty in the pursuit of the color of the greatest power

roH = the interpreter of pine's faith in oH

r𝒪𝒪 = to succeed in avoiding uncovering one's inner self

rs = grief and hardship (astral)

ruH = horoscope

ruw = a suffering that persists

rw = level

ryss = the prison gates may be opened

rys = to die from one's self

S

s = to take on the leaden bonds of matter and the release from the H

s = a sin arising from turning away from the spartan life and yearning for physical pleasure

s = cross, trials, despair, physical pain

s = faithlessness, dubiousness, indifference in spiritual matters; taking up residence with lower creatures who cannot help us rise upward

s = defenses within oneself. Symbol of the small-mindedness that restrains others but conceals how the Yssean interior protests against this.

s = struggle to abandon the world (material) and thus the joy of Easter Eve.

s in the middle of a word = the dissolution of difficulties

samuH = to feel joy in the core of one's being

sass = to be dazzled

savu = diminishing powers

sav = women

sear = astral mediumistic building materials

seH = buoyancy from the joy of faith, which may also seem like anger toward the uninitiated

seH = a completely white flower

seove = a very prominent image

ses = the first existence of the ascetic and vestal within matter

sev = in the service of light. Free from the risk of repressing and being repressed.

ses = yearning, humility, fear of hostile spiritual beings

sg = I am the servant of the Lord. May it be unto me according to your word.

sgs = the day of Easter Eve's oH

sleH = bright, ethereal beings are guiding you

slove = a prominent image

soH = a desperate, impotent struggle during the time of wheat, in the service of spiritual forces

spaH = the work on the day of Easter Eve, freethinking beings

sreHes = the righteous

ss = all troubles both material and spiritual, especially the mission of anguish during the material struggle

suH = to keep faith during the struggle

sus = other people's helpful thoughts when engaged in the brave work of faith

suv = *00*

swa = mouth, hand, heart

swaH = rose-colored

swoH = Devachanic happiness, eagerness to give

swus = blue spirituality

syH = an insufficient answer

sys = Easter Eve's oH

sw = to appear as a messenger in word and action

Ss = a formula by which the transgressions are overcome

T

t = beneath the beds of dust the seed will grow

tjw = from its burdens the spirit of Ysseen shall become bright and pure

U

U = the spiritual forces of life

U = everything in the world of the spirit. Truth, freedom, tranquility, the reality of light, sacred desire, rebirth, the woman

U = the bond between the god within us and the soul

U = the wheat, Devachan. Destination of development, where evolution's warriors belong

U.B. = good, solid brotherhood

Udes = the struggle between man and woman

UgHn = a matter of the heart

UH = the lords of Lustrum were bound on earth to the brothers of Ararat during their work

UH = the time between two earthly existences

UH = the soul's connection to U

Umar = the bond between the ascetic and vestal

Ummu = to see oneself in another

Unes = shackled to the dual half

Unns = to spread peace

Urw = a hero's astral victory over the self

Us = Easter Sunday. Dual work's continuation

Us = to have the faith and courage to follow the guides

Us = childlike soul

Us = the circle encompassing the lower seven of the twelve principles

Us = carrying the cross during the searing of the soul, troubles during the sanctifying struggle. Futile ambition, winter, death

U.S. = the purpose of the lustrum

Uss = the evolution of the world

Uss = to receive the word of knowledge

Uss = the source of life

Uss = to call forth the color blue through faith and tenderness

Us wy
Usy $\Big\}$ = joyful ambition

Uv = to interpret

Uvw = the Pleiades' series

Uw = yearning for light; life and the word within the self

Uw = lily

Uw = the part of the chain that stands between the completion of the dual truth and the soul merging with the spiritual

Uw = the raising of the cross by the body's obedience to the spirit

uw
dw $\Big\}$ = symbol of the dual truth
aH

U.W. = the descent of the H

Uws = Easter Eve is over

Uy = instruction

Uyo = worldly time

v = the site of liberation for the Akasha element; occupied by worldly elementary spirits who are preparing the evolution of the world

v = a desire to serve the H, to renunciate, to give without taking, to obey without seeing, to pass the test, to give offerings to Easter Eve

v = spartan courage, a desire for change and for the Ysseian work

v = desire to meditate; youthful feelings, the fulfillment of fine promises

v° = the fruit of the work

vaH = to improve rapidly

vaH = to capture a bright thought's counterpart in matter (dual truth), and to be told of a love culture of the past (soul molecule) for the sake of construction

vaH = an appeal to pass the test and become the child of the spirit

vaH = the color ultramarine

vaH = the task of preparation in the outer realm

vaHeHe = to journey under tight circumstances

vav = the path of the evolution of wheat

veH = to leave everything to the H

veH = the pictorial language of Eros

veH = the sleep that God allowed to descend upon man

veH = the strange influence of the soul's world; mediumistic work

vejav = bright belief

ves = the prayer book of the stronghold

ves = a journey undertaken with firm belief in the guides

vg = the journey's hardships

vo = to be painted with blood

vos = an imperative force

vrvs = Ararat's faith

vs = the workday's victory, life's culmination

vs = the archetype, perfect harmony

vu = when mankind reaches the destination where joy awaits

vu = to prepare and bind to the school of the cross

vuH = to brace the physical part

vur = to fix the mind especially on the backdrop of light

vus = darkness and yet faith

vuv = the H's servants' servants' servants

vw = bodily defeats

w = to fight cunning and vanity

w = the bond between heaven and earth

w = the song the spirit sings; desire for freedom, submissiveness; the concept of light—not its reality

w = the dark side of the cross

w = everything that could be called a burden

w = the body, the concealing shadow; everything in the world of forms

w = unease; life's material struggle and battle

w = the place where the H's servants live; the dematerialization of the world; the dwelling of a rich evolution of the world

waH = to prepare for a celebration; to mature

waHa = to receive help

waraH = frozen ground thawed by the guidance given to Ovatius by Gidro

waes ⎫
wus ⎬ = failed efforts
wys ⎭

wasw = to finish

we = the enemies of light may appear large but are very small

weH = to calmly sever bonds

weH = to not suffer from the absence of the messengers

wg = faith in life's path (the evolution of the world)

wH = struggle and battle

wHer = days shall no more be stained by earthly work

wm = spirit of virtue

woH = vestal [last letter crossed out in red]

wraH = chromatic ? see p. 522

wras = law enacted by adversaries

wru = a sign for evolution regarding the symbol for nervous desire

wru = spiritual pride

wru = w8 = a malevolent act

ws = life's evolution in matter

ws ⎫
us ⎬ = fulfillment of dual truth
es ⎭

wsy = joyful ambition

wu = the color is pink

wu = the chain of evolution that takes place during the struggle inside and outside of humanity, also faith in development

wu = pink rose and white lily

wu = a duty that is partly Ysseian and partly Spartan

wu = the mystic name of the temple

wu = $\begin{cases} \text{w = lighthearted} \\ \text{u = fighting spirit} \end{cases}$

wu = image of the struggle in the middle ages

wu = logos; w has the same meaning here as Eoames, i.e., the bond between heaven and earth. u = the bond between the god within us and our selves.

wu = indescribable, inscrutable. The sacred vessel is invisible, it contains and encompasses aH.

wu = what could be the pioneering garment of lustrum

wu = unfathomable is

wu = sacred is

wu = eternal is   the prayer of Ararat's chalice

wu = God is

wuH = love has much to consider

wuH = your kingdom is infinite, and love rules it

wuH = the opposite of ys

wu + uw = soon the wheel will be turned

wuH = the knight of virtue

wuH = everything within the form binds the soul until the H have delivered it to freedom

wur = the beginning of a new course for evolution during the faith of Easter Eve

wus = the sevenfold within humanity

wus = to lead the work by use of the universal brothers' (the Mahatmas') intervening thoughts. They are.

wus = the intensification of experience through the descent into matter

wus = certain gentle caged bird concepts; Easter Eve is here

wwH = special circumstances within dazzling matter

ww^{oo} = the fundamental truth

ww = not able to understand

ww^{s} = to be troubled

wvs = the apostle of the spirit

wy = obedience to the promptings of the H

wyH = plentiful, useless elements

wyH = the bible of the stronghold; ves = the prayer book of the stronghold, which is included in the idea of Brahma

wyss = the evolution of the spirit under strain

wyss = to be mediumistically guided

wu = aH

w is a symbol of a life of astral force = in constant activity.

X

x = frost, cold

Y

y = the pull of material forces

ygs = incorrect

yH = the hell of prison is doubt, which eventually becomes faith

yHg = contributes to the sharpness of mind in vision

ym = the cloister work

yn8 = the time of rest free of work

yo = a grand work

yrH = misapprehension

ys = the struggle for the victory of light in the world, supported by prayer. Boomerang. Purity's first day's work

yws = to fulfill your task with gratitude

ywo =

Ö = the end of everything

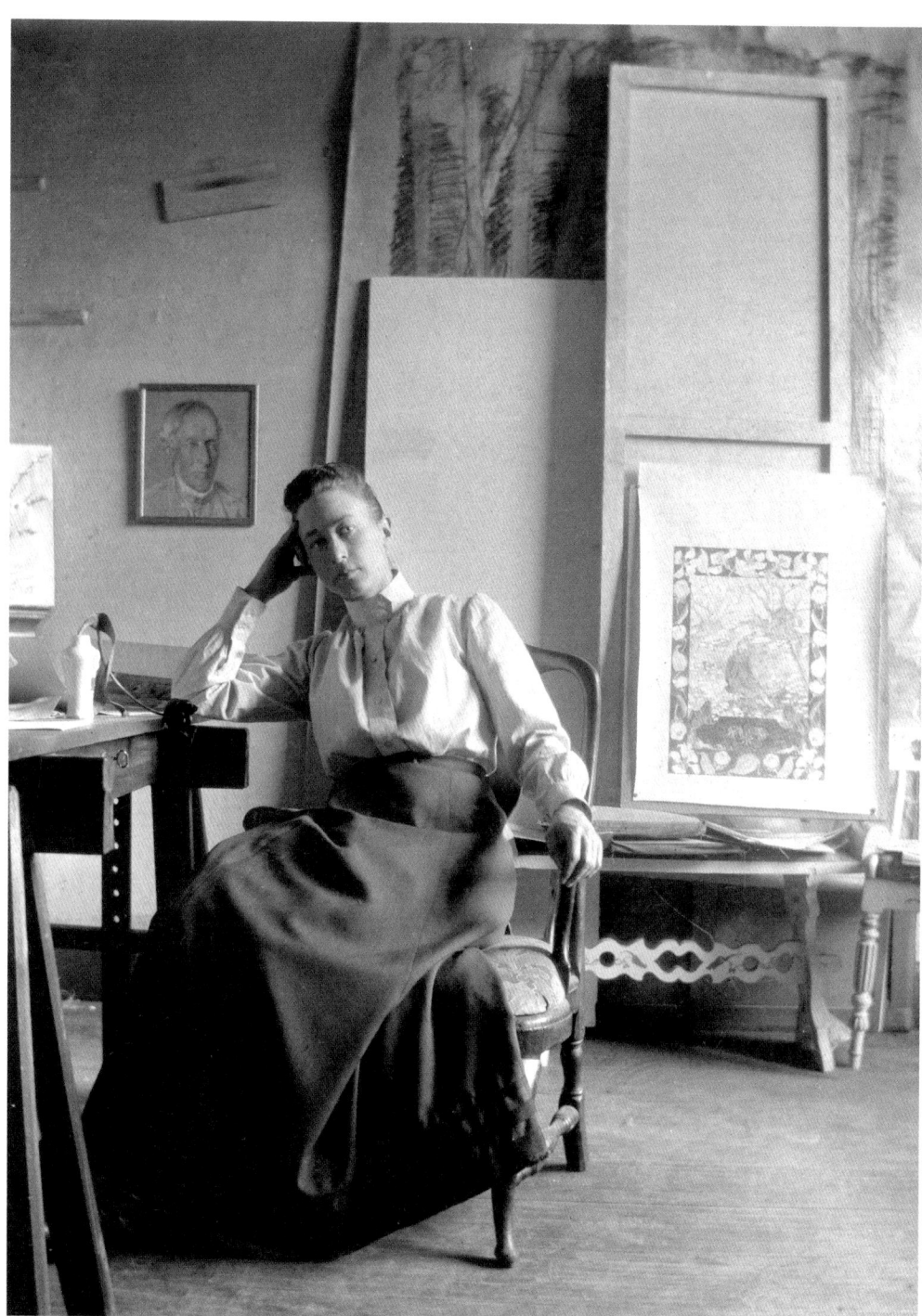

Afterword

Hilma af Klint (1862–1944) was an academically trained Swedish artist who began to paint abstractly in 1906. In her work, she gave physical form to mental aspects: complex philosophical ideas, spiritual concepts, and religious experience. Hilma af Klint developed her own ideas and concepts and in doing so became a forerunner of abstract painting.

Hilma af Klint changed her mode of painting several times during her life. After receiving her degree from the Royal Academy of Fine Arts in Stockholm in 1887, she worked as a conventional painter. From 1906 onward, influenced by the Rosicrucian tradition, Theosophy, and Christian thought, she began to create abstract forms in her work such as *The Paintings for the Temple*. In 1922 she started to paint with "floating colors," a method resulting from her studies of Goethe's color theory and of Anthroposophy. This method of painting would occupy her for the rest of her life.

Iris Müller-Westermann was the initiator and curator of the 2013 exhibition *Hilma af Klint: A Pioneer of Abstraction* at the Moderna Museet in Stockholm. She was instrumental in cultivating international recognition of Hilma af Klint's work. With this publication of the artist's notebooks, Müller-Westermann continues her important contributions to the academic research about Hilma af Klint and her works—for which we are much obliged.

Hilma af Klint painted for the future—and the future is now!

Johan af Klint
Member of the Board of Directors
The Hilma af Klint Foundation

Hilma af Klint in her studio at Hamngatan 5, c. 1895

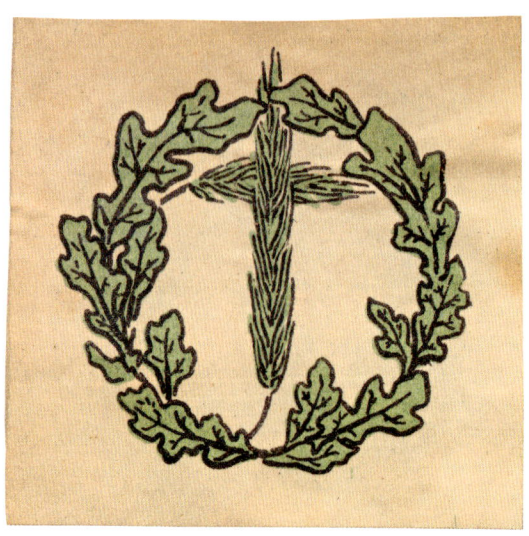

Acknowledgments

With special thanks to Johan af Klint and the Hilma af Klint Foundation, Susan Bielstein, Kerstin Lind Bonnier, Jason Burch, Albin Dahlström, David Horowitz, Simona Jansons, Don Kennison, Olga Krzeszowiec, Laura Lindgren, Josiah McElheny, the Moderna Museet, Nina Øverli, Anne Posten, R. H. Quaytman, Ken Swezey, James Whitman Toftness, and Elizabeth Clark Wessel.

Above: Hilma af Klint's ex libris